SELF-DETERMINATION

AND WOMEN'S RIGHTS

IN MUSLIM SOCIETIES

BRANDEIS SERIES ON GENDER, CULTURE, RELIGION, AND LAW

SERIES EDITORS: LISA FISHBAYN JOFFE AND SYLVIA NEIL

This series focuses on the conflict between women's claims to gender
equality and legal norms justified in terms of religious and cultural traditions. It seeks work
that develops new theoretical tools for conceptualizing feminist projects for transforming the
interpretation and justification of religious law, examines the interaction or application of civil law
or remedies to gender issues in a religious context, and engages in analysis of conflicts over gender
and culture/religion in a particular religious legal tradition, cultural community, or nation. Created
under the auspices of the Hadassah-Brandeis Institute in conjunction with its Project on Gender,
Culture, Religion, and the Law, this series emphasizes cross-cultural and interdisciplinary
scholarship concerning Judaism, Islam, Christianity, and other religious traditions.

For a complete list of books that are available in the series, visit www.upne.com

Chitra Raghavan and James P. Levine, editors,
Self-Determination and Women's Rights in Muslim Societies

Janet Bennion, *Polygamy in Primetime:*
Media, Gender, and Politics in Mormon Fundamentalism

Ronit Irshai, *Fertility and Jewish Law: Feminist Perspectives on Orthodox Responsa Literature*

Jan Feldman, *Citizenship, Faith, and Feminism: Jewish and*
Muslim Women Reclaim Their Rights

Self-Determination
and Women's Rights
in Muslim Societies

EDITED BY CHITRA RAGHAVAN AND JAMES P. LEVINE

BRANDEIS UNIVERSITY PRESS   WALTHAM, MASSACHUSETTS

Brandeis University Press

An imprint of University Press of New England

www.upne.com

© 2012 Brandeis University

All rights reserved

Manufactured in the United States of America

Designed by Mindy Basinger Hill

Typeset in 10.35/14 pt. Parkinson Electra by Copperline Book Services, Inc.

University Press of New England is a member of the Green Press
Initiative. The paper used in this book meets their minimum
requirement for recycled paper.

For permission to reproduce any of the material in this book, contact
Permissions, University Press of New England, One Court Street,
Suite 250, Lebanon NH 03766; or visit www.upne.com

Library of Congress Cataloging-in-Publication Data

Self-determination and women's rights in Muslim societies /
edited by Chitra Raghavan and James P. Levine.

p. cm.—(Brandeis series on gender, culture, religion, and law)

Includes index.

ISBN 978-1-61168-279-3 (cloth : alk. paper)—ISBN 978-1-61168-280-9
(pbk. : alk. paper)—ISBN 978-1-61168-281-6 (ebook)

1. Women—Legal status, laws, etc.—Islamic countries.   2. Women's rights—
Islamic countries.   3. Women's rights—Religious aspects—Islam.   4. Equality
before the law—Islamic countries.   I. Raghavan, Chitra.   II. Levine, James P.

K644.S45 2012

323.3′4091767—dc23   2012010139

5   4   3   2   1

CONTENTS

FOREWORD

When John Jay College of Criminal Justice was founded in 1964 as a liberal arts college for police officers, it would have been virtually unimaginable that the college would be sponsoring an edited volume on the topics of self-determination and women's rights in Muslim societies. Seen from this perspective, the existence of this book, artfully edited by James P. Levine, John Jay College's former dean of research, and Chitra Raghavan, a member of our Psychology Department, is a testament both to the maturation of the idea of criminal justice education and the expanded reach of scholarly inquiry on the questions of justice. In this sense, this book reflects the enduring power of the promise inherent in John Jay's mission of "educating for justice."

Yet given recent events, a broader perspective seems relevant. Today, as we are riveted by the forces of rebellion in the Middle East and northern Africa and inspired by the role of women fighting for democracy, it is equally unimaginable that these topics would be considered anything but central to an understanding of our modern era. The world is facing new challenges that had not emerged on the research agenda a half- century ago. Although the role of women in our society is a topic of timeless importance, the valiant struggles for self-determination in the modern era and the complex struggle for gender equality in the Muslim world combine to give scholarly treatments of women's rights in Muslim societies a vibrant immediacy. Likewise, although the relationship between different religious institutions and the ideals of a pluralistic society is a topic that has occupied scholarly and public attention for centuries, the modern challenge posed by the emergence of vibrant Muslim communities in Western democracies has acquired an urgency that calls for objective reflection and academic analysis. I know I speak for the editors and authors of this volume when I express the hope that this book will contribute to a deeper understanding of these crosscurrents in our global village.

As president of John Jay College of Criminal Justice, I am particularly proud that this volume reflects the scholarly contributions of the college's Ninth Biennial International Conference, held in Marrakesh, Morocco, in June 2010. This conference was designed and sponsored in close collaboration with our Moroccan partners, the Advisory Council on Human Rights, the Hassan II University in Casablanca, and Cadi Ayyad University in Marrakesh. The conference brought together scholars from twenty-nine countries to address the theme of "Societies in Transition: Balancing Security, Social Justice, and Tradition." The presentations at this multidisciplinary conference covered a remarkable array of topics, ranging from the reform of policing in Nepal to female suicide bombers and the international criminal record exchange. From this rich collection of presentations, we invited several presenters to transform their work into the chapters represented in this thematic volume. When we first approached our leading partner—Ahmed Herzenni at the Advisory Council on Human Rights—we realized we had a common goal: that our conference would make lasting and substantive contributions to the research literature on the issues embodied in the conference theme. I trust that this book represents a fulfillment of that aspiration.

As John Jay College approaches its fiftieth anniversary, the topics addressed in this volume resonate with the modern educational activities of the institution. We have recently created a gender studies major and a human rights minor. In 2008 we hosted a research conference on femicide that was attended by 450 people. Our students have traveled to Africa, Asia, Europe, and Latin America for faculty-led study-abroad programs. Our faculty members are engaged in research activities in Muslim countries, on topics ranging from women police officers in Bahrain to Sharia reform in the Republic of Maldives. Last year, inspired in part by our experience in Morocco, we created a collegewide series of lectures, artistic presentations, and student activities titled "Mosques, Veils and Madrasses: Muslims and Institutions of Justice in Pluralistic Societies." So, knowing that this volume will also have ongoing relevance to the education of our students and the research of our faculty, I wish to express my thanks, on behalf of our college, for the scholarly contributions represented in this exemplary book.

Jeremy Travis

PRESIDENT, JOHN JAY COLLEGE OF CRIMINAL JUSTICE
CITY UNIVERSITY OF NEW YORK

CHITRA RAGHAVAN AND JAMES P. LEVINE

Introduction

GENDER EQUALITY, CHANGE, AND THE QUEST

FOR SOCIAL JUSTICE FOR WOMEN IN MUSLIM SOCIETIES

The struggle for gender equality is neither new nor confined to Muslim so-cieties. Non-Muslim women have endured long histories of very particular-ized oppression justified by both religious and secular male-driven laws (for example, Mir-Hosseini and Hamzić 2010). Nonetheless, for a complex set of social, political, and economic reasons, Muslim states have among the weakest human rights records, including those pertaining to gender equality (Baderin 2007; Moustafa 2011).

While Islam is neither the cause of nor the solution to Muslim women's gender inequality (Chase 2007), religion has been increasingly recognized as a key element of human identity (Moustafa 2011; Gates and Steane 2009) rather than a completely separate and private sphere of ideology or faith. Religion cannot be ignored, sidestepped, or minimized in the quest for change. Fur-thermore, in virtually all Muslim societies and Muslim states, family structures and personal status codes crucial to attaining gender equality are influenced by Islamic codes to some degree (Baderin 2007). Thus, any attempt to change women's rights in these key areas must engage with Muslim cultural contexts and Islamic discourse (Modizardeh 2006). Finally, because Islamic discourse has always historically privileged social justice and has been traditionally used as a call for action (Waardenberg 1985), such discourses can help provide a familiar and trusted platform from which to orient improvement in women's rights.

The twelve essays in this volume present the struggles to end oppression against women from multidisciplinary perspectives in Muslim contexts spanning the globe. While there are excellent books that cover comparative approaches to Muslim law from a jurisprudence standpoint or from the view of a single culture (for example, Welchman 2007; Esposito and DeLong-Bas 2004), this is the first volume to consider the topic from diverse methodologies in a wide range of countries. We present studies that move beyond narrow conceptions of Muslim societies within the Arab world to include Muslim majority and minority countries in Asia and North Africa, such as India, Thailand, the Maldives, and Uganda. Scholars are drawn from both the humanities and the social sciences — from anthropology, law, political science, history, and psychology.

The use of ethnographic methodology drawn from these disciplines in several essays is especially noteworthy. Ethnographic method — which relies on original field data and interviews — has been slow to enter the discourse on Islam and women's rights, in part because of methodological differences across disciplines, and in part because of difficulty of access to grass-roots women's voices. By using original field data on issues pertaining to marriage, divorce, property rights, and women's sexuality, authors in this volume explore how the debates around rights discourse, local cultures, and varying interpretations of Islamic legal traditions are lived and challenged every day. Ethnographic data brings readers closer to the lived world of women in Muslim societies and allows readers to understand the changes women desire, how change happens, what obstacles confront women, and how they challenge them. This focus on local realities can illuminate surprising disjunctions between politico-legal reforms on the one hand and daily life on the other hand: diverse opinions at the local level help explain why politico-legal reforms can have limited effect, how supposedly feminist legislation can backfire (especially when the voices of women are not included in drafting the reforms), and how popular Western assumptions about the slow pace of change in Muslim societies are faulty.

This collection is also unique in that it brings larger theoretical frameworks of change crucial to development in all types of societies to bear on specific Muslim contexts. This is an especially important contribution to the literature on this topic, as it serves to correct two interconnected Western prejudices. First, since 9/11, Western media and politicians have primarily depicted Islam to be a dangerous and backward religion. These negative depictions have sometimes served Western political ends. Lila Abu-Lughod (2002) describes how Laura Bush, during her radio address on November 17, 2001, rejoiced that the War on Terrorism in Afghanistan had freed Muslim women from hateful Taliban oppression, thus justifying the invasion and occupation. In 2008, Geert Wilders, an anti-Islam member of the Dutch Parliament, produced a short video called *Fitna* that depicted Islam as a religion that inherently oppresses and continues to oppress women, a message that Muslim women denounced almost immediately (Vis, van Zoonen, and Mihelj 2011). Popular literature, too, validates "Islamofascism" (Gurel 2009): Ayaan Hirsi Ali's controversial novels, such as *The Infidel* and *Caged Virgin*, are tales of Islamic oppression as told by a courageous Muslim woman who has suffered from it. Works such as these reinforce the stereotype of Islam as retrograde, oppressive, and an enemy of women's rights (Mayer 2007).

These and dozens, if not hundreds, of other attacks against Islam render the religion in the form of caricatures. They promote the false belief that Muslim states are so different from Western ones that the former are impervious to academic analysis and interpretation. This denies the impressive scholarly output of the twentieth century on the history of change and development across Islamic societies. More specifically, it erases the complex, vivid, and ever-changing relationship between Islam and feminism. Instead of a rich, dialogic debate that brings diverse aspects of Islamic women's religious beliefs, lives, and culture in conversation with top-down politico-legal reform, we are trapped in an intractable set of dichotomies with Islam on the one side and women's rights on the other. When politicians, religious figures, the media, and others create dualistic categories (modern versus traditional, insider versus outsider, developed versus backward, secular versus Islamic), they simply reinforce a set of biased Western assumptions (which are shared to some extent by non-Western non-Muslim nations) and attitudes that inhibit real change for women.

A central issue in these debates is whether there is a pure Islam and, if there is, what it says about women's rights. Contemporary Muslim scholars argue that the Quran and the hadith (the words and deeds of Prophet Muhammad) can and should be reinterpreted according to current customs and that contemporary fatwas (opinions) issued by religious scholars can serve as important sources of guidance. Thus, the presumed rigidity and immutability of Islam on the position of women, a stereotype embraced by antireligious liberals and right-wing religious fundamentalists alike, is being actively challenged as erroneous (Ahmed 1992; Mernissi 1987; Mir-Hosseini 2003; Mir-Hosseini and Hamzic 2010).

Although prominent scholars of Muslim culture and law have repeatedly provided evidence that Islam and human (and women's) rights are compatible and in fact have argued that Muslim nations have contributed to the universal development of human rights (for example, Mayer 2007; Waltz, 2004), negative stereotypes of Islam infamously typified by Samuel Huntington in his article "The Clash of Civilizations?" (1993) persist.

Scholars who contest the dualistic schism between Islam and feminism nonetheless note that these are contested practices (Mir-Hosseini 2003): they mean different things to different people in different settings and at different times. From this perspective, Ali's novels can be interpreted as presenting a monolithic view of Islam influenced by a less mature form of Western feminism built on the artificial dichotomy of us (all women) versus them (mostly brown men, but some white men too) (Gurel 2009). In this spirit, the essays in this volume challenge the static views of Islam and feminism presented by Ali, Bush, and Wilders. Inspired by the current transnational feminism that grapples with women's material and cultural differences throughout the world and the rich, ever-mutable relationships among religion, rights, and real life, this volume encourages a vision of complexity that recognizes the inherent diversity in Muslim societies and neither conflates culture and religion nor dichotomizes them simplistically.

Islamic Legal Tradition, Feminism, and Human Rights Discourse

The 2010 *Encyclopedia Britannica Book of the Year* estimates that there were approximately one and a half billion Muslims in the world as of mid-2009 (Table I-1). Islam thus has the second largest number of adherents worldwide, after Christianity. Although there are practicing Muslims on all continents, including forty million in Europe, the overwhelming preponderance of Muslims (97 percent) reside in Asia or Africa.

Many very large nations are comprised almost exclusively of Muslims (Table 1-2). In eleven of the twenty countries with the largest Muslim populations, Islam is the religion of at least 95 percent of the residents. In two other countries, Muslims constitute between 85 percent and 95 percent of the national population.

However, these numbers should not mislead us into thinking that the populations across these nations or even within a nation are homogeneous. Rather, there is a notable diversity in religious interpretation and practice. At the religious helm is the Quran, the holy book of Islam, viewed as divine by those who believe that it is the exact word of Allah (God) as revealed to the Prophet Muhammad. In addition, the Sunnah — the will, behaviors, and practices of the Prophet Muhammad as derived from the hadith, or his sayings — is also relied on to provide divine guidance (Esposito and DeLong-Bas 2004). Most Muslims are either Shi'a or Sunni, branches of Islam that originated from different beliefs concerning the spiritual leadership of Islam after the death in 632 of the Prophet Muhammad, the founder of Islam. The Shi'a believe that leaders cannot be elected and that only the descendants of the Prophet can assume legitimate leadership of the Muslim world; in contrast, the Sunni believe that election through correct political practice is legitimate (Nasir 2009).

Approximately 85 percent of the Muslim world is Sunni. The Sh'ia are found primarily in Iran, Pakistan, India, and Iraq, although their numbers are difficult to estimate as many countries do not acknowledge them. In addition to the major Sunni and Sh'ia schools of thought, there are also splinter groups such as the Alawites, the Druse, and the Sufis; each has a distinctive orientation. Textual interpretations by Islamic scholars have led to several schools of Islamic law; the best known include Shafi'i, Maliki, Hanbali, and Hanafi in the Sunni tradition and the Twelvers in the Shi'a tradition.

Although conservative Islamic scholars, right-wing fundamentalists, and oppressive Muslim states hold the laws derived by these multiple schools as sacred and therefore immutable, feminists sharply reject the notion that there is such a thing as pure Islamic law (for example, Mernissi 1987; Ahmed 1992. Feminists argue instead that existing laws are male-oriented sociopolitical interpretations of Islamic sacred texts. As such, these legal codes and statutes are more accurately referred to as Islamic legal traditions rather than Islamic

TABLE I.1

Geographical Distribution of Muslims, Mid-2009

Africa	408,001,000
Asia	1,066,329,000
Europe	40,836,000
Latin America	1,836,000
North America	5,647,000
Oceania	563,000
Total	1,523,212,000

Source: *The World Almanac and Book of Facts 2011* (taken from the *2010 Encyclopedia Britanica Book of the Year*). All figures are estimates.

TABLE I.2

World's Largest Muslim Populations, 2009

RANK	COUNTRY	MUSLIM POPULATION	MUSLIMS AS A PERCENT OF TOTAL
1.	Indonesia	202,867,000	88.2
2.	Pakistan	174,082,000	96.3
3.	India	160,945,000	13.4
4.	Bangladesh	145,312,000	89.6
5.	Egypt	78,513,000	94.6
6.	Nigeria	78,056.000	50.4
7.	Iran	73,777,000	99.4
8.	Turkey	73,619,000	98.0
9.	Algeria	34,199,000	98.0
10.	Morocco	31,993,000	99.0
11.	Iraq	30,428,000	99.0
12.	Sudan	30,121,000	71.3
13.	Afghanistan	28,072,000	99.7
14.	Ethiopia	28,063,000	33.9
15.	Uzbekistan	26,469,000	96.3
16.	Saudi Arabia	24,949,000	97.0
17.	Yemen	23,363,000	99.1
18.	China	21,667,000	1.6
19.	Syria	20,196,000	92.2
20.	Malaysia	16,581,000	60.4

Source: *The World Almanac and Book of Facts 2011* (taken from the Pew Research Center). All figures are estimates.

law. The latter implies immutable and sacred codes that have been divinely determined; the former emphasizes that these traditions are cultural products of time and place (Barazangi 2008; Mir-Hosseini 2003, 23; Mir-Hosseini and Hamzić 2010).

Feminists make a distinction between the Sharia (divine guidance for humankind as told to the Prophet Muhammad) and *fiqh* (the process of understanding and codifying Muslim religious scriptures into jurisprudence). This distinction is a crucial one for women's rights because it challenges the notion that women's subjugated position in Islamic legal traditions is divinely ordained (that is, contained in the Quran or derived from the hadith) and therefore incontestable, arguing that instead it is encoded in interpretations produced and managed by the patriarchy and therefore open to debate and change (Ahmad 1992); Mernissi 1987; Mir-Hosseini 2003; Mir-Hosseini and Hamzić 2010). These distinctions are highlighted by Anissa Hélie in her essay in this volume on abortion in multiple Muslim cultures. She analyzes how women's bodies are defined, redefined, and identified as conforming (or not) to Islam depending on vestiges of colonial law, local politics, and current economics, with such assessments rarely based on Islamic jurisprudence as is stereotypically assumed. Similarly, William Clarence-Smith discusses how the practice of female circumcision — neither mandated by Islam nor traditionally culturally practiced — has been introduced into Indonesia by conservative misinterpretations of Islamic law.

Many of the chapters in this book grapple with the religious diversity and plural interpretations of Islamic law in an individual society. Of particular interest is the discussion of feminist interpretations of Islamic legal traditions. Importantly, current debates about women's rights across these varied schools rely on new interpretations of the Quran and hadith and are remarkably similar in their exhortation of women's equal rights under Muslim law (Nasir 2009).

Feminist interpretation of Islamic legal traditions are finding increasing support as a legitimate and necessary endeavor both in local Muslim communities and externally from influential states and international decision-making bodies. The encouragement and integration of women's rights in general, and the feminist interpretations of Islam in particular, come at a time when the structure and mechanism of the international rights discourse itself has undergone substantial change. In the past thirty years, civil society — including grass-roots nongovernmental organizations, local activists, celebrities, and independent media — has gained a powerful and legitimate voice in representing local interests internationally rather than depending primarily on state politicians and international organizations with state political affiliations (Moustafa, 2011). This "multi-vocalization" (Merry 2006) has led to a familiarity with and acceptance of the messages contained with the rights struggle for women. As the discourse has normalized, it has led to the reframing of rights discourse as a contemporary product of multiple actors. Equally important, this reinterpretation has moved away from privileging the rights discourse from any particular point of origin, including a suspicious imperialistic Western one (Chase 2007).

This multivocalization of human rights has had important consequences for the partnering of rights discourse and Muslim realities. From a sociopsychological viewpoint, Muslim proponents of gender equality are able to garner more support for a discourse that is less and less viewed as an imperialist one imposed by wealthier states on developing ones. Thus, the bitter memories of Muslims watching American invasions in Afghanistan and Iraq — which were presented in part as a liberation of women, leading to an intense suspicion of anything akin to Western-based feminism — are slowly being superseded by a more collectively defined set of feminist values. Muslim women and their advocates are more able to argue against a culturally relativistic discourse conveniently adopted by state powers that enable violations of gender equality in the name of religion by pointing to grass-roots changes and rights discourse that are being produced by and integrated into local belief systems. Further, as rights discourse matures, the view that human rights exist as an all or nothing utopia is being recognized as a convenient fiction of the West (Chase 2007).

Instead, there is a wider recognition that in any reality, most feminist positions exist in a contested and constantly changing sociopolitical and legal reality, with feminists from Muslim contexts allied with secular feminists and gay rights advocates, among others, to widen the scope of human rights (Mayer 2007). Detailing the evolution of feminism in Iran from its inception to contemporary times, Roja Fazaeli shows the changing nature of the discourse and the differential importance given to Islamic legal traditions throughout the dialogue in Iran. Indeed, as Roja Fazaeli and Claudia Merli demonstrate, cultural norms — including those defined by issues of gender — are neither monolithic nor static, and internal debates of change and resistance are as prolific (Volpp 2001) as external ones. Katja Zvan Elliott demonstrates the same point rather differently: although she is concerned about women's right to own property in a small Berber village in Morocco and to have homes separate from those of their husband's family, the women she interviews are much more focused on the right to work after marriage. They are unimpressed by Zvan Elliott's worries that they are "unable" to exercise marital independence in the ways that she expects.

Claudia Merli's essay on female circumcision in southern Thailand reinforces how nonmonolithic Islamic law and traditions can be. She shows how feminist positions on female circumcision vary in distinct ways across men and women. When women choose whether or not and how to circumcise their daughters, they find multivocal and flexible interpretations of Islamic legal traditions that can provide legitimacy for their personal positions. Conflicts between these differing positions can be misinterpreted as irresoluble (Okin 1999), with each group needing to dominate the others or be defeated. Such a position problematizes these debates into binaries that box Islam in as traditional, religious, and backward, with rights seen as modern, secular, and progressive. This tendency to view differing positions as intractable and categorically opposed to each other seriously obscures the complexity of change and women's multiple positions. Instead, these tensions should be seen for what they are: a living out of social realities and of pluralism, as well as evidence of constant change. In a rather dramatic turn of events, Claudia Merli illustrates how female family members noisily dispute the views of the current elder who believes that female circumcision is not required by Islam, a view that most other women she interviews support rather than oppose. In an equally complicated tangle at the state level, Aziza Ahmed demonstrates how a multiplicity of actors with differing investments impede change for increased rights for Muslim women in India. No different from any other sets of relationships, feminist currents must grapple with different actors on different levels and manage the myriad subtle ways that power is traded at each of these levels.

The Politics of Change

A common misperception of the struggle for gender equality in Muslim nations is that it is not radical enough or is too slow. Many of the chapters in this book indirectly counter these assumptions by illustrating how these processes painstakingly unfold. We are reminded in these essays that social change is a dialectical process. Rarely does progress occur in linear fashion; it happens in fits and starts. The quest to rectify the shortcomings of a society almost invariably entails forward movement followed by backsliding. This is especially the case where deeply entrenched interests are threatened and where power relations deeply embedded in society are called into question. This in fact was one of the great truths revealed by Marx and Engels (2008): correcting the abuses of both feudal society and unfettered capitalism involved explosive activities upending established economic structures, changes that harnessed the energy released, counterattacks by those being displaced, and a partial return to the previous status quo, only to be followed by a resumption of anti-establishment forays. Things move forward, then backward, and then forward again; the eventual result is a new social order.

The effective realization of gender equality is no different. The chapters in this volume show that the pathways to social justice for Muslim women are fraught with complications and subject to many of the same social forces that have been at work historically when people pursue improvement in their lives. While long-standing social practices have occasionally been swept rapidly away to produce a radically different world, these cases have been the exceptions and not the rule. Establishing women's rights in societies that are patriarchal, sexist, or misogynous has not been easy anywhere in the world. As a case in point, at the time this book was written, the United States had still not ratified the Convention to Eliminate All Forms of Discrimination Against Women.

Two intertwined forces are argued to be necessary for successful rights change — the sociocultural approach and the politico-legal approach (Baderin 2007). The sociocultural approach is a bottom-up process where local actors working alone (that is, local celebrities or community activists) or with global colleagues hybridize rights values with existing practices in local cultures (Merry 2006) so that new norms are created and shaped to fit with local customs. The sociocultural approach may be particularly relevant for violations of gender equality that tend to occur in the private sphere of the family, violations that are difficult to track and impossible to correct without widespread norm change.

The politico-legal approach (Baderin 2007), generally privileged in the human rights arguments and seen as an index of success or failure, is a top-down approach where states enact changes by passing laws that on the books ensure equality. Baderin argues that the top-down and bottom-up approaches are complementary and that both are necessary for introducing and successfully maintaining human rights change. Several essays in this volume confirm this view. Stephanie Bordat and Saida Kouzzi's work with the marriage contract exemplifies using sociocultural approaches that utilize Islamic tradition and local customs to create new norms as well as shape old ones to better women's lives. However, these changes would not have been possible without the state's sweeping, top-down legal reforms of 2004 in Morocco that guaranteed gender equality in many but not all domains of personal life in Morocco.

Analyses that combine the sociocultural and politico-legal approach seem best able to address the ambivalent nature of change. While women may harbor deep-seated discontent about their exclusion from crucial aspects of daily life, they also may be uneasy about the prospect of changing a way of life to which they are accustomed. They may be apprehensive about the social disarray that such changes might occasion. In short, the devil you know may be preferable to the one you don't know. Reservations about change may be exacerbated by fears of adopting Western mores (Chase 2007), independent of whether the proposed changes are in fact driven by Western or other value schemes. Most Muslim countries experienced centuries of colonialism and missionary crusades that attempted to undercut if not destroy indigenous religious and cultural norms. While there may be eagerness on the part of many Muslim women to have more opportunities and to end male domination, they may well be loath to fight for a whole panoply of rights if these changes are defined as a betrayal of their way of life (Mir-Hosseini and Hamzić 2010). Sociocultural approaches by creating hybridized localized norms, such as using Muslim marriage contracts to improve women's economic situation, can reframe these changes as belonging to the people whom they are intended to benefit. Indeed, as fundamentalist groups and oppressive state regimes use anti-Western rhetoric to impose social control over women, widespread local agitating rather than state-based mandates may be the most effective way to counter such propaganda.

Indeed, in their work on changing a law on violence against women in Morocco, Kouzzi and Bordat challenge the view that women are ambivalent about change — suggesting that this view is a neoliberal Western depiction of women in non-Western states. The authors find that when there is opposition, it comes from members of the elite and educated class, who desire to protect their position, and not from rural and working-class women, who in fact passionately desire change. As proponents of the sociocultural approach argue, most of the rural and working-class urban North African women described in this chapter, when involved at the grass-roots level and given opportunities to shape decisions, advocate for increased rights and change.

Critics of the sociocultural approach to change say that it takes too long and is dependent on maverick leadership, and that microlevel success, especially in private relationships, is difficult to evaluate. In contrast, politico-legal approaches are more transparent and can achieve the same changes more efficiently. However, proponents of sociocultural approaches argue that they are tailored for local realities, whereas top-down processes may miss their mark. Both sides have a point. In her essay on whether the Moudwanna reforms have improved rural women's lives, Zvan Elliott notes that rapid change that occurs top-down rarely considers the social realities of women and may be irrelevant or poorly attuned to their needs. She finds that the proposed changes in the Moroccan Family Code are completely irrelevant to the realities of life in rural Amazigh; as a result, few women are interested in the reform. Their lack of enthusiasm for these changes may be incorrectly interpreted as a reluctance to embrace reform; rather, it stems from a disconnection between the reform and the people it is intended to benefit. In his chapter on the Maldives, Anthony Marcus points out that the top-down legislation is hurting Maldivian women who enjoyed sexual freedom for centuries before so-called feminist legislation crept into the state. In contrast, Anthony Kafumbe makes a strong case for a dramatic overhaul in the Ugandan law, which has dragged its feet where women's property rights are concerned, and argues that these changes need to occur top-down. In fact, many Muslim states — including Indonesia, Pakistan, and Turkey — use top-down approaches (with varying degrees of success) to curtail localized new and oppressive practices against women (Mir-Hosseini and Hamzić 2010).

The tensions of reform, whether moving from top down or bottom up, pose keen dilemmas about the most efficacious means of fomenting change. Evaluating the pace of change and assessing which reforms are acceptable and for who is a very delicate undertaking. Taken together, these different chapters provide a nuanced understanding of these complex processes.

Overall, though, they confirm the wisdom of a growing trend in social policies to encourage gradualism in enforcing change as a way to maintain stability, based on the assumption that rapid change is unwelcome and therefore destabilizing.

Law in Action

As alluded to above, one of the important insights emerging from sociological inquiry is that the politico-legal approach — or the law on the books, the formal law enshrined in constitutions and codes — does not automatically get translated into the law that affects people's lives. The renowned German sociologist Max Weber noted well over a century ago in his classic work *Politics as a Vocation* (1965) that there are competing authorities that can command the allegiance and acquiescence of a society. Legal authority competes with traditional authority and charismatic authority to win the respect and obedience of the people. Legal mandates in themselves may go unheeded if they are at odds with the dictates of respected popular leaders or contrary to deep-seated traditions.

This insight was amplified by Eugen Ehrlich, an Austrian scholar credited by many with being the founder of the sociology of law. He claimed that the "living law" that controls human life may depart significantly from the rules propounded by legislatures and interpreted by courts (Ehrlich 1936). The laws that govern life are socially accepted norms of conduct that may draw on formal law but often supersede it. The weight of custom, therefore, determines the law in action.

This helps explain why legal reforms sometimes are ineffectual in achieving their intended effects. If there are substantial misgivings or outright opposition to changes, those who have the obligation to enforce the law may do so half-heartedly or not at all. And citizens targeted for control by the new legal dictates but who disagree with them may ignore them, especially if they think they can do so with impunity.

Women in many Muslim societies, especially in countries with a history of colonial rule, have to grapple with the legal pluralism of customary law, civil and penal codes, and Islamic law. The classic assumption that the law on the books is in fact the best law (better than customary or traditional law) for the people it governs rarely holds true when examined closely; this is especially the case for minority groups whose members have not been included or consulted in the original formulation. In some cases, a set of laws may treat men and women in more egalitarian ways in one area but not another. When the laws are in conflict, interested political parties and special interest groups are motivated to assign superiority to one set of laws over another, using whatever means and arguments available. Ahmed deconstructs both the assumption of superiority of so-called secular law and the religious authority of the Indian Shariat, arguing that both are intimately tied to British colonial rule, privileging the current dominant (Hindu) groups and consequently marginalizing Muslim minorities. Yüksel Sezgin compares and contrasts different multicultural societies and how the legal and secular interact. Thus, multiple overlays and definitions of legal norms in current political contexts tremendously complicate the legal status of women.

Nevertheless, penal codes and civil codes in some Muslim countries have been amended in furtherance of women's interests and in some cases offer the most effective option to end discrimination against women. But local politics in many areas have transcended these legal advances, and authorities have been lax in putting new regulations into practice. Lip service is given to the modified laws on the books, but enforcement is half-hearted, and the laws are largely unheeded. Moreover, some regimes have picked and chosen which laws best legitimize their rules. In the case of clashes between old and new or secular and religious, such regimes usually select what feels defensibly traditional and therefore authentic, at high cost to women. Both Clarence-Smith, writing primarily on Indonesia, and Merli, discussing southern Thailand, navigate these waters by exploring the position of female circumcision or female genital cutting in Muslim jurisprudence and the current sociopolitical climate that encourages and discourages cutting in these communities.

These cautions and tensions do not mean that the imposition of new laws is to no avail or that new laws can never be written to be genuinely protective of women's rights. Women who have support and the means to fight for their rights can take advantage of the legal protections on the books and occasionally get redress of their grievances. Bordat and Kouzzi demonstrate just this, and Kafumbe argues for new written laws to supersede customary law. Moreover, laws on the books can have the effect of tempering and modifying the local politics and social customs that jeopardize the interests of women. Ultimately, a well-defined and forceful law can still be a potent force in the advancement of women's rights.

Yet there remains a seemingly simple but actually quite provocative question: What does it mean to be a woman, who defines that meaning, and for whom? To a very great extent, the future of women's rights in Muslim societies depends on how this very profound question is answered. Although politics and law are critical ingredients of social transformation, ultimately the driving force that liberates women is their ability to have their voices heard in defining the nature of a fair and humane society. While activism and agitation can bring about change, free and democratically informed self-determination of women is the key to sustaining social justice.

Editors' Note

Many thanks to our wonderful students Jillian C. Dispoto, Karyna Pryiomka, Chelsea Shotwell-Tabke, Keila Simons, Todd Squitieri, Julie Sriken, and Rosa Viñas-Racionero for their hard work on the glossary. Special thanks to Julie Sriken for her contributions to the early part of the project. We are indebted to Jeanne Ferris for her meticulous copyediting of the manuscript. And finally, we owe a warm note of gratitude to Phyllis Deutsch for her constructive criticism, unending support, and encouragement to complete this project.

References

Abu-Lughod, L. 2002. "Do Muslim Women Really Need Saving? Anthropological Reflections on Cultural Relativism and Its Others." *American Anthropologist* 104 (3): 783–90.

Ahmed, L. 1992. *Women and Gender in Islam: Historical Roots of a Modern Debate*. New Haven: Yale University Press.

Baderin, M. A. 2007. "Islam and the Realization of Human Rights in the Muslim World: A Reflection on Two Essential Approaches and Two Divergent Perspectives." *Muslim World Journal of Human Rights* 4 (1): 1–25.

Barazangi, N. 2008. "The Absence of Muslim Women in Shaping Islamic Thought:

Foundations of Muslims' Peaceful and Just Co-Existence." *Journal of Law and Religion* 24 (2): 403–32.

Chase, A. 2007. "The Transnational Muslim World, the Foundations and Origins of Human Rights, and Their Ongoing Intersections." *Muslim Journal of Human Rights* 4 (1): 1–14.

Ehrlich, E. 1936. *Fundamental Principles of the Sociology of Law.* Translated by Walter Moll. Cambridge: Harvard University Press.

Esposito, J. L., and N. J. DeLong-Bas. 2004. *Women in Muslim Family Law*. Syracuse, NY: Syracuse University Press.

Gates, D. K., and P. Steane. 2009. "Political Religion — The Influence of Ideological and Identity Orientation." *Totalitarian Movements and Political Religions* 10 (3–4): 303–25.

Gurel, P. 2009. "Transnational Feminism, Islam, and the Other Woman: How to Teach." *Radical Teacher*, no. 86, 66–70.

Huntington, S. 1993. "The Clash of Civilizations?" *Foreign Affairs* 42 (3): 22–49.

Marx, K., and F. Engels. 2008. *The Communist Manifesto*. Edited by David McLellan. New York: Oxford University Press.

Mayer, A. E. 2007. "The Islam and Human Rights Nexus: Shifting Dimensions." *Muslim Journal of Human Rights* 4 (1): 1–27.

Mernissi, F. 1987. *The Veil and the Male Elite: A Feminist Interpretation of Women's Rights in Islam.* New York: Basic.

Merry, S. E. 2006. "Transnational Human Rights and Local Activism: Mapping the Middle." *American Anthropologist* 108 (1): 38–51.

Mir-Hosseini, Z. 2003. "The Construction of Gender in Islamic Legal Thought and Strategies for Reform." *Hawwa* 1 (1): 1–28.

Mir-Hosseini, Z., and V. Hamzić, V. 2010. *Control and Sexuality: The Revival of Zina Laws in Muslim Contexts*. London: Women Living under Muslim Laws.

Modirzadeh, N. K. 2006. "Taking Islamic Law Seriously: INGOs and the Battle for Muslim Hearts and Minds." *Harvard Human Rights Journal* 19:192–233.

Moustafa, Y. 2011. "The Islamisation of Human Rights: Implications for Gender and Politics in the Middle East." *IDS Bulletin* 42 (1): 21–25.

Nasir, J. J. 2009. *The Status of Women under Islamic Law and Modern Islamic Legislation*. Leiden: Brill.

Okin, S. M. 1999. "Is Multiculturalism Bad for Women?" In Susan Moller Okin with respondents, *Is Multiculturalism Bad for Women?*, edited by Joshua Cohen, Matthew Howard, and Martha C. Nussbaum, 7–24. Princeton: Princeton University Press.

Vis, F., L. van Zoonen, and S. Mihelj. 2011. "Women Responding to the Anti-Islam Film *Fitna*: Voices and Acts of Citizenship on YouTube." *Feminist Review*, no. 97, 110–29.

Volpp, L. 2001. "Feminism versus Multiculturalism." *Columbia Law Review* 101:1181–1218.

Waardenburg, J. 1985. "Islam as a Vehicle of Protest." In *Islamic Dilemmas: Reformers, Nationalists, Industrialization; The Southern Shore of the Mediterranean*, edited by E. Gellner, 22–48. Berlin: Mouton.

Waltz, S. E. 2004. "Universal Human Rights: The Contribution of Muslim States." *Human Rights Quarterly* 26 (4): 799–844.

Weber, M. 1965. *Politics as a Vocation*. Philadelphia: Fortress Press.

Welchman, L. 2007. *Women and Muslim Family Laws in Arab States: A Comparative Overview of Textual Development and Advocacy*. Amsterdam: Amsterdam University Press.

PART ONE

Politics of Change

ANISSA HÉLIE

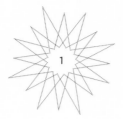

The Politics of Abortion Policy in the Heterogeneous "Muslim World"

Legal frameworks in part inspired by Muslim jurisprudence (also referred to as Sharia laws) regulate the lives of as many as 600 million women around the world, a majority of them living in Asia. Personal Status Codes, known in some contexts as Family Codes, affect various aspects of women's status as citizens, professionals, sexual beings, and so forth. This paper examines and compares contemporary laws, policies, and theological debates relating to abortion in a range of Muslim countries. It is timely because reductionist commentaries—present especially in the media of the United States and other Western countries, but also finding their way into academic writing—often fail to recognize the diversity that exists across Muslim societies.

Apart from the widespread reference to the so-called Muslim world—a term that erroneously suggests some sort of homogeneity—neoconservative discourses in particular place emphasis on women's status, presenting it as uniformly subordinate. In fact, the sheer geographical, cultural, and political scope of Muslim societies implies that legal approaches and national policies (including those relevant to women's bodily rights and abortion) are likely to be more varied than is usually portrayed. The confusion that leads to constructing homogenized, and hence inaccurate, views of "Muslim laws" and "Muslim women" must be clarified. This chapter is intended to operate as an intervention into these debates: focusing on one particular aspect within the reproductive rights arena—abortion—it provides concrete data that challenge ongoing generalizations and misperceptions. My hope is that it will contribute to a larger, critically important project aimed at making the realities and complexities of Muslim societies more intelligible to an often inadequately informed audience.

Section 1 frames the issue of abortion in a global context, providing statistical evidence of the connections between unsafe abortion and maternal mortality. It then briefly evokes how, over the past several decades, interventions to increase access to abortion have been linked to a neo-imperialist agenda and have provided ideological fodder to sections of the Muslim religious right. Finally, section 1 refers to the controversy over rights, looking at some of the key confrontations in the international arena between opponents and advocates of women's reproductive rights in the 1990s, and examining current efforts by the international community to improve maternal health.

Section 2 looks at Muslim jurisprudence and examines how theological considerations are reflected, or not, in the legal arena. Presenting various Muslim scholars' legal opinions, it inquires whether these evidence a unanimous view regarding the permissibility of voluntary termination of pregnancy across Muslim societies. Section 2 also provides an overview of forms of legislation related to abortion in Muslim-majority countries and includes specific examples of state policies enacted in nations ranging from Algeria to Malaysia and Bangladesh. And it inquires to what extent governments appear to be readjusting their abortion policies and guidelines on the basis of concrete socioeconomic realities.

Section 3 pays attention to a claim urged by a number of women's rights defenders from Muslim societies: that laws (including abortion laws) become more restrictive where conservative religious voices are able to influence, more or less overtly, state policies and institutions. Among these religious groups, those associated with political Islam have been identified as particularly concerned with curtailing women's autonomy and control over their reproductive capacities. Looking at contexts as varied as Nigeria, Kyrgyzstan, Iran, and

Bangladesh, section 3 raises the question of whether politico-religious (or fundamentalist) groups are indeed increasingly powerful in shaping national legal frameworks.

1. Abortion in a Globalized Context: Public Health Concern, Problem of Imperialism, or Question of Rights?

In both Muslim and non-Muslim societies, questions linked to women's bodies tend to generate especially fierce debates in the arena of reproductive rights. The issue of abortion in particular has been for decades, and remains, a controversial and highly politicized issue around the world. We first examine the issue from a public health perspective, revealing the links between illegal, unsafe abortion and its impact on maternal mortality worldwide. The political implications of the abortion debate are then considered, with an emphasis on the criticisms formulated by Muslim politico-religious groups — criticisms that are seemingly directed against imperialist policies yet that are ultimately geared toward limiting women's reproductive options. Finally, the long-standing relevance of abortion debates in international forums is highlighted, as we review key reproductive rights agreements made at UN conferences held in Cairo and Beijing in the 1990s, and highlight recent attempts by governments worldwide to curb maternal mortality, notably through the Millennium Development Goals.

ABORTION AND PUBLIC HEALTH: UNSAFE ABORTION AND MATERNAL MORTALITY

Pregnancy-related problems can pose serious risks to women's health, but these issues have long been overlooked or made invisible, despite their prevalence in some regions and the fact that most are medically preventable. Actually, women's lives are most at risk when minimal infrastructure and a lack of basic training for health care providers combine with legal restrictions. This is particularly true with regard to abortion in contexts where it is outlawed or practiced in precarious conditions. The World Health Organization (WHO) currently defines "unsafe abortion" as "a procedure for terminating an unintended pregnancy that is carried out either by a person lacking the necessary skills or in an environment that does not conform to the minimal medical standards, or both."[1]

Country-specific data show that women seek and undergo abortion even where access is illegal.[2] For example, Pakistan and Indonesia—two Muslim countries where abortion is outlawed and considered a criminal offense—have some of the highest rates of unsafe abortions. In Indonesia in 1989 there were "an estimated 750,000 to 1 million abortions performed per year or a ratio of 16.7–22.2 abortions per 100 live births."[3] A decade later, the trend had increased: it is estimated that in 2000, about two million abortions were taking place every year in Indonesia.[4] In Pakistan, 2004 statistics showed that "890,000 unwanted pregnancies (or one in six pregnancies) end in induced abortions per year."[5] Because the legal grounds for abortion are severely restricted in both these countries, the procedures are often performed by unqualified individuals in substandard medical conditions. As a result, health risks are great, ranging from infection to lifelong complications, infertility, and death—despite the fact that safe and effective abortion methods are available.

The high prevalence of unsafe abortion therefore constitutes a major public health problem—not only in Muslim countries but globally. In 2000, WHO estimated that the annual number of abortions worldwide was 42 million[6]—22 million occurring safely and 20 million unsafely.[7] Of the 20 million unsafe abortions, 19 million (a staggering 97 percent) occurred in developing countries.[8] The latest WHO figures indicate a rise in unsafe abortion worldwide, with data for 2008 reaching 21.6 million.[9] In addition, unsafe abortion accounts each year for 47,000 maternal deaths (13 percent of all maternal deaths) and causes a further 5 million women to suffer temporary or permanent disability. The relationship between restrictive legislation and medical complications related to illegal abortion—including increased maternal mortality ratios[10]—has been documented throughout the world. In 2010, the UN High Commissioner on Human Rights identified unsafe abortion as "one of the five major direct causes of maternal deaths,"[11] resulting in about one in eight pregnancy-related deaths.[12]

It must be noted that current maternal mortality ratios vary drastically from one region to another—but they overwhelmingly affect the "low and middle income countries of the economic South where 98 percent of maternal deaths occur."[13] Pregnancy-related deaths are contingent on many factors, but they skyrocket in conflict zones and in conditions of extreme poverty. In Muslim-majority countries, 2008 data show that incidence is as high as 1,400 for 100,000 live births in Afghanistan—among the highest in the world—but

TABLE 1.1

Maternal Mortality Ratios in Muslim-Majority Countries, 2009

MIDDLE EAST	NORTHERN AFRICA	SUB-SAHARAN AFRICA
Bahrain 19	Algeria 120	Burkina Faso 560
Iran 30	Egypt 82	Chad 1,200
Iraq 75	Libya 64	Djibouti 300
Jordan 59	Morocco 110	Eritrea 280
Kuwait 9	Sudan 750	Gambia 400
Lebanon 26	Tunisia 60	Mali 830
Oman 20		Mauritania 550
Saudi Arabia 24		Niger 820
Qatar 8		Nigeria 840
Syria 46		Senegal 410
Turkey 23		Sierra Leone 970
United Arab Emirates 10		Somalia 1,200
Yemen 210		

CENTRAL ASIA	SOUTH AND SOUTHEASTERN ASIA	EUROPE
Kyrgyzstan 81	Afghanistan 1,400	Albania 31
Tajikistan 64	Bangladesh 340	
Turkmenistan 77	Indonesia 240	
Uzbekistan 30	Malaysia 31	
	Pakistan 260	

Note: Numbers refer to maternal deaths per 100,000 live births.

Source: World Health Organization, Global Health Observatory. 2008.
"World Health Statistics: Cause-Specific Mortality and Morbidity; Maternal Mortality Ratio."
Geneva: World Health Organization. http://apps.who.int/ghodata.

as low as 18 in Saudi Arabia.[14] Maternal mortality ratios tend to be very high in sub-Saharan Africa[15] but much lower in former Soviet republics or the Middle East and North Africa regions (MENA). Table 1.1 highlights these discrepancies between Muslim countries, although it does not reflect the fact that ratios also tend to vary within countries.[16]

ABORTION AS AN "IMPERIALIST PROJECT":
THE MUSLIM RELIGIOUS RIGHT'S DISCOURSES
AND FEMINIST RESPONSES

Despite the severe toll of unsafe procedures on women's bodies and lives, the abortion issue has nevertheless been instrumentalized for political purposes. Particularly relevant to examine here is the rhetoric used by Islamists and the Muslim religious right over the last several decades—specifically, the religious right's alleged anti-imperialist stand—but we also briefly touch on the counter-arguments developed by advocates of reproductive rights in Muslim contexts.

Starting with coercive population policies implemented beginning in the late 1960s and continuing until—though to a lesser extent—the 1990s,[17] "popu-lation control" referred to the regulation of fertility enacted as a government strategy. This involved a range of practices—including forced sterilization, forced abortion, and coercive use of contraceptives—that were at times carried out without the consent (or even the knowledge) of the women concerned. The reality of neocolonialism (particularly Western pressure exercised over the Third World to endorse population control policies, and the funding made available for these purposes) has long been used to lend power to the anti-abortion argument of those in Muslim countries whose aim is in fact to curtail women's reproductive rights. For example, in post-1979 Iran, abortion access was denounced by the new Islamist regime as an imperialist strategy promoted by the West to limit the growth of Muslim populations.

This argument, based on defining abortion as an imperialist project, re-mains alive. Interestingly, commentaries currently available on websites that promote comparable conceptions of Islam—and of women as reproductive engines—continue to issue similar warnings. For example, *Mission Islam* (whose stated goal, as stated on the organization's home page, is to denounce "the conspiracy that exists to exterminate Muslims and the religion of Islam from the face of the Earth") contains highly sensationalist rhetoric. An article on population control discusses alleged Western attempts to deplete Muslim populations in Nigeria, the Gambia and Indonesia in the 1990s. Providing ap-parently pertinent data, the unnamed author asserts that "the Muslim world is the primary focal point for the demographic fears of the West."[18] The argument is then carefully crafted to provoke dismay and anger, with an explosive con-spiracy theory involving the UN Population Fund, the International Planned

Parenthood Federation, a pro-Israel think tank, outside financiers, mass media manipulation, and psychological warfare. To those familiar with the Muslim religious right discourse, the conclusion reached by the author is predictable: the final section advocates "a return to militancy: Fighting back against the enemies of Islam."[19] In other words, a Muslim using family planning methods or resorting to abortion is a pawn of hostile foreign powers—and by extension an enemy of Islam. In section 3 I will come back to this manipulation of religious beliefs—a strategy that remains effective even as it has little to do with theological debates and much more to do with a desire on the part of male clerics to control women's agency over their bodies.

It is not within the scope of this chapter to elaborate on the criticisms of coercive population policies formulated by women's rights advocates in Muslim societies—that is, by social actors who are clearly at the opposite end of the political spectrum from the religious right. Yet it must be noted that in the 1980s and 1990s, feminists from various Muslim countries and communities also condemned measures aiming at curbing birth rates. These feminists criticized population control policies on the basis that they were heavily promoted from abroad without securing the involvement of those concerned, particularly women, and that they reflected a hegemonic agenda on the part of institutions such as the World Bank, the Rockefeller Foundation, or Pathfinder. While concerned about donor-driven agendas and how these shaped national health programs, however, feminist critique has particularly emphasized the impact of these agendas on women's bodies and lives. Activists have focused as much on denouncing coercion (forced abortions and sterilizations) as on condemning prohibition (of contraceptives or abortion). While feminists' analysis took stock of the complexities at stake, their approach was often undermined by simplistic yet powerful allegations that they were colluding with foreign powers. The religious right and conservatives also accused them of undermining religious and cultural values.

ABORTION AS A HUMAN RIGHT? FROM THE UNITED NATIONS CONFERENCES OF THE 1990S TO THE MILLENNIUM DEVELOPMENT GOALS (2000–2015)

The United Nations Conferences of the 1990s: Cairo and Beijing Confrontations between advocates of access to abortion and those who opposed a "woman's right to choose" culminated during the UN-sponsored international conferences of the 1990s. Overt conflicts emerged regarding whether control of women's reproductive functions should lie primarily with the individual, the state, or the community (with religious leaders being particularly vocal spokespersons). While these political tensions had been ongoing, they reached a peak during two key events: the International Conference on Population and Development (ICPD) held in Cairo in 1994 and the World Conference on Women that took place in Beijing the following year. To this day, both Cairo and Beijing remain landmarks in the history of reproductive rights.

Crucially, in 1994 the ICPD established the close relationship between reproductive rights and human rights. The final document stated that reproductive rights "rest on the recognition of the basic right of all couples and individuals to decide freely and responsibly the number, spacing and timing of their children and to have the information and means to do so, and the right to attain the highest standard of sexual and reproductive health."[20] It insisted that the principle of "informed free choice" was "essential" and advised governments to "remove unnecessary legal, medical, clinical and regulatory barriers to information and to access" to the "full range of modern family planning methods."[21] Further, it urged decision makers to "deal with the health impact of unsafe abortion as a major public health concern."[22] A most significant step was achieved at the next UN conference, in 1995, when the Beijing Platform for Action (the final document of the United Nations Fourth World Conference on Women) linked improved women's health to legal reform, recommending that governments "consider reviewing laws containing punitive measures against women who have undergone illegal abortions."[23]

Yet, in spite of these outcomes of the Cairo and Beijing conferences, which focused on the identification of individual women's human rights, conservative religious actors of various faiths ensured that abortion would not be recognized by the conferences as part of reproductive health and rights, in deference to existing national laws.[24] Conservative Muslim governments (alongside their allies from other religious faiths) were particularly forceful in their opposition, and they resorted to a familiar anti-imperialist rhetoric. For example, "the Saudi Arabian 'Council of Ulama,' that nation's highest body of religious authorities, condemned the Cairo conference as a 'ferocious assault on Islamic society' and forbade Muslims from attending. Sudan, Lebanon and Iraq then joined Saudi Arabia in announcing that they would not send delegates to Cairo. . . [I]ssues of family planning and birth control [were] seen as an imposition of western values on the Muslim people and an attempt to revive 'colonial and imperial ambition'."[25]

As established earlier, the anti-imperialist claim deployed by the Muslim religious right disguises its motives, which are primarily centered on its core objection to women's autonomy over their fertility and, more broadly, gender equality. Indeed, the same voices that opposed abortion (along with other gender equity provisions) back in the 1990s continue to be vocal now in condemning foreign interference in the reproductive health arena.[26] Tellingly, they do not similarly characterize other trends adversely affecting reproductive health and health care in general—such as the lack of trained providers, shrinking state support for public health systems, privatization of health care,[27] and the pharmaceutical industry's prohibitive pricing of medicines—all of which undermine access to essential services and result in increased mortality rates. Instead, the selective use of the foreign interference theme works precisely to undermine recognition of women as subjects with human rights. Despite the carefully crafted argumentation, the issue at stake is clearly not about resisting bullying by foreign powers: it is about the control of women's bodies and agency. Even as advocates for women have responded powerfully to the failure to recognize reproductive rights as human rights,[28] the issue remains highly contested.

The Millennium Developments Goals (2000-2015) Since the 1990s, the health risks associated with a legal ban on abortion have been emphasized further. In particular, the correlation between unsafe abortion and maternal mortality has gained visibility in the context of the Millennium Developments Goals (MDFS),[29] a set of eight concrete development benchmarks identified by the UN Development Program and aiming at eradicating global poverty. Governments agreed on the MDFS in 2000, with quantifiable outcomes to be achieved by 2015. Increasingly aware of the scope and gravity of maternal mortality, the international community came together to try to collectively address the issue: MDF5 focuses on "improving maternal health,"[30] and several other MDFS are seen as relevant to abortion.[31]

While the MDFS constitute a major step forward in terms of international awareness, there is increasing concern that the benchmarks may not be achieved by 2015. Also, feminist critique of MDF5 has pointed to its limitations, including the shift in focus, political intent, and language from earlier international forums. For example, the emphasis in Cairo and Beijing on reproductive *rights* is replaced in MDF5 by milder and politically less controversial references to reproductive *health*. Without explicitly raising the issue of abortion, MDF5 nevertheless specifically encompasses the availability of contraceptives and tackles teenage pregnancy. MDF5 addresses abortion in that, as experts agree, the goal "is unlikely to be achieved without addressing unsafe abortion and associated mortality and morbidity"[32] in a context where unsafe abortions account for 13 percent of maternal deaths globally.[33] In her comprehensive report on abortion worldwide, Susan Cohen points out: "In the developed and developing world alike, antiabortion advocates and policymakers refuse to acknowledge the facts that abortion's legal status has much less to do with how often it occurs than with whether or not it is safe, and that the surest way to actually reduce the incidence of abortion is to reduce the incidence of unintended pregnancy. While they debate, obfuscate and insist on legal prohibitions, the consequences for women, their families and society as a whole continue to be severe and undeniable."[34] Indeed, there is urgency as tens of thousands of lives are lost each year due to complications linked to unsafe abortion.

2. Religious Discourses and State Policies

As the human cost of unsafe abortion is increasingly acknowledged, various social actors—ranging from international agencies to governments, and from nongovernmental organizations (NGOs) to nonstate actors—are stakeholders in the politically and ethically charged abortion debate. Around the world, the increased involvement of religious actors and institutions in policy matters has raised concern among human rights defenders, partly because the "tendency to treat religious condemnations of abortion as irrefutable"[35] can leave little room for more nuanced views. A full understanding of Muslim laws regarding abortion requires both a highlighting of the main religious stands on abortion and an examination of how laws are formalized on the ground.

THEOLOGICAL DEBATES:
BETWEEN JUSTIFICATION AND PROHIBITION

With respect to Muslim contexts, references to "the correct Islamic position" on abortion are common in media as diverse as secular Western newspapers and broadcasts, literature distributed in mosques, and extremist Internet sites.

The often-quoted assertion that "Islam prohibits abortion" does not, as will be demonstrated, reflect the wide range of Muslim scholars' opinions on the matter. This misconception derives from a broader framework of reference to "Islamic law," which suggests the existence of a unified normative legal system common to all Muslims. Using the term "Muslim laws" may better reflect the fact that there is no centralized authority in Islam. Traditionally, guidance is provided by theologians whose carefully considered opinions (fatwas, which are not legally binding[36]) carry varying weight depending on the theologian's status and knowledge. Apart from Shi'a-Sunni differences in jurisprudence, the four main schools of thought within Sunni Islam ensure de facto diversity in terms of religious interpretation. Further, the principle of *ijtihad*[37]—or the use of reason to apply Islamic teachings to modern contexts—allows for legitimate debate among learned scholars. It is worth reiterating the point made by the Pakistani sociologist Farida Shaheed, currently a UN independent expert on cultural rights, who calls attention to the interplay between "religious continuity and social change." Shaheed notes that it should not be "presumed that religion is uni-dimensional or fixed in time." In addition to ongoing theological debates, beliefs also fluctuate: "Within one sub-group religious attitudes and practices vary with ethnic and class identity, and with time, these undergo changes."[38]

Muslim Jurisprudence—Varying Legal Doctrines Regarding Abortion The Quran does not explicitly address abortion, and religious scholars therefore consider other sources—such as relevant hadith or the Sunnah—in forging their opinions. As noted by Sa'diyya Shaikh, a professor of Islamic studies at Cape Town University, "historically the Muslim legal positions range from unqualified permissibility of an abortion before 120 days into the pregnancy on the one hand to categorical prohibition of abortion altogether on the other. Even within a single legal school the majority position was often accompanied by dissenting minority positions."[39] Today, some jurists continue to reject abortion entirely as incompatible with Islam, while others tolerate it. The latter may endorse a range of valid reasons, including the health of the fetus (for example, fetal impairment), the circumstances of the pregnancy (for example, rape or incest) or its impact on the woman (for example, danger to a woman's life or to her mental health, but also economic or social reasons, or when a new pregnancy threatens the life of a suckling infant).

In all legal schools, prohibition of abortion is contingent on the gestational age of the fetus. The above reference to 120 days is related to ensoulment, the belief that a fetus becomes fully human when "an angel is sent and breathes the *ruh* (spirit) into it." While the timing of "ensoulment is not specified in the Qur'an,"[40] Quranic verses discuss various stages of fetal development. The relevant "passages describe the formation of *nutfa*, *'alaqa*, and *mudgha* (semen, a bloody clot, and a lump of flesh)" and are read alongside with the *"hadith* in which these stages are divided into periods of 40 days."[41] Theologians' varying assessments of when abortion is prohibited (becoming a criminal offense) are linked to the series of changes the fetus undergoes from conception to 120 days—shifting from a simple organism to a human being.

Ensoulment is just one question on which jurists differ as they debate either previously established matters or issues prompted by recent developments. For example, an ongoing discussion centers on whether abortion for rape or incest victims is *haram* (prohibited) or justified.[42] Prominent clerics and religious institutions—such as the Grand Sheikh of Al-Azhar in Egypt in 2008[43] and the Indonesian Council of Ulemas (MUI)[44] in 2005—have recently supported the right of raped women to seek abortion. Indeed, several countries—such as the Sudan, Iraq, and Qatar,[45] among others—have recently incorporated similar opinions into their legal provisions, allowing abortion for rape victims.

Interestingly, both opponents and advocates of family planning and/or abortion (not all of them learned scholars) can justify their preferred position by referring to the same sources. For example, one often-quoted Quranic verse is: "Do not kill your children for fear of poverty for it is We who shall provide sustenance for you as well as for them."[46] On the one hand, this is seen as corroborating the so-called "traditional Muslim rejection of birth control";[47] as such, it is interpreted as meaning that "the greatest reward Allah gives a person for his commitment to God, right in this world, is to give him various children... This is why the Prophet clearly stressed that Muslims should marry and generate for He will be proud of their large number in the last day."[48] On the other hand, it is analyzed in relation to its original context by feminist theologians (such as the Pakistani Riffat Hassan), who interpret it as a reference to—and a rejection of—the customary infanticide of girls at the time of the Prophet. These dissenting interpretations highlight the need to avoid conflating "Islamic" and "Muslim." As the Nigerian researcher Ayesha Imam notes, "Islam is the religion or faith (the way of Allah), while Muslims are those who believe in Islam and attempt to practice it... The recognition that Islamic and Muslim are not synonymous is important because it helps avoid essentialising Islam and reifying it as an a-historical, disembodied ideal which is more-or-less imperfectly actualized in this or that community."[49] It is a fact that Islam has merged with diverse cultural traditions across the world, ensuring local variations in terms of religious beliefs and practices, as well as in terms of interpretations of the scriptures.

ABORTION LAW IN APPLICATION
IN MUSLIM-MAJORITY STATE POLICIES

How do these theological debates influence actual legislations, and are they reflected at national policy levels? In 2009, "70 countries, representing more than 60 percent of the world's population, permit[ted] abortion without restriction . . . or on broad grounds."[50] Table 1.2 shows where Muslim-majority countries stand with regard to abortion (if allowed, it should be performed during the first four months of gestation; beyond this, certain countries make provisions for abortion to save a mother's life). National laws are generally justified with reference to Islam, but combinations of theological, cultural, historical, and political factors translate into different legal prescriptions at the country level. Indeed, despite the emphasis on religion as their main framework, Muslim laws are not the sole parameter affecting legal prescriptions related to abortion. Other factors intervene: in most countries, a complex mix of customary practices, civil codes partly inherited from colonial times, *fiqh* (Muslim jurisprudence), and so forth is likely to be at play. In fact, one reproductive rights expert has noted that "the majority of abortion laws in the North African and Middle Eastern region are based on antiquated civil laws (primarily French, British and Italian), not Islamic law (except for Sudan, Iran and Saudi Arabia)."[51]

As the data above make clear, laws range from total prohibition from the time of conception to different levels of permissibility (generally during the first four months of pregnancy). It is beyond the scope of this paper to examine the complexities involved in each context, but it must be remembered that legal prescriptions, practical considerations, and social norms combine to enhance, limit, or criminalize women's ability to access abortion services. For example, where abortion is illegal, penal and criminal codes often include sanctions against both the person performing the abortion and the woman seeking it (as in Oman or Pakistan). Where abortion is legal, there may nonetheless be little awareness about abortion access among the public or little willingness to apply the law among health practitioners, or both. (A case in point is Malaysia, where

TABLE 1.2

Abortion Laws in Muslim-Majority Countries: Grounds on Which Abortion Is Permitted (as of September 2009)

COUNTRY	TO SAVE THE WOMAN'S LIFE OR PROHIBITED ALTOGETHER	TO PRESERVE PHYSICAL HEALTH	TO PRESERVE MENTAL HEALTH	ON SOCIO-ECONOMIC GROUNDS	WITHOUT RESTRICTION OR ON REQUEST
Afghanistan*	•				
Bangladesh*	•				
Egypt	•				
Indonesia*	•				
Iran* (F)	•				
Iraq	•				
Lebanon*	•				
Libya* (PA)	•				
Mali*	•				
Mauritania	•				
Nigeria*	•				
Oman	•				
Senegal	•				
Somalia	•				
Sudan (R)*	•				
Syria (SA/PA)*	•				
United Arab Emirates (SA/PA)*	•				
West Bank & Gaza Strip*	•				
Yemen*	•				
Burkina Faso (R/I/F)	•	•			
Chad (F)	•	•			
Djibouti	•	•			
Eritrea (R/I)	•	•			
Jordan	•	•			
Kuwait (SA/PA/F)	•	•			
Morocco (SA)	•	•			
Niger (F)	•	•			
Pakistan	•	•			
Qatar (F)	•	•			

COUNTRY	TO SAVE THE WOMAN'S LIFE OR PROHIBITED ALTOGETHER	TO PRESERVE PHYSICAL HEALTH	TO PRESERVE MENTAL HEALTH	ON SOCIO-ECONOMIC GROUNDS	WITHOUT RESTRICTION OR ON REQUEST
Saudi Arabia (SA/PA)	•	•			
Algeria	•	•	•		
Gambia	•	•	•		
Malaysia	•	•	•		
Sierra Leone	•	•	•		
Albania	•	•	•	•	•
Azerbaijan	•	•	•	•	•
Kyrgyzstan	•	•	•	•	•
Tajikistan	•	•	•	•	•
Tunisia	•	•	•	•	•
Turkey (SA/PA)	•	•	•	•	•
Turkmenistan	•	•	•	•	•
Uzbekistan	•	•	•	•	•

* Exception only to save woman's life   *Italics* | No exception to save woman's life
F | Abortion permitted in cases of fetal impairment   I | Abortion permitted in cases of incest
PA | Parental authorization required   R | Abortion permitted in cases of rape
SA | Spousal authorization required

Source: The format of this table is borrowed from the Asian-Pacific Resource and Research Centre for Women 2009; the data is excerpted from the Center for Reproductive Rights 2009.

a progressive law recognizes physical and mental health as grounds for abortion and the National Fatwa Committee endorsed abortion during the first 120 days of pregnancy, yet a monitoring study carried out by Asian-Pacific Resource and Research Centre for Women [ARROW] in 2009 shows that "there is a strong anecdotal evidence of restricted accessibility in several public hospitals."[52]) On the other hand, Tunisia—the first MENA country to liberalize its abortion law, which it did in 1973—has taken bold steps, introducing adolescent-friendly clinics and making abortion available to unmarried women.[53]

Bangladesh: The Case of "Menstrual Regulation" Bangladesh's innovative policy needs to be briefly addressed as an example of the pragmatic accommodation that a state's health services and conservative religious forces can make to one another. Abortion is illegal in Bangladesh (except to save a woman's life), but in the early 1970s the government became concerned about the country's growing population. In 1974 the state introduced menstrual regulation (MR, also known as ME, for menstrual extraction) for women at risk of being pregnant. The procedure is allowed up to ten weeks "following a missed menstrual period," but because the pregnancy is not technically verified, MR is not regulated by the penal code. It is usually referred to as a "postcontraceptive method" or an "interim method of establishing nonpregnancy." By 1979 the government had "included MR in the national family planning program"[54] and, "over the last 20 years, has trained over 10,000 physicians and other health care providers to provide MR services."[55] Beyond MR's being "a crucial strategy to circumvent anti-abortion laws,"[56] the Bangladeshi case illustrates that women's reproductive rights are not only contingent on religious and ethical considerations but also on sociopolitical matters. Bangladesh's matter-of-factness is certainly not unique, as Carla Makhlouf Obermeyer shows in her discussion of changing population policies in Iran. She makes a point that has a wider relevance: "While the [religious] doctrine has a degree of flexibility on issues of reproduction, the political context is a key factor for understanding the way in which religious doctrine is interpreted."[57] In other words, governments that claim adherence to Islamic doctrine tend to either use or reject religious arguments when suitable to justify adjustments in policy. They may also engage with religious authorities to secure more liberal interpretations, or more conservative ones, that fit their needs at a given time. As a result of this pragmatism, reproductive laws and policies are far from static.

Algeria: Dealing with Wartime Rapes Algeria is another good example of pragmatic politics. Until the 1970s, abortion was outlawed, and family planning information was not available. However, when confronted with a spiraling population (and an average of 7.9 *living* children per woman[58]), the government launched a public awareness campaign focusing on the compatibility of contraception with Islam. Officially, abortion was still rejected on religious grounds: "The opinion (15 February 1973) of sheikh Ahmad Hammani, at the time President of the Higher Muslim Council of Algeria, was very rigid, with abortion being a crime for him and the abortionist a murderer who exposes himself to revenge and the law of retaliation."[59] A couple of decades later, however, another contingency needed to be dealt with—namely, the fact that during the 1990s, fundamentalist armed groups kidnapped and raped several thousand young women (estimates vary between 1,000 and 3,000), forcibly impregnating them. When planning its response, the government felt it needed to take into account the reactions of a socially conservative society where raped women were considered as having "lost their virginity" and, as such, were often rejected by their families. In 1998, the government secured a fatwa from the High Islamic Council allowing abortion for rape victims[60]—an edict requiring that each victim of sexual violence be considered "a chaste and honorable woman, that no one should blame or punish [or the false accuser may be sued]."[61] Furthermore, once the rape was confirmed by testimonies, no doctor could invoke his or her freedom of conscience to refuse to perform an abortion. Worth noting is the fact that religious authorities did not initiate this fatwa: it was the "Ministry of National Solidarity and the Family [an Algerian governmental agency] which took the initiative in requesting the ruling."[62] National needs and concerns took precedence over earlier religious considerations.

Concretely, when specific developments—such as economic trends or war—require a large pool of labor at a particular juncture, contraception and abortion become unavailable and, often, are deemed un-Islamic. But when governments become alarmed by the threat of overpopulation, religious support is often enrolled so that abortion laws may be liberalized. In such situations, conservative religious forces cooperate without exercising dominant power in their relationship with the state. Sometimes, however, in strong collusion and coalition building with fundamentalist forces, governments in Muslim-majority states effectively bow to the dominant forces of the religious right and advance their generally more restrictive policies.

3. Fundamentalist Politics

Reproductive health and rights continue to be sites of negotiations between states and civil society, as well as sites of conflicts between the religious right and women's reproductive rights advocates. In contexts where fundamentalist forces[63] are vocal and increasingly affect national political agendas, women's rights (in particular, sexual or reproductive rights) tend to be denounced as a crime against Islam—or as an offense to Muslim culture or a threat to Muslim values. Following a regional consultation in 2007, a prominent activist from Sisters in Islam in Malaysia noted that "religious interpretations that do not support women's sexual and reproductive rights and gender equality are having an increasing impact in many countries of our region. This extends from negatively influencing sexuality and reproductive policies and laws and their implementation, to actual access to health services, as well as morality norms."[64] The Asian and Pacific region is indeed not the only part of the world affected by the rise of these sectarian and authoritarian forces: a number of feminists from other Muslim contexts have documented this trend over the last several decades. A few selected examples from Nigeria, Bangladesh, Kyrgyzstan, and Iran stress the impact that fundamentalist discourses—and practices—have had on women's reproductive self-determination.

ISLAMIZATION PROCESSES AND THEIR IMPACT ON ABORTION POLICIES IN NIGERIA, BANGLADESH, KYRGYZSTAN, AND IRAN

Nigeria "No good Muslim will ever accept any human directive which contravenes the laws of Allah" begins a pamphlet published "in response to the national population control program adopted by the Nigerian military government in 1988." The writer is presented as a "one-time governor [and] highly respected religious leader" who "discuss[es] the divinely ordained balance between male and female and between human numbers and resources" and objects to "those who support anti-natalist programmes [and] fail to take into consideration the resources that are made available to righteous people as a result of divine providence."[65] In a couple of sentences, the anonymous commentator exemplifies several arguments commonly used by fundamentalist leaders to challenge those who do not share their views. First, "human directives" (that is, man-made laws—in this case, government family planning policies) are presented as contradicting or even undermining what are otherwise perceived as God-given injunctions; this establishes a hierarchy that no true believer can challenge in good faith. Second, popular resentment against an authoritarian regime comes as a helpful reminder that "the military government" should not be trusted. Third, the author's social and religious standing is legitimized to ensure greater support. Fourth, gender norms are clearly presented as immutable and the product of God's will. Finally, repeated references to "divine providence" and to the role that "good Muslims" and "righteous people" have to play help clarify the way: real Muslims cannot resort to family planning, lest they betray their faith. This conveys a potent threat that suggests to those tempted to follow another path that they will face God's wrath. Furthermore, such discourse creates a climate that incites human rights violations, legitimizing punishment (including extrajudicial punishment) of perceived deviations from religious teachings.

Bangladesh The processes of Islamization in various Muslim countries and communities provides a fertile ground to both state and nonstate actors who, claiming to uphold moral values and religious prescriptions, feel entitled to unleash their own wrath on individuals. Bangladesh has witnessed a strengthening of politico-religious forces over the last decades and attests to the pervasiveness of fundamentalist discourse at the community level. Issues such as reproductive rights provided a platform for the religious right's increased mobilization. In the 1980s, birth control campaigns were aggressively promoted by the Bangladeshi government. By the early 1990s, the prominent feminist lawyer Salma Sobhan noted that conservative male community figures started "arrogating to themselves the privilege of pronouncing *fatwas*,"[66] although they were not qualified to pronounce religious edicts. By hijacking and subverting traditional, informal village tribunals (*shalish* or *salish*[67]), these coalitions of elders and/or clerics appointed themselves as judicial authorities, pronouncing sentences and even enforcing punishments. The edicts they pronounced targeted women especially and focused on enforcing narrow definitions of cultural and moral norms. While alleged offenses varied (ranging from working outside the home to exercising agency in sexual matters), the sociologist Sajeda Amin and the lawyer Sara Hossain noted in the mid-1990s that a series of fatwas were directed at local women who used family planning. These fatwas imposed harsh sanctions, including "social ostracization, refusal to burial, and lashings and other sentences."[68] The authors also observe: "Interestingly, while Muslim fundamentalists have not directly threatened family planning programs, they have reacted to the assertion of women's reproductive rights within the context of such programs. In this effort to challenge the ability of women to assert their reproductive rights, fundamentalist groups have sought to impose a monolithic and repressive interpretation of religious laws and religious views."[69] To specifically target women is a feature common to many religious fundamentalisms.

Kyrgyzstan An additional way to curtail women's rights (reproductive or otherwise) is through legal reform—another avenue used by fundamentalists in various regions. As in most former Soviet republics, termination of pregnancy is legal in Kyrgyzstan: *women can obtain an abortion on request up to the twelfth week of pregnancy, and up to the twenty-second week for socioeconomic and medical reasons. An additional guarantee is enshrined in the* reproductive rights law, which states in article 12 that "a woman cannot be forced by anyone to pregnancy, abortion, or delivery. Such actions are qualified as violence against women."[70] But since the mid-1990s, the government has faced pressure from Islamic groups seeking to restrict abortion. Furthermore, in June 2006, the government ombudsman tried to introduce criminal liability for women and medical staff terminating pregnancies between twelve and twenty-two weeks for social reasons. In response, a coalition of women's NGOs launched a campaign to defeat this initiative, first organizing hearings locally and then mobilizing their colleagues in the region[71] and beyond. The liberal abortion law remained in place, but in January 2010, Olga Djanaeva, from the Rural Women's Union (ALGA, an NGO whose mission is to improve rural women's quality of life), was still issuing warnings regarding the pervasive pressure exercised by religious anti-abortion advocates on the government in Kyrgyzstan.[72]

Iran Lastly, the example of Iran may challenge commonly held assumptions. As noted by Lynn Freedman, a leading expert on maternal mortality and former board member of Women Living under Muslim Laws: "Although fundamentalists are intensely concerned with the control of women, this does not necessarily mean that all fundamentalists are inherently opposed to contraception. Indeed, the experience of Iran shows that fundamentalists, particularly when in power, will continue to be pragmatic and, using the tools of scriptural interpretation, accomplished a 180-degree reversal from a pro-natalist [post-1979] to an anti-natalist policy."[73] One of the Islamic Republic's first steps after 1979 was to reject family planning programs that had been implemented under the shah and outlawing sterilization and abortion on religious grounds. As a result, the following decade witnessed a drastic population increase, in line with the demands placed by the Iran-Iraq War (1980–88) at the time. However, the war (along with other factors, such as the declining price of oil) left the country's economy depleted. By 1989, the government revised its ideological stand, with the Parliament (also known as the Islamic Consultative Assembly) formulating a National Birth Control Policy in order to curb the fertility rate and increase access to contraception. Both these instances, primarily motivated by the economic impact of population growth, were justified with reference to Quranic teachings and hadiths. More recently, in 2005, the Iranian Parliament passed the Therapeutic Abortion Act, which permits abortion before sixteen weeks of pregnancy under limited circumstances, including medical conditions related to fetal and maternal health.[74] In views of these various policy changes, Makhlouf Obermeyer noted that "even an Islamic regime such as Iran's can come—however grudgingly—to support reforms that result in improvements of women's options, and can justify its position with reference to Islamic texts, clearly demonstrat[ing] the flexibility of the doctrine."[75] The changes in Iranian law also illustrate the ideological gymnastics (theological, in this case) that politicians engage in when confronted with harsh demographic and economic realities.

Abortion Access: Forgotten Constituencies? While the legality of abortion varies from country to country, and while policies vary within countries depending on political and historical contingencies, feminist analysis has long asserted that women do not constitute a homogeneous group. It therefore comes as no surprise that Muslim women (among others) experience differential access to abortion services. It is necessary to acknowledge some of the groups that are underprivileged in this regard—regardless of whether abortion is legalized in their particular context. Among those whose reproductive needs tend to be ignored, some are particularly disadvantaged due to their specific social circumstances: in particular, low-income women (who are especially affected by the privatization of health care), youth (especially where parental consent is required), mentally and physically disabled women (who face sexual assault and are also denied sexual agency), incarcerated women, rural women, undocumented migrants, women facing domestic violence and those whose mobility is curtailed, HIV-positive women, and refugees and internally displaced persons.

Furthermore, feminist scholars and advocates have also pointed out that with regard to the voluntary termination of pregnancy, the central issue is not so much one of choice as one of access (at least in contexts where abortion is not criminalized—that is, where legal choice is available). A variety of factors, ranging from social to economic, come into play and affect the accessibility of abortion services—including seclusion, female literacy rate, knowledge related to sex education, financial means, available means of transportation to medical centers, and the opposition and stigma women may face within their communities. These considerations, seemingly centered on the micro level, actually provide further ways to help deconstruct homogenized views of women in Muslim countries and to show how their lives and reproductive options are affected not only by Muslim laws but also by other factors. The complexities they reveal have a broader relevance in that they challenge stereotyping and hence offer a more nuanced picture of abortion trends—and of Muslim societies in general.

Conclusion: Unholy Alliances

By providing tangible data related to Muslim religious views and state policies on abortion, as well as evidence of evolving legal patterns in a variety of contexts, this chapter has helped to document the changing nature of abortion politics. Beyond pointing at the multilevel realities of reproductive rights in Muslim contexts, it has also highlighted one phenomenon that threatens women's rights in Muslim societies—that is, the impact of the religious right. To avoid casting the Muslim religious right as an isolated force, it is useful to conclude with a reminder that politico-religious movements operate at a global level and strengthen each others' agendas.

Especially in the post-9/11 context, fundamentalist leaders from various creeds are often portrayed as sworn enemies of one another, but the development of a shared political agenda can be seen over the last couple of decades. This increasing collaboration was denounced early on by women's rights advocates, and scholars have since documented cross-religious alliances among religious extremists, especially with respect to the United Nations arena.[76] As early as 1999, the Iranian scholar Janet Afary noted that "revival movements do not operate in isolation from each other," and she pointed to the 1994 UN conference in Cairo as a turning point.[77] That conference, Afary noted, "became the scene of a new type of alliance between the Roman Catholic Church and a host of Muslim fundamentalist groups. Both opposed any reference to abortion rights in the UN documents. Since Muslim jurisprudence has historically been tolerant of birth control methods, one wonders whether Islamist movements are learning new arguments from the Catholic Church or from Christian fundamentalist groups in the United States."[78] Following Cairo, an international Christian and Muslim religious right alliance continued to develop at other UN conferences, with Mormons,[79] fundamentalist Christians, and conservative Arab heads of states strategizing to oppose liberal social policies. Representative of other such successes, one of the results of this coalition building was to oppose including a reference to reproductive health care services in the final declaration of the UN Summit on Children in 2002.[80] Over the years, a series of networking meetings[81] has brought together Mormons, representatives of the Vatican, and fundamentalist Muslims; some of these gatherings also welcomed envoys from Sudan, Libya, Iran, and the United States. The coalition—which has grown to include a powerful bloc of more than fifty governments—is now able to mobilize a critical mass that successfully lobbies the United Nations. In 2002 Austin Ruse, the founder and president of the New York–based Catholic Family and Human Rights Institute, noted: "We have realized that without countries like Sudan, abortion would have been recognized as a universal human right in a UN document."[82]

Conservatives and extremists continue to collaborate at the UN level on this as well as on other issues, with a key battleground being sexuality. However, local gains have been made at the national level to limit unsafe abortion. For example, among the seventeen countries worldwide that liberalized their abortion laws between 1995 and 2007, four are Muslim-majority countries and one has a large Muslim minority: Albania, South Africa, and Burkina Faso liberalized their laws in 1996, as did Chad and Mali in 2002.[83] Despite these significant steps, however, women's unmet needs for reproductive health services remain massive in many Muslim countries, and unsafe abortion practices continue to claim tens of thousands of lives every year.

Notes

I would like to thank the following friends and colleagues for their comments on the draft version of this paper: Marie Ashe, professor of law at Suffolk University Law School, in Boston; Marge Berer, editor of *Reproductive Health Matters*, in London, and chair of the International Consortium for Medical Abortion's Steering Committee; and Neloufer de Mel, professor of English at the University of Colombo.

1 The current WHO definition (World Health Organization, Department of Re-

productive Health and Research 2008, 3) derives from the original WHO formulation, which dates back to 1992 and defined unsafe abortion as follows: "characterized by the lack or inadequacy of skills of the provider, hazardous techniques and unsanitary facilities" (World Health Organization, Maternal Health and Safe Motherhood Programme 1993).

2 There is inherent difficulty in securing reliable evidence regarding the prevalence of illegal procedures, but Susan Davis, former executive director of the Women's Environment and Development Organization, warns that abortion opponents tend to inflate global data on illegal abortions, quoting a range "from 150 to 500 million a year" (Davis 1999). For more reliable statistics, see World Health Organization 2004.

3 See also Hull, Sarwono, and Widyantoro 1993, 243.

4 Utomo B et al. 2001.

5 Pakistan Population Council data for 2004, quoted in Hamdani 2006, 4.

6 This figure represents about 22 percent of all pregnancies, but the percentage relates to a slightly higher estimate of forty-six million abortions yearly (Guttmacher Institute 2011).

7 Åhman and Shah 2004.

8 World Health Organization, Department of Reproductive Health and Research 2007.

9 The 21.6 million figure for 2008 indicates an increase from 19.7 million in 2003, "a rise due almost entirely to the increasing number of women of reproductive age globally" (Shah and Åhman 2010, 1). This article usefully details trends in all regions and subregions.

10 Maternal death is currently defined as follows: "the death of a woman while pregnant or within 42 days of termination of pregnancy, irrespective of the duration and site of the pregnancy, from any cause related to or aggravated by the pregnancy or its management but not from accidental or incidental causes" (World Health Organization 2004).

11 United Nations General Assembly, Human Rights Council 2010.

12 Cohen 2009.

13 Development Alternatives with Women for a New Era 2010.

14 World Health Organization, Global Health Observatory 2008.

15 As noted by WHO experts, two regions bear most of the burden of maternal mortality: in 2005 sub-Saharan Africa and South Asia accounted for 86 percent of all maternal deaths (Say and Shah 2008).

16 For example, in the Philippines, "the maternal mortality ratio is below 15 in high-income urban areas but up to 94 in Region 8 (Eastern Visayas) and reaches 165 in the Autonomous Region of Muslim Mindanao" (Estrada-Claudio 2010). Among other factors, Estrada-Claudio points to the fact that there are only 500 midwives in the Autonomous Region of Muslim Mindanao.

17 Feminist scholars have noted again recently that indigenous peoples and communities of color are subjected to population control to this day (Silliman, Fried, Ross, and Guttierez 2004). However, mainstream debates have shifted since the glory days of population control: nowadays, population growth is seen less as a threat to economic and social development, and more as a potential economic booster guaranteeing increased market opportunities.

18 "Population Control," n.d.

19 Ibid.

20 United Nations International Conference on Population and Development 1994, 156.

21 Ibid., 158–60.

22 Ibid., 167.

23 United Nations Fourth World Conference on Women 1995, 174.

24 Petchesky 2003, 44.

25 Shaikh 2003.

26 The argument that posits contraception and abortion as plots promoted by racist Western states to enhance their hegemony is not limited to Muslim countries. An illuminating article highlights its appeal among subjugated communities in the West as well (Prisock 2003).

27 For a discussion regarding the growth of private health care and its impact worldwide, see "Privatisation of Sexual and Reproductive Health Services" 2010.

28 In the context of the Cairo conference, for example, women's groups organized a range of responses, from the unequivocal support for a woman's right to choose to the international network Women Living under Muslim Laws (Women Living under Muslim Laws 1994) to the Los Angeles–based Muslim Women's League's support for "issues that are embraced by Islam, namely . . . providing access to birth control so married couples can have some influence on the size of their families" (Muslim Women's League 1994).

29 For a short but comprehensive overview of the MDFs, see the UN Development Program website (www.undp.org/mdg/basics.shtml).

30 MDF5 aims to improve maternal health by 2015 through "reducing maternal mor-

tality ratio by three quarters" and "achieving universal access to reproductive health" (ibid.).

31 Advocates and experts agree that at least MDF1 (on the "Elimination of poverty and hunger") and MDF3 (on "Promoting gender equality and empowerment of women") also have relevance to access to abortion.

32 Shah and Åhman 2009, 1149.

33 World Health Organization, Maternal Health and Safe Motherhood Programme, 1994.

34 Cohen 2009.

35 Center for Reproductive Rights 2005, 1.

36 See note 66 for a complete definition of fatwas.

37 The excellent article on family planning by Shaikh (2003) offers a comprehensive definition of *ijtihad* and its usefulness with regard to abortion: "Ijtihadi issues . . . are issues that require independent intellectual exertion and moral circumspection in light of a changing context and varying individual circumstances. Ijtihad is based on the assumption that in dealing with issues that are not explicitly addressed in the primary sources, jurists, informed by the spirit of the Qu'ran, use their moral capacities for creative reasoning and judgment to arrive at relevant legal solutions. Thus this opens up the possibilities for more dynamic Islamic approaches to understanding the issues of family planning in the current context."

38 Shaheed 1988–89.

39 Shaikh (2003) refers to one of the most prominent jurists at Al-Azhar (based in Cairo, this university is one of the most respected institutions in Sunni Islam) to provide a concise description of the positions held various school of thought.

40 Atighetchi 2008, 93. Note that chapter 5 of Atighetchi's book, devoted to abortion, provides a critical analysis of relevant sources and an erudite review of opinions from prominent jurists regarding ensoulment; the various valid reasons considered for allowing abortion; and the differences between, and within, various schools of thought.

41 Zuhur 2005, 52. Interestingly, Shaikh notes the correlation between "scriptural teachings" in Islam and the "prophetic teachings from Greek medicine which had a corresponding understanding of the stage of fetal development" (2003,11).

42 A significant contribution to this debate is the fact that "in October 1988, a *fatwa* by Nasr Farid Wassel, Grand *Mufti* of Egypt, stated that in the case of rape it is lawful (*halal*) for a woman to abort within the first 120 days of pregnancy as rape is the equivalent to psychological murder in a cultural and religious context where female

virginity is an essential condition for marriage... On the contrary, the present Grand *Mufti* of Egypt, Ali Gumaa, has defined killing an innocent fetus which is the result of incest or rape as sacrilege" (Atighetchi 2008), 115, 117). While Atighetchi refers to the 1990s rapes in Bosnia and Kosovo as having "reopened the question of the lawfulness of abortion," abortion for rape victims has fairly consistently preoccupied legal scholars. For example, in 1972 in Bangladesh the prohibition on abortion was waived for women raped during the 1971 war of liberation (against Pakistan); in Algeria in 1998, the Supreme Islamic Council issued a fatwa supporting a similar provision, in reaction to Islamist fighters holding women in sexual slavery.

43 Muhamed S. Tantawi, who died in 2010, was the top Egyptian cleric at the time (Ramadan Al Sherbini, "Row over Abortion Right for Rape Victims in Egypt," *Gulf News*, 1 January 2008, http://gulfnews.com/news/region/egypt/row-over-abortion-right-for -rape-victims-in-egypt-1.75832).

44 Asian-Pacific Resource and Research Centre for Women 2008, 143.

45 Zuhur 2005, 53.

46 Quran, Surah 6:151.

47 "Population Control" n.d.

48 Ibrahim N. Sada, quoted in ibid., is introduced there as the "head of the Department of Islamic Law at Ahmadu Bello University."

49 Imam 1997, 7.

50 Center for Reproductive Rights 2007, 1.

51 Leila Hessini, director of women's organizing and community outreach at Ipas (a global organization that promotes women's sexual and reproductive rights), e-mail message to author, 4 March 2008.

52 Asian-Pacific Resource and Research Centre for Women 2009, 74.

53 Hessini 2007, 3. These are bold steps in the sense that both unmarried women and teenagers constitute contentious constituencies with regard to access to abortion.

54 Quoted in Asia Safe Abortion Partnership n.d.

55 Quoted in Asian-Pacific Resource and Research Centre for Women 2009, 72.

56 Joffe 1999.

57 Makhlouf Obermeyer 1994, 59.

58 Laws 1988–89)

59 Atighetchi 2008, 114.

60 For details regarding these rapes and the ensuing fatwa liberalizing abortion in Algeria, see Luerssen Crowther (2000, especially 612–13) and Chelala (1998).

61 "Algérie: le Haut Conseil Islamique autorise les femmes à avorter," *Libération*,

28 April 1998 (www.liberation.fr/monde/0101243363-algerie-le-haut-conseil-islamique -autorise-les-femmes-violees-a-avorter). The translation is my own.

62 "Algeria Islamic Body Rules on 'Terror Rape,'" *Reuters*, 12 April 1998, www.mediter raneas.org/article.php3?id_article=545.

63 "Fundamentalism" is a disputed term; it is taken here to refer to those who blend theology and politics and rely on the use of religion to further their political purposes or cultural legitimacy.

64 Abdullah 2008, 72.

65 "Population Control" n.d.

66 Sobhan 1994, 11. Sobhan clarified the definition of a "fatwa" as "an opinion on a point of law [that should be] rendered by a mufti (i.e. a competent legal scholar) in response to questions submitted to him by a private individual or a *qadi* [judge]. The function of a mufti was essentially private and consultative and so a fatwa was not legally binding (unless it was) utilized by a *qadi* and incorporated into his decision" (ibid.).

67 *Salish* are "a centuries-old method of alternative dispute resolution, traditionally called upon to negotiate and mediate family or land disputes or petty criminal matters. [In the 1990s,] *shalish* contravened this customary practice and appropriated the right of judicial punishment" (Amin and Hossain 1995, 22). See also *Eclipse (Grahanka)* 1994. This documentary highlights the political roots, range of alleged offenses, and scope of *salish*-decreted fatwas in Bangladesh.

68 Amin and Hossain 1995.

69 Ibid.

70 See Women Living under Muslim Laws 2006.

71 In particular, via ASTRA (the Central and Eastern European Women's Network for Sexual and Reproductive Health and Rights). See ASTRA 2006.

72 Djanaeva 2010.

73 Freedman 1998, 65.

74 Larijani and Zahedi 2006. See also Hedayat, Shooshtarizadeh, and Raza 2006.

75 Makhlouf Obermeyer 1994, 71.

76 See, for example, Bayes and Tohidi 2001.

77 Afary 1999, 11. On the Cairo conference as a site of a "high-profile alliance among conservative forces," see also Freedman (1998, 55). For a review of the period 1975–2005, see Sen 2005.

78 Afary 1999, 11.

79 Notably, the Mormons' World Family Policy Center (and its director, Richard

Wilkins) was instrumental in linking with Saudi representatives. See Brian Whitaker, "Fundamental Union," *Guardian*, 25 January 2005 (www.guardian.uk/world/2005/jan/25/worlddispatch.brianwhitaker).

80 Colum Lynch, "Islamic Bloc, Christian Right Team Up to Lobby U.N.," *Washington Post*, 17 June 2002.

81 One significant meeting of this sort took place in Doha, Qatar, in 2004. See Whitaker, "Fundamental Union." See also Goldberg 2009, especially 163–65.

82 Quoted by Lynch, "Islamic Bloc."

83 Center for Reproductive Rights 2007, 4–5.

References

Abdullah, R. 2008. "Challenging Religious Fundamentalisms: Ways Forward." In *Surfacing — Selected Papers on Religious Fundamentalisms and Their Impact on Women's Sexual and Reproductive Health and Rights*. Kuala Lumpur: Asian-Pacific Resource and Research Centre for Women, 72–75.

Afary, J. 1999. "The War against Feminism in the Name of the Almighty: Making Sense of Gender and Muslim Fundamentalism." Grabels, France: Women Living Under Muslim Laws. http://www.wluml.org/sites/wluml.org/files/import/english/pubs/pdf/dossier21/D21.pdf.

Åhman, E., and I. Shah. 2004. "Unsafe Abortion: Global and Regional Estimates of Incidence of Mortality Due to Unsafe Abortion and Associated Mortality in 2000." 4th ed. Geneva: World Health Organization.

Amin, S., and S. Hossain. 1995. "Women's Reproductive Rights and the Politics of Fundamentalism: A View from Bangladesh." *American University Law Review* 44 (4): 1319–43.

Asia Safe Abortion Partnership. n.d. "Legal Status of Abortion in Bangladesh." www.asap-asia.org/country-profile-bangladesh.htm.

Asian-Pacific Resource and Research Centre for Women. 2008. *Surfacing — Selected Papers on Religious Fundamentalisms and Their Impact on Women's Sexual and Reproductive Health and Rights*. Kuala Lumpur: Asian-Pacific Resource and Research Centre for Women.

——. 2009. *Reclaiming and Redefining Rights — ICPD + 15: Status of Sexual and Reproductive Rights in Asia*. Kuala Lumpur: Asian-Pacific Resource and Research Centre for Women.

ASTRA [Central and Eastern European Women's Network for Sexual and Reproductive Health and Rights]. 2006. "Support Letter." Warsaw: ASTRA. www.astra.org.pl/kyrgyz_abortion.pdf.

Atighetchi, D. 2008. *Islamic Bioethics: Problems and Perspectives.* New York: Springer-Verlag.

Bayes, J., and N. Tohidi, eds. 2001. *Globalization, Gender, and Religion: The Politics of Women's Rights in Catholic and Muslim Contexts.* New York: Palgrave Macmillan.

Center for Reproductive Rights. 2005. "Religious Voices Worldwide Support Choice: Pro-Choice Perspectives in Five World Religions." New York: Center for Reproductive Rights, September. www.reproductiverights.org.

———. 2007. *Abortion Worldwide: Twelve Years of Reform.* New York: Center for Reproductive Rights, July.

Chelala, C. 1998. "Algerian Abortion Controversy Highlights Rape of War Victims." *Lancet* 351 (9113): 1413.

Cohen, S. A. 2009. "Facts and Consequences: Legality, Incidence and Safety of Abortion Worldwide." *Guttmacher Policy Review* 12 (4). www.guttmacher.org/pubs/gpr/12/4/gpr120402.html

Davis, S. 1999. "Are There Too Many People on the Planet? An Overview of Cairo +5." *Linkages* 4(1). www.iisd.ca/journal/davis.html.

Development Alternatives with Women for a New Era. 2010. "Maternal Mortality: In Need of Rescuing from the Depths of a Silo." 22 September. www.dawnnet.org.

Djanaeva, O. 2010. "Central Asia Reproductive and Sexual Rights and Health: Situation Overview." Paper presented at the Women's Global Network for Reproductive Rights Regional Consultation, Bangkok, Thailand, 17–19 January.

Eclipse. 1994. Bangladeshi with English subtitles. Dhaka, Bangladesh: Ain O Salish Kendra.

Estrada-Claudio, S. 2010. "Reproductive Health Services in the 21st Century: Is Anyone Shortchanged?" Presentation delivered at Repoliticizing Sexual and Reproductive Health & Rights—A Transformative Framework: Beyond ICPD and the MDFS conference, organized by Asian-Pacific Resource and Research Centre for Women and Reproductive Health Matters, Langkawi, Malaysia, 4 August.

Freedman, L. 1996. "The Challenge of Fundamentalism" *Reproductive Health Matters* 4 (8): 55–69.

Goldberg, M. 2009. *The Means of Reproduction: Sex, Power, and the Future of the World.* New York: Penguin.

Guttmacher Institute. 2011. "Induced Abortion Worldwide." New York: Guttmacher Institute, February. www.guttmacher.org/pubs/fb_IAW.html.

Hamdani, I. 2006. "Providing Safe, Clandestine Abortions Services in Pakistan." *ARROWs for Change*, 12 (3): 4-5.

Hedayat, K. M., P. Shooshtarizadeh, and M. Raza. 2006. "Therapeutic Abortion in Islam: Contemporary Views of Muslim Shiite Scholars and the Effect of Recent Iranian legislation." *Journal of Medical Ethics* 32 (11):652-57.

Hessini, L. 2007. "What Do Muslims Say about Abortion? Policies in the Middle East and the North African Region." Unpublished manuscript, October.

Hull, T. H., S. W. Sarwono, and N. Widyantoro. 1993. "Induced Abortion in Indonesia." *Studies in Family Planning* 24 (4): 241-51.

Imam, A. M. 1997. "The Muslim Religious Right ('Fundamentalists') and Sexuality." Grabels, France: Women Living Under Muslim Laws. www.wluml.org/sites/wluml .org/files/D-17.pdf.

Joffe, C. 1999. "Abortion in Historical Perspective." Reprinted from *A Clinician's Guide to Medical and Surgical Abortion*, edited by M. Paul et al. Philadelphia: Churchill Livingstone. www.prochoice.org/education/resources/surg_history_overview.html.

Larijani, B., and F. Zahedi. 2006. "Changing Parameters for Abortion in Iran." *Indian Journal of Medical Ethics* 3(4). www.ijme.in/144ie130.html.

Laws, S. 1988-89. "Bound and Gagged by the Family Code—An Interview with Marieme Hélie-Lucas." Grabels, France: Women Living Under Muslim Laws. www.wluml.org/node/5620.

Luerssen Crowther, A. 2000. "Empty Gestures: The (In)Significance of Recent Attempts to Liberalize Algerian Family Law." *William and Mary Journal of Women and the Law* 6 (3): 611-43.

Makhlouf Obermeyer, C. 1994. "Religious Doctrine, State Ideology, and Reproductive Options in Islam." In *Power and Decision—The Social Control of Reproduction*, edited by G. Sen and R. C. Snow, 59-75. Cambridge: Harvard University Press.

Muslim Women's League. 1994. "Muslim Women Call for Critical Review of UN Document on Population Control and Development." Los Angeles: Muslim Women's League, September. www.mwlusa.org/topics/rights/population_control.html.

Petchesky, R. 2003. Global Prescriptions: Gendering Health and Human Rights. London: Zed.

"Population Control: Centrepiece of Imperialist Aggression against the Muslim World." n.d. *Mission Islam*. http://missionislam.com/conissues/popcontrol.htm.

Prisock, L. 2003. "If You Love Children, Say So: The African American Anti-Abortion Movement." *Public Eye* l7 (3): 1, 3–15.

"Privatisation of Sexual and Reproductive Health Services." 2010. Special issue. *Reproductive Health Matters* 18:36.

Say, L., and I. Shah. 2008. "Maternal Mortality and Unsafe Abortion: Preventable yet Persistent." *IPPF Medical Bulletin* 42 (2). www.ippf.org/NR/rdonlyres/F1EB2F20-77AD -4ADD-9428-C9D5A75BD783/0/42_2_June08.pdf.

Sen, G. 2005. "Neolibs, Neocons and Gender Justice: Lessons from Global Negotiations." Geneva: United Nations Research Institute for Social Development, September.

Shah, I., and E. Åhman. 2009. "Unsafe Abortion: Global and Regional Incidence, Trends, Consequences, and Challenges." *Journal of Obstetrics and Gynaecology Canada* 31 (12): 1149–58.

———. 2010. "*Unsafe Abortion in 2008: Global and Regional Levels and Trends.*" *Reproductive Health Matters* 18 (36): 1–12.

Shaheed , F. 1988–89. "Women, Religion and Social Change in Pakistan: A Proposed Framework for Research." Grabels, France: Women Living Under Muslim Laws. www.wluml.org/node/261.

Shaikh, S. 2003. "*Family Planning, Contraception and Abortion in Islam: Undertaking Khilafah: Moral Agency, Justice and Compassion.*" *In Sacred Choices: The Case for Contraception and Abortion in World Religions, edited by D. Maguire, 105–28. New York: Oxford University Press.* www.religiousconsultation.org/family_planning_in _Islam_by_Shaikh_p1.htm.

Silliman, J., M. Fried, L. Ross, and E. Guttierez. 2004. *Undivided Rights: Women of Color Organizing for Reproductive Justice.* Cambridge, MA: South End.

Sobhan, S. 1994. "What Is a Fatwa?" In *Fatwas against Women in Bangladesh*, edited by Women Living under Muslim Laws, 11. www.wluml.org/node/363.

United Nations Fourth World Conference on Women. 1995. "Beijing Declaration and the Platform for Action." un Doc. A/CONF.177/20. Reprinted in *Women and Human Rights: The Basic Documents*, edited by Paul Martin and Mary Lesley Carson. New York: Columbia University, Center for the Study of Human Rights, 1996.

United Nations General Assembly, Human Rights Council. 2010. "Report of the Office of the United Nations High Commissioner for Human Rights on Preventable Maternal Mortality and Morbidity and Human Rights." Document A/HRC/14/39. N.p.: United Nations, April. http://www2.ohchr.org/english/bodies/hrcouncil/ docs/14session/A.HRC.14.39.pdf.

United Nations International Conference on Population and Development. 1994. "Program of Action." UN Doc. A/CONF. 171/13. Reprinted in *Women and Human Rights: The Basic Documents*, edited by Paul Martin and Mary Lesley Carson, 156, 158–60, 167. New York: Columbia University, Center for the Study of Human Rights, 1996.

Utomo, B., et al. 2001. "*Incidence and Social-Psychological Aspects of Abortion in Indonesia: A Community-Based Survey in 10 Major Cities and 6 Districts—Year 2000.*" Jakarta: Center for Health Research, University of Indonesia.

Women Living Under Muslim Laws. 1994. "Statement on Reproductive Rights/NGO Forum/ ICPD." In *Women's Reproductive Rights in Muslim Countries and Communities—Issues and Resources*. Grabels, France: Women Living Under Muslim Laws.

——. 2006. "Kyrgyzstan: Support the Campaign to Ensure Continued Access to Abortion." London: Women Living Under Muslims Laws. www.wluml.org/action/kyrgyzstan-support-campaign-ensure-continued-access-abortion.

World Health Organization. 2004. "Health Statistics and Health Information Systems: Maternal Mortality Ratio." Geneva: World Health Organization. www.who.int/healthinfo/statistics/indmaternalmortality/en/index.html.

World Health Organization, Department of Reproductive Health and Research. 2004. *Unsafe Abortion: Global and Regional Estimates of Incidence of Unsafe Abortion and Associated Mortality in 2000.4th ed. Geneva: World Health Organization.* www.who.int/reproductivehealth/publications/unsafe_abortion/9241591803/en/index.html.

World Health Organization, Department of Reproductive Health and Research. 2007. "Unsafe Abortion: Global and Regional Estimates of Incidence of Unsafe Abortion and Associated Mortality in 2003." Geneva: World Health Organization. www.who.int/reproductivehealth/publications/unsafe_abortion/9789241596121/en/index.html.

World Health Organization, Department of Reproductive Health and Research. 2008. "Improving Sexual and Reproductive Health Is at the Core of Achieving Millennium Development Goal 5." Geneva: World Health Organization. www.who.int/making_pregnancy_safer/events/2008/mdg5/srhand_mdg5_facts.pdf.

World Health Organization, Global Health Observatory. 2008. "World Health Statistics: Cause-Specific Mortality and Morbidity; Maternal Mortality Ratio." Geneva: World Health Organization. http://apps.who.int/ghodata.

World Health Organization, Maternal Health and Safe Motherhood Programme. 1993. *The Prevention and Management of Unsafe Abortion: Report of a Technical Work-*

ing Group, Geneva, 12–15 April 1992. Geneva: World Health Organization. http://whqlibdoc.who.int/hq/1992/wнo_MSM_92.5.pdf.

World Health Organization, Maternal Health and Safe Motherhood Programme. 1994. *Abortion: A Tabulation of Available Data on the Frequency and Mortality of Unsafe Abortion*. 2nd ed. Geneva: World Health Organization.

Zuhur, S. 2005. *Gender, Sexuality and the Criminal Laws in the Middle East and North Africa: A Comparative Study*. Istanbul: Women for Women's Human Rights—New Ways.

SAIDA KOUZZI WITH STEPHANIE WILLMAN BORDAT

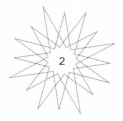

Promoting a Violence against Women Law in Morocco

LEGISLATIVE ADVOCACY BY GRASSROOTS-LEVEL NGOS

This chapter describes an ongoing, grassroots-level legislative advocacy campaign to promote a violence against women law in Morocco. Both the approach and the country raise interesting and timely questions about the processes of legal reform and the strategies of local nongovernmental organizations (NGOS) to address violence against women. While this chapter focuses on an initiative in Morocco, the political and law-making framework and social norms surrounding violence against women are similar to those in other countries in the Middle East and North Africa (MENA) region. Democracy building, parliamentary strengthening, and women's human rights in the region have all recently been the focus of much attention by the international community, foreign governments, donors, and NGOS.

The 2004 Family Code reforms in Morocco were initially hailed as a victory for women's rights, particularly in the international arena. However, reports analyzing implementation of the law in the seven years since its promulgation describe obstacles both among the population and from the authorities charged with enforcing the law. High illiteracy rates, discrepancies in its application across the country, and remaining gaps and discrimination prevent the Family Code from really protecting women.[1] Implementation problems with the law also reveal the disadvantages of a top-down reform process.

The chapter illustrates how local NGOs in Morocco are now working from the ground up to promote a violence against women law. The multifaceted set of project activities carried out in this campaign includes a series of community consultations with women at the grassroots level, mobilization and awareness raising among women and local authorities and other stakeholders in the community, and legislative advocacy to national decision makers.

Based on the firsthand experiences of the authors and representatives of participating NGOs, this chapter focuses on the process of developing and advocating for a violence against women law and the main practical challenges encountered when working with the different stakeholders targeted in the campaign. Certain lessons learned call into question frequently held stereotypes and misconceptions about grassroots-level mobilization among people with limited education and about women in the MENA region. They also reveal obstacles to law reform from members of the traditional elite, who are typically considered the decision makers responsible for leading the country forward.

The authors hope that this experience in Morocco — which would be among the first countries in the MENA region to pass a violence against women law — will be useful for advocates across the region who are working to eradicate violence against women through law reform efforts. In particular, the challenges involved in the process of lobbying for such a law and the lessons learned about the interactions between diverse stakeholders may help to identify issues that must be addressed and to develop effective strategies for lobbying for such legislation in the MENA region.

Violence against Women in Morocco: An Overview

Few would dispute the fact that violence against women constitutes a serious problem in Morocco, as it does worldwide. Official statistics from the Ministry of Justice indicate that 41,000 cases of violence against women were brought before Moroccan courts in 2007. The Casablanca Court of Appeals received the largest number of such cases—28,375, including seven premeditated murders and more than 15,597 acts of violence that resulted in more than twenty days of disability for the victim.[2] In its 2009 report, the Ministry of Social Development, the Family, and Solidarity notes that roughly 30,000 cases of violence against women had been reported that year, 79.80 percent of these involving conjugal violence.[3]

Similarly, the first report of the Casablanca-based NGO Women's Eyes, in November 2004, included statistics revealing that 18 women had committed suicide, 121 had become permanent invalids, and 13 had to abort as a result of violence. Moreover, 2,728 women were battered and another 1,139 were seriously injured. Such violence also caused at least 1,299 women to lose their homes and 858 women to lose their jobs, and provoked nervous breakdowns among 1,181 women.[4] These figures are only partial given the universal culture of silence surrounding, and the underreported nature of, domestic violence crimes. Moreover, the statistics reflect the situation only in the country's large urban areas, where assistance centers for women victims of violence are located. Small towns, villages, and rural areas are not included.

<hr>

During a consultation meeting in Casablanca with women on
their experiences with conjugal violence, one participant described
how "one of my friends has a daughter who is about to get married.
During the henna ceremony, the mother of the bride asked the other
women who among them had not experienced conjugal violence so that
she may have the honor of beautifying the bride with henna. However,
all the women, without exception, admitted that they had suffered
conjugal violence." (A facilitator, Casablanca)

<hr>

There is no specific legislation in Morocco addressing violence against women. Rather, violence against women is covered by the general provisions of the Penal Code, which are inadequate and incapable of preventing domestic violence and other forms of violence against women. Additionally, current laws are insufficient to investigate such violence, punish the offender, or protect and compensate the victim.

Victims must demonstrate actual physical injury in order to prove that violence occurred. Penal Code provisions apply only to grievous bodily injury and focus on the concrete consequences of the violence rather than on the acts committed. Indeed, the law provides for the mitigation of penalties depending on the extent of the injuries sustained.[5] In reality, police do not respond to complaints of domestic violence when no blood has been shed. Similarly, courts seldom punish offenders who commit serious offenses resulting in less than twenty days of disability, or low-level misdemeanors common to domestic violence, such as slaps, scratches, threats, insults, and choking (which may cause bruises but normally does not break the skin).

While the Penal Procedure Code authorizes the use of all forms of evidence, in reality, courts require women to produce medical certificates and the testimony of witnesses to prove violence. Because the violence often occurs in the privacy of the home, with no witnesses, or because witnesses refuse to testify on the ground that what happens between a husband and wife is a personal matter that should not be interfered with, there are typically no witnesses to testify, and most perpetrators get away with their crimes. Current legislation lacks any provisions for compelling witnesses to testify or holding them liable for not reporting violence. According to the Moroccan Penal Code, harboring or hiding a married woman who has left the conjugal home without her husband's consent is a misdemeanor punishable by the same penalty as kidnapping a married woman.[6] As a result, family members, friends, and members of NGOs risk prosecution for providing shelter to a battered woman who has fled a violent husband. In addition, the Family Code provides that a wife who leaves the conjugal home and refuses to return under a court order loses her right to financial support.[7] The Penal Code retains the concept of the husband's legal authority over his wife, despite the fact that the current Family Code has eliminated the wife's duty of obedience to her husband and places the household under the joint responsibility of the spouses.

Under the Family Code, women may seek a judicial divorce for cause on the grounds of harm or prejudice, defined as "any ignominious behaviour by the husband or act against good character that causes the wife material or moral harm such that the continuance of the conjugal relationship is rendered unendurable."[8] Moroccan laws once again link harm to its consequences and not to the acts that caused them. Moreover, such a moral definition is interpreted differently by different judges, some of whom consider that beating one's wife is normal behavior and thus is not against good character, and others even permit it on supposedly religious grounds.

Given the lack of a precise definition of "prejudice," the difficulties proving it even in cases of severe beatings, the length of divorce proceedings for cause, and the many instances of acts perpetrated that were not deemed ignominious or against good character, women victims of violence frequently apply for divorce for irreconcilable differences rather than for cause. As a result, they lose many of their rights, and perpetrators are not held accountable for their acts.

Rape is defined in the law as a crime against morality—an offense against honor, rather than a crime against a woman's physical and moral integrity. Since rape is linked to "the absence of consent," victims find it extremely hard to prove. If a woman reports rape yet cannot meet the high threshold of proof, she may then be prosecuted for having had illegitimate sexual intercourse. Marital rape is not even criminalized, on the ground that consent to have sexual intercourse is the basis of marriage.

In addition, Moroccan law does not provide any protection for women before, during, or after the violence. There are no civil remedies or mechanisms such as temporary or long-term restraining or protection orders to remove the offender from the home in order to prevent future violence. Police frequently do not intervene promptly in domestic violence cases, on the ground that the violence has taken place within the private sphere in the home. Moreover, the law gives women no compensation—material or otherwise—for the harm suffered or financial resources necessary to cover costs involved in securing a medical certificate, filing a complaint, or bringing a lawsuit.

As a result of this situation, local women's rights NGOs have increasingly worked to combat violence against women by establishing counseling and legal assistance centers for victims. They also strive to break the wall of silence around such violence by publishing annual reports and statistics in an attempt to motivate the competent authorities to take action to address it.

In addition to local civil society campaigns, international human rights institutions have repeatedly reminded the government of Morocco of its obligations to eradicate all forms of violence against women and urged it to swiftly enact legislation on violence against women and girls.[9] The government continues to make declarations to international bodies such as the Human Rights Council and the Committee on the Elimination of Discrimination against Women (CEDAW) of its intention to promulgate such legislation.

Increasing local and international attention has forced the government to recognize the rampant nature of violence against women in Morocco and take steps to combat it. In 1998 the State Secretariat in Charge of Social Affairs, Family and Children, now the Ministry in Charge of Social Development, Family, and Solidarity, launched a national campaign for the prevention of violence against women. This was followed by other governmental initiatives, notably the 2002 National Strategy for the Prevention of Violence against Women, launched by the State Secretariat in Charge of the Family, Children and Persons with Disabilities, and the 2006 Fourth National Campaign "Towards a Law on Violence against Women."[10] The same agency also established the National Observatory for the Prevention of Violence against Women in 2006, and then as a government ministry launched the Sixth National Campaign in 2008 with the slogan "For the Sake of a Law That Protects Me and My Family." Along the same lines, in 2004 the Ministry of Justice issued a National Strategy to Combat Violence against Women.

In the meantime, the Moroccan government has also repeatedly made public declarations of its intent to promulgate a violence against women law. Indeed, in 2006 the State Secretariat in Charge of the Family, Children and Disabled Persons prepared a bill and submitted it to the Government General Secretariat (the first step in the legislative process). However, this bill was withdrawn by the succeeding minister. And in the most recent national campaign (2010), the minister in charge of Social Development, Family, and Solidarity announced the end of September 2009 as the date for presenting a violence against women bill to the competent authorities for debate and adoption. Nevertheless, as of October 2011, the purported bill had not yet been introduced into the legislative process or made public.[11] In the meantime declarations on the imminence of such a law continue to be made without adequate transparency and clarity as to its content and focus.

Campaigning for a Violence against Women Law in Morocco

Since 2007, a national network of local NGOs with the technical assistance of the Maghreb office of Global Rights, an international human rights capacity-building NGO,[12] has conducted a multifaceted campaign for a violence against women law in Morocco. This grassroots-level initiative aims to promote comprehensive legislation with both criminal and civil measures that take into account the specific nature of violence against women and are designed to prevent such violence, protect victims, hold perpetrators accountable, and promote a culture of zero tolerance for violence against women.

The project strategy is to generate broad-based support for, and solicit input into the content of, an eventual violence against law from women at the grassroots level as well as other local stakeholders, from the beginning of and throughout the process.

Recent experiences with the 2004 Moroccan Family Code taught the organizers of this current initiative several critical lessons. The seven years since the promulgation of that law have demonstrated several disadvantages of a top-down law reform process.[13] Studies illustrate the lack of public knowledge about the new law, as well as how it is vulnerable to criticism and propaganda and disinformation campaigns. They also describe problems with its implementation, and how it is frequently not applied by those officials charged with enforcing it. In addition, the content of the law is not necessarily responsive to social realities.[14] It is in this context that the grassroots-level legislative advocacy campaign to promote a violence against women law in Morocco was designed. Campaign organizers hope to prevent the problems with the 2004 law from happening with an eventual violence against women law through widespread public participation in the process of drafting the law. Creating a sense of ownership over future reforms, it is hoped, will contribute to their credibility and acceptance, and therefore their application and sustainability.

The project also aims to promote dialogue between civil society and local and national decision makers; develop legislative advocacy and lobbying skills among local women's organizations across the country; promote government responsiveness and accountability to citizens' concerns; and ensure that the eventual law reflects international human rights standards.

The ten local partner NGOs from across Morocco have simultaneously implemented the program in their respective regions and engaged in collective advocacy at the national level. They are nontraditional, youth-led NGOs from generally underserved and remote regions of the country. The diversity of the local partners and the communities they serve permits the inclusion of a wide range of cultures, languages, and experiences and ensures the participation of and widespread support from the largest possible number of women and local and national authorities and other stakeholders.[15]

Engaging Grassroots-Level
Women in the Campaign

Taking a bottom-up approach, the campaign started with activities designed to engage women at the grassroots level in the development of the content of a violence against women law. Organizers felt that this approach was necessary to ensure that women's voices were heard and their experiences and opinions incorporated in the law, resulting in legislation that would respond to the reality of their lives and therefore be more effective in protecting the interests of victims of violence. Such participation was also designed to create an educational and empowering process for the women involved.

COMMUNITY CONSULTATIONS

Based on a training workshop organized by Global Rights in September 2007[16] to launch this initiative, the ten local partner NGOs collaborated with thirty-nine additional local associations in their respective communities to train ninety-four of their young women members as community consultations facilitators. In addition to presenting violence against women issues, these workshops focused on participatory group facilitation methods, communication skills, and pedagogical methods appropriate for working with adult women with limited literacy.[17]

The partner NGOs then conducted a series of consultations with groups of women at the grassroots level in their communities to discuss and debate their experiences, priorities, concerns, and needs related to violence against women and solicit their suggestions for the content of an ideal violence against women law in Morocco. They held 161 such sessions in thirty-five cities, towns, and rural villages across Morocco, involving 1,836 women. The women who participated in the consultations came from a cross-section of the population and a variety of experiences. They were of different ages and socioeconomic statuses and from diverse rural and urban regions of Morocco, and both Amazigh (Berber) and Arab women were included.[18]

The first hour of each meeting was frequently marked by long silences. At the beginning, most women would deny that they had been subjected to violence, adding that their knowledge was limited to what they had heard about other women's stories. However, toward the end of the discussion, women would often rush to take the floor to relate their personal experiences with violence. Facilitators usually had a difficult time concluding the sessions, some of which lasted four hours longer than planned.

> Women were reluctant to speak in public on the grounds that their stories would set the tongues of the village-dwellers wagging. Indeed, such reluctance was so common that when one woman volunteered to speak, the other women would prevent her from doing so. But women were very eager to talk individually to the facilitators, who devoted some of the time at the end of every session to receive women privately and listen to their stories and their problems related to violence. (A facilitator, Agadir)

By and large, the meetings were not only successful from the organizers' viewpoint but also were greatly appreciated by the women. Some of the women, especially in rural areas, remarked that they had never before been consulted or asked their opinion on any topic whatsoever, adding that the few such prior meetings had always been held around election time. More than 100 women participated in some of the meetings, when the organizers had expected only thirty women at most.

These meetings were an opportunity for women to share their experiences with violence and to express their opinions and ideas about change. At the end of each session, the facilitator noted all of the suggestions that women deemed necessary for future violence against women legislation. These included the need to punish offenders and to protect and compensate women victims of violence and their children.

> How could I be thrown out of a home where I have lived for roughly twenty-two years? My husband threatened to cut my throat if I did not leave the home—which he may well do, for he beats me on a daily basis in front of my children. (A woman, Tetouan)

The women were very bold in their suggestions, with one significant common denominator among them being distrust in the enforcement of the law and disappointment with the institutions charged with applying it. Participants also expressed their desire to see improved treatment of women in institutions such as police stations, Gendarmerie Royale (part of the armed forces, the gendarmes have police powers over the civilian population, usually in rural areas) stations, hospitals, and courts.

Global Rights Maghreb then collected, analyzed, and evaluated some thirty proposals for legislative reforms on violence against women submitted by the partner NGOs and selected and refined twelve of them.[19] These themes were then redistributed among the partner NGOs to develop a visual representation of each one through collaboration between the NGOs and the participating women. In some instances, a volunteer local artist listened to the women provide suggestions for visuals; in other cases, women did the drawings themselves. This process resulted in illustrations for twelve proposals for legal reform — eight for criminal law provisions and four for civil law provisions.

GRASSROOTS-LEVEL AWARENESS RAISING

Based on the reforms desired by women, the Global Rights team then created a poster—titled "Pénalisation, Protection, Pas de Tolérance: Revendications des femmes pour une loi contre les violences" (Criminalization, protection, no tolerance: demands of women for a law against violence). — that combined the twelve illustrations, each captioned with Arabic, Tamazight, and French summaries. The team and local NGOs also developed an Arabic language discussion booklet on violence against women with information and talking points to accompany the poster.[20] More than 2,000 copies of the poster and an accompanying discussion booklet were printed and distributed in less than a year, and both had to be reprinted to meet local demand.

Using the poster as a primary tool, since January 2008 local NGOs have organized ongoing small-group awareness-raising activities with women and larger public mobilization events in their communities, including informational tents in public areas, open-door days, outreach caravans to surrounding villages, and interviews on local radio stations. One even conducted a drive-through campaign in the local market with the poster taped on car hoods and antiviolence messages broadcast from a bullhorn. These reached thousands of women in the first three months of the campaign alone.[21]

We organized an awareness-raising campaign about domestic violence for three days, by pitching a large tent in the Sidi Youssef Ibn

Ali neighborhood. We used the poster and accompanying booklet, in
addition to international conventions in order to convey the message
that violence perpetrated against women is a violation of human
rights. (An NGO member, Marrakech)

In addition to awareness raising about violence against women through
distribution of the poster, these activities were intended to maintain contact
with the women who had participated in the community consultations, brief
them on the results of their participation, and update them on the status of the
campaign, as well as opening up the discussions to additional women to obtain
their suggestions and support for a violence against women law.

Women appreciated the facts that they continued to be involved in and
updated on developments in the program, and that they were able to see the
results of their suggestions — rather than having the consultation meetings
being single events with no follow-up. The women reiterated their support
for the suggestions in the poster and even participated in meetings with local
officials to provide personal testimonies and express their demands directly.

We had to rent buses to bring women from the neighboring villages
into the city because the women all insisted on participating in a meeting
with local authorities and the region's MP [member of Parliament].
(An NGO member, Agadir)

THE NATIONAL MOBILIZATION CARAVAN

In collaboration with the ten partner NGOs and more than forty additional local
nongovernmental human rights, economic development, cultural, and women's
associations, in October 2009 the Global Rights team organized a three-week
National Mobilization Caravan, which toured Morocco to launch the third
year of this legislative advocacy campaign for a violence against women law.

One of the primary objectives of the caravan was to inform and mobilize
women from remote, marginalized areas of the country and other regions not
yet reached by the campaign. The caravan team presented the poster and led
discussions with large groups of women in local communities in order to ex-

plain the initiative—both its activities and the reasons behind it—and to generate a wider, truly national understanding of the need for a violence against women law, as well as national support for such legislation. This also helped the team members gain a greater understanding of the diverse nature and extent of women's situation and realities across Morocco and the problems they face in their daily lives.

During the twenty-one-day caravan, the team travelled more than 4,000 kilometers in a circle around the country, stopping in thirty-three cities, towns, and rural villages.[22] The diverse activities organized each day included seventeen grassroots-level awareness-raising meetings on women's right to freedom from violence that included a presentation of the campaign for a law, in which more than 1,100 women participated. The sessions were cofacilitated by members of partner NGOs from other parts of Morocco traveling with the caravan team, in collaboration with members of the local associations hosting the event.

At the beginning of the meetings, in response to the question of whether women in the region suffered domestic violence, the answer was usually negative. However, as soon as we gave examples of stories of women from other parts of Morocco, women began to recount their own stories. (An NGO member, Nador)

Women participated actively in the meetings. They showed such keen interest that some who first declared that they would be unable to attend the entire session because they had other obligations ended up staying until late in the evening to participate in the discussion. Even when the facilitators were ready to leave, women would continue to approach them to recount stories they dared not share with the entire group.

One of the women did not attend the meeting, but on hearing about the event, she came in a hurry only to find that it had just ended. Still she insisted on talking to us about her own experiences of violence. She described how she had remained silent for twenty-two years of violence. (A facilitator, Tarmikt, near Ouarzazate)

Women's participation in the caravan awareness raising was massive, with over 100 women participating in many sessions. This indicated the women's enthusiasm for participating in initiatives related to their concerns and their eagerness for such meetings, presumably due to long-standing suffering from violence and lack of any prior such activities. On one notable occasion, a planned traditional celebration for the birth of a baby was actually postponed by consensus among the village women so that they could all attend the session.

The number of women participating in meetings reached 120.
Many had to walk for about two hours in order to attend.
(A facilitator, Mhamid Al-Ghizlane)

Women expressed their appreciation for the activity, in the majority of cases the first time a discussion on the topic had ever been organized in their community, or their opinions on the subject solicited. They also were very eager to hear about similar experiences of women from other far-away regions of Morocco and enthusiastic about meeting the caravan team, particularly because (in the words of the participants) the team were all (relatively) young women, who came from various other parts of the country, and who had traveled so far to meet with them. One group of women in a village at a desert oasis in southeastern Morocco asked if they could come to Rabat on a bus and stand outside the Parliament building the next time the associations met with members of Parliament.

The women supported all of the proposals for reform in the poster, backing them up with personal testimonials. Participants insisted in particular on the need for a law to protect women in small, remote communities like theirs, where there are no support and counseling centers for victims of violence. They raised a number of specific problems they had with the local police forces in dealing with their cases, which exacerbated the violence perpetrated against them. Tamazight-speaking women requested that different languages be accommodated, as they all suffered from language barriers in courts and hospitals: "We are obligated to travel as far as Zagora to lodge our complaint, but most of the time, we get no hearing or we are asked to come back at some later time, knowing that the distance is considerable and that the road is blocked."

Integrating Other Local Stakeholders
into the Campaign

In addition to the activities organized with women, the campaign also aimed at generating support from the largest possible number of local stakeholders, such as community-level associations. These included not only organizations focused on women's legal rights, violence against women, and human rights, but also a diverse range of nontraditional but potential ally associations working on economic development, Amazigh rights, culture and sports, cooperatives, clubs, and other organizations directly serving women. The goal was to reach out to the women beneficiaries of these organizations to include their experiences and mobilize their support, as well as to create alliances with these associations and encourage them to integrate women's human rights issues into their activities.

Local partner NGOs also conducted significant outreach to local stakeholders from the public health, law enforcement, justice, and education sectors, initially to present the campaign and later to keep them regularly informed of developments. They also solicited the assistance of these stakeholders in holding the community consultations with women and organized other joint activities between local associations and specialists such as lawyers and medical doctors. This strategy aimed not just at eliciting additional opinions and suggestions for the violence against women legislation, but also to enhance collaboration and coordination among local stakeholders and mobilize communities to participate in government decision making.

During the poster launch from January to March 2008, more than 317 local stakeholders—including lawyers, judges, trade unionists, association members, health professionals, and journalists—jointly organized or participated in several public meetings and activities held by local NGO partners. At these meetings, participants analyzed domestic violence in their communities, identified various obstacles to legal action for and protection of women, and developed local solutions for violence against women cases.

Thanks to collaboration with local medical specialists, we have
established good relations with the director of the local hospital in El
Hajeb. It has thus become easier for us to get free medical certificates for

women victims of violence who come to our association. Moreover, we
have secured the assistance of a lady lawyer who voluntarily helps
us receive and counsel the women who come to our association.
(An NGO member, El Hajeb)

During the National Mobilization Caravan in October 2009, more than
forty local NGOs from different regions of Morocco, especially remote and underserved towns, partnered with the caravan team to organize twenty conferences and round-table discussions in which 700 members of local associations
and local public and private stakeholders from different sectors participated.
These events included presentations on violence against women by Global
Rights staff members on the caravan team and local partner lawyers and NGO
members, followed by discussion and debate among the participants.

We are very pleased and enthusiastic about our participation in this
meeting. For us this is the first such meeting in the region consecrated to
the human rights of women. (A participant, Bab Berrad)

Many participants stressed the urgency of intensifying services and actions
in remote areas. They also noted that these round-table discussions were a big
event, especially since they were the first of their kind to have ever been held
in many of the communities reached by the caravan.

OUTREACH AND ADVOCACY TO LOCAL PUBLIC AUTHORITIES

Following the community consultations with women, the Global Rights team
and ten partner NGOs launched the campaign for a violence against women law
by conducting mass distribution of the poster and accompanying discussion
book to diverse local authorities and decision makers, including members of
Parliament, members of municipal councils, police, hospital staff members,
employees in the justice sector, political party officials, ministry delegations,
and the media. In the first year, partner NGOs held more than 490 individual
meetings with local representatives of these different sectors.[23]

These meetings were designed to sensitize local authorities—in particular
those authorities who came into direct contact with victims of violence—to

women's rights issues; to convey the demands of women, as featured on the poster, to staff members of all local public services and administrations; and to explore ways of enhancing local cooperation and coordination to improve services for women victims of violence. Indeed, throughout the campaign the team was often pleasantly surprised to enter public buildings and find the poster displayed prominently on the wall, including at the entrance of a local courthouse in a remote town and in the office of a high-placed national ministry official.

Several women came to our association after they saw the poster on the wall in the police station. (An NGO member, Tetouan)[24]

In addition to individual lobbying, partner NGOs organized local town-hall meetings, designed to bring members of local associations and the women who had participated in the community consultations together with members of Parliament from the district, political party officials, local authorities, health professionals, lawyers, judges, and the local press. The town-hall meetings were designed to initiate and promote ongoing communication between local associations and stakeholders on this initiative and convey women's voices to local decision makers.

Indeed, the town-hall meetings gave women a unique opportunity to address officials directly in public. Women gave personal testimonies, emphasized the need for a violence against women law, and frequently directly addressed the members of Parliament and other local officials, speaking frankly about "what we are asking from you."

These were followed by open discussions that frequently lasted longer than three hours. From March to May 2008, more than 1,000 individuals participated in the town-hall meetings.[25]

These meetings helped us create a unit for women victims of violence, made up of a representative of every sector (the police, gendarmes, healthcare, and justice), in addition to the association. This makes it easy for us to give support to women. (An NGO member, Taza)[26]

In contrast to the grassroots-level meetings, in which women described the diverse forms of violence committed against them and were unanimous about the need for a law to protect them, the round-table discussions and town-hall meetings with local stakeholders were marked by divergences of opinion and mixed reactions to demands for change. Resistance to reforms can be attributed to a general lack of faith in the rule of law,[27] elitist stereotypes about the uneducated general population, sexist attitudes toward women, and a desire to protect male privilege.

Participants most frequently expressed reservations about the effectiveness of any new law, especially if the law were simply added to the existing legal arsenal without any serious guarantees of its enforcement, and they cited the lack of implementation to date of the 2004 Family Code reforms. Some underscored the lack of trust in law-enforcement authorities, given the lack of judicial independence and widespread corruption among public officials charged with protecting women victims of violence. The belief that the current laws, having been imported from the West, are not binding is also, in their view, an obstacle to the application of existing laws and fair treatment of women.

Many participants pointed out that various considerations make violence perpetrated against women seem acceptable to most parties, including local authorities. For example, prevailing misogynistic beliefs and behaviors allow the man of the family—the father, brother, uncle, nephew, or husband—to discipline female family members under his authority. Others suggested adopting a modern approach based on new interpretations of religious texts, to counter the prevailing popular culture dominated by misinterpretations that condone or even encourage violence against women.

Comments made by participants in the meetings revealed that a good number of them only supported amending certain articles of the Penal Code, an initiative that had been under way for several years at the Ministry of Justice, rather than promulgating a specific violence against women law. The organizing NGOs had to emphasize the fact that the campaign advocated a comprehensive law that would be gender-specific and address all forms of violence against women, with both criminal and civil provisions.

Participants also expressed concerns that a new law would be difficult to implement, owing to the allegedly spiteful attitudes of some women who lied and unjustly accused their husbands of rape and domestic violence. In the view of these participants, women wishing to take revenge might well falsely accuse men of violence or rape.

Often participants insisted that any law should take into account the causes of violence against women, which they then proceeded to explain included poverty, ignorance, unemployment, political violence exercised by the state against men, and substance abuse. There was significant resistance to an understanding of violence against women as caused by gender inequality or power dynamics characterized by male domination.

A few people questioned the credibility of the associations leading such initiatives and their real intentions. According to these individuals, the solution was not in importing laws from abroad, as associations organizing the campaign were accused of trying to do. Rather, questions of violence against women should be directed to local religious authorities, namely the *faqih* (cleric) who, according to some, would have the most appropriate answer to such social problems. Finally, local stakeholders often expressed doubts about the need for a law, declaring that the population needed awareness raising and sensitization rather than a law. This view was notable given that most of those who expressed conservative views about women and skepticism about the value of the law were people with high levels of education, including lawyers and other legal professionals. Organizers frequently had to remind participants that the twelve proposals for a special law to prevent violence against women had been made by 1,836 women from the population. One wonders who really needs awareness raising and sensitization—the population or certain members of the elite?

THEMATIC WORKING GROUPS: MOBILIZING LOCAL EXPERTISE AND SUPPORT

Meetings with local authorities and other stakeholders revealed the necessity and value of engaging with supportive representatives of key public sectors concerned with violence against women—notably the justice, health, law enforcement, and education sectors—in the campaign for a specific law. Accordingly, during the third year of the campaign, local partner NGOs established and facilitated thematic working groups in their respective communities, holding 132 meetings in fifteen towns and villages in diverse remote and traditionally underserved parts of Morocco. More than 318 representatives of different sectors participated.[28]

The thematic working groups were designed to gather opinions about and experiences with violence against women cases from local professionals in each sector, focusing on identifying the obstacles and challenges confronting them in their daily work. The working groups also collected a list of sector-specific proposals and suggestions for concrete legal reform in a proposed violence against women law.

This approach presumed that local public authorities wanted to assist women victims of violence but that current laws did not provide them with the tools to do so—a strategy that organizers found more effective than sensitization training or criticism. The hope was that allies in the public sector would serve as a positive influence on their more resistant colleagues. And the hope was also that an eventual violence against women law would be more effective if the professionals who would eventually be charged with implementing it were involved in its creation from the beginning, by making reforms relevant to them and valuing their contributions.

Partner NGOs used a variety of methodologies to organize thematic working groups, according to the local context and their relationships with the local authorities and aimed at ensuring the broadest possible participation by representatives of the different sectors, from their own communities as well as neighboring regions. In some regions, representatives worked together in joint cross-sector meetings. These were often organized by the local general prosecutor, and local NGOs distributed roles and facilitated the development of action plans and work schedules. In order to solicit the input of the largest number of local actors from the different sectors, survey forms were distributed to the representatives at the working group meetings, to be completed by their colleagues.

It was necessary to organize the meetings jointly with the vice general prosecutor to ensure the participation of all the sectors. He sent the invitations himself and established contacts with officials in charge of other sectors to urge them to participate. (An NGO member, Taza)

In other places, it was easier to organize separate meetings with officials in charge of each of the different sectors individually, who distributed the surveys among their regional colleagues and facilitated meetings with the partner NGOS.

We were able to organize meetings with law enforcement sector
personnel in El Hajeb, Meknes, and Khenifra, thanks to the help of a
national security official in El Hajeb. (An NGO member, El Hajeb)

Still others organized individual meetings with officials in charge of the different sectors by relying essentially on personal contacts. Interviewers here completed the survey forms themselves during the meetings, assuring the interviewee that his or her participation would be kept anonymous. This approach had the advantage of eliciting quite forthright concerns and suggestions from the persons interviewed, due to the fact that the meetings were held outside of the workplace, and the interviewees were not subjected to any hierarchical oversight since their participation was informal and voluntary.

Holding such meetings and engaging with local public authorities, and in the relatively short time span of mere months, was an unusual and unique experience. Usually when NGOs seek to engage public officials, the process necessitates excessive formalities and lengthy administrative procedures to obtain authorizations from the central authorities in Rabat.

The most serious obstacle encountered in our work is the problem
of administrative hierarchy, which prevented interviewees from making
suggestions freely, on the grounds that they needed to consult with
central authorities. This necessitated our organizing many of
our meetings in cafes and arranging them through our
personal relationships. (An NGO member, Agadir)

Thematic working group members agreed that current Moroccan law does not allow them to discharge their duties fully and that a violence against women law was long overdue to address the specific nature of this violence and enable them to intervene promptly and in optimal conditions. Numerous local public sector representatives expressed their gratitude for the organization of such meetings, describing their desire to help women victims of violence and the previous absence of anybody willing to listen to them and their opinions.

This is the first time anyone has asked me for my view on the issue!
(A recurrent statement at many of the meetings)

Representatives from different sectors participating in the thematic working groups identified numerous common obstacles in their daily work with women victims of violence, related both to the content of current laws (a point that is beyond the scope of this chapter) and to systems and practices. The latter were related to inadequate infrastructure and financial and human resources, and the absence of coordination among the different sectors, as well as lack of communication and even occasional estrangement between local authorities and local civil society organizations.

Thematic working groups also generated suggestions from the participating stakeholders for provisions to be included in a law that would make it easier for them to help women victims of violence. In addition to substantive changes to the content of the laws, the most frequent proposals included the need for ongoing training for all officials concerned to help them work effectively with women victims of violence, as well as enhanced communication and coordination among the different sectors.

Thematic working group members also suggested the creation of additional infrastructure to increase proximity to women in more communities, and specialized units with trained staff—particularly more female personnel—in each relevant sector to provide support for women victims of violence. They described the need for sufficient facilities in good condition to receive women victims, give them emotional support, and encourage them to speak freely. Local partner NGOs drafted reports combining the working group recommendations and shared them with all of the other campaign partners and Global Rights for analysis and integration into the campaign objectives.

National Legislative Advocacy

In parallel to the above activities, since the opening of the fall 2008 session of Parliament, the local partner NGOs have traveled to Rabat from their respective communities on regular, collective lobbying missions. As part of intensive legislative advocacy for a violence against women law, they meet as a group with members of Parliament, ministry officials, other national authorities and decision makers, and the press.[29]

By June 2010, the NGOs had made eleven collective advocacy trips to Rabat and met with representatives of over ten different parliamentary groups, including the major ones, with meetings actually held inside the Parliament building. They met with high-level officials from numerous ministries—including the key ones concerned with this legislation, such as the Ministries of Health; Justice; Social Development, Solidarity, and the Family; and National Education. In addition, they had meetings with the national security director and the president of the Consultative Council on Human Rights.

During the first year of national lobbying, partner NGOs focused on introducing the campaign for a violence against women law, conveying the voices of women from the local community consultations to national decision makers by distributing the poster and accompanying discussion booklet, and exploring possible avenues to transform women's demands into comprehensive legislation on violence against women. These meetings were also an occasion for local partner NGOs to create a network of alliances in Parliament and the relevant ministries, as well as to try to obtain updated information on the government's intentions about and steps taken for the promulgation of a specific violence against women law.

It was quite difficult at first for the local partner NGOs to organize meetings with national decision makers. In addition to their geographic distance from the capital—some NGO representatives traveled more than twelve hours by bus to reach Rabat—the partner NGOs are grassroots-level organizations from small, remote, and underserved regions of the country. The fact that the organizations are usually represented by relatively young women was also new to national decision makers. The decision makers were usually surprised by the initial contact, since they were simply not used to this type of lobbying meeting initiated by local NGOs, especially those from outside the usual privileged urban elite.

Partner NGOs often had to contact an official numerous times and by a variety of different means (telephone calls, faxes, and e-mail messages) in order to obtain an appointment. It was also difficult to plan dates of lobbying missions and meetings to ensure attendance by members of Parliament and avoid conflicts with their schedule. Often a parliamentary or a major government activity necessitating their presence would come up unexpectedly. Meetings were frequently canceled at the last minute, or partner NGOs would arrive at the designated time and place but the official would not show up at all.

In order to overcome these obstacles, partner NGOs often requested their local political party representatives to organize meetings with their party's national members of Parliament as a group. Another effective strategy was to ask a local official or other prominent figure in the community to intervene and facilitate a meeting with national decision makers. Frequently partner NGOs would send official written correspondence to the secretariats of parliamentary groups to request a meeting, which necessitated significant following up by phone. In other cases, partner NGOs were able to obtain the mobile phone numbers of some members of Parliament and contact them directly. They would also telephone the main number of a relevant ministry and ask to meet with the person in charge of women's affairs in that ministry. Finally, a particularly effective strategy was to ask people the NGOs had met with to arrange for appointments with other decision makers from the same political party.

> Most of the time we would inform the parliamentary group we
> sought a meeting with that we had also organized a series of meetings
> with other groups so as to make the most of the competition between the
> groups. To confirm and remind the person of the scheduled meeting,
> we usually had to phone again the day before and even again half
> an hour before the actual meeting. (An NGO member, Agadir)

After returning from each lobbying trip to Rabat, the partner organizations organized local town-hall meetings in their communities, inviting local authorities, members of the different concerned sectors (health, justice, law enforcement, and education), women participants in the community consultations and other beneficiaries of the NGOs' services, representatives of other local nongovernmental associations, the local media, and the general public. During these town-hall meetings, the local NGOs reported to their communities on the outcomes of the legislative advocacy meetings in Rabat and provided information on the status of the violence against women law. The aim was to ensure that local communities had updated information and were continually mobilized in support of the campaign, and to generate a sense of local links to national decision making.

During the first year of the legislative advocacy to national decision makers, parliamentary groups declared their appreciation for the meetings for helping them to foster ties with civil society representatives. They also said that it was the first time local NGO representatives had asked to meet with them to discuss women's human rights issues. However, notwithstanding the numerous meetings held with diverse national decision makers from both the legislative and executive branches, the local partner NGOs were unable to obtain any information as to the outcome of the supposedly forthcoming violence against women bill proclaimed in numerous government declarations.

Indeed, ministerial and parliamentary meetings revealed that many national decision makers were completely unaware of any such bill. It is interesting to note that during the lobbying meetings with national decision makers, as well as at local meetings and consultations with local authorities, the NGOs actually served an important information transmission function. Most frequently, rather than obtaining any real updates, it was the NGOs themselves who provided government officials on both the national and local levels with information on laws, policies, and reform initiatives that normally they should have already received either horizontally or vertically from the government they worked for.

The majority of members of Parliament—from a wide spectrum of opinions among all of the major political parties—at least verbally supported the campaign for a violence against women bill. They proposed to set up committees either in Parliament or in their communities with the civil society stakeholders to follow up on this initiative. Several also pledged not only the support of their political party and parliamentary group, but the support of a other parliamentary groups as well. One even promised to write a draft law including all the proposals on the poster, although this draft never materialized.

As a result of the first year of NGO lobbying, three oral questions were posed by twenty-eight members of Parliament belonging to five different parliamentary groups during the regular questioning sessions whereby the government is held accountable to the Parliament. One parliamentary group even submitted a written question. These questions focused on violence against women and were addressed to the Minister of Social Development, Family, and Solidarity. It was significant both that violence against women was introduced as an issue in parliamentary sessions, and that the members began exercising their prerogatives more actively than they typically do in Morocco.

However, the majority of parliamentary groups said that they did not have the material or human resources to write a law themselves, and requested that local NGOs draft a comprehensive text for them to adopt and present as a bill. This is noteworthy because the overwhelming majority of legislation in Morocco originates as a *projet de loi*, or a bill drafted by the executive branch, rather than as a *proposition de loi*, or a bill drafted by the legislative branch. As one member of Parliament asked, "Why should [we] be always be waiting for the executive branch to write the bills instead of doing it ourselves?"

One national ministry agreed to issue special directives to its local delegations across the country, urging them to give more importance to cases of violence against women and to cooperate with local NGOs in this initiative. In meetings, representatives of the Ministry of Social Development, Family, and Solidarity restated its promise to presenting a draft violence against women bill, but without providing any details as to whether the bill had been completed or was still being developed.

Given the apparent lack of movement by the government to abide by its numerous declarations that a violence against women bill was imminent, partner NGOs continued and intensified their national lobbying efforts from September 2009 to June 2010. This second year of lobbying focused on follow-up and accountability, as partner NGOs inquired about steps national decision makers had pledged to take in previous meetings, updated them on developments in the campaign and recent statements by the ministry charged with drafting the government bill, and informed them that local NGOs would be preparing a violence against women bill themselves in March 2010. Local partners were able to broaden their support base by establishing new contacts with parliamentary groups and other ministry officials and gain access to more higher-level officials, including several ministers or their special advisors.

Special attention was paid to participating in national and local conferences across Morocco organized by the Ministry of Social Development, Family, and Solidarity, to ask direct questions about the status of the violence against women bill, which the ministry continued to declare was completed and about to start the formal legislative process. Partner NGOs actively participated in these conferences, despite the facts that they were usually announced with merely a day or two's notice; and that invitations were issued—usually only informally, by word of mouth—to a limited number of elite NGOs. At the national conference in Rabat, the partner NGOs presented the minister personally with the poster and discussion booklet.[30]

In contrast to the first year of national legislative advocacy, during which parliamentary groups had been somewhat surprised by local NGO requests for meetings, in the second year, parliamentary groups themselves initiated contacts with local NGOs to support the initiative and request meetings about the issue. Members of Parliament once again asked the NGOs to draft a bill and giving it to them so that they could adopt it and present it as a bill—*proposition de loi*—themselves, rather than wait for the ministry bill.

On arriving at some of the meetings, partner NGOs were surprised to find national television station cameras or print media journalists, who had been invited to cover the meeting. While the parliamentary groups saw this as a public relations tactic to promote their political party, NGOs welcomed it as an opportunity to obtain explicit commitments from the group and document them through a TV broadcast or newspaper article.[31]

In the second year, ten members of Parliament, representing five parliamentary groups, addressed four oral questions on the status of the violence against women bill to the Minister of Social Development, Family, and Solidarity. In addition, two parliamentary groups submitted two written questions to the minister, again asking about the status of the often-announced bill.[32]

After three meetings with staff members of the Ministry of Social Development, Family and Solidarity, a meeting with the general secretary of the minister's political party, a meeting with the parliamentary group of the same party, countless phone calls to the minister's special advisor, and the last-minute cancellation of a couple of scheduled meetings, the partner NGOs were finally able to meet with the minister in the second half of the second year of national lobbying efforts. They requested a copy of the violence against women bill, which at that point had been publicly declared to have been filed at the Secrétariat General du Gouvernement, and hence started the legislative process.

However, the minister adamantly refused to share the bill with the partner NGOs and indeed was unclear as to the current status of such a bill. When partner NGOs informed the minister that they would then just draft a bill themselves, offering to collaborate with her and suggesting that their work could reinforce and enrich her bill, she promised that there would be an official ministerial note outlining the provisions of her bill on 8 March. On that date, the minister again declared that the bill was imminent but did not provide any further details.

After more than two years of legislative advocacy to various parliamentary and ministerial representatives, including at the Ministry of Parliamentary Relations, as of February 2010, no violence against women bill had been presented publicly or reached any clear step in the law-making process. As a result of the governmental inaction and express requests by members of Parliament for a draft text for them to use to sponsor such a bill, the campaign organizers and partner NGOS decided to draft a violence against women law themselves.

Bringing It All Together: The NGO Draft Law on Violence against Women

> For many years we have heard governmental declarations about a law on violence against women and how it will be promulgated shortly. However, up until now we have seen only a legislative void, to say nothing of the fact that the authorities concerned remain silent on the issue. For this reason, we, as part of civil society, have decided to take the initiative and write the law ourselves. (An NGO member, Marrakech)

The Global Rights Maghreb team, along with its local partner NGOS, organized an intensive weeklong working group meeting in March 2010 in the small southeastern town of Errachidia, with the express purpose of working in *huis clos*[33] to collectively draft a comprehensive bill on violence against women.

In addition to the team and representatives of local partner NGOS—primarily young women members of grassroots-level NGOS providing legal assistance and advice to women in their communities—the working group included lawyers, three legal drafting consultants, three experts—one Moroccan and two foreign—on international rights-based approaches to violence against women legislation, and a vice general prosecutor, family court judge, court clerk, police inspector, hospital director, social worker, director of a hospital violence against women unit, and education ministry counselor. Members of the group were chosen to provide a diverse range of professional expertise as well as to foster collaboration between NGOS and local public officials.

The composition of this working group was unique not just in the professional diversity of the members, but also because participants came from various areas of the country—many quite remote or marginalized—rather than from the capital city. It was also quite exciting to benefit from the presence of local public officials, in light of the usual hierarchical administrative constraints on their participation in such activities, as previously noted.

As a basis for drafting a violence against women law, participants studied the conclusions and recommendations of the local thematic working groups described above and both international standards and comparative examples of violence against women bills or laws from other countries, including Bulgaria, France, Spain, Jordan, Turkey, and the United States.

On the first day, participants worked in four sector-specific groups—law enforcement, health, education, and justice. They reviewed the relevant conclusions and recommendations made by the local thematic working groups, identified common obstacles impeding local professionals in each sector from effectively working on violence against women, and outlined suggestions for provisions of a violence against women law.

As a result of this review, the participants agreed on a list of important topics to be addressed. These were grouped into ten themes to be covered in sections of the law: objectives of the law, acts covered by it, relationships covered by it, civil protective measures, support and assistance for women victims of violence, police complaints and investigations, criminal procedures, court structure and jurisdiction, evidence, and crimes and sanctions.

Throughout the week, participants worked in small groups, each comprised of both NGO members and local public officials and jointly guided by a legal drafting expert and an expert in women's international human rights. Each group was assigned a specific theme from the list and charged with drafting a section of the law to address it. In this way the groups worked their way through the list of topics to prepare a fairly comprehensive violence against women bill. At the end of each working day, participants united in a plenary session to present the section(s) of the law they had drafted and receive feedback and additions from members of the other groups and outside experts.

The working group dynamics were unique. At times participants worked in complete harmony, striving to complete a comprehensive and ideal violence against women bill. At other times, intervention from the organizers was necessary to find common ground for different participants to agree on or to rebalance power dynamics in the group. Every participant had a special agenda that he or she defended and tried to make a priority in the discussion. In addition, participants came from quite diverse professional, educational, and geographic backgrounds. For instance, a judge would discuss certain issues from the perspective of the applicability of domestic legislation, while NGO representatives discussed matters based on their fieldwork and human rights culture. Power dynamics related to the novel, mixed nature of the groups in terms of gender, age, and socioeconomic status also created challenges to effective discussion that were new to some of the participants.

I protest strongly against the fact that we are constantly being eliminated from discussion. While it is true that we are not legal experts, we are expressing the voices of women concerned about a violence against women law. For this reason, I request that discussion here not be limited to legal experts or those who have legal knowledge because of their job. (An NGO member, Tetouan)

Nonetheless, intense and ongoing work throughout the week among the participants from different regions and backgrounds created strong relationships between them and provided opportunities to share knowledge and experiences. Every participant was given an opportunity to understand the realities and working conditions of the others, as well as to share their own with nontraditional allies.

One remarkable incident occurred during a discussion over a point of law that could not be settled in terms of legal formulation, despite the presence of two lawyers and a legal expert in the group. Strangely, the breakthrough was made by medical doctor who made a suggestion that was accepted by everyone. The doctor then remarked laughingly that, once back at his hospital, he feared he might address his patients using legal jargon instead of the usual medical terms. And the vice general prosecutor joked that "all that I have learned in my life in terms of law and legal concepts have been undone or lost during this week!"

At the end of the week, participants were both pleased and somewhat overwhelmed by the fact that they—grassroots-level members of local civil society and stakeholders, few of whom were legal professionals—had actually drafted a comprehensive violence against women bill. Collectively edited and finalized over the following months, the final text has 111 criminal and civil provisions. A press conference held in Rabat in December 2010 to present the NGO bill and kick off public distribution of the text drew over 130 members of local NGOs, the press, members of Parliament, and governmental representatives.[34] The third year of legislative advocacy, launched with the fall 2010 parliamentary session, is focusing on widely distributing the NGO draft bill and advocating its promulgation.

Conclusion

The discourse of the relatively well-educated traditional elite—those charged with assisting and making decisions for the general public—in the different round-table discussions, conferences, and town-hall meetings was quite astounding. Legal professionals, local authorities, and even many civil society activists consistently described the problem of violence against women as primarily one of "ignorance among the population." As a result, in their view the appropriate solution was not legislation but rather public education and awareness raising—directed of course at the same purportedly "ignorant population" that actually formulated the law reform framework under discussion.

During advocacy at the national level, members of Parliament at least voiced enthusiastic support (it is interesting to note that not one actually explicitly said that he or she opposed such a law), yet they claimed an inability to fulfill their legislative function. On the ministerial level, local NGOs continually cited the lack of transparency and collaboration. All of the officials seemed surprised and bewildered at the idea that they would actually be held accountable by their constituents for the public declarations that had been made, frequently for their public relations value alone.

It is also interesting to note that, based on anecdotal evidence, the majority of the people who expressed the most sexist opinions were legal professionals and members of the educated elite (lawyers, local NGO members, and political party representatives)—but usually not elected officials (who are eager to be reelected), officials in the law enforcement and justice sectors (who are eager to exercise their authority), or the women who attended the activities.

Women who participated in the different campaign activities were for the most part not from the geographic, educational, or socioeconomic elite that one might expect would be more aware of the issues or modern or progressive in its attitudes. However, in activity after activity women spoke openly about violence, and many sought individual assistance from facilitators after sessions for their own problems. They agreed that a violence against women law was necessary and desirable, and they suggested provisions for an ideal law that organizers found to be quite strong in the punishment they proposed and bold in their content. The problem, it seemed, was not one of awareness of violence as a rights violation, or of reluctance to participate in public policy debates, but the lack of any previous forum to speak out at.

In one event in the town of Agdz, the 126 women present did not mind the presence of a gendarme, since they wanted to take advantage of the opportunity to express their problems with the gendarmes directly to a representative of the group. After many participants told their own stories, at one point the gendarme was apparently so ashamed that he left the session, claiming he had an urgent phone call. In one small and remote desert town, participants surprised the facilitators by announcing that in advance of and in preparation for the session, they had prepared a short play on violence against women to depict their suffering. In yet another small desert town, women prayed for God to help the NGOs with their activism and even asked if they could accompany them to meet with members of Parliament. Time and again, women across the country repeated a refrain heard in Nador during the caravan: "When is this law going to be ready? We need it now!"

Notes

The authors would like to thank Houda Benmbarek, program officer for Global Rights Maghreb, for her valuable research assistance, support, and helpful comments on this chapter. They also thank Chitra Raghavan and James Levine for their support and thoughtful comments on early drafts; the Advocates for Human Rights in Minnesota for their years of inspiring and invaluable expert technical support with this project; their local partner nongovernmental organizations in Morocco for their collaboration, energy, and creativity in promoting women's rights at the grassroots level in their local communities; and the donors who have so generously supported this project.

1 For more details and sources for this assertion, see, for example, Ligue Démocra-

tique des Droits des Femmes, *Rapports annuels sur l'application du Code de la Famille* (Casablanca: Ligue Démocratique des Droits des Femmes, 2004, 2005, 2006, and 2007); *Le Code de la famille: Perceptions et pratique judiciaire* (Morocco: Friedrich Ebert Stiftung, January 2007); Association démocratique des femmes du Maroc, "Implementation of the CEDAW Convention: Non-Governmental Organisations' Shadow Report to the Third and the Fourth Periodic Report of the Moroccan Government," November 2007 (http://www2.ohchr.org/english/bodies/cedaw/cedaws40.htm).

2 A medical certificate attesting to at least twenty days of disability resulting from the violence is necessary to bring a criminal case for assault. Statistics are from the http://amanjordan.org/a-news/wmview.php?ArtID=22640.

3 Statistics are from http://laghzal.maktoobblog.com/1285.

4 Statistics are from http://maghress.com/almaghribia/97317.

5 See Articles 400–404 of the Moroccan Penal Code.

6 Article 495 of the Penal Code: "Shall be liable to a prison term of 1 to 5 years and a fine ranging from 200 to 2000 *dirhams* whoever willfully hides a married woman that has been kidnapped or seduced or helps her run away while she is being searched for." Article 496: "Shall be liable to the same aforementioned penalty any person that willfully hides a married woman that has run away from the authority of whoever has legal guardianship over her. The same applies to a person that enables her to run away while she is being searched for."

7 Article 195 of the Family Code.

8 Article 99 of the Family Code.

9 See, for example, Committee on the Elimination of Discrimination against Women, "Concluding Comments to the Most Recent Moroccan State Party Report (Combined 3rd and 4th Periodic Reports)," February 2008, http://www2.ohchr.org/english/bodies/cedaw/docs/co/CEDAW.C.MAR.CO.4.pdf.

10 For more information about the Fourth Campaign, see www.almaghribia.ma/Reports/Articles.asp?idr&id=31669.

11 In October 2010, the minister stated on national television that a violence against women bill would be presented to Parliament before the end of the year.

12 For more information, see www.globalrights.org.

13 The Family Code was reformed based on recommendations submitted to the palace by a royal commission after thirty months of deliberations, and a bill was then presented by King Mohamed VI to Parliament in October 2003.

14 See, for example, Ligue Démocratique des Droits des Femmes, *Rapports annuels sur l'application du Code de la Famille*; *Le Code de la famille*; Association

démocratique des femmes du Maroc, "Implementation of the CEDAW Convention; "Investigation: Over 91% Of Illiterate Women Lack Information on Family Code," *Morocco Times*, 31 December 2005.

15 The ten partners in this initiative are the Association Amal pour la femme et le développement (El Hajeb), Association el Amane pour le développement de la femme (Marrakech), Association Tawaza pour le plaidoyer de la femme (Tétouan), Association Tafiil Moubadarat (Taza), Association Tafoukt Souss pour le développement de la femme (Agadir), La Voix de la femme amazighe (national), Espace Draa de la femme et du développement (Zagora), Association Bades (Al Hoceima), Association des jeunes avocats (Khemisset), and Espace Oasis Tafilalet pour le développement (Rissani).

16 This workshop benefited from the expert participation of local lawyers and of women's rights activists from different countries with violence against women laws. The partner NGOs examined causes and theories of domestic violence and analyzed current Moroccan laws dealing with violence against women and other national legislation from a human rights perspective. They also reviewed international standards on violence against women and case studies of campaigns for violence against women laws in other countries. The detailed training workshop report is available in Arabic and English at www.globalrights.org/.

17 According to the *2009 Human Development Report* (New York: United Nations Development Program, 2009), 56.8 percent of Moroccan women aged fifteen and older are illiterate.

18 Community consultations were held in El-Hajeb, Meknes, Azrou, Martil, Mdiq, Tetouan, Dchira, Taddart, Agadir, Anza, Aourir, Marrakech, Harbil, Ghenass, Tamekrout, Agdz, Zagora, Fezouata, Tamtek, Amzrou, El-Hoceima, Imzourn, Rabat, Temara, Casablanca, Khemisset, Tiflet, Tidass, Rissani, Oulad Abdelhalim, Merzouga, Ahedhad, Ouirlane, Oulad Youssef, and Taza.

19 The twelve proposals made by the women participants for both civil and penal legislative reforms are: order violent offenders out of the family home; do not allow mediation in domestic violence cases; guarantee financial support during domestic violence cases; guarantee protection for victims of violence through protection orders against offenders; require police to prepare a written report at all suspected scenes of domestic violence; increase penalties for domestic violence; criminalize marital rape; criminalize all forms of sexual harassment; prosecute domestic violence offenders without the need for witnesses; increase the police's power to intervene immediately in domestic violence cases; punish low-level misdemeanors in domestic violence cases; and increase penalties for repeated acts of violence.

20 The booklet is available as a PDF at www.globalrights.org.

21 See "Year One Final Report," on the first year of this program, available in Arabic and English at www.globalrights.org.

22 For more information, see the Daily Caravan Blog (in Arabic, English, and French) at http://caravaneglobalrights.bloguez.com.

23 For more information about these individual meetings, see "Year One Final Report."

24 The testimonies and facts presented in this thematic section are quoted from the periodic reports sent by the partner NGOs.

25 For more information about these meetings, see "Year One Final Report."

26 The cells or units are created following circulars issued by the Ministry and sent to various services stressing the necessity of coordinating with associations to create local entities, under the supervision of the General Prosecutor. These cells work on the files of women victimized by violence. However, such cells have not been created in most regions up to now.

27 A legal tenet that provides that no person is above the law, that no one can be punished by the state unless they have violated the law, and that no one can be convicted of breaching the law except in the manner set forth by the law itself.

28 Full reports on all the thematic meetings are available in Arabic at the Global Rights offices in Morocco.

29 Global Rights has organized several workshops over the years of the initiative to provide partner NGOs with training on topics and skills such as legislative procedure, a human rights approach to violence against women, comparative laws from around the world, and legislative advocacy.

30 Reports on all these meetings are available at the Global Rights office in Rabat.

31 See, for example, a double issue of *Bayan Al-Yawm*, 13-14 February 2010; *Al-Alam*, 25 January 2010.

32 For more information about the contents of the oral questions and the written one, as well as the names of the parliamentary groups and members who posed the questions, see www.mcrp.gov.ma/Default.aspx (for oral questions) and http://mcrp .gov.ma/QuestEcrite.aspx (for the written question).

33 The French phrase literally means "closed doors." The expression is generally used to describe a meeting that no one can leave before the next step is agreed on.

34 The complete Arabic text of the NGO bill, as well as summaries of key provisions in French and English, can be found at www.globalrights.org/site/PageServer ?pagename=www_africa_morocco.

AZIZA AHMED

No Way Out

THE DUAL SUBORDINATION OF MUSLIM WOMEN

IN INDIAN LEGAL CULTURE

Muslims in India account for 12 percent of the population (approximately 102 million people) and are India's largest religious minority. Despite some progress toward a more inclusive state, the large Muslim minority in India continues to be trapped between two legal paradigms that offer little access to justice. This chapter focuses on Muslim women in particular, who face the burden of what I call dual subordination: the simultaneous subordination by two legal paradigms. The first of the legal paradigms is the state courts rooted in a more formal secular legal regime. The second is the religious legal mechanisms enacted at the local level. Often the secular and the religious rely on each other to reinforce gender norms. Muslim women experience this reality especially with regard to assertions of sexual rights. This is an important paradox to understand: it teaches us the instability of viewing secularism as a "way out" of religious personal law to advance women's rights.

Section 1 of the chapter begins with an explanation of relevant legal frameworks, including the role of Islamic law in India and the international human rights framework for sexual rights. Section 2 locates the sexual rights of Muslim women within domestic and secular discourse by presenting and analyzing the various ways in which scholars have located rights within Islam. This analysis acknowledges that activism in the arena of women's rights is not necessarily a site of resistance for a broader movement for gender identity and gender expression. Rather, the construction of women's rights has often encoded the definition of "woman" premised on a common experience of subordination.[1] Finally, while the struggle over national identity co-opted by the Hindu Right is not discussed as a section on its own, it is understood that a conversation about Muslim rights in India cannot ignore a fundamentally violent and anti-Muslim movement that remains authoritative in legal, policy, social, and cultural realms.[2]

1. Legal Frameworks

A BRIEF HISTORY OF ISLAMIC LAW IN INDIA

In present-day India, there are several schools of interpretation of Islamic law, including the Hanafi, Maliki, Hanbali, Shafi'i, Zahiri, and Shi'i.[3] In India the majority of Muslims are Hanafi, However, there are several large Shi'i communities, including the Dawoodi Bohra[4] and Ismaili communities. In western India, members of the lower castes generally converted to Sunni Islam, while individuals belonging to intermediate castes generally became Shias. Today Shias make up approximately 10–15 percent of the total Muslim population.[5] There are over 350 regional or ethno-linguistic Muslim groups. India's Muslims have always been closely connected to the Hindu communities and have maintained many similarities in practice and custom.[6]

The development of Sharia law in India is partly a product of India's colonial legacy. In *Gender and Community: Muslim Women's Rights in India*, Vrinda Narain argues that while the British asserted that the establishment of personal law was to "facilitate the freedom of the individual in the marketplace," the underlying objective was to utilize a decentralized power structure vis-à-vis scriptural and religious norms to maintain strict constraints on individuals in families and communities.[7] In doing so, the British were able to maintain power and the political and economic goals of the colonial state through supporting a framework that allowed for the religious elite to maintain its own power.[8]

Narain further argues that one cannot see Indian Muslim law as representative of Sharia law. Rather, one must recognize that Islamic law as influenced by British rule is substantially different from strict Islamic Sharia law and could more appropriately be called Anglo-Mohammedan law[9] as it diverges significantly from its sources. The effort of the British to create a formal space for Muslim Personal Law was codified in the Muslim Personal Law (Sharia) Application Act of 1937.[10]

THE CURRENT STATUS OF MUSLIM LAW IN INDIA

Partition saw the division of South Asia into countries primarily distinct on the basis of religion. Muslim law in India, and in particular the status of women in Muslim law, has evolved into a complex mixture of religious freedom, minority rights, and state policy toward the "accommodation of difference."[11]

The constitution of India safeguards minority rights. Article 14 of the Constitution grants equality to all citizens regardless of caste, language, or religion.[12] Articles 26, 27, and 28 state that minorities have the right to manage their own religious affairs and are not compelled to attend state-funded religious institutions, and that minority-managed institutions must receive equal treatment.[13] Article 44 includes provision for a Uniform Civil Code (ucc) that was initially introduced when the Congress Party appointed a National Planning Committee in 1939 to plan for economic and social development in the future independent India.[14] Designed by the women's subcommittee, the idea was that a ucc would eventually replace the personal law system. Women's rights groups consistently advocated for the eradication of the personal law system through the 1940s. In 1947 the formal proposal to enact a ucc was introduced to the Constituent Assembly. Although conceptualized as a fundamental right, the provision was included in the constitution as a directive principle. Through Article 37, the constitution establishes that it is the duty of the state to apply the directive principles in order to bring about "positive social change."[15] It has been argued that the inability during the time of independence to forward the ucc as a fundamental right was largely due to the fears of Muslims and Sikhs that their religious rights would be overridden in the context of partition.

A foundational moment in the state's validation of Islamic law is the oft-cited case of *Mohd. Ahmed Khan vs. Shah Bano Begum & Ors (Shah Bano)*, decided in the Supreme Court of India in 1985. Shah Bano, a seventy-three-year-old Muslim woman who had been divorced by her husband, brought a petition for maintenance against her husband under Section 125 of the Criminal Procedure Code (CPC).[16] In accordance with Muslim personal law (as asserted by Muslim scholars), she would have been entitled to maintenance for the period of *iddat*, defined as the period three months after the divorce.[17] The Supreme Court overrode the interpretation of the Sharia by Muslim leaders and ruled that under Section 125 of the CPC, Shah Bano was entitled to maintenance beyond the period of *iddat*.[18] The Muslim community, led by conservative and orthodox Muslims, protested the decision on the ground that Islam was in danger because the court had overstepped its bounds, given that the view of Muslim theologians that they alone were able to interpret the Quran.

Largely due to the backlash inspired by the *Shah Bano* decision, an independent member of Parliament introduced the Muslim Women's (Protection of Rights on Divorce) Act, which provided that Section 125 of the CPC does not apply to divorced Muslim women. A strange political pairing of feminists and members of the Hindu Right campaigned against the bill, with the Hindu Right often co-opting the feminists' arguments. Feminists specifically opposed the bill because they believed it to exemplify the government's "pandering to minorities."[19] The active involvement of the Hindu Right in opposing the *Shah Bano* decision added to the suspicion felt by Muslims that the judgment was intended to undermine Islamic law in accordance with the agenda of the Right.

In the *Danial Latifi & Anr. vs. Union of India* decision of 1985, the court found that the liability of a Muslim husband to pay maintenance to his divorced wife is not confined to the *iddat* period. In *Danial Latifi*, the court held that the Muslim Women's (Protection of Rights on Divorce) Act would be unconstitutional if it was not understood to mean that women would get a reasonable and fair provision of maintenance. However, despite reasoning that the bill actually contained a provision for Muslim women's maintenance beyond *iddat*, the court stopped short of declaring the act unconstitutional.[20] In 1991 the High Court of Bombay declared that the "constitution's framers did not intend to exclude personal laws from the ambit of Article 13[21] of the constitution,"[22] while also acknowledging that personal laws are subject to fundamental rights.

The Panchayat system also plays a key role in governing Muslims' lives. Panchayats are codified in the Indian Constitution in Part IX, Section 243. There is evidence to suggest that Panchayats in India date back to 1200 BCE. Joti Sekhon outlines their history:

These councils, usually controlled by upper-caste men, were responsible for governing village affairs and managing land and taxes... Initially the British, who consolidated their rule in India in the 18th century, did not pay much attention to the villages as long as the local elite collected and paid taxes, but after the revolts of 1857, the British initiated a series of measures to decentralize local government. However, the administrative structure remained very hierarchical with little effective control at the local level.[23]

After independence, calls for greater local participation in development projects led to the government's establishment of commissions that "recommended measures to facilitate local involvement through Panchayats." In 1993 the seventy-third amendment to the Indian Constitution provided a three-tiered structure of elected representation: the village, the intermediate (group of villages), and the district levels. The amendment requires that one-third of the total seats be reserved for women and includes a separate reservation for members of scheduled castes and tribal groups.[24] Despite this constitutional provision, many Muslim women's rights activists have decried the lack of representation of women and the subsequent lack of monitoring of the Panchayat system by the government.

Several other private groups have had a key role in advocating for the formalization of Islamic Personal Law. One such organization is the All India Muslim Personal Law Board (AIMPLB), which claims to have been formed in 1973 "at a time when the Government of India was trying to subvert Sharia law applicable to Indian Muslims."[25] The AIMPLB has argued in court that in accordance with Sharia law, Muslim women should not be given maintenance beyond the *iddat* period.[26] The AIMPLB's role as an actor in the shaping of Islamic Personal Law is self-appointed.[27]

More recently the All India Muslim Women Personal Law Board (AIMWPLB) has been established and has rebutted the advocacy of the AIMPLB to further the role of Sharia law and separate courts,[28] while also openly rejecting fatwas by Islamic seminaries.[29]

SEXUALITY AND SEXUAL RIGHTS: INTERNATIONAL NORMS

The standards established through international human rights documents provide a context through which to assess the realization of sexual rights and critically consider the assumptions made about sexuality by the law. In a discussion on sexual rights in the context of sexual and reproductive health and rights, Alice Miller defines "sexual rights" as the right to life, liberty, security of person, equality, nondiscrimination, bodily integrity, freedom of information, access to health care, protection from epidemic diseases, and equality within the family, as well as the right to marry and found a family and to have the highest attainable standard of mental and physical health.[30] She also acknowledges that sexual rights might include freedom from torture, arbitrary killing and execution, and arbitrary detention.[31] Sherifa Zuhur outlines some of the issues of sexual rights pertaining to Muslim women: "Sexual rights are matters of sex, sexuality, and bodily integrity because it is [sic] concerned with issues such as rape, adultery, honor killings, battery and wife-beating, murder, abortion, infanticide, sex trafficking, sex work, sexual abuse, incest, homosexuality, [transgender,] and transexuality."[32] Miller argues that sexual rights must go beyond those involved in reproductive health to include those pertaining to nonheterosexual and nonprocreative sex. She broadly locates sexual rights in human rights documents, recognizing the problematic history of sexual rights as the desire of the state to "uphold social norms regarding honor and chastity."[33] Several international documents and treaties touch on sexual rights from both an empowerment and a protective perspective, including the UN Convention on the Elimination of Discrimination against Women (CEDAW),[34] corresponding general recommendations, and the Convention on Rights of the Child (CRC).[35] Applicable provisions of CEDAW include General Recommendation 19, which calls for protections against sexual violence and exploitation. The CRC contains "protections"[36] against sexual exploitation and sexual abuse as well as the traffic of children.

India has made reservations to CEDAW in reference to Articles 5[37] and 16(1),[38] stating that the "Government of India declares that it shall abide by and endure these provisions in conformity with its policy of non-interference in the personal affairs of any community without its initiative and consent."[39] The reservation is demonstrative of India's desire to accommodate religious preference at the cost of women's rights. The specific reference to "initiative and consent" from religious communities begs the obvious question of whose consent represents the consensus and attitudes of a community.

Although nonbinding, several human rights documents provide further guidance on the realization of sexual rights. For example, the Beijing Declaration and Platform for Action extends reproductive rights to cover sexuality: "The human rights of women include the right to have control over and decide freely and responsibly on matters related to their sexuality, including sexual and reproductive health, free of coercion, discrimination, and violence."[40] More recently, human rights groups issued a statement called the Yogyakarta Principles, which outline a range of human rights standards and their applicability to sexual orientation and gender identity. The Yogyakarta Principles acknowledge that states and societies "impose gender and sexual orientation norms on individuals through custom, law, and violence and seek to control how they experience personal relationships and how they identity themselves."[41] When interpreting the International Covenant on Civil and Political Rights—ratified by India on 10 July 1979—the UN Human Rights Committee has identified sexual orientation as a protected category.[42]

2. Locating Sexual Rights in Domestic
Religious and Secular Discourse

MUSLIM FEMINISTS AND THE STRUGGLE
WITH STATE AND RELIGION

Feminist Analysis of Sexuality and the Law In *Danial Latifi & Anr. vs. Union of India*, the Supreme Court was tasked with interpreting the Muslim Women's (Protection ofRights on Divorce) Act of 1986. As noted above, the court held that the act, which limited maintenance for women after divorce, would be unconstitutional if not interpreted to grant fair provision and maintenance.[43] The court considered several perspectives represented by various constituencies in making their decision, including the AIMPLB. The court summarized the input of that group:

> The aim of the [Muslim Women's (Protection of Rights on Divorce)] Act
> is not to penalize the husband but to avoid vagrancy and in this context Section 4
> of the act is good enough to take care of such a situation and he, after making
> reference to several works on interpretation and religious thoughts as
> applicable to Muslims, submitted that [the] social ethos of Muslim
> society spreads a wider net to take care of a Muslim divorced wife
> and [that she is] not at all dependent on the husband.[44]

The AIMPLB argued for a limited maintenance requirement for men, signifying their role in defining discourse around women's sexuality. Here the AIMPLB reveals that it is not only the man, the family, the state, and the joint family[45] that have a role to play in Muslim sexuality in India, but also the structures that govern the discourse of the Muslim community vis-à-vis the Islamic Personal Legal Code.[46] Building on one another, the secular and the religious courts reinforced gender norms that subordinate Muslim women.

Zuhur notes that Islamic law consistently reminds us that the primary social identification of women is as reproductive and sexual beings constrained by men, the family, and the state.[47] While Mernissi speaks to Islamic law, the Indian secular context only serves to validate her point, as seen in the court's description of the *Shah Bano* case in the *Danial Latifi* decision. As stated by Justice Rajendra Babu:

> The important feature of the case was that the wife had managed the matrimonial home for more than 40 years and had borne and reared 5 children. . .
> The husband, a successful Advocate with an approximate income of Rs 5000 per month provided Rs 200 per month to the divorced wife, who had shared his life for over half a century and mother [sic] his five children and was in desperate need of money to survive.[48]

There are several ironies embedded in the state's discussion of the *Shah Bano* and *Danial Latifi* decisions. First, we have the secular courts attempting to reconcile injustice toward Muslim women vis-à-vis maintenance as pre-scribed by Islamic law but, in doing so, the courts reinforced gender norms that underlie women's inequality. These assumptions define the standards of what it means to be a "good wife and sacrificing mother," reinforcing the roles of economic dependence through rewarding, in this case, a good Muslim wife with alimony.[49] Ratna Kapur and Brenda Cossman assert that beyond rewarding behavior, judges are able to "mediate the legal code they admin-ister" through invoking shared cultural assumptions regarding the "nature of sexuality and the act of procreation."[50] The *Shah Bano* and *Danial Latifi* cases exemplify the assumptions about women's roles and identity in family that are embedded in the law. Here the secular state court rewards Shah Bano (and Danial Latifi) for fulfilling their obligations as reproductive and child-rearing agents facilitated by economic support from their husbands, men who are also forced to fulfill their role in the state-encouraged heteronormative and procre-ative family structure.

Legal discourse is a site of political struggle over sex difference and whether the creation of rules is based on natural differences between sexes or differences produced by the rules themselves.[51] The status of Muslim women and the rhetoric of difference between Muslim men and women (compared to one another and to members of the Hindu majority) employed by the state and community leaders exemplify the production of culture and norms through legal discourse. For the Muslim community in India, Muslim women have become markers of the cultural community. The separation of the public and private spheres has been maintained by the state and religious leaders. Religious leaders, in particular, maintain group autonomy as defined through these cultural markers.[52] Although the Indian Constitution guarantees all citizens equality and freedom from discrimination, personal law determines whether women have equal rights in the family and community and thus whether the experience of Muslim women is one of inequality and subordination. In turn, any claim for Muslim women's rights confronts religious hierarchy and traditions as well as state policies that have protected dominant religious traditions and the patriarchal structures of authority.[53]

2005's notorious *Imrana* case exemplifies the extremity of enforcing strict "religious" community norms. When she was twenty-eight years old, Imrana was raped by her father-in-law. When she took the case to the Panchayat, the body of men ruled that she must now marry her father-in-law and treat her husband as her son. The prominent Islamic seminary Darul-uloom Deoband supported this judgment.[54]

In India rape is a crime that typically is under the jurisdiction of the criminal courts.[55] However, individuals sometimes opt to have judgment for the accused administered through a personal law system. While there is a lack of data to suggest how Panchayats normally rule on such decisions, critiques of Muslim court decisions by Muslim feminists regarding rape in general, as well as specific examples such as the *Imrana* case, are illustrative of underlying norms pertaining to sexuality regulated by the personal law system. In Islamic law, for example, rape is treated both as an act of physical damage and a theft of sexual property that alters a virgin's financial worth. Each Islamic legal school differs in its approach to rape. The Hanafi school spells out the notion of this injury as being one to a man's property, rather than to the woman herself.[56] In the *Imrana* decision, Imrana is treated as property of the men in the family at large, and her rape represents the taking of property from son to father when the rape occurs.[57] Zuhur points out that marriage of the man to his rape victim—which is considered to save the woman from shame—is an "escape hatch" for men who rape. She further points out that this complicated system for handling rape represents the patriarchal management of female sexuality.[58] Other cases are also indicative of the desire for a religious structure that controls the sexuality of women. In Lucknow, for example, the case of another young woman whose fiancé visited her in the evening led to the Panchayat ruling that as punishment she must parade naked through her community; she was, in fact, forced to do so.[59]

The desire to pacify the Muslim minority for political reasons has resulted in the state's acceptance of fundamentalists as representatives of Muslim interests and has aided in the subordination of Muslim women. For example, the right of Muslim women to a monogamous marriage is not protected. Muslim men, in deference to personal law, are exempt from the provision of the Indian Penal Code that criminalizes bigamy.[60] Muslim women do not have equal rights of inheritance and succession: generally, female heirs receive half the share of male heirs. Widows only take a quarter share in the property of their husband if there are no children. This rule applies regardless of the number of wives that a man has. A Muslim mother can never be the legal guardian of her children; if the father dies, guardianship passes to the paternal grandfather or the paternal grandfather's executor. Muslim women do not have the freedom to choose whom to marry. Muslim men can marry non-*kitabbiya* (not "of the book"—that is, the Quran) women, and the marriage is seen as irregular but not void. But if a Muslim woman marries a non-Muslim man, the marriage is void.[61]

The refusal of state agents to intervene for the sake of more equal judgments is demonstrated by the experience of one Muslim women's rights activist in India. She told *Frontline* magazine of approaching the State Women's Commission in Uttar Pradesh after the *Imrana* Panchayat decision. The magazine's reporter wrote: "When Tehriq [Tehreek], a Lucknow-based organization working on violence among the urban poor, especially Muslim women, approached the State Women's Commission, it was told that as the matter concerned 'them,' that it is Muslim women, the Commission could not intervene beyond a point . . . They told us, *'yeh aap logon ka maamla hai'* [this is your community's problem]."[62] The denial of access to justice experienced by Muslim women and Muslim women's rights groups is reflective of the tacit support of the state for the continued sexual subordination of Muslim women. As Narain argues, "the Indian state has retained personal law as a means to regulate gender roles, the family and the community." In addition, the privileging of group rights over individual rights has resulted in the subsuming of Muslim women's rights and interests under the presumed need of the Muslim collective. In this way, the state reinforces women's subordination by reaffirming patriarchal structures of authority vis-à-vis personal law.[63] Furthermore, the lack of concern for women in the private spaces regulated by religious laws leads to what Kapur and Cossman have described as a space of cultural production and reinscription of sexual norms consistent with ideas of women's sexual purity. Also exemplifying these norms is the provision in section 497 of the Indian Penal Code: "Whoever has sexual intercourse with a person who is and whom he knows or has reason to believe to be the wife of another man, without the consent or connivance of that man, such sexual intercourse not amounting to the offense of rape, is guilty of the offense of adultery." The state's assumptions about female sexuality manifest themselves in a more nuanced way in this section, with its lack of punishment for the woman involved in adultery: in the law, women lack total agency. In fact, women are seen as victims of adultery.[64] Here the state seeks to protect a woman for her lack of agency in sexual decision making.

Women's sexuality in India is defined vis-à-vis the state and religious governing bodies. Both the secular and religious entities promote a patriarchal and heteronormative view of sexuality that values traditional roles for women and their sexual subordination. The state's relegation of sexuality largely to the religious legal sphere does not answer the question of who has been chosen to be the representative of culture and community, leaving decisions to self-appointed Muslim authorities — most of whom are men.

National Discourse and Muslim Sexuality Defining the boundaries of cultural and religious identity through women's bodies and lives has also been reinforced by the rhetoric and action of Hindu nationalists.

Acts of violence committed by agents of the Hindu Right serve as examples not only of the state's failure to protect but also of its active role in violating sexual rights. This is best exemplified through the recent pogrom against Muslims in Gujarat that left over 2,000 people dead and 160,000 displaced.[65] Much of the violence was targeted specifically toward women and was inspired by the hate rhetoric of Hindu nationalists, who urged Hindus to destroy communities of Muslims by raping and killing women.[66] Women's bodies become carriers of nations as well as children. A report by the People's Union for Democratic

Rights titled *Maaro! Baalo! Kaato!* (Kill! Burn! Hack!) documented numerous acts of sexual violence, including the raping of women in front of their families, the cutting off of their breasts, and the destruction of fetuses through attacking pregnant women's bodies.[67] A women's panel noted that women were subject to unimaginable "inhuman and barbaric" sexual violence.[68] The harm associated with rape becomes harm to the community, rather than a violation of an individual woman's right to bodily autonomy or bodily integrity.[69]

The extreme amount of violence experienced by the Muslim community and existing levels of discrimination may foster Muslims' distrust of the state and thereby strengthen the community's insularity and help revive a nationalistic discourse that defines women as carriers of culture. These community-based norms, as defined by self-appointed Muslim leaders, define the good Muslim woman as one who is chaste and virginal, while placing a high value on marriage.[70]

ISLAM AND RIGHTS

How can we begin to reconcile people's sexual rights with Islam? In the context of conducting a religious analysis of human rights, the notion of the "authority," or the person who makes a right binding, may be the most contentious. Secular theoretical frameworks define rights as granted and protected vis-à-vis the state[71] in which individuals reside, rather than as granted and protected by God.[72] The secular human rights paradigm largely rests on the following assumptions: people have rights simply because they are human; human rights are universal; human rights treat all people as equals; human rights are primarily the rights of individuals; human rights encompass the fundamental principles of humanity; and the promotion and protection of human rights are not bound by the frontiers of national states.[73]

When reconciling the secular human rights discourse with Islamic law, scholars have attempted to locate the notion of rights within Islam. Reformist Islamic scholars have tended to ground human rights values within the Islamic law framework, thereby acknowledging a divine granting of duties and rights.[74] In doing so, these scholars have outlined various methodologies for preserving human rights and human dignity within the Islamic legal and secular[75] context, while recognizing the interactions of Islam through, as, and with state mechanisms.

The traditional approach to locating rights in the Islamic legal tradition is to revisit Sharia, or divine law. Mohammed Hashim Kamali, a noted Muslim legal scholar, identifies the predominant difference between Western and Islamic law in this way:

> Both assume that right and wrong are not a matter of relative convenience for the individual, but derive from an eternally valid standard that is ultimately independent of human cognizance and adherence. But natural law differs from divine law in its assumption that right and wrong are inherent in nature. From an Islamic perspective, right and wrong are determined, not by reference to the nature of things, but because God has determined them as such.[76]

Notwithstanding their different approaches to determining right and wrong, natural law and the divine law of Islam uphold substantially the same values, according to Kamali.[77] The concept of equity (*istihsan*),[78] from which the notion of rights might be derived in Islamic law, is similar to the Western notion of a right in that they are both inspired by principles of "fairness and conscience," while authorizing "a departure from a rule of positive law when its enforcement leads to unfair results."[79] *Istihsan* offers a methodology that allows for the exercising of personal opinion in order to avoid rigidity and unfairness that might result from the literal enforcement of existing law; it has allowed for adaptation of Islamic law to the changing needs of society.[80] The concept of *istihsan* does not recognize the superiority of any other law over divine revelation, and the solutions it offers are largely based on the principles that are upheld by divine law; therefore, it does not constitute an independent authority from Sharia.[81]

Istihsan is not a concept that has been accepted by all Muslims: the Hanafi, Maliki, and Hanbali jurists have validated *istihsan* as a subsidiary source of law, while the Shafii, Zahiri, and Shi'i *ulama* have rejected it altogether and have refused to give it any credence in their formulation of legal theory.[82] For those who accept the reasoning of *istihsan*, Kamali argues that a well-defined role for the methodology could potentially create a space for evolutionary thinking in the context of Islamic law.[83]

In addition to finding philosophical underpinnings for human rights principles within the Islamic legal and religious traditions, scholars have specifically identified the sources of rights in linguistic and historic Islamic discourse. In his analysis, Ebrahim Moosa first locates the concept of a right in the Arabic word *haqq*, while acknowledging that *haqq* is considered "polysemous or multivalent" and thus could mean right, claim, duty, or truth, depending on the specific context and the use of the word in that context.[84] Moosa writes: "The relationship between rights and duties is an interpersonal and correlative one. In the enforcement of a right jurists understand that one party has a claim to have a 'right' and another 'obligation' to honor a right: every right thus has a reciprocal obligation."[85] After identifying the location of rights in Arabic, Moosa then traces the concept of *haqq* in Islamic history. In doing so, he highlights the methodological flaw in Islamic historical analysis: it is not inclusive of the notions of rights in pre-Islamic history, which may have influenced the practice of rights after the beginning of Islam. Moosa writes that during the reign of the Prophet and the caliphate (632–61), landmark events such as the Prophet's farewell sermon to his followers at the last pilgrimage; passages from the Quran dealing with the sanctity of life, property, dignity, and honor; and actions taken by the Prophet's successors to rectify rights violations of their subjects are early examples of a rights discourse in Islam.[86]

Abdullahi An-Na'im argues that one cannot derive human rights discourse from the framework of the Sharia. While acknowledging Islam as the ideal model of scriptural religion, he argues for a more radical departure from Sharia.[87] An-Na'im's methodology and critique is rooted in his belief that Sharia itself is not divine—rather, it is based on "human interpretation of divine sources . . . clearly established by the actual historical evolution of Shari'a and techniques used by its founding jurists."[88] He draws on the work of Ustadh Mahmoud Mohamed Taha, who states that there are two messages in Islam, one transitional and the other universal. The former was created for the immediate application of the universal theme in the immediate time; the second is to be interpreted by a process appropriate for today, potentially abrogating past historical formulations of Sharia.[89] His work is grounded in rereading the Quran in such a way that the Suras of the Meccan period contain the eternal theological message of Islam, while the Suras of the Medina period refer mostly to the specific needs and circumstances of the first Muslim community and cannot immediately be applied to modern circumstances.[90]

An-Na'im argues that in order to best reconcile differences between Islam and human rights, there must be a reformation of the historical Sharia necessitated by the "modern world": "large interpersonal urban centers, complex political relations, and globalized economies."[91] For An-Na'im, such a world requires a more specific structure for "political relations, forms of social interaction and control, and types of economic relations" that are not accounted for in traditional Islamic legal reasoning. He acknowledges classifications inherent in Islam that define gender and religion[92]—outlining, for example, the roles of women and men within Sharia that prevent the full realization of human rights.[93] Attempts to rework the relationship between Islam and human rights provide ground on which activists and reformers can build a reform agenda for Islamic law, but this has not translated into real change.

Conclusion

Despite ongoing efforts, activists have been unable to break down the dominant ideologies and cultural assumptions that obstruct the realization of rights in India for many Muslim women.[94] Islamic and secular law in India (both separately and, often, in reliance on one another) prevent Muslim women from fully realizing their sexual rights. While international human rights agreements provide some framework, language, and context to assess the situation of Muslim women's rights, India's reservations on grounds of noninterference in the personal affairs of any community weaken the ability to rely solely on human rights mechanisms for change. This chapter demonstrates the need to continue critical engagement with both secular and religious legal frameworks with regard to Islam and sexuality, and makes it clear that the secular state has not proved itself to be free of the gendered logic relied on by Islamic law.

Notes

I would like to thank Anthony Chase and Kathryn Abrams for their assistance with earlier versions of this chapter. Many thanks to the *Muslim World Journal of Human Rights* and the Berkeley Electronic Press for allowing the reprint of portions of this paper, Berkeley Electronic Press © 2007.

1 Wendy Brown, "Suffering the Paradoxes of Rights," in *Left Legalism, Left Critique*, edited by Wendy Brown and Janet Halley (Durham: Duke University Press, 2002), 422.

2 Hindu Unity (www.hinduunity.org); Vishva Hindu Parishad, *Why Vishva Hindu Parishad?* (www.vhp.org/englishsite/a-origin_growth/whyvhp.htm); Human Rights

Watch, *We Have No Orders to Save You: State Participation and Complicity in Communal Violence in Gujarat* (http://hrw.org/reports/2002/india/).

3 Ibid.

4 A subsect of Shi'a Islam based in India. This belief system originates in Yemen, where it evolved from the Fatimid Caliphate and its members were persecuted due to their differences from mainstream Sunni Islam—leading the group to move to India.

5 Minority Rights Group International, *Muslim Women in India* (United Kingdom: Minority Rights Group, 1999).

6 Flavia Agnes, *Law and Gender Inequality: The Politics of Women's Rights in India* (Delhi: Oxford University Press, 1999).

7 Vrinda Narain, *Gender and Community: Muslim Women's Rights in India* (Toronto: University of Toronto Press, 2001).

8 Ibid.

9 Ibid.

10 "All questions regarding intestate succession, special property of females, including personal property inherited or obtained under contract or gift or any other provision of Personal law, marriage, dissolution of marriage, including talaq, ila, zihar, lian, khula and mabaraat, maintenance, dower, guardianship, gifts, trusts and trust properties, and wakfs (other than charities and charitable institutions and charitable and religious endowments) the rule of decision in case where the parties are Muslims shall be the Muslim Personal Law (Shariat)" (Muslim Personal Law [Sharia] Application Act of 1937).

11 Narain. *Gender and Community*.

12 "Equality before law.—The State shall not deny any person equality before the law or the equal protection of the laws within the territory of India" (Indian Constitution, Article 14).

13 "Freedom to manage religious affairs.—Subject to public order, morality and health, every religious denomination or any section thereof shall have the right—(a) to establish and maintain institutions for religious and charitable purposes; (b) to manage its own affairs in matters of religion; (c) to own and acquire movable and immovable property; and (d) to administer such property in accordance with law" (Ibid., Article 26)."Freedom as to payment of taxes for promotion of any particular religion.—No person shall be compelled to pay any taxes, the proceeds of which are specifically appropriated in payment of expenses for the promotion or maintenance of any particular religion or religious denomination" (Ibid., Article 27). "Freedom as to attendance at religious instruction or religious worship in certain educational institutions.—(1) No

religious instruction shall be provided in any educational institution wholly maintained out of State funds. (2) Nothing in clause (1) shall apply to an educational institution which is administered by the State but has been established under any endowment or trust which requires that religious instruction shall be imparted in such institution. (3) No person attending any educational institution recognised by the State or receiving aid out of State funds shall be required to take part in any religious instruction that may be imparted in such institution or to attend any religious worship that may be conducted in such institution or in any premises attached thereto unless such person or, if such person is a minor, his guardian has given his consent thereto" (Ibid., Article 28).

14 "Uniform civil code for the citizens. — The State shall endeavor to secure for the citizens a uniform civil code throughout the territory of India" (Ibid., Article 44).

15 Narain, *Gender and Community*.

16 *Danial Latifi & Anr. vs. Union of India*, 1985 (2) SCC 556.

17 Muslim Women's (Protection of Rights on Divorce) Act, 1986.

18 *Mohd. Ahmed Khan vs. Shah Bano Begum & Ors*, 1985 (2) SCC 556.

19 Ratna Kapur and Brenda Crossman, *Subversive Sites: Feminist Engagements with Law in India* (New Delhi: Sage, 1996).

20 "Hullaballoo over Triple Talaq in India," South Asian's Citizen's Wire (www .wluml.org/english/newsfulltxt.shtml?cmd percent5B157 percent5D=x-157-64559).

21 "Laws inconsistent with or in derogation of the fundamental rights. — (1) All laws in force in the territory of India immediately before the commencement of this Constitution, in so far as they are inconsistent with the provisions of this Part, shall, to the extent of such inconsistency, be void. (2) The State shall not make any law which takes away or abridges the rights conferred by this Part and any law made in contravention of this clause shall, to the extent of the contravention, be void. (3) In this article, unless the context otherwise requires, — (*a*) "law" includes any Ordinance, order, bye-law, rule, regulation, notification, custom or usage having in the territory of India the force of law; (*b*) "laws in force" includes laws passed or made by a Legislature or other competent authority in the territory of India before the commencement of this Constitution and not previously repealed, notwithstanding that any such law or any part thereof may not be then in operation either at all or in particular areas. (4) Nothing in this article shall apply to any amendment of this Constitution made under article 368" (Indian Constitution, Article 13).

22 *In re, Smt. Amina*. In the High Court of Bombay. Manu/MH/0039/1992.

23 Joti Sekhon, "Engendering Grassroots Democracy: Research, Training, and Net-

working for Women in Local Self-Governance in India," *National Women's Studies Association* 18, no. 2 (2006): 105.

24 Ibid.

25 All India Muslim Personal Law Board (www.aimplboard.org/).

26 *Danial Latifi & Anr. vs. Union of India*, 1985 (2) SCC 556.

27 Another such organization is the Islamic Sharia Board, which also advocated that women not be given maintenance beyond the *iddat* period in the *Danial Latifi* case.

28 "Plea against Muslim Personal Law Board Setting Up Parallel System," *The Hindu*, 17 August 2005 (www.hindu.com/2005/08/17/stories/2005081703311300.htm).

29 "Muslim Women's Law Board Rejects Fatwa on Imrana," Rediff.com, 30 June 2005 (www.rediff.com/news/2005/jun/30rape1.htm).

30 Alice M. Miller, "Sexual But Not Reproductive: Exploring the Junction and Disjunction of Sexual and Reproductive Rights," *Health and Human Rights* 4, no. 2 (2000): 17–29.

31 Ibid.

32 Sherifa Zuhur, *Gender, Sexuality, and the Criminal Laws in the Middle East and North Africa: A Comparative Study* (Istanbul: Women for Women's Human Rights, 2005; www.wwhr.org/images/GenderSexualityandCriminalLaws.pdf).

33 Miller, "Sexual But Not Reproductive."

34 India ratified CEDAW on 9 July 1993.

35 India ratified the CRC on 11 December 1992.

36 Miller, "Sexual But Not Reproductive."

37 "States Parties shall take all appropriate measures: (a) To modify the social and cultural patterns of conduct of men and women, with a view to achieving the elimination of prejudices and customary and all other practices which are based on the idea of the inferiority or the superiority of either of the sexes or on stereotyped roles for men and women; (b) To ensure that family education includes a proper understanding of maternity as a social function and the recognition of the common responsibility of men and women in the upbringing and development of their children, it being understood that the interest of the children is the primordial consideration in all cases" (CEDAW, Article 5).

38 "1. States Parties shall take all appropriate measures to eliminate discrimination against women in all matters relating to marriage and family relations and in particular shall ensure, on a basis of equality of men and women: (a) The same right to enter into marriage; (b) The same right freely to choose a spouse and to enter into marriage only with their free and full consent; (c) The same rights and responsibilities during marriage and at its dissolution; (d) The same rights and responsibilities as parents, irrespective

of their marital status, in matters relating to their children; in all cases the interests of the children shall be paramount; (e) The same rights to decide freely and responsibly on the number and spacing of their children and to have access to the information, education and means to enable them to exercise these rights; (f) The same rights and responsibilities with regard to guardianship, wardship, trusteeship and adoption of children, or similar institutions where these concepts exist in national legislation; in all cases the interests of the children shall be paramount; (g) The same personal rights as husband and wife, including the right to choose a family name, a profession and an occupation; (h) The same rights for both spouses in respect of the ownership, acquisition, management, administration, enjoyment and disposition of property, whether free of charge or for a valuable consideration. 2. The betrothal and the marriage of a child shall have no legal effect, and all necessary action, including legislation, shall be taken to specify a minimum age for marriage and to make the registration of marriages in an official registry compulsory" (CEDAW, Article 16).

39 Quoted in National Commission for Women (India), *CEDAW, The Reservations and the Optional Protocol* (National Commission for Women, January 2006; http://ncw.nic.in/pdfreports/CEDAW percent20The percent20Reservations percent20And percent20Optional percent20Protocol.pdf).

40 Fourth World Conference on Women, Beijing, China. www.un.org/women watch/daw/beijing/beijingdeclaration.html.

41 "Yogyakarta Principles on the Application of International Human Rights Law in Relation to Sexual Orientation and Gender Identity" (www.yogyakartaprinciples .org/index.php?item=25).

42 *Toonen v. Australia*, Communication No. 488/1992, U.N. Doc CCPR/C/50/D/488/1992 (New York: United Nations, 1994).

43 "All Unjust Personal Laws Have to Go, Be They Hindu, Muslim, or Christian," South Asian's Citizen's Wire (www.wluml.org/english/newsfulltxt.shtml?cmd percent5B157 percent5D=x-157-64559).

44 *Danial Latifi & Anr. vs. Union of India*, 1985 (2) SCC 556.

45 Kapur and Crossman, *Subversive Sites.*

46 Feminists have argued that many Sharia law provisions that are applied in a retrogressive manner toward women must be understood in their historical context, in order to extract the lessons of progressive values toward women that these rules originally represented.

47 Zuhur, *Gender, Sexuality, and the Criminal Laws in the Middle East and North Africa.*

48 *Danial Latifi & Anr. vs. Union of India*, 1985 (2) SCC 556.

49 Kapur and Crossman, *Subversive Sites*, 87.

50 Ibid.

51 Mary Joe Frug, cited in ibid., 34.

52 Narain, *Gender and Community*.

53 Ibid.

54 Pervez Iqbal Siddiqui, "Father-in-Law Gets 10 Years for Imrana rape," *Times of India*, 20 October 2006 (http://timesofindia.indiatimes.com/articleshow/2210881.cms).

55 Indian Penal Code, section 375.

56 Zuhur, *Gender, Sexuality, and the Criminal Laws in the Middle East and North Africa*, 30-34.

57 Until 2006, India's Penal Code section 375, which outlaws rape, excluded from its definition of rape "sexual intercourse by a man with his own wife, the wife not being under sixteen years of age," supporting the notion of women as property in the secular legal code.

58 Zuhur. *Gender, Sexuality, and the Criminal Laws in the Middle East and North Africa*, 30-34. Zuhur also talks about how this challenge exists in all Abrahamic traditions.

59 Naish Hasan conversation with author.

60 Narain, *Gender and Community*, 25.

61 Ibid., 25-28.

62 T. K. Rajalakshmi, "*Fighting for Imrana*," *Frontline*, 29 July 2005 (www.hinduonnet .com/fline/fl2215/stories/20050729006512100.htm).

63 Narain, *Gender and Community*, 25.

64 Kapur and Crossman, *Subversive Sites*.

65 Human Rights Watch, *We Have No Orders to Save You: State Participation and Complicity in Communal Violence in Gujarat* (Human Rights Watch, 2002; http://hrw .org/reports/2002/india/).

66 Ratna Kapur, *Erotic Justice: Law and the New Politics of Post Colonialism* (London: Glasshouse, 2005).

67 People's Union for Democratic Rights. *Maaro! Kaapo! Baalo!* (People's Union for Democratic Rights, 2002; www.pucl.org/Topics/Religion-communalism/2002/ maro_kapo_balo.pdf). See also Human Rights Watch, *We Have No Orders to Save You*.

68 Jyotsna Singh, "Gujarat Muslim Women Rape Victims," BBC News, 16 April 2002 (http://news.bbc.co.uk/2/hi/south_asia/1933521.stm).

69 Kapur and Crossman, *Subversive Sites*.

70 Ibid. Kapur and Crossman are discussing Agnes talking about the state, but I apply their discussion to Muslim community leadership.

71 Ebrahim Moosa writes: "A deeper paradox of the role of the state in protecting rights is the idea that rights exist as a mechanism designed to protect individuals from the overwhelming powers of the bureaucratic state . . . The notion of human rights as we know it today arises in the context of the evolution of the nation-state as a political system, even though some may claim a more ancient pedigree for it to date back to the Magna Carta and the French Revolution" ("The Dilemma of Islamic Human Rights Schemes," *Journal of Law and Religion* 15, nos. 1-2 [2000-2001]: 185-215).

72 Moosa, "The Dilemma of Islamic Human Rights Schemes," 185-215.

73 International Federation of Red Cross and Red Crescent Societies and Fracois-Xavior Bagnoud Center for Health and Human Rights, "Human Rights: An Introduction," in *Health and Human Rights A Reader*, edited by Jonathan Mann and Sofia Gruskin (New York: Routledge, 1999), 21.

74 See Heiner Bielefeldt, "Muslim Voices in the Human Rights Debate," *Human Rights Quarterly* 17, no. 4 (1995): 587-617.

75 Abdullahi Ahmed An-Naim argues for the creation of a specifically Islamic secularism ("A Kinder, Gentler Islam?," *Transition* 52 (1991): 4-16).

76 Kamali, *Principles of Islamic Juriprudence.*

77 Ibid.

78 Roja Fazaeli discusses *istihsan* as a type of *itjihad*. She notes that Al-Shafii concludes that there is no canonical grounding for *itijihad* and *istihsan*. However, the views of Islamic legal scholars and Sunni religious scholars differ: some reject *itjihad*, while some use it in a much wider context or restrict the scope of its application while recognizing its legitimacy. See Roza Fazeli, "Islamic Feminism and the Issues of Dependency," *Feminism and Legal Theory Project: All in the Family? Islam, Women, and Human Rights* (Atlanta: Emory University Law School, 2-4 March 2006).

79 Kamali, *Principles of Islamic Jurisprudence.*

80 Ibid.

81 Ibid.

82 Ibid.

83 Ibid.

84 Moosa. "The Dilemma of Islamic Human Rights Schemes."

85 Ibid.

86 Ibid.

87 An-Naim, "A Kinder, Gentler Islam?"

88 Ibid.

89 Anthony Tirado Chase and Abdul Karim Alaug, "Health, Human Rights, and Islam: A Focus on Yemen." *Health and Human Rights* 8, no. 1 (2004).

90 See Bielefeldt, "Muslim Voices in the Human Rights Debate."

91 An-Naim, "A Kinder, Gentler Islam?," 4-16.

92 This is also discussed by Bielefeldt, "Muslim Voices in the Human Rights Debate."

93 An-Naim, "A Kinder, Gentler Islam?"

94 Kapur. *Erotic Justice*, 92.

PART TWO

Law and Culture

ANTHONY MARCUS

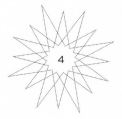

Reconsidering *Talaq*

MARRIAGE, DIVORCE, AND SHARIA REFORM
IN THE REPUBLIC OF MALDIVES

The Maldives, an entirely Muslim society that is reputed to have the highest divorce rate in the world, enacted comprehensive family law reform in 2001 designed to create greater equality between men and women. One of the key aspects of this reform was new restrictions on the verbal male divorce prerogative known as *talaq*. This chapter takes up this key issue in the Maldives as a case study to reveal some of the contradictions between de jure reform and de facto outcomes. Although the reforms created near-equality of the sexes before the law, the chapter argues that the two constituent components—Western secular law and Islamic religious law—created a dialectic between two forms of patriarchy that endangers the customary rights and freedoms that Maldivians understand to be their peculiarly national version of "folk Islam." With regard to marriage and divorce, this folk Islam contains surprising spaces for women's quotidian social and sexual agency that may be endangered by largely top-down attempts to reform family law, make it more gender equal, and bring the Maldives in line with international norms governing the nexus between family, property, and the state.

On 1 July 2001 the Republic of Maldives—an atoll-based Muslim nation of roughly 350,000 people, located about 600 kilometers south of Sri Lanka in the Indian Ocean—followed Algeria, Turkey, Tunisia, and other Islamic nations in enacting a comprehensive family law reform. As with other such programs in the Muslim world, the Maldives reform was presented as an attempt to reconcile the aspirations of women, particularly educated ones, with the conflicting demands of national development and neotraditional nationalist ideologies that hold Islamic Sharia to be both custom and culture in the countries of the world's Islamic community, or *ummah*. The Maldivian reforms granted women nearly complete de jure equality with men, in a country already known for the greatest equality between the sexes in South Asia. As was the case with the sweeping family law reform of 2004 in Morocco, members of the international community and Maldivian civil society advocates for women's rights who were connected to institutions involved in the Convention for the Elimination of All Forms of Discrimination against Women (CEDAW) hailed the Maldivian family law reform as an important step forward.

However, as has been the case for family law reform in both the West and the East, de facto outcomes often relate in confusing and contradictory ways to de jure statutes, and many Maldivian women are unable or unwilling to access their new rights, often leaving them in similar circumstances—or worse ones—due to patriarchal backlash (Moghadam 2008). In the Maldives, nearly a decade after family law reform, there has been very little research about on-the-ground outcomes of this crucial moment in Maldivian gender relations and legal history.[1] This chapter, based on nine months of ethnographic research in the Maldives in 2006-7, will attempt to begin a discussion of the relationship between Maldivian family law reform and social practice by looking at the way in which some of the changes that were ostensibly designed to provide greater equality for women may have actually reduced their ability to exert agency over their role in family life.

Divorce, which is more common in the Maldives than anywhere else in the Muslim world,[2] (Warren 2006; United Nations, Population Division 2009) is viewed as a key social problem by both neotraditionalists and secular progressives (Hama Jamiyya 2007). It has been described by liberal observers both within and external to the Maldives as being responsible for everything from high rates of child abuse and juvenile delinquency to disease, sickness, and poverty (Asian Development Bank 2007; United Nations, Committee on the Rights of the Child 1998; World Health Organization 2006). Islamicists are equally disturbed by the Maldivian disregard for the most sacred of Islamic institutions, the family. For this reason, divorce reform was a key part of the 2001 family law reform, which sought to change divorce from a prerogative of a husband—who needed only say "I divorce you" in front of two witnesses—to an institution encompassing the rights and responsibilities of both parties to a marriage.

Under the new law, divorce may be initiated by either aggrieved party and is mediated and decided by a judge whose charge is to provide equal protection to both sides. As with similar reforms in other Islamic countries, the right to prenuptial agreements limiting polygamy was built into the law. However, unlike reforms in other Islamic countries, where divorce is less common, Maldivian couples are now expected to take prenuptial classes on effective marital communication and what is called the "expectations of marriage."

While there was a radical drop in divorce rates in the year after family law reform, in the following three to four years the divorce rate returned to pre-2001 levels (Republic of Maldives 2005, 2008; United Nations, Population Division 2009). It will be my argument in this chapter that this is because the 2001 family law reform, like others in the Islamic world, was driven by a largely top-down politico-legal process, involving a dialectic between two relatively static visions of development: secular Western and Muslim traditionalist. This process, which is not dissimilar to other Islamic family law reforms, has involved a variety of combinations of Western style legal codes, neotraditional religious beliefs, and religious reinterpretation, meant to better fit contemporary society and economy (Amado 2006; Moghadam 2008). In some cases, the outcomes have been described as largely secular, as in the case of Turkey and Tunisia (Mogahadam 2008); more religiously based, as in the case of Jordan and Iran (Mir-Hosseini 2000; Moghadam 2008); or balanced, as in the case of Morocco (Mir-Hosseini 2007).

Regardless of the methodology or particular balance between West and East, or secular and religious, this dialectic may obscure on-the-ground social realities and quotidian life concerns of the women that advocates of family law reform claim to want to address. In the absence of a mass feminist movement that might make demands for women's rights that come from a combination of a conscious program of liberation and the immediate needs of daily life, family law reform is almost inherently a cold transformation, largely driven from above by special interests. While this often means that serious and well-intentioned civil society actors work with and for international institutions and progressive elites (Mir-Hosseini 2007), the net effect may be to weaken one form of socioeconomic patriarchy, that of Islam, by adding another, that of the secular West.

None of this is to say that family law reform in the Islamic world is not a generally positive process. The elimination of agrarian codes of patriarchy that continue to restrict women in modern capitalist economies has been a crucial development for those who can access their new rights. Furthermore, the entire process has democratized the practice of interpreting the Quran and hadith, as has been observed by the Maldivian Islamic law scholar Abdullah Saeed (2006). However, the use of this dialectic between two systems of patriarchy for recasting family law may also be endangering customary and interstitial behaviour, typically referred to as "folk Islam." It will be my contention that divorce in the Maldives, far from being one of the nation's central social problems, is a vibrant part of that folk Islam that has much to teach us about what women (and men) want in both the Islamic and Western worlds.

Patriarchy East and West

Marriage, according to structuralist anthropological accounts (Lévi-Strauss 1969; Needham 1971; White 1959), is universal to human life and represents an alliance between families. However, the form taken by that alliance and the rules governing it are believed to be determined by the specific structuring factors predominant in a given society, such as the social division of labor, property relations, and subsistence technologies (Collier 1988; Coontz and Henderson; 1986; Leacock 1972; Reed 1975; Sacks 1975). This approach to the historically changing relationship between marriage and society is based on the social evolutionism of nineteenth-century kinship theorists such as Johann Bachofen (1992), Friedrich Engels (1972), and John McLennan (2001) and twentieth-century sociocultural evolutionists such as V. Gordon Childe (1951) and Leslie White (1959).[3]

Drawing on the ethnographic and historical record of prestate, pre-agricultural societies, this approach has suggested a structural tie between the lack of agriculture—which produces the first storable accumulated surplus in human history—and loose, relatively gender-equal, marital bonds. Whether the postulated instrument for the rise of gender inequality is inheritance and patrimony (Engels 1972), the existence of commodifiable male property (Sacks 1975), scarcity of women (McLennan 2001), sedentarism (Draper 1975), or the greater politico-economic power of polygyny (accumulating women through marriage) over polyandry (accumulating men through marriage) when women's agricultural labor is the basis of the social surplus (Coontz 1986), virtually all schools of thought in this approach see a connection between agriculture, property, and changing family forms that, in various ways, control women—the first producers of surplus. This worldwide historical change is seen as contrasting agrarian societies with hunter-gatherer societies, in which there is little value to be gained by controlling the labor of women since they produce no storable surplus that can be accumulated—and for the same reason, there is little to be gained in controlling their children, whose future labor and social alliances also will not produce significant storable or accumulated surpluses. This, it is argued, inherently makes sexually based kinship—usually based on something called marriage—typically weaker, more fluid, and more egalitarian (Coontz 1986; Engels 1972; Leacock 1972; Mies 1999; Reed 1975; Shostak 2000).

According to this approach, the rise of tributary or feudal agrarian societies put tremendous stress on sexually based kinship and made the marriage bond the crucial stress-bearing intersection between family property and inheritance (Mies 1999). Until the rise of a ubiquitous market economy and the legal codification of the modern corporation—defined as a coalition of investors acting as one legal person—marital kinship was the primary means by which property could be concentrated, investment made possible, and subsistence or expansion realized. With little to no means of modern accounting, the existence of nearly all property in unsalable forms, such as use rights to land, labor, and resources; and a common pattern of primary producers who were bound to the land, marriage was the crucial foundation of inheritance and must have been, almost by definition "till death do us part" (Mies 1999; Sangari and Vaid 1990). This is regardless of the comparative status of women in varied agrarian social formations and the power of individual women over their own dowries and inheritances (Talwar-Oldenburg 2002).

According to this same perspective, the new freedoms of capitalism gave individuals the right to buy and sell their labor in the open market, replacing the elite family with the modern publicly owned corporation and the family farm, with the quasi-voluntary cooperation of two independent wage earners—typically referred to as the "modern companionate marriage" (D'Emilio 1983; Coontz 1988). This has changed marriage and the family from a necessary institution that nobody can live without into a social ideal to which most individuals, even same-sex couples, aspire—creating opportunities for women, who are no longer simply factors of production and the property of men who rule the agrarian family domestic unit.

However, the new companionate corporation of two wage earners, whose accumulated family property can be easily commodified and divided, has also made marital kinship more voluntary, and therefore an emotionally charged site of civic, social, and political combat in which the control of women, whose voluntary rights are in question, has often come to be a key symbol of social order and economic advancement (D'Emilio 1983; Sangari and Vaid 1990; Smith 1985). This has yielded a situation in which the attenuation of such marital forms has sparked culture wars between the traditional and the modern in all but the most isolated, distant, and marginal parts of the world, where those agrarian feudal or tributary norms never fully penetrated.

The Maldives is, in some respects, one of those marginal places. It has no history of agrarian property, and its accompanying social codes of honor and shame, a semi-nomadic male maritime population, an endless ocean frontier, a historically weak mercantilist sultanate, and an ocean that acts as a buffer from Old World feudal or tributary agrarian states and their accompanying patriarchal social relations. It has, for the last thirty years, been in a process of leapfrogging from the pre-agrarian to the postindustrial without experiencing an agricultural or industrial phase. The remainder of this chapter will address the possibility that the legal dialectic between the two contemporary scions of Old World agrarian patriarchy—neotraditionalist Islam and modern liberal capitalism—yields potentially different results in a sociocultural environment such as this, lacking a history of agrarian state formation and separated from the mainland core of the *ummah*.

Background

The Maldives is a low-lying archipelago, stretching across twenty atoll adminis-trative units with roughly 1,200 islands, of which some 200 are inhabited. Sitting in the middle of the Indian Ocean's sea lanes, the Maldives stretches almost 1,000 kilometers, north to south. The population is primarily South Asian de-scendants of the modern-day Sinhalese in Sri Lanka; it is entirely Muslim—converted from Buddhism in the twelfth century—and speaks one language, Divehi.

The Maldives was known to premodern Indian Ocean travelers as a curious land where women held political power, had remarkable sexual license, and were reputed to prefer temporary to permanent marriage. The most famous Maldivian sultana was Rehendi Khadeeja, who ruled from 1343 to 1379. How-ever, she may be famous simply because she was on the throne during the visit of the Islamic traveller and writer Ibn Battuta. Due to its strategic location and abundance of natural resources, the country was tremendously wealthy, producing cowries for the slave trade, coir rope, dried tuna fish, ambergris, and *coco de mer*, in addition to providing a site for ships to replenish their supplies, wait out poor sailing conditions, and transfer slaves and manufactured goods between India, Southeast Asia, the Arabian Peninsula, and Africa.

The rise of North Atlantic capitalism and the growth of European colo-nialism in the eighteenth and nineteenth centuries shifted the focus of the world economy away from Indian Ocean commerce, and the Maldives ex-perienced a long period of poverty and isolation. Though some Maldivians in the northern atolls identify themselves as descendants of sixteenth-century Portuguese slavers, the Maldives missed much of the experience of European colonialism, becoming a barely noticed British protectorate in 1885. The coun-try gained independence in 1965, and an international airport—built in the late 1970s—brought in a trickle of tourists, but the Maldives remained relatively isolated until the last two decades.

Since the late 1990s, tourism and foreign direct investment in tourist infra-structure and properties have boomed spectacularly, with Maldivian honey-moon vacations becoming famous worldwide and over 700,000 tourists—more than twice the population of the country—arriving in 2007. This has made the Maldives one of the fastest growing economies in the world since 2000 and driven a real estate, construction, and banking boom that has raised the country into the ranks of the United Nations' category of "middle income." The Maldives is the only country in South Asia with universal literacy and the only Muslim country where men and women are roughly equal in health, education, and other common social development indicators. Maldivians often cite these facts as proof of the endurance of their ancient tradition of Indian Ocean cosmopolitanism and folk Islam in face of the neotraditionalism—which they typically refer to as "gulf-oriented" Islam—that seems to be gaining ground across the region.

The Maldives had no international development or policy organizations for the first four decades after independence, with the exception of a tiny, barely operational, UN duty station. However, the Indian Ocean tsunami of December 2005 changed this, flooding nearly all of the 200 inhabited islands and spreading international reconstruction and development projects staffed by young, foreign-educated Maldivians and expatriate development workers to the most distant islands. The uniquely national impact of the tsunami—combined with the arrival of large numbers of outside observers, agitators, and collaborators—empowered the opposition Maldivian Democratic Party in the post-tsunami period and forced the government to begin a democratization process that has been planned for many years, but never been acted on.

This confluence of a multibillion-dollar post-tsunami reconstruction and democratization has created a dynamic and volatile sociopolitical environment in which young Maldivian men and women have gained remarkable opportunities and skills as entrepreneurs in the booming tourist economy, researchers and professional staff members in international agencies, and leaders in the political opposition. It has also accelerated a population concentration in Malé, the capital city, which is on an island of less than two square kilometers and which currently has roughly 150,000 residents, making it the most densely populated city on earth and producing a boom in apartment building and a rise in social problems connected to space and housing. Famous for its maritime nomadism, the Maldives now has more than a third of its national population permanently living in the capital city in housing densities that average over seven people per room.

Field Methods

My interest as a researcher in questions of marriage and divorce in the Maldives began during a seminar on gender and development in the University of Melbourne's Development Studies Programme in July 2005. There a Maldivian student, whose master's thesis I later supervised, raised the question of the high divorce rates in the Maldives as part of a discussion of the rarity of divorce in Islam, despite the relative ease of the divorce process. When my study leave arrived at the end of 2006, I moved to the Maldives to study post-tsunami reconstruction and development and lived in Henveeru, one of the wealthier seafront neighbourhoods of Malé, between October 2006 and June 2007. My partner worked as the country director for an Australian Red Cross waste management program that was being delivered to seventy-four islands across the Maldives.

My initial contacts were through two Maldivian former students, one who was well connected in the Maldivian government and another who worked for the United Nations. My partner, whose program had close relations with the Canadian, French, American, German, and British Red Cross, gave me access to their projects and large contingents of Maldivian and foreign development workers in exchange for my help with monitoring and evaluation. This enabled me to participate in events, workshops, and work trips to the many islands where projects were being administered.

Using interpreters, who were trained in social sciences at Anglophone universities abroad, I did extensive interviews, usually in Divehi, the Maldivian national language, on these islands with up to 200 families. I talked with ordinary people, island chiefs, and members of the women's development committees that were the beneficiaries of the waste management program. I spent seemingly endless hours of ethnographic time on speedboats and tiny islands where there was nothing for national and international development staff members from Malé to do at night except talk, joke, and compare their cultures.

I also obtained consulting work with UNICEF, which had a largely Maldivian staff of some fifty people—all of whom spoke English fluently.[4] I spent several months working from 9:00 to 6:00 at a desk in their offices and developed close contacts with Maldivian and expatriate co-workers. Through UNICEF I was able to access the staff and work of affiliated organizations in the Maldives, such as the United Nations Development Program, United Nations Population Fund, and World Health Organization. Finally, my residence in the Maldives afforded me many opportunities to observe the minutiae of everyday life and interact with Maldivian merchants, weight-lifting partners at the local gymnasium, colleagues in educational faculties and research centers, and expatriates trying to meet their deadlines for reconstruction projects, while struggling to understand and respect Maldivian cultural norms.

Divorce, Maldivian Style

The Republic of the Maldives, which officially describes itself as 100 percent Muslim, is believed to have the highest divorce rate in the world, at 10.97 divorces per 1,000 population in 2004. This is in comparison with barely more than 4 per 1,000 for Guam, Belarus, Russia, and the United States, the countries with the next four highest divorce rates in the same year (Kotlikoff and Burns 2005). It has been repeatedly estimated that the average Maldivian woman is married four times (Asian Development Bank 2001).[5] While many foreigners identify this as a new problem, involving modernity, selfishness, and the disruption of traditional patterns of life (Warren 2006), most Maldivians view it as neither alien and Western nor modern, but rather as an eternal national cultural essence tied to the general traditions of Indian Ocean mobility and mercantilism, liberal Islamic rules allowing temporary marriage and easy face-to-face divorce, a frontier mentality produced by disparate settlement across some 1,200 islands, and a peculiar and legendary curse of uncontrollable sexual promiscuity among Maldivian women.

Many Maldivians take great nationalist pride in their liberality and native cosmopolitanism. However, the last-named characteristic—female sexual promiscuity—appears to be more what Michael Herzfeld calls cultural intimacy: "the recognition of those aspects of a cultural identity that are considered a source of external embarrassment but that nevertheless provide insiders with their assurance of common sociality" (2004, 3). The relatively general consensus among both Maldivian men and women that sexual loyalty may not be possible for Maldivian women sits within the Islamic *ummah* as an almost textbook case of Herzfeld's observation that cultural intimacy represents "alleged national traits . . . that offer citizens a sense of defiant pride in the face of a more formal or official morality" and take the form of "self-stereotypes that insiders express ostensibly at their own collective expense" (ibid.). Or, as many Maldivians lament, "we just aren't very good Muslims, no matter how hard we try."

Maldivians commonly refer to the fourteenth-century Islamic scholar, traveler, and politician Ibn Battuta's travelog about his visit to the Maldives—the key historical record of their preindustrial past—as a way of affirming that the national character these self-stereotypes refer to is ancient. In the story, as told by Maldivians in informal social settings and national media,[6] Ibn Battuta shows up expecting to spend only days, but he passes nine months married to several Maldivian women. One of these women—who was royal—convinces him to become the kingdom's chief justice. As the culturally intimate nationalist story goes, ibn Battuta struggles heroically but unsuccessfully to make good Muslims out of the recently converted Maldivians.

He decries the amoral penchant for serial marriages, observing that the problem is that people marry for pleasure rather than exchange of property and the creation of household wealth—which he views, through his patriarchal agrarian lens, as the purpose of marriage. He tries to institute the largely uncontroversial mainland practice of cutting off the hands of thieves, but the Maldivians prove too weak and complain that the punishment is too severe for theft. When he finally manages to arrange such a dismemberment, Maldivian men faint at the sight. Finally, in the name of Islam, he passes a kingdom-wide law demanding sexual modesty of women and requiring them to cover their breasts in public. He is able to get only a few particularly powerless slave women to comply, and they don't do it correctly. He leaves and later returns briefly, hoping to use South Indian Muslim armies to conquer the country, but in the end he is conquered by Maldivian incorrigibility, or at least so goes the nationalist story of Maldivian folk Islam and the hanging judge.

Ibn Battuta's text has the strange feel of an early anthropological study of first contact, highlighting the many differences that existed between the agrarian social relations that he would have seen in his travels around the world and relations in the peculiar nonagrarian Maldives, which had the religious ideologies of Islam but different social relations dealing with property—be it stolen or exchanged in marriage.

Modern popular texts written by Maldivians express similar sentiments. The main opposition newspaper, *Minivan News*, ran a story in 2006 on the increasing concern of many Maldivians that "rich Arab donors" have too much influence, as evidenced by the introduction of female head covering to a country where it was not customary and women only recently started covering their breasts in public.[7] The author observes: "Hijab or no hijab . . . if someone preys on another's wife, in the Maldives, the tendency is to pay back in the same coin. Since the Maldives has the highest divorce rate in the world, there is little need to speak about the wantonness of our women, or our men, for that matter." The author continues in an intimate vein, discussing the time the president's wife left him for a cabinet member and speculating about whether the president got revenge by sleeping with that cabinet member's wife. And the author concludes by stating that "the Maldives is not becoming another Afghanistan. For most Maldivians, sex is like a second language."[8]

The government-sanctioned media are a bit more circumspect but also often identify ubiquitous divorce as a national metanym. The *Evening Weekly*, for example, ran an article in 2004 on the effects of the new family law reform titled "Despite New Legislative Measure, Divorce Rate Increases," which stated that "a high divorce rate is not something new to Maldivian society and . . . divorce is not understood as something with a lot of negativity attached to it." Sounding much like Battuta, this modern author bemoaned the fact that "liking each other seems the sole factor [in marriage] . . . [A]s long as the attraction lasts, so does the marriage."[9]

The few ethnographic sources that exist concur. In the scholarly literature, the only recent major anthropological work on the Maldives, *People of the Maldive Islands,* by Clarence Maloney (1980) cites the statistic that 85 out of every 100 marriages in 1974 ended in divorce, giving the country the highest divorce rate in the world. Arguing that Maldivian kinship bears a striking resemblance to that of the Lakshadivip in Kerala, India, who have even higher contemporary divorce rates, Maloney identifies a set of traits that he believes contribute to making marital ties weak. Among them are semimatriarchal political systems, involving female sultanas, matrilineal kinship, and postmarital residence rules that favor women; the seasonal and traditionally temporary residence of male partners in multiple female homes; and a near-total lack of concern about virginity on marriage. In fact, it seems that modernity, globalization, and economic affluence have probably reduced the divorce rate in the Maldives.[10]

Despite these unusual cultural traits, the pre-2001 Maldivian divorce code was relatively unremarkable for the Islamic world. Divorce was a male prerogative, and marriages were typically dissolved through the Islamic *talaq*, in which husbands had the right to the famous unilateral verbal divorce decree. A husband simply announced "I divorce you" (*talaq*) in front of two witnesses and paid an *iddah*, a relatively standard Islamic version of alimony, for a period equivalent to three menstrual cycles if the woman was not pregnant, or until she gave birth if she was. There were no legal protections for a woman who did not want a divorce and feared the financial, emotional, and social strains of abandonment by her husband.

Since the family law reform, divorce in the Maldives has become something that men and women have equal right to initiate, and, in order to reduce the capricious use of this power to break up families, it must involve a judgment in family court, along with the payment of court fees by one or both parties. While the fees (about $400) are not extravagant, they are relatively high for a country with a middle-income per capita gross domestic product, making divorce something that must be considered more seriously than it was in the past. This has been combined with the requirement that all new couples attend a prenuptial class, designed to reduce divorce.

In 2002 the whole country waited expectantly for the government's statistics on divorce. To everybody's amazement, the divorce numbers dropped substantially, to under 1,000 in the capital city (Republic of Maldives 2005). However, in 2003 the numbers jumped up from those of the previous year and thereafter crept up until they were at roughly the same level as they had been before the reforms. This confirmed the sense of many Maldivians that there was something inescapable about their version of folk Islam. They had made a good-faith effort, using the best international partners, to be more Islamic and more Western and had failed at both.

The Ministry of Family and Gender and its international partner agencies struggled with the issue of divorce in all its facets: the ease of getting it, the means of initiating it, the expectations in marriage—individuals' commitment to more than pleasure—and postdivorce outcomes. However, what was never discussed in ministry documents, statements by nongovernmental organizations working within the CEDAW framework, or by either the Muslim or Western development assistance community is the possibility that Maldivian marriage and divorce laws, which do not appear substantially different from those of the rest of the Islamic world, are not actually that opposed to the spirit of CEDAW. Instead, it may be—as ibn Battuta observed—that marital bonds that are based on pleasure (read desire, love, companionship, and so forth) are inherently loose. Thus modern Maldivian marriage may remain more companionate and less tied to property management and exchange than marriage in even the most advanced industrial societies. In such a situation, the *talaq*, with all its patriarchal language and assumptions, may be better equipped to meet the daily needs of women than the Western version of marriage and divorce law that stresses equality before the law.

The Maldives did not have an agrarian property regime (Bell 1882; Maloney 1980; Romero-Frias 1999) of the type common to the "patriarchy belt"—typically described as stretching from China to Spain, where a father might legitimately will three limbs of an olive tree to three different sons, thus tying three families related by marriage together. In the Maldives, where women have traditionally had the right to own various forms of real property, an endless frontier of small islands made land property of little value, and patrimony was barely important, even to the royal family—which at the time of ibn Battuta was led by a sultana and therefore had clear lines of inheritance regardless of sexual propriety. In the following pages, I will examine some of the contours of a contemporary marriage regime that combines pre-agrarian social relations, capitalism, and the norms and thought patterns of the Western-Eastern dialectic with which I began this chapter.

Maldivian Marriage Lite

In meetings of staff members working on international projects, the need to strengthen families was generally regarded as part of the development outcomes. At such gatherings, Maldivian staffers typically seemed to take the issue quite seriously. However, in rap sessions late at night, an innocent expatriate comment about the possibility that the high divorce rate led to child abuse—a remark that would have fit smoothly into an earlier meeting—often got dismissive responses. The most common one was the humorous comment that "yes, it is true that the majority of the bad fathers in the Maldives are stepparents, but then a majority of the good fathers are also stepparents." Somebody might typically chime in with another silly statistic, like "the majority of grocery store owners and fishermen are also stepparents."

For expatriates like me working in the development sector, the contradictions inherent in this version of cultural intimacy were often difficult to reconcile. However, as Kirk Dombrowski (2001) points out, few people are not ambivalent about their culture. It seemed that Maldivians were sincere in their workday desire to reduce and soften the worst financial and emotional outcomes of divorce—an often painful and disruptive personal experience— but that they also clearly realized that a penchant for divorce is an important part of who they are and how they build their life courses. Thus, the commitment to antidivorce policies and activities in both Western and Islamic-oriented international agencies seemed to create a type of irony that most often emerged in informal settings, where the dictates of employers and international politics faded.

Late one night, over Coca-Colas, I was standing in a street on a medium-size regional island with a group of expatriate and national development workers who were on a trip to investigate water and sanitation issues. Water and sanitation is famously the most masculine area of international development, and there were no women around, which led after work conversations toward the ribald. An expatriate international development consultant from India made a comment about the need to reduce rampant divorce in the Maldives, which was answered by a stream of ribald observations by a Maldivian engineer with a Western education and a high-level position in a nongovernmental organization. Then in his thirties, this man has several stepparents and half and step siblings on both sides; he has been married twice himself. "Do you know how tough it is to get a single Western woman to fuck when she doesn't want to and to stop her when she wants it?" he asked. "Well, Maldivian women are worse. They are just as bad even when they're married: my mother, my sister, my daughter, someday. They just do it when they want with whomever they want—well, except for with you foreigners [pointing particularly to the Westerners in the group]—they don't want to be called prostitutes or perverts. If they want a divorce, they just cut you off and find somebody else. Their mothers let them move back home and what can you do? Give them a divorce and then you have to pay them too. Sometimes I can hardly believe we're really Muslims."

Similar discussions, with less sexual invective, were overheard among expatriate and Maldivian women in the communications office of UNICEF, where I was the only male staffer. In response to a mild comment about the problems of divorce by an expatriate development worker, a discussion ensued in which two Maldivian women in their late twenties asserted that when their husbands did not contribute income to the household, did not show enough interest in their children, became sexually selfish, tried to stop the women from seeing their friends, committed adultery, or became physically abusive, the women simply left them and moved back in with their natal families.

On one occasion, a young Maldivian woman working in communications — who, then in her early twenties, had recently married for the first time and had started wearing a hijab while studying overseas in Malaysia (she was the only one in the group who covered her head — expressed disdain for these sentiments. The senior woman of the group, who was in her early thirties, had been married three times, and lived with her divorced mother, stated forcefully: "You'll see how men are. It's usually better to take your children and find another one [man]. That is what they will do to you eventually if you don't do it first." In response to the young woman's contention that *talaq* is a sacred male responsibility, a passing woman staffer observed that getting a man to say *talaq* is as easy as closing your legs — possibly the most common joke I heard from Maldivians of both sexes. Afterward the older woman confided that she feared this new generation was becoming "gulf-oriented."[11]

As several of my Maldivian colleagues pointed out separately, Maldivians are rationalists when it comes to a wedding and unconcerned with the kind of expensive, time-consuming, and wasteful ceremonies that they identify as Western. Weddings are arranged by the couple getting married, and the traditional ceremony is very simple. The bride and groom get a certificate, find a public space, and have a quick buffet dinner with their guests. Many Maldivian women I met could barely remember where they had held weddings, who had attended, or what they had done that might have been special.

Maldivians do not ignore the simplicity of their wedding ceremonies, or how different they are from the global standard set by Hollywood, Bollywood, and international fashion magazines. Many Maldivian women are quite conscious of the connection between the lack of expensive weddings, large dowries and bride prices, and complex interfamilial negotiations and their relative freedom to make and break marriages.[12] This approach dovetails with the historical feminist preference for civil marriages at city hall.

A foreign Muslim male expressed to me and a female Maldivian colleague of mine his anxieties about his upcoming arranged marriage — which was to be held at great expense to his family in a hotel in Dubai, with hundreds of family members and friends coming from around the world and the gift giving expected to provide money for a down payment on a home in Canada. Afterward my colleague, who had already been married to two men before the age of twenty-four, commented: "I'm glad we don't have that kind of pressure. He'll have to spend his whole life with her no matter how bad it is. I planned my first marriage in one afternoon."[13]

In line with this woman's observation, it has been suggested in much of the historical and anthropological literature on dowry and bride price that no matter which family pays for the wedding, which family delivers money or resources to the other, or which family takes the financial responsibility for the couple's residence after the wedding, women typically remain the most vulnerable partners in a patriarchal society when significant resources are invested in the uniting of the two families (Talwar-Oldenburg 2002). The simplicity of Maldivian weddings is changing somewhat, as globalization brings in more money, more property, and more possibilities for the big rituals that Maldivians see on satellite television. In particular, the honeymoon has become a Maldivian rite of passage, and couples save their money to go to exotic places like the United Arab Emirates, Thailand, Europe, and Sri Lanka—although most often end up settling for places nearer to home.

Like nearly every place on the planet, the Maldives has worse financial outcomes, on average, for women than for men after divorce (UNICEF 2004). Although men are required to help support women for a time after divorce, as happens elsewhere in the world, they often do not. For this reason, many of the liberal policy concerns that drove the 2001 family law were directed toward protecting women from the reduced income that is typical after divorce, particularly for the most visibly poor women in the crowded slums of the capital city—where the modern salaries of the capitalist tourist boom are often very high for men and quite a bit lower for women. For some of these women, the *talaq* may seem, as it does to financially dependent women across the *ummah*, like a death threat. However, for most Maldivian women it does not, and for many Maldivians, as suggested earlier by my informant late one night over Coca-Colas, it smooths a return to the natal home, through the claim that it was the husband's fault—"he threw me out." While this is certainly not the feminist ideal in which equal citizens make decisions about their lives, it can provide Maldivian women with space for remarkable agency in marital and sexual choices.

The fact that these women often have not only natal homes to return to, but also the homes of stepparents, half-siblings and other kin produced by their parents' multiple marriages and divorces, often provides a form of social capital (Putnam 1995) or postmarital "weak ties" (Granovetter 1973) that gives greater agency to women in forcing divorces, regardless of juridical rights or "gulf-oriented" parents. An Indian schoolteacher's wife whom I interviewed in a small city outside the capital observed that most of the girls did not care what their legal status was, and that others living at home had plenty of opportunity to save their money to get a divorce eventually, after they met their next husband. As she put it, "the reason that the reform didn't stop these girls from getting divorced is that divorce is now part of marriage. If you are a gentleman, you pay the 2,000 Rufiyaa [$400] so your beloved [next wife] can get her divorce."

Several of my female informants who were in their late twenties and early thirties had quickly ended early marriages after high school against the will of their husbands, who the women claimed took the relationships more seriously than they had. If these women's self-interested accounts are to be believed, they had made the marriages to have more freedom to have sex, stay out late, and party with their friends, without having to hide their activities from or answer to parents or older siblings. When they were actually married, they found that their freedom was reduced by their young husbands, who often had dreams of patrimonial Islamic families with children and of wives with ladylike decorum. As the young men's and young women's aspirations came into conflict, the contradictions became heightened, with the men becoming more controlling and the women becoming increasingly less respectful of their young husbands' demands. The final blow to these marriages was often the discovery of infidelity, by either party, at which point the aggrieved spouse would claim betrayal and initiate the breakup. As one woman once said to me about the new family law and its focus on judges, courts, and fees, "you just tell your husband you've had enough, move back home, and what judge is going to try to get a Maldivian woman to move back in with some guy that she hasn't been with in months. This is not the gulf—not yet, at least."

For most of the women I knew, divorce initiated a period of casual dating and sex, followed by a series of more serious relationships, one of which seemed inevitably to end in a marriage—often at the urging of the mother, whose job was usually to cover for the daughter's sexual escapades, while often pretending not to know about them. Second marriages were usually described as more successful, more equal, and less driven by conflicting fantasies on the part of the principals. The sense that most of these women gave was that each marriage involved more maturity and more ability for the life ambitions of the two partners to correspond. Although many Maldivians do have children in the first marriage, the educated urban sophisticates that I was working with often put off childbearing until their late twenties, which often meant during a second or third marriage. For those who had gone to college overseas, the entire pattern was somewhat different, with the first marriage occurring later, the level of communication between the spouses being greater, and a sense of seriousness and permanence about marriage being driven by the influence of the Western or Islamic milieu in which they had studied and lived.

While Maldivian men often seem to be proud of their relative lack of honor—as demonstrated by their easy ability to discuss the lack of chasteness and sexual modesty on the part of "their" women—the de facto power that women have to initiate divorce can also be a source of shame for them in front of men from other Muslim countries. The absence of strong traditions of exchange of real property in marriage, combined with the freedom that most Maldivian women have to return to their natal homes made any sanctions that might be imposed by the husband or his family inherently weak. For Maldivian men, this stood in contrast to the situation in the rest of the Muslim world, where they understood men to have nearly untrammeled power to subordinate their wives. As is often the case with Maldivian views of what is and is not proper Islam, Maldivian men typically invoked an image of patriarchy in the Arab Gulf as both their nightmare of what the Maldives might someday become and their vision of how a well-ordered Islamic society should function.

Conclusion: The Dialectic of Patriarchy

We are now roughly a decade past the Maldives family law reform, and few people in the Maldives seem to be happy with it. The Islamicists continue their relentless propagandizing against the manifest chaos of secular life,[14] and many people listen to their vision of an alternate modernity with interest, while also typically expressing concern about their attempts to transform what they see as a liberal Indian Ocean republic built on Buddhist foundations and folk Islam. Those who are connected to the global economy—which means India and Dubai as much as Australia and the United States—continue to press for greater openness in the economy and lament the capricious, arbitrary, and sloppy nature of Maldivian marriage.

A recent oral statement to the CEDAW committee that was prepared by Hama Jamiyya—a coalition of nine Maldivian nongovernmental organizations and five Maldivian community-based organizations that work on issues of women's rights in the Maldives—complained that very little substantive work has been done in regard to protecting women's rights since the Maldives signed CEDAW in 1993 (Hama Jamiyya 2007). The statement began by complaining that most Maldivians (including women) do not believe that women are discriminated against, and they base this belief on the fact that there is more gender equality in the Maldives than in other countries (they may be referring to the Middle East and South Asia). This is despite the facts that domestic violence in the Maldives is still common and typically treated as a private matter, rather than a criminal one, and that men still occupy all the top positions in the government and judiciary.

The statement goes on to assess the decade since the family law reform and draws the conclusion that the reform has accomplished little since polygamy continues, albeit as a rarity among the wealthy; girls under eighteen still regularly request, and are granted, the right to get married, although this is now against the law; not a single couple has taken advantage of the right to prenuptial agreements limiting a husband's power; there is still no provision for joint property; the Gender Equality Council has met only once in six years; and divorce remains ubiquitous and entirely initiated by men (Hama Jamiyya 2007). So why has family law reform been such a failure, according to many of the people who helped institute it? They claim the answer is inaction by a state with little commitment to the spirit of CEDAW. This begs the questions why the state cares about the body but not the spirit of CEDAW, and why a complex and modern family law reform was enacted in a country where the vast majority of men and women believed that equality already existed. More research is required to answer these questions. However, a few possible avenues for inquiry are presented in the final pages of this chapter.

As with other nations across the developing world, the Republic of Maldives has been under heavy pressure from international agencies, institutional investors, and other members of the international community to make its legal, governance, and financial accounting practices more "transparent and accountable," to use the common terminology of international governance assistance programs. Marriage, one of the key means by which property is still combined, transferred, and turned into capital around the world, is a famously opaque institution. However, in the Maldives it is not only personal, opaque, and informal but still largely uncontrollable by the state.

A decade-long economic boom has made the capital, Malé, the most densely populated city on earth, created vast wealth disparities, and made previously rare forms of private property ubiquitous. A social layer of young Maldivians has been made rich from joint ventures with international tourist resorts, spreading their wealth and debt across vast multiple marriage and kin networks. This may have driven a need by those who have access to these opportunities and the Western and Arab banks that are investing in this development to define, regularize, and guarantee the continuity, debt obligation, inheritance patterns, and political responsibilities of this greatly expanded and only recently titled property and the resources that they put into creating it. From this perspective, family law reform is an important part of governance.[15]

The salaried new middle classes in the capital, like my former students and their families, are equally dependent on these expanded forms of property. The huge economic growth has driven a real estate boom in Malé that has such families aspiring to build their own apartment buildings, which has led to a dense skyline filled with six- to twelve-story, partially completed concrete shells. These Maldivian skyscrapers and the land they sit on have been financed through some of the highest levels of family debt in the world[16] — typically to foreign banks. These apartment buildings, which are typically inhabited on the lower floors, are built with elevator shafts but rarely have an elevator; contain concrete stairwells that flood during rainstorms because there is often no roof; and multiple floors, typically near the top, with neither exterior nor interior walls.

Even the outlying islands with little or no tourist development are increasingly being brought into the property boom by international exporters who have begun fishing according to an industrial model, which requires greater capital inputs—also provided by Western and Islamic banking interests. And the national government is following, bringing its authority to the distant atolls. Inhabitable islands that have not had their water fouled by rising sea levels are being developed by international hotel chains as honeymoon resorts or staked off and claimed by government ministers, through the use of a variety of family connections.

This is a complex world where issues of family, children, marriage, residence, and property are increasingly taking on the life or death significance that they typically have in most of the world and are being decided by complex property arrangements that require title records, birth certificates, clear lines of kinship demarcation, and legal precedents for resolving conflict in the courts. In such a situation of rapid development and change, relying on family dynamics, personal relations, and customary patterns of folk Islam that were already attenuated when the boom began to adjudicate complicated and high-stakes issues of property, social relations, and politics is not sufficient for the needs of the international financial community, Maldivian entrepreneurs seeking credit and investment, or international agencies like UNICEF that depend on standardized and comparable statistics for measuring social development outcomes for women and children.

Such connections between expanding private property, globalization, the interventions of the international community, and the drive to enact Islamic family law reform suggest some of the durable interests of state actors and the private sector. However, the people who actually participated in writing these new laws were largely well-intentioned participants in a developing civil society sector that genuinely seeks gender equity through progressive compromise between Islamic traditionalism and Western democracy. As Hama Jamiyya (2007) points out, much of what they have created floats high above everyday Maldivian family life with little direct impact on it. Meanwhile, we may guess that the new forms of property are being rapidly accumulated by male members of families, largely to the exclusion of their female kin.

This question of property may well be the crucial question that underlies every other social issue in the Maldives, but who owns what is not likely to be decided or changed based on family law reform. As titled property becomes increasingly important in everyday life, it seems likely that Maldivian women will occupy ever narrower spaces within which they must negotiate the intersection of family, law, marriage, and the dissolution of marriage. In an environment of such rapid change and modernization, it is difficult to imagine how they will avoid the disadvantaging dialectic between Islamic ideologies of male dominance in marriage and Western ideologies of individual equality by law, shackled to de facto subordination by gendered socioeconomics.

Regardless of how this dialectic plays out, the institution of family law reforms that, a priori and top-down, assume that the relative freedom of the Islamic *talaq* is purely a male sexual prerogative and of little value to the cause of women's equality inscribes a bias toward the Western semipermanent protective legal corporation of two individuals—husband and wife. In both urban and rural sites in Morocco, Tunisia, Jordan, Turkey, Egypt, and other regions where land and labor have a long history of well-defined ownership, states have ancient histories of absolute power; local governance has been enforced through agrarian codes of honor, shame, and retribution; and the corporate entities created by marriage have always involved well-defined property drawn from two kin networks with a "till death do you part" ethos, the patriarchal bargain of trading freedom for protection is written in the landscape. From the perspective of women's liberation, the contemporary compromises of family law reform are generally a form of "trading up" (Moghadam 2008). With regard to divorce, this typically means protecting women from the capricious power of their husbands to use the *talaq* and various restrictions on mobility, full citizenship, and property ownership.

However, in these discussions of compromise between Islam and the West, the implied goal is nearly always to produce a more just form of patriarchy. It is not even clear that this vision of balancing one form of patriarchy against another is always a positive approach in the more mainstream Islamic countries, where the study of outlying regions far from national capitals sometimes reveals surprisingly liberal and egalitarian customary behavior hidden behind the Islamic ideologies of male dominance—as has been argued is the case with some of the social relations of the Alevi in Anatolia (Erdimir 2005) and other outlying folk minorities.

In this regard, the above-mentioned statement (Hama Jamiyya 2007) is revealing, not so much for what it criticizes about the implementation of family law, but for what it does not criticize. It does not challenge the notion that preserving a marital family—even one governed by the patriarchy "lite" of Western civil society—is positive. It demands that divorce rates be lowered, restrictions on immediate divorce be enforced, and marriage as a whole be strengthened. It assumes that marriage is to the benefit of women because of the protections it affords them and that divorce is to the benefit of men because of the sexual license it gives them. And it assumes that property must be individual and partible—therefore, divisible. These are all assumptions that were long ago hardwired into the dialectic of patriarchy that informs the reform process and the CEDAW approach that has influenced Islamic family law reform.

The statement never questions whether a girl under eighteen who gets married is an example of a female being traded by her family to a despotic polygamist or of a young adult escaping her parents' home and claiming her own life and sexuality; and it certainly does not question the value and functionality of modern notions of adolescence. Instead, the women of Hama Jamiyya demand that the restriction on under-age marriages be enforced, thus affirming a Western secular vision of an attenuated patriarchy in which families have a form of ownership over female sexuality with an eighteen-year use-by date that is governed by the sanctification of childhood and contemporary views on the proper course of education. The underlying implication is that a young woman must trade her freedom to her natal family for education and protection from would-be husbands until she is eighteen, and that thereafter she must trade her freedom for the protection of a husband—albeit under hopefully more equal terms than is now the case.

The ability to strip away a woman's crucial socioeconomic protections and rights to marital property are the predominant threat lying under the *talaq* in most times and places in the *ummah*. Such a threat is indeed, for many women around the world, akin to a threat of death—either social or physical. However, the assumption that the women inherently need the protection of men in marriage is the basis of the Western contract that Islamic family law reform seeks to substitute for the *talaq*.

Underlying this substitution is the notion that the sick body of Islamic family law may be healed through the introduction of homeopathic doses of the poison of the patriarchal Western legal contract of marriage. Despite ten years of experimenting, this remains as unrealistic as the opposite idea that the problems of the Western family can be solved through the introduction of the Islamic *talaq*. In contrast to the goal of reforming and restricting the *talaq*, the ideal that sexually and procreatively based kinship should be a free association of individuals, terminable immediately on the desire of the self-governing parties involved—one of the key ideas promoted by the nineteenth-century feminist movement—remains far more compelling to most Maldivians (both male and female), at least at the folk level, after hours, and far away from the pressures of trying to participate in the Western international community or the Islamic *ummah*.

Notes

In writing this chapter, I am intellectually indebted to Antonia Antonopolis, whom I met at the United Nations duty station in Malé. It was her combative Socratic approach to friendship that forced me to focus my thoughts about this topic. Nadeem Malik, one of my former PhD students, contributed greatly to my thinking about the topic and continues to inspire me to take the long view of social inquiry. Professor Ann Sanson of the University of Melbourne, helped me understand the discussions around divorce outcomes. Jo Sanson, my partner, provided plenty of her own Socratic challenges, along with the opportunity to go to the Maldives and the companionship to enjoy the experience. Finally, the University of Melbourne gave me study leave for the research, and the Department of Anthropology and Deviance Studies at John Jay College of the City University of New York has given me an extremely fertile environment for intellectual and scholarly work.

1 With the exception of Fulu (2007), which assessed the gendered implications of the international response to the 2005 Indian Ocean tsunami, the scholarly literature on the Maldives has been largely restricted to climate science, population health, and tourism management.

2 Currently, the Republic of Maldives has the highest divorce rate in the world, typically estimated above 10 per 1,000 by a variety of sources.

3 Given the topic of this chapter, it seems worth noting that this approach is often attributed to the fourteenth-century Islamic sociologist Ibn Khaldun.

4 The United Nations technically does business in six languages, making English the de facto language of the Maldivian duty station, with an occasional nod to French.

5 Given the changes in record keeping regarding divorce and the frequency with which many Maldivians divorce without reporting it, take up with new partners, and eventually return to an earlier partner, it is not clear whether this estimate reflects more or less than four different husbands, on average.

6 The following story is an amalgam of numerous versions I have heard in informal conversations and interviews, all of which stressed some particular aspect of the story to describe Maldivians as Muslims who were "liberal," "sloppy," and so forth. A review of Ibn Battuta (2003) suggests that this national metonymic story is quite close to the original text.

7 While I never witnessed any women with uncovered breasts, both long-standing expatriate residents and Maldivians who remember the 1980s assured me that such a sight was not unusual as recently as the late 1980s.

8 Ali Rasheed, "Islam, Maldives & the Reform Movement," *Minivan News*, 7 October, 2006.

9 Noora Ali, "Despite New Legislative Measure, Divorce Rate Increases," *Evening Weekly*, 8 February 2004.

10 The first official United Nations statistics for the Maldives, from 1975, show a far higher divorce rate than at any time since.

11 A recent communication revealed that this idealistic young woman had gotten divorced, been involved with another man, and finally remarried her husband and had a child—all between 2007 and 2009.

12 Sex outside of marriage is strictly forbidden by Islamic law, but teenage sex seems to be rampant, as demonstrated by a night-time walk around the island where Malé is located and the popular observation that the courtship period is three trips around the capital on a motorcycle. This yields a "don't ask, don't tell" policy that has parents grateful when daughters who have been sexually active marry.

13 Since writing this chapter, I have learned that this woman has had a second divorce and married a third husband, with whom she now lives in Malé.

14 Taimour Lay, "Is Islam a Threat to the Maldives?," *Minivan News*, 8 October 2006.

15 The difficulties of negotiating such investment and property management were first suggested to me by a low-level government minister I interviewed.

16 This is according to a World Bank economist I interviewed.

References

Amado, L. 2006. "Gender, Sexuality and Law Reform in Muslim Societies." *Development* 49 (1): 96–98.

Asian Development Bank. 2001. *Women in the Maldives: A Country Briefing Paper*. Manila: Asian Development Bank. www.adb.org.

——. 2007. *Maldives: Gender and Development Assessment*. Manila: Asian Development Bank. www.adb.org.

Bachofen, J. J. 1992. *Myth, Religion, and Mother Right*. Translated by R. Mannheim. Princeton: Princeton University Press.

Bell, H. C. P. 1882. *The Maldive Islands, An Account of the Physical Features, History, Inhabitants, Productions and Trade*. Colombo: Ceylon Government Printer.

Childe, V. G. 1951. *Social Evolution*. New York: Henry Schuman.

Collier, J. 1988. *Marriage and Inequality in Classless Societies.* Stanford, CA: Stanford University Press.

Coontz, S. 1986. "Property Forms, Political Power and Female Labour in the Origins of Class and State Societies." In *Women's Work, Men's Property: On the Origins of Gender and Class,* edited by S. Coontz and P. Henderson, 108-55. London: Verso.

———. 1988. *The Social Origins of Private Life: A History of American Families.* New York: Verso.

———and P. Henderson. 1986. *Women's Work, Men's Property: On the Origins of Gender and Class.* London: Verso.D'Emilio, J. 1983. "Capitalism and Gay Identity." In *Powers of Desire: The Politics of Sexuality,* edited by A. Snitow, C. Stansell, and S. Thompson, 100-113. New York: Monthly Review.

Dombrowski, K. 2001. *Against Culture: Development, Politics and Religion in Indian Alaska.* Lincoln: University of Nebraska Press.

Draper, P. 1975. "!Kung Women: Contrasts in Sexual Egalitarianism in Foraging and Sedentary Contexts." In *Toward an Anthropology of Women,* edited by R. Reiter, 77-109. New York: Monthly Review.

Engels, F. 1972. *The Origin of the Family, Private Property, and the State, in the Light of the Researches of Lewis H. Morgan.* New York: International Publishers.

Erdimir, A. 2005. "Tradition and Modernity: Alevis' Ambiguous Terms and Turkey's Ambivalent Subjects." *Middle Eastern Studies* 41 (6): 937-51.

Fulu, E. 2007. "Gender, Vulnerability, and the Experts: Responding to the Maldives Tsunami." *Development and Change* 38 (5): 843-64.

Granovetter, M. 1973. "The Strength of Weak Ties." *American Journal of Sociology* 78 (6): 1360-80.

Hama Jamiyya. 2007. "Maldives NGO Statement to the CEDAW Committee." Malé. www.iwraw-ap.org/resources/pdf/Maldives percent20oral percent20statement.pdf.

Herzfeld, M. 2004; *Cultural Intimacy: Social Poetics in the Nation-State.* New York: Routledge.

Ibn Battuta. 2003. *The Travels of Ibn Battuta.* Abridged, introduced, and annotated by Tim Mackintosh-Smith. London: Picador.

Kotlikoff, J. and S. Burns. 2005. *The Coming Generational Storm: What You Need to Know about America's Economic Future.* Cambridge: MIT Press.

Leacock, E. 1972. Introduction to F.Engels, *The Origins of the Family, Private Property and the State, in the Light of the Researches of Lewis H. Morgan.* New York: International Publishers.

Lévi-Strauss, C. 1969. *The Elementary Structures of Kinship*. Edited by R. Needham. Translated by J. H. Bell, J. R. von Sturmer, and R. Needham. Boston: Beacon.

Maloney, C. 1980. *People of the Maldive Islands*. Hyderabad, India: Orient Longman.

McLennan, J. F. 2001. *The Patriarchal Theory: Based on the Papers of the Late John Ferguson McLennan*. Edited and completed by Donal McLennan. Kitchener, ON: Batoche.

Mies, M. 1999. *Patriarchy and Accumulation on a World Scale: Women in the International Division of Labour*. London: Zed.

Mir-Hosseini, Z. 2000. *Marriage on Trial: Islamic Family Law in Iran and Morocco*. 2nd ed. London: Tauris.

———. 2007. "How the Door of Ijtihad Was Opened and Closed: A Comparative Analysis of Recent Family Law Reforms in Iran and Morocco." *Washington and Lee Law Review* 64:1499-511.

Moghadam, V. 2008. "Feminism, Legal Reform and Women's Empowerment in the Middle East and North Africa." *International Social Science Journal* 59 (91): 9-16.

Needham, R., ed. 1971. *Rethinking Kinship and Marriage*. London: Tavistock.

Putnam, R. 1995. "Bowling Alone: America's Declining Social Capital." *Journal of Democracy* 6 (1): 65-78.

Reed, E. 1975. *Women's Evolution: From Matriarchal Clan to Patriarchal Family*. New York: Pathfinder.

Republic of Maldives. 2005. *Twenty-Five Years of Statistics*. Malé: Ministry of Planning and National Development.

———. 2008. *Statistical Yearbook*. Malé: Ministry of Planning and National Development.

Romero-Frias, X. 1999. *The Maldive Islanders: A Study of the Popular Culture of an Ancient Ocean Kingdom*. Barcelona. Nova Ethnographia Indica.

Sacks, K. 1975. "Engels Revisited: Women, the Organization of Production, and Private Property." In *Toward an Anthropology of Women*, edited by R. Reiter, 211-34. New York: Monthly Review.

Saeed, A. 2006. *Interpreting the Qu'ran: Towards a Contemporary Approach*. New York: Routledge.

Sangari, K., and S. Vaid eds.1990. *Recasting Women: Essays in Indian Colonial History*. New Brunswick, NJ: Rutgers University Press.

Shostak, M. 2000. *Nisa: The Life and Words of a !Kung Woman*. Cambridge: Harvard University Press.

Smith, G. 1985. "Reflections on the Social Relations of Simple Commodity Production." *Journal of Peasant Studies* 13 (1): 99-108.

Talwar-Oldenburg, V. 2002. *Dowry Murder: The Imperial Origins of a Cultural Crime*. Oxford: Oxford University Press.

UNICEF. 2004. *Maldives Poverty Report*. New York: United Nations.

United Nations, Committee on the Rights of the Child. 1998. "Summary Record of the 467th meeting : Maldives." New York: United Nations, 19 October.

United Nations, Population Division. 2009. *Demographic Yearbook*. New York: United Nations.

Warren, M. 2006. "Country Profile: Maldives." *New Internationalist*, June 2006, 38

White, L. 1959. *The Evolution of Culture*. New York: McGraw-Hill.

World Health Organization. 2006. "Country Office for Maldives: General Information." Geneva: World Health Organization. www.who.org.mv/EN/Section15.htm.

WILLIAM G. CLARENCE-SMITH

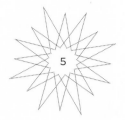

5

Female Circumcision
in Southeast Asia since
the Coming of Islam

The current program to eradicate female circumcision in Islamic Southeast Asia is weakened by ignorance of its history. It is argued here that female circumcision is not a pre-Islamic custom but was brought to the region with Islam. The scriptural bases for the practice are weak, but so-called orthodox Muslims of the Shafi school of law, which predominates in Southeast Asia, consider female circumcision to be obligatory. Nevertheless, Southeast Asian Muslims have generally followed the Prophet's alleged command to cut sparingly. Syncretist Muslims, who are numerous on Java, have been more hesitant to adopt the procedure. All significant Islamic movements have been unable to agree on the issue since the 1910s. Recently, some Muslims have called not only for all women to be circumcised, but also for deeper cutting, and at an earlier age.

Female circumcision is frequently portrayed as a custom predating the advent of world religions, but the practice almost certainly arrived in and spread throughout Southeast Asia with Islam, beginning in the thirteenth century.

Female circumcision has been more or less as widespread there as in other Muslim societies that adhere to the Shafii school of Sunni Islam. However, the procedure in Southeast Asia has traditionally consisted of a mere nick, producing a single drop of blood, and has sometimes been reduced to a symbolic gesture that draws no blood at all. The impact on women's bodies has been far less severe than in the Nile Valley or the Horn of Africa, where midwives remove the whole clitoris and a large part of the labia and infibulate (sew up) a woman's orifices (Boddy 2008). Thus, the expression "female circumcision" is more appropriate for Southeast Asia than "female genital cutting," let alone "female genital mutilation."

However, current trends, including the rise of fundamentalist or literalist Islam, are influencing the practice in Southeast Asia, leading to more radical surgery, at a younger age, and in a more public and collective manner. The conclusion to this chapter argues that reformists probably need to step back from the World Health Organization's zero-tolerance approach, which results in head-on confrontations with devout believers, and should rather work along the grain of reformist Islam. While this chapter considers Muslim communities in Malaysia, southern Thailand, and the southern Philippines, the principal focus is on Indonesia because it contains the great majority of Southeast Asian Muslims, some 200 million in all. Indeed, this sprawling island country boasts the largest number of Muslims of any nation in the modern world.

The island of Java is of special importance to the story, partly because about two-thirds of all Southeast Asian Muslims live on this fertile volcanic island, and partly because many of them practice syncretic forms of Islam. Preexisting animism (paganism), Hinduism, and Buddhism have heavily influenced syncretic Islam, known to foreign scholars as Javanism and to locals by a variety of names, including *kejawen*. Syncretism, which may have more practitioners than orthodox Islam across Southeast Asia, is strongest in east and central Java, where the Javanese language is predominant. Beginning in the 1750s, this region was divided between the two most powerful precolonial Islamic states of Southeast Asia, based in Yogyakarta and Surakarta. These two states were retained by the Dutch to the end of the colonial era and have often been represented as bulwarks of syncretism, although they were also centers of reformist Islam. Syncretist Muslims also existed elsewhere, notably in Lombok and South Sulawesi in Indonesia, and among the Cham of Vietnam and Cambodia.

Bastions of Islamic orthodoxy were scattered around Southeast Asia. The Sundanese-speaking western part of the island of Java and the Madurese-speaking island of Madura were the most significant. In the larger but less populated island of Sumatra, the torch of orthodoxy lay in the hands of the Minangkabau of the west and the Acehnese of the north, both speaking their own languages. The Malay-speaking northern part of the Malay Peninsula, including southern Thailand, was the chief center of orthodoxy outside Indonesia. All the languages mentioned here belong to the Austronesian family, and Malay forms the basis of the official language of Indonesia (Clarence-Smith 2010; Hefner 2010).

The global literature on female circumcision generally disregards or marginalizes Southeast Asia. The second edition of the *Encyclopaedia of Islam* merely acknowledges the existence of the practice among Malays (Bosworth et al. 1978, 913). Kecia Ali includes Southeast Asia but admits that she found little information on this far-flung periphery of the Islamic world (Ali 2006, 100). The *Encyclopedia of Women and Islamic Cultures* restricts itself to Africa and the Middle East (Kassamali 2006). Similarly, Jonathan Berkey's learned and informative survey of female circumcision in the early centuries of Islam includes comparative material on Africa and Central Asia but leaves out Southeast Asia (Berkey 1996).

My sources are secondary in nature and partial in their coverage, and my conclusions must therefore remain tentative. For historical data, I have relied heavily on a seminal article, largely based on fifty-six local reports collected by the Dutch colonial authorities from across Indonesia (Feillard and Marcoes 1998). For modern times, I have used sociological surveys, especially those conducted in Yogyakarta and Madura by Basilica Putranti, as well as anthropological inquiries. Newspaper articles, encyclopedia entries, and Internet sites have filled some gaps. I have elicited further information directly from authors, and I am grateful for the help I received from Andrée Feillard on Indonesia, Basilica Putranti and Subhani Kusuma Dewi on central Java, Lynda Newland and Chiara Formichi on west Java, Lyn Parker on west Sumatra, and Claudia Merli on south Thailand.

Islam and the Origins of
Female Circumcision in Southeast Asia

The Southeast Asian case undermines a widespread notion that female circumcision is a pre-Islamic custom that has merely been tolerated by the newer faith (Bosworth et al. 1978; Hodgson 1974, 1:324). In contrast to other regions, female circumcision seems to have been introduced into Southeast Asia as part of the inhabitants' conversion to Islam from the thirteenth century on (Ali 2006, 100; Feillard and Marcoes 1998, 340, 342–43). Indeed, for Tomás Ortiz, writing about the southern Philippines in the early eighteenth century, female circumcision was not only a Muslim innovation, but also one that had spread to some degree to non-Muslims (see Blair and Robertson 1903–07, 43:110).

Authors who suggest that forms of female circumcision existed before the arrival of Islam cite vague references, possibly relating to cutting males rather than females (Putranti 2008, 25; Putranti, Faturochman, Muhadjir, and Purwatiningsih 2003, 19; Laderman 1983, 206). There is no convincing evidence that any speakers of Austronesian languages practiced female circumcision prior to the advent of Islam. In south Sulawesi, a region that had only recently and partially converted to Islam in the 1680s, Muslim girls alone were circumcised (Gervaise 1701/1971, 139–40). B. J. O. Schrieke, a Dutch official who consulted reports from around Indonesia, affirmed that no animists anywhere in the archipelago ever circumcised girls (see Feillard and Marcoes 1998, 345–8). Only on the southeastern marches of the region, among non-Austronesian-speaking peoples in New Guinea and Australia, are there animist traditions of cutting girls' genitalia, and those are in ways that diverge considerably from the traditions prevalent in Southeast Asia (*New Encyclopaedia Britannica* 1993, 2:318, 3:390).

The spread of Hindu and Buddhist beliefs during the first millennium BCE, which were especially deeply rooted in Java, makes it even less likely that female circumcision preceded the advent of Islam (Hefner 1985; Koentjaraningrat 1988). Hindu beliefs would have entailed a prohibition of genital mutilation, as they do in modern India (Ghadially 1991, 20). Hindus and Buddhists in today's Southeast Asia reject the circumcision of either boys or girls, although they may go along with the practice in majority Muslim areas (Hanks 1968, 126, 128; Putranti, Faturochman, Muhadjir, and Purwatiningsih 2003, 44; Putranti 2008, 27). People in east Java's Tengger Mountains, who have clung to Hindu beliefs through the centuries, shunned male circumcision (Hefner 1985, 34, 143–45, 256).

Indeed, Christiaan Snouck Hurgronje, a great Dutch scholar of Islam, opined in the early 1890s that numerous Javanese women were not circumcised, because so many syncretists opposed the practice (Snouck Hurgronje 1923–24, 4:205). Some Javanists certainly turned their backs on female circumcision altogether, seeing the practice as a symbol of adherence to the orthodoxy that they so disliked (Koentjaraningrat 1988, 361). Indeed, opponents of female circumcision referred to it as an "Arab custom" (Lyn Parker, personal communication, 2 October 2006). This is significant, because Arab mores were among the greatest bêtes noires of nineteenth-century militant syncretists.

However, most syncretist Muslims did not completely reject female circumcision. Some declared it to be optional, as with so much else in the Islamic canon, and accepted the fact that it was honorable or recommended (Snouck Hurgronje 1923–24, 4:205). Many of Java's *priyayi* (nobles), strongly influenced by Hindu beliefs, none the less circumcised their daughters. Indeed, female circumcision has survived to this day at the court of Yogyakarta, as a ritual associated with a complex set of ceremonies (Putranti, Faturochman, Muhadjir, and Purwatiningsih 2003: 21, 37–39; Putranti 2008). The royal families of Java, treading a fine line between their roles as guardians of Islam and leaders of the Hindu warrior *varna* (caste), often sought cultural compromises (Carey 2007). In addition, Javanists preferred to employ non-Arabic descriptors for female circumcision, such as *kres* in central Java (Dewi 2007). More common is *tetesan*, from the archaic Javanese root *tetes*, meaning hatching or pricking, possibly to convey the notion that pricking a girl results in enhanced fertility (Putranti 2008, 25).

A mixed vocabulary prevails among the *santri* (the orthodox Muslims). A common Malay term is *sunat perempuan*, with *sunna* the Arabic for "tradition" or "recommended action," and *perempuan* a Malay term for girl. Similarly, *khitan perempuan* and *khitan wanita* are expressions in which a Malay word for girl or woman follows the generic Arabic word for the circumcision of either men or women (Feillard and Marcoes 1998, 339–41; Koentjaraningrat 1988, 361; Moore 1981, 182–85; Newland 2006, 399; Putranti, Faturochman, Muhadjir, and Purwatiningsih. 2003, 16–17). In contrast, *khafd* or *khifad*, the specific Arabic term for female circumcision, with the root meaning of "lowering," is rarely employed in Southeast Asia.

Justifications for Female Circumcision

The Shafii school of law, widespread in the Indian Ocean, is unique in Sunni Islam for declaring female circumcision to be obligatory. In the fivefold ethical terminology of Islam, this ranks above the term for honorable or recommended, which is applied to female circumcision by the other three surviving Sunni schools of law as well as by the Shi'a. The obligatory nature of female circumcision was clearly spelled out by the revered Syrian scholar Muhi al-Din Yahya al-Nawawi (1234–78), who claimed the authority of Imam Shafi'i himself (Berkey 1996, 25; Kassamali 2006, 131). In Egypt, the spiritual home of Shafii Islam, the necessity of female circumcision was stressed as late as 1958 (Masry 1962, 45).

Shafii belief in the compulsory nature of female circumcision may reflect pre-Islamic cultural norms in the Nile Valley, for the scriptural bases for the procedure in the holy texts of Islam are extremely weak. The Quran is silent on the matter, and all that can be said with certainty about other scriptures is that they do not prohibit the practice (Berkey 1996, 20; Awde 2000, 192, note 28). There are hadiths—sayings and deeds of the Prophet and his companions—that are cited to support female circumcision, but they are either of dubious authenticity or hard to interpret. Sound traditions are those that are included in all or most of the six canonical collections, and that are given the imprimatur of the compiler. One such tradition imposes ritual ablution when the two circumcised parts have touched in sexual congress, but this does not clearly imply an obligation to circumcise (Ali 2006, 105–6; Berkey 1996, 22). Another sound hadith commands circumcision in a general sense, but it also enjoins trimming one's moustache, suggesting that the hadith was not directed at women (Awde 2000, 199, note 8; Berkey 1996, 24–25).

The most commonly cited hadith over the centuries appears in only one of the six canonical collections, and Abu Da'ud, the compiler, brands it as unreliable in terms of its transmission. The Prophet is said to have told a female circumciser: "Do not cut severely, as that is better for a woman and more desirable for a husband." While seeming to give authority to the practice, it is also restricts the extent of cutting (Ali 2006, 105; Berkey 1996, 25, 28; Davis 2006, 359, note 1).

Other texts, occasionally cited, are of less substance. A hadith collected by Ibn Hanbal says that female circumcision is noble but not mandatory (Berkey 1996, 25; Ali 2006, 105). There is also a folk tale that Sarah, in a fit of jealousy, circumcised Hagar (Hajar), the servant concubine of Abraham (Ibrahim). Hagar was the mythical mother of all Arabs and, by extension, of all Muslims (Kassamali 2006, 131; Berkey 1996, 22).

In Southeast Asia, as elsewhere in the Islamic world, a logical link with male circumcision can be discerned. Thus, in south Sulawesi in the 1680s, a boy to whom a girl was promised in marriage would preferably be circumcised on the same day as she was, albeit in a different location (Gervaise 1701/1971, 139-40). In western Malaya in the 1830s, it was noted that pious inhabitants circumcised both their sons and daughters (Moor 1837/1968, 250; Newbold 1839/1971, 1:247). The same was true among the Yakan of Basilan Island, in the southern Philippines, in the 1960s (Wulff 1974, 252).

Indeed, the main reason for circumcising women that was advanced by both female and male Muslims in Southeast Asia was that it marked the entry of a woman into the Islamic faith (Budiharsana, Amaliah, Utomo, and Erwinia 2003, 24; Feillard and Marcoes 1998, 340-41, 360; Putranti, Faturochman, Muhadjir, and Purwatiningsih 2003, 10; Snouck Hurgronje 1923-24, 4:205; Dewi 2007). Circumcision enables women to enter mosques, marry, and bear legitimate children. A nebulous but powerful notion of cleansing, *kebersihan*, is frequently asserted, related to the idea that someone who is unclean cannot pray (Feillard and Marcoes 1998, 360-61; Merli 2008, 271; Moore 1981, 182; Newland 2006, 399-401; Putranti 2008, 26; Islamic Religious Council of Singapore 2007) In southern Thailand, it is said that uncircumcised girls become "stubborn" (Merli 2008, 272).

Syncretists advance arguments of a similar nature, but with typical twists. As well as indicating a general adherence to religion, circumcision marks the transition to adulthood at the time of menstruation, facilitates marriage and childbirth, protects from bad luck, and averts various kinds of pollution and harmful energy. Female circumcision is also at times portrayed as an ancient Javanese custom, especially in royal circles (Putranti, Faturochman, Muhadjir, and Purwatiningsih 2003: 18-19, 22, 26, 37; Dewi 2007).

Circumcision has also long been said to regulate women's lust, which is naturally excessive and which thus threatens the stability of families and the moral order of society. Male religious specialists typically hold such views, but many women share them (Feillard and Marcoes 1998, 348-50, 361; Newland 2006, 401; Putranti, Faturochman, Muhadjir, and Purwatiningsih 2003, 48; US State Department 2001; Isa, Shuib, and Othman 1999). In Negeri Sembilan, southwestern Malaya, circumcision allegedly prevents a girl's clitoris from continuing to grow and becoming too big (Peletz 1996, 208). In Yogyakarta in 2002, one woman expressed the belief that not having enough of her clitoris cut could lead her into homosexuality (Putranti 2008, 30). Enhancing a man's sexual pleasure, and thus strengthening family bonds, has also been regularly advanced as a reason for circumcising women (Isa et al. 1999; Moore 1981, 183; Putranti 2008, 30).

Anthony Reid further suggests that female circumcision was a pre-Islamic custom, intended to increase women's sexual enjoyment (Reid 1988, 148–49). However, he not only generalizes from a single modern case from the late 1970s, but he also incorrectly cites Ruth Moore's observations on Sulu, in the southern Philippines. In reality, Moore's Tausug informants told her that female circumcision enhanced sexual proficiency and insisted that it was a classically Islamic procedure (Moore 1981, 183).

Nevertheless, there are tentative signs of concern with women's sexual pleasure (Feillard and Marcoes 1998, 361; Newland 2006, 401). An article appearing in a West Sumatran newspaper, probably *Singgalang*, on 17 September 2004 alleged that women who had been circumcised were more easily stimulated and aroused when touched, and were thus more loved and honored by their husbands (Lyn Parker, personal communication, 2 October 2006).

The Incidence of Female Circumcision

The incidence of female circumcision has regularly been reported to be higher in orthodox Islamic areas, as in a Dutch colonial compilation of the 1920s (see Feillard and Marcoes 1998, 349). Sociological sampling techniques and anthropological participant observation reveal a general prevalence of female circumcision in Indonesia's Islamic strongholds, where women foresee the same fate for their daughters and granddaughters. This is the case notably in Madura, west Java, and west and north Sumatra, but also in southeast Sumatra, north-central Sulawesi, and south Sulawesi (Putranti, Faturochman, Muhadjir, and Purwatin-ingsih 2003; Budiharsana, Amaliah, Utomo, and Erwinia 2003, 12, 22; Newland 2006, 396–97; US State Department 2001; Lyn Parker, personal communication, 2 October 2006; Chiara Formichi, personal communication, 3 October 2008). One exception to this pattern is east Kalimantan (Borneo), where the procedure is less common (Budiharsana, Amaliah, Utomo, and Erwinia. 2003, 22). In Malaysia, all Muslim women in a sample of 262 in Kelantan, a bastion of orthodoxy, claimed to have been circumcised (Isa, Shuib, and Othman 1999).

In contrast, even orthodox Muslims did not always cut their daughters in east and central Java in colonial times (Feillard and Marcoes 1998, 349). In 2002, only 43.5 percent of female respondents in Yogyakarta claimed to have been circumcised, a figure that fell as low as 31 percent elsewhere in the same publication. Moreover, some older girls and women attending *pesantren*—rural Javanese Islamic boarding schools of an orthodox bent—declared that they had "not yet" been circumcised (Putranti, Faturochman, Muhadjir, and Purwatiningsih 2003, 18, 22, 25). The standard Indonesian locution for "not yet," *belum*, can imply not intending to do anything about something and can even be a polite way of saying no.

The Severity of Female Circumcision

Female circumcision in Southeast Asia generally followed al-Nawawi's dictum: "it is obligatory to cut off a small part of the skin in the highest part of the genitals" (quoted in Wensinck 1986, 20). The first known report, dating from around the 1680s, states that in south Sulawesi circumcised girls could walk about again the next day, indicating that it was not a major operation (Gervaise 1701/1971, 139–40). Similarly, Tomás Ortiz recounted that for Muslims in the southern Philippines in the early eighteenth century, female circumcision was a minor procedure (Blair and Robertson 1903–7, 43:110).

Evidence is most abundant from the 1950s, when social anthropologists began to record the procedure in detail. It was part of a complex of ceremonies, ending in a ritual meal. A midwife or female healer was typically entrusted with the job, and she made a minor cut, prick, scratch, rubbing, or stretching, to the clitoris, the labia minora, or both. A sharp piece of bamboo was the traditional instrument, but *pandanus* thorns, needles, pen knives, kitchen knives, finger knives used to harvest ears of rice, razor blades, and scissors might be used. Witnessing a single drop of blood was the usual sign that the operation had been successfully performed. A small piece of flesh, said to be no larger than a grain of rice, might be removed, and it was then ceremonially buried (Budiharsana, Amaliah, Utomo, and Erwinia 2003, 29–38; Feillard and Marcoes

1998, 339-45, 359-60; Hanks 1968, 128; Jaspan and Hill 1987, 22; Laderman 1983, 205-7; Merli 2008, 270-73; Moore 1981, 182-85; Newland 2006, 394-400; Putranti, Faturochman, Muhadjir, and Purwatiningsih 2003, 32-33; Strange 1981, 58; US State Department 2001; Isa, Shuib, and Othman 1999).

A few references to more severe procedures exist, but they are of dubious validity. James Peacock writes about "clitoridectomy" in Singapore, but the context indicates that he is actually referring to standard Southeast Asian circumcision (Peacock 1978a, 160). Jeff Hadler, in a contribution dated 6 April 1998, mentions statements about the complete excision of the clitoris in north Sumatra but admits that they are unconfirmed ("Women in Indonesia" 1998). Meiwita Budiharsana's team reported that 22 percent of their sample in west Sumatra had suffered "excisions," but they used the word to refer to any removal of flesh, however small (Budiharsana, Amaliah, Utomo, and Erwinia 2003, viii, 28). Indeed, Malay villagers in southern Thailand boycotted one midwife because she had the reputation of cutting too deeply (Merli 2008, 271).

Syncretists might perform no more than a symbolic operation. In Java, a peeled turmeric root was placed over the girl's clitoris, and the root was cut instead of the flesh. The turmeric was then buried or thrown into the sea. The yellow color of the root symbolized a yellow spirit, which removes bad luck from children, cleansing them of the dirt adhering to them because of the curse of the god Batara Kala (Putranti, Faturochman, Muhadjir, and Purwatiningsih 2003, 19, 31; Putranti 2008, 27). This substitution may have evolved from an older practice of using turmeric root as an antiseptic and burying root and flesh together after the procedure (Feillard and Marcoes 1998, 343; Jaspan and Hill 1987, 13, 22). In recent times in Java, a doctor might simply cleanse the girl's genitalia with an antiseptic while a female healer blew over them (Putranti 2008, 28; Chiara Formichi, personal communication, 3 October 2008). In Basilica Putranti's sample in the Yogyakarta area in 2002, symbolic procedures accounted for just under half of all interventions (Putranti 2008, 26).

Elsewhere, other symbolic objects could be substituted. In south Sulawesi, a cock's comb was cut, at times wrapped in a betel leaf, and the blood was smeared on the girl's clitoris (Budiharsana, Amaliah, Utomo, and Erwinia 2003, 34, 37). Betel leaves had numerous ritual associations, as well as antiseptic properties similar to those of clove oil (Clarence-Smith, forthcoming). Bohra Isma'ili Muslims in India sometimes cut betel leaves when girls were "born circumcised," whatever that expression might mean (Ghadially 1991, 19).

Snouck Hurgronje stressed the obsessive secrecy surrounding the circumcision of girls among orthodox Muslims in both Java and north Sumatra, but this was something of an exaggeration. To be sure, the procedure was usually hidden from the eyes of men, celebration was muted, and the only outsider certain to be present was the officiating midwife or female healer (Snouck Hurgronje 1923-24, 4:206, and 1906, 1:395). Already in the 1680s in south Sulawesi, this was a private and unostentatious ceremony, reserved for female family members (Gervaise 1701/1971, 139-40). Female relatives and neighbors from outside the household might be invited, however, and fathers or grandfathers were present on occasion. Moreover, it could be made widely known in the community that the ceremony had taken place (Feillard and Marcoes 1998, 343; Merli 2008, 271).

Snouck Hurgronje himself reported that Javanese syncretists celebrated the occasion more than the *santri*. Although the operation itself remained private, a gamelan orchestra would signal to the local community that the deed had been done. Afterward, the family would offer a ritual feast, which, among noble families, could be on the same sumptuous scale as that for a circumcised boy (Snouck Hurgronje 1923-24, 4:206-7).

The Age of Girls at the Time of Circumcision

Debates have long existed about the age at which a girl should be circumcised, with a marked tendency for it to come down from adolescence to babyhood over time. Al-Nawawi already recommended in the thirteenth century that it should happen shortly after birth, while recognizing divergent opinions on this point (Wensinck 1986, 20). In south Sulawesi in the 1680s, the fact that circumcised girls could walk about again the next day indicates that they were not infants (Gervaise 1701/1971, 139-40).

In the nineteenth and early twentieth centuries, Southeast Asian girls were most commonly circumcised between about six and ten years of age, typically prior to making their formal declaration of the faith and beginning to learn to recite the Quran (Feillard and Marcoes 1998, 339-40, 343-49). The onset of puberty might also be chosen, notably if it was desired that the event should coincide with a brother's circumcision. In Sundanese-speaking west Java, circumcision accompanied the filing of a girl's teeth at puberty, and the two practices were known by the same name, *gusaran* (Snouck Hurgronje 1923-24, 4:206).

Arabs, mainly from Hadhramaut in today's eastern Yemen, transmitted some of the earliest reformist impulses of the modern era to Southeast Asia (Freitag and Clarence-Smith 1997). Some may have argued in favor of lowering the age at which the procedure was carried out, for *khafd* was practiced in parts of Hadhramaut shortly after birth, together with piercing the ears and nose of babies (Ingrams 1949, 99; Rodionov 2007, 144-45; Snouck Hurgronje 1931, 113).

In any event, the age of circumcision tended to fall in Southeast Asia. In the early twentieth century, particularly pious Muslims were already likely to circumcise girls before the age of two, notably in west Java and parts of Indonesia's outer islands (Feillard and Marcoes 1998, 342-48; Snouck Hurgronje 1906, 1:395). In the 1960s, the Yakan of the southern Philippines circumcised their girls at the age of three (Wulff 1974, 252). Muslim mothers progressively assimilated circumcision into the ceremonies that marked the end of the postpartum phase of a girl baby's life, celebrated some forty days after birth, although it could still occur as late as ten years of age (Berlie 1983, 88, note 42; Feillard and Marcoes 1998, 357; Jaspan and Hill 1987, 13, 22; Merli 2008, 270; Newland 2006, 399-400; US State Department 2001; Isa, Shuib, and Othman 1999). Increasingly, circumcision is being medicalized and commercially packaged with piercing a baby girl's ears, inserting gold studs into the ears, the first cutting of hair, and massages, which are all seen as bodily rites of passage.(Budiharsana, Amaliah, Utomo, and Erwinia 2003: 27-28; Putranti 2008, 29).

Syncretists are those most likely to resist the trend of circumcising early, preferring to wait for a girl's first menstruation (Koentjaraningrat 1988, 361). While fifteen is still mentioned as a possible age, eight has become more common (Putranti 2008, 28; Dewi 2007). At the royal court of Yogyakarta, girls are usually circumcised at around this age, with a tendency for it to occur even earlier (Putranti, Faturochman, Muhadjir, and Purwatiningsih 2003, 21, 37-39; Putranti 2008, 28).

According to the anthropologist James Siegel, in Aceh, an area whose residents are renowned for Islamic piety, girls were circumcised around the age of twelve in the 1960s, but this is doubtful. It would have meant that they were being cut later than boys, who underwent the operation at around eight years of age (Siegel 1978, 154-55). Girls were usually circumcised at a younger age than boys in Southeast Asia (Koentjaraningrat 1988, 359, 361; Peacock 1978a, 62–65, 160; Wulff 1974, 252). In addition, adult women are expected to undergo circumcision on conversion to Islam, according to reports dating from at least the fifteenth century in Southeast Asia (Feillard and Marcoes 1998, 347). This practice was justified by the example of the rightly guided Caliph 'Uthman, who ordered the circumcision of captive Byzantine women converting to Islam, as a form of ritual purification (Abdu'r-Razzaq 1998, 48, 53; Berkey 1996, 25). Circumcision thus became common, notably in Shafii areas, when slave women came over to the faith (Clarence-Smith 2006, 81, 158). Thus, animist Dayak women, stolen in raids or purchased from the interior of Borneo in the 1840s, were circumcised on conversion (Low 1848/1968, 119).

As marrying a Muslim man entails the adoption of Islam, this has become the most common occasion on which an adult woman is circumcised. This is routinely expected in the southern Philippines, where Catholic women commonly wed Muslims, and in north Sulawesi, where wives might be Protestant or animist (Budiharsana, Amaliah, Utomo, and Erwinia 2003, 35; Moore 1981, 135, 196, note 7). Similarly, a Balinese Hindu woman would be cut on marrying a Javanese Muslim (Putranti 2008, 27). However, circumcision is apparently demanded only of male converts in the Lesser Sunda Islands, which contains many Christians and animists (Feillard and Marcoes 1998, 346). In southern Thailand, when Theravada Buddhist women marry Muslim men, both spouses are allowed to decide whether the woman should be circumcised (Merli 2008, 271–72).

The circumcision of an adult woman can also result from deepening one's faith. Putranti recounts how one Javanese woman, after studying Islam intensely, decided to undergo the procedure. She took this decision even though she considered circumcision to be recommended rather than obligatory. Moreover, she asked a woman doctor to cut her slightly, with sterilized scissors, rather than going to a midwife or a female healer (Putranti 2008, 26).

Divisions in Reformist
and Conservative Movements

Logically, syncretic Javanese movements might have been expected to provide the most obvious home for opponents of female circumcision (Koentjaraningrat

1988, 361). Budi Utomo, the first Javanese nationalist party, and Taman Siswa, a Javanese educational movement, were both syncretist. Members were deeply imbued with secularism and a fascination with Western modernity, while glorifying Java's ancient Hindu and Buddhist kingdoms (Nagazumi 1972; Tsuchiya 1987).

Nevertheless, there were discordant voices. A Taman Siswa student in the 1930s explained that circumcision was necessary to reduce female libido and thus to maintain fidelity in marriage, especially when a man had more than one wife (Feillard and Marcoes 1998, 349-50). A male "native doctor," associated with Budi Utomo, expressed similar ideas in a Dutch survey. Abdul Rajid, active in Tapanuli, west Sumatra, declared that female circumcision diminished a woman's sexual desire, which was necessary because women were naturally much more lustful than men. He also opined that the procedure fattened women, thus making them more attractive — an idea that does not occur elsewhere in the literature (Feillard and Marcoes 1998, 348).

Orthodox Islamic movements, emerging at around the same time, were just as divided over the issue. Everywhere, modernists (*kaum muda*, a young or new group) challenged conservatives (*kaum tua*, an old group) (Hefner 2010). The *kaum muda* might have been expected to oppose female circumcision, and the *kaum tua* to defend it. This has indeed occasionally been the case, as in southern Thailand today (Merli 2008, 272-75).

Surprisingly, however, sharp divisions over female circumcision surfaced and persisted within every significant orthodox movement. Divergent views are revealed in contradictory fatwas (opinions on Islamic law) (Feillard and Marcoes 1998, 361-66). Religious leaders have typically disagreed about whether female circumcision is obligatory, merely honourable, or recommended (us State Department 2001).

Modernist orthodox Muslims initially avoided discussing the issue. Muhammadiyah, founded in Java in 1912 and claiming tens of millions of members after 1945, was strongly influenced by Egypt, a traditional center of female circumcision in the Middle East (Alfian 1989; Peacock 1978b). Although the leaders of Muhammadiyah generally did not circumcise their own girls, they relegated the practice to the sphere of harmless folklore (Feillard and Marcoes 1998, 355-57, 363-64).

In more recent times, modernist opinion has remained divided. Some contemporary leaders of Muhammadiyah in Yogyakarta state that there is no backing for the practice, either in the Quran nor in the canonical collections of hadith. Others state that female circumcision is merely recommended. Others again rarely impose it on their own girls and leave the decision up to mothers and other female relatives. Yet others relegate the practice to the domain of acceptable Javanese custom (Putranti, Faturochman, Muhadjir, and Purwatiningsih 2003, 25–26; Putranti 2008, 26).

Sarekat Islam, founded at about the same time as Muhammadiyah, was much influenced by the Islam of British India (Melayu 2002; Shiraishi 1990). The movement's main ideologue was Haji Agus Salim (Kahfi 1997). Although it is not clear whether he ever pronounced on this issue, a medical student who was close to him, Ahmad Ramali, published a dissertation in 1951, dealing with health and Islamic law. Ramali did not condemn female circumcision but explained that it was obligatory in Shafii law, and that devout Muslims circumcised their girls earlier than others. He further noted that female circumcision was essential for a woman to be considered a Muslim, although touching the clitoris and labia with a knife might be the equivalent of actual cutting. He cited some dubious medical notions about improving female hygiene, removing repulsive odors, restricting female libido, lessening the chance of premature ejaculation for male sexual partners, and feminizing a woman in Freudian terms (Feillard and Marcoes 1998, 350–52).

Modernists were especially strong in west Sumatra, where they made repeated attempts to reform or abolish the matrilineal customary law of the Minangkabau people (Noer 1973, 31–56). However, an article appearing in a local newspaper, probably *Singgalang*, on 17 September 2004 decreed that Islam and custom were at one in this matter, and that female circumcision was an acceptable practice for local Muslims (Lyn Parker, personal communication, 2 October 2006).

From the other side of the divide, the logical conservative defenders of female circumcision would have been the *ulama* of the Shafii school of law. They formed Nahdatul Ulama (NU) in 1926, which today claims tens of millions of members (Barton and Fealy 1996). Yet some early NU leaders publicly declared that they did not circumcise their girls, whereas others clung to the notion that it was obligatory to do so prior to puberty. A compromise fatwa of 1928 merely termed the practice "permitted," which must have raised the eyebrows of their colleagues in Cairo (Feillard and Marcoes 1998, 351, 355–56).

The NU has remained divided in present times. Abdurrahman Wahid (Gus

Dur) set his face against female circumcision, and this was especially important because he was president of Indonesia from 1999 to 2001. However, most
NU *ulama* went no further than to downgrade the practice of female circumcision from obligatory to recommended status (Feillard and Marcoes 1998,
362–63). Another stance has been to refuse to prohibit female circumcision,
as the Prophet did not do so, while insisting that it be carried out hygienically
(Putranti 2008, 30). Most NU *ulama* in socially conservative Madura continue
to consider female circumcision to be compulsory, and many NU activists in
east Java cling to the same position (Feillard and Marcoes 1998, 356; Putranti,
Faturochman, Muhadjir, and Purwatiningsih. 2003, 23–25).

Islamic organizations on the Malayan Peninsula, closely supervised by the
state, have at times defended female circumcision as a requirement of Shafii
law, while insisting on cutting as little as possible. This was the position of the
chief mufti (an Islamic legal expert) of Singapore in 1994, and it was repeated
in 2007 in a fatwa on the website of the city-state's Islamic Religious Council
(Mardiana 1994; Islamic Religious Council of Singapore 2007). The chief mufti
of Kuala Lumpur, the capital of Malaysia, when pressed by the World Health
Organization in 1979, opined that the practice was recommended rather than
compulsory (Strange 1981, 58).

The Majlis Ulama Indonesia (Council of Indonesian Ulama) long avoided
issuing a formal fatwa on the matter, but a woman on the council declared female circumcision to be obligatory (Feillard and Marcoes 1998, 364). The more
general stance has been one of reform rather than repression, accepting that
the practice is halal (permitted) in Islamic law (Putranti 2008, 30). When, beginning in November 2000, the council cooperated in a National Action Plan
to end violence against women, it took the stance that ritualistic—or at least
noninvasive—techniques of female circumcision should be promoted, during
an initial phase of raising social awareness (U.S. State Department 2001).

On the ground, local Islamic experts often clash over the issue. In the 2000s,
in one village situated in central Java near Surakarta, a private religious teacher
from outside the region, married to a woman medical doctor, rejected female
circumcision as a superstitious relic from the *jahiliyya* (the age of ignorance
before the advent of the Prophet). He was contradicted by the *modin* (elected
religious official), who taught that it was allowed by both Islamic law and Javanese custom (Dewi 2007).

Fundamentalist movements have been slow to develop in the region, and even they have remained curiously undecided as to how to handle the issue. Persatuan Islam (Persis) was refounded on such lines in 1926, with strong South Asian influence (Federspiel 2001). For some in this movement, female circumcision was reprehensible, a throwback to the age of ignorance before Islam (Feillard and Marcoes 1998, 364). However, one Persis scholar in the 1990s took the position that since the Prophet had ordered that his wives be circumcised, this should be the model for the faithful of all ages. Female circumcision was necessary to perform acts of devotion, and it also exemplified cleanliness and hygiene. In addition, it was said to enhance sexual enjoyment (Newland 2006, 401).

Recently, a new kind of fundamentalism has emerged in Southeast Asia, notably the currents that go under the name of Jemaah Islamiyah (Barton 2005). Although some of these fundamentalists merely treat female circumcision as honorable, others, including women, call for it to be observed more strictly, due to the need to reduce or regulate women's excessive lust. This involves cutting, rather than mere pricking (Putranti, Faturochman, Muhadjir, and Purwatiningsih 2003, 26, 48). Such fundamentalists issue guidelines for doctors on how to practice female circumcision in conformity with a literalist reading of hadith (Putranti 2008, 28). In southern Thailand, envoys from South Asia are also preaching the need for deeper cutting (Merli 2008, 273). Fundamentalists remain a minority among Southeast Asian Muslims, however, and it is unclear how many of them adopt such a position.

An Intensifying Practice?

In the past few decades, there have been signs that female circumcision has become more widespread and invasive in Southeast Asia. There are no good data that can clearly estimate the extent of any change, because the practice is private and embarrassing and is now technically illegal. However, limited surveys, together with anecdotal evidence, suggest that female circumcision is on the increase, and that the extent of cutting is becoming more serious.

Such a change can only partly be attributed to the rise of the new kind of fundamentalism, and it seems to be more broadly linked to the wave of Islamic revivalism that began in the 1970s, when both socialism and secular nationalism were deemed to have failed. The apparent rise in the incidence of female circumcision has been most striking in densely populated east and central Java, the traditional heartland of syncretism. Unfortunately, Indonesia's steadfast refusal to allow syncretists to be separately counted in the census makes it impossible to know whether this strand of Islam is shrinking. In addition, the ritual seems to be more frequently performed on infants than in the past, often as part of a wider postnatal package. Moreover, even if most circumcision is still so minor as to leave no physical trace, there is a growing stress on cutting more deeply, associated with more talk of reducing female lust. The invasive nature of the operation has grown through medicalization and commercialization, with the greatest impact in urban areas (Budiharsana, Amaliah, Utomo, and Erwinia 2003, viii-ix, 25; Feillard and Marcoes 1998, 354, 356; Newland 2006, 395-96, 401-2; Putranti, Faturochman, Muhadjir, and Purwatiningsih 2003, 24, 47-48; Putranti 2008, 28; US State Department 2001).

A new and surprising development is the mass circumcision of young girls, which has been reported in west Java and which may parallel the rising popularity of similar revivalist mass rituals for boys. In 2001, an advertisement in a local paper, *Pikiran Rakyat*, called attention to a general ceremony for girls, organized by the Assalam Foundation (Budiharsana, Amaliah, Utomo, and Erwinia 2003, 10). By 2006, this Islamic foundation, dedicated to education and social services, was circumcising large groups of girls in the city of Bandung, west Java, where it had its own mosque. Every spring, in the lunar month marking the birth of the Prophet, numerous girls, many under the age of five, come together in prayer halls or classrooms. Women circumcisers, who have served an apprenticeship, use sterilized scissors to cut a small piece of the prepuce. The procedure is free, and afterward each girl receives a small gift and a cup of milk to drink. The foundation's chairman explained that female circumcision would stabilize a girl's libido, make her more beautiful in the eyes of her husband, and balance her psychology (Corbett 2008). Cutting, rather than merely pricking, was one of the novelties involved in this ceremony (Lynda Newland, personal communication, 26 January 2008).

Conclusion

The policy of zero tolerance of female genital mutilation, adopted by the United Nations and the World Health Organization in 1998 and reluctantly accepted by a hesitant Indonesian government, is probably the wrong response to such recent trends. There has been almost no enforcement of the law against female circumcision, and the fact that the infidel is seen as having imposed this concession on the government appears to have stiffened the resolve of the pious to continue with the practice (Newland 2006). The attempt to eliminate female circumcision in both Indonesia and Malaysia can all too easily be made to look like an assault on Islam itself. Such campaigns play into the hands of noisy fundamentalist minorities (Putranti 2008, 29; Isa Shuib, and Othman 1999).

A better strategy might be to encourage Southeast Asian Muslims to probe and evaluate the underpinnings of female circumcision in Islam, as there are excellent scriptural grounds for declaring the practice to be unacceptable. Some reformists in the wider Islamic world have come to reject female circumcision entirely, condemning it as a survival from the *jahiliyya* (Abdu'r-Razzaq 1998, 39; Ali 2006, chapter 6; Bosworth et al. 1978, 913–14). Manifold divisions, which have rent every Southeast Asian strand of Islam over the issue, suggest that many Muslims in the region might well be prepared to repudiate an imported Arab custom derived from the Middle East's pre-Islamic culture, as long as this was seen to be an inherent aspect of reforming and strengthening their religion, and not an imposition by an international community dominated by insensitive nonbelievers.

Notes

This chapter is a much revised and updated version of "Islam and Female Genital Cutting in Southeast Asia: The Weight of the Past," published in the *Finnish Journal of Ethnicity and Migration* 3, no. 2 (2008): 14–22, a special issue on "Female Genital Cutting in the Past and Today," edited by Marja Tiilikainen (www.etmu.fi). My thanks are due to the editor and the journal for allowing me to use material from that article.

References

Abdu'r-Razzaq, Abu Bakr. 1998. *Circumcision in Islam*. Translated by Aisha Bewley. London: Dar al-Taqwa.

Alfian. 1989. *Muhammadiyah: The Political Behaviour of a Muslim Modernist Organi-*

zation under Dutch Colonialism. Yogyakarta, Indonesia: Gadjah Mada University Press.

Ali, Kecia. 2006. *Sexual Ethics and Islam: Feminist Reflections on Qur'an, Hadith, and Jurisprudence*. Oxford: Oneworld.Awde, Nicholas. 2000. *Women in Islam: An Anthology from the Quran and Hadiths*. New York: St. Martin's.

Barton, Greg. 2005. *Jemaah Islamiyah: Radical Islamism in Indonesia*. Singapore: Ridge.

Barton, Greg, and Greg Fealy, eds. 1996. *Nahdlatul Ulama, Traditional Islam and Modernity in Indonesia*. Clayton, Victoria, Australia: Monash Asia Institute.

Berkey, Jonathan P. 1996. "Circumcision Circumscribed: Female Excision and Cultural Accommodation in the Medieval Near East." *International Journal of Middle East Studies* 28 (1):19-38.

Berlie, Jean. 1983. *Tepi Laut, un village malais au bord de la mer*. Paris: de la Maisnie.

Blair, E. H., and J. A. Robertson. 1903-7. *The Philippine Islands*. 55 vols. Cleveland, OH: Arthur H. Clark.

Boddy, Janice. 2008. "Clash of Selves: Gender, Personhood, and Human Rights Discourse in Colonial Sudan." *Finnish Journal of Ethnicity and Migration* 3 (2): 4-13.

Bosworth, C. E., et al. 1978. "Khafd." In *Encyclopaedia of Islam*, 4:913-14. 2nd ed. Leiden: E. J. Brill.

Budiharsana, Meiwita, Lila Amaliah, Budi Utomo, and Erwinia. 2003. *Female Circumcision in Indonesia: Extent, Implications and Possible Interventions to Uphold Women's Health Rights*. Jakarta: Population Council.

Carey, Peter. 2007. *The Power of Prophecy: Prince Dipanagara and the End of an Old Order in Java, 1785-1855*, Leiden: KITLV Press.

Clarence-Smith, William G. 2006. *Islam and the Abolition of Slavery*. London: Hurst.

——. 2010. "South-East Asia and China to 1910." In *The New Cambridge History of Islam*, vol. 5: *The Islamic World in the Age of Western Dominance*, edited by Francis Robinson, 240-68. Cambridge: Cambridge University Press.

——. Forthcoming. "From Betel to Beverages: A Gustatory Revolution." In *Senses in Southeast Asia*, edited by Raquel Reyes and Peter Boomgaard.

Corbett, Sarah. 2008. "A Cutting Tradition." *New York Times*. 20 January.

Davis, Natalie Zemon. 2006. *Trickster Travels: A Sixteenth-Century Muslim between Worlds*. New York: Hill and Wang.

Dewi, Subhani K. 2007. "The Role of Ulama in Indonesia Contesting FGC and Advocating Women's Sexual Identity." Paper presented at the Fourth FOKO Conference, "Female Genital Cutting in the Past and Today," Hanasaari, Finland, 7-8 September.

Federspiel, Howard M. 2001. *Islam and Ideology in the Emerging Indonesian State*. Leiden: E. J. Brill.

Feillard, Andrée, and Lies Marcoes. 1998. "Female Circumcision in Indonesia: To 'Islamize' in Ceremony or Secrecy." *Archipel* 56:339–67.

Freitag, Ulrike, and William G. Clarence-Smith, eds. 1997. *Hadhrami Traders, Scholars and Statesmen in the Indian Ocean, 1750s-1960s*. Leiden: Brill.

Gervaise, Nicolas. 1701/1971. *An Historical Description of the Kingdom of Macasar in the East Indies*. Reprint. Westmead, Hampshire, England: Gregg International.

Ghadially, R. 1991. "All for 'Izzat': The Practice of Female Circumcision among Bohra Muslims." *Manushi* 66:17–20.

Hanks, Jane R. 1968. *Maternity and Its Rituals in Bang Chan*. Ithaca, NY: Cornell University Press.

Hefner, Robert W. 1985. *Hindu Javanese: Tengger Tradition and Islam*. Princeton: Princeton University Press.

———. 2010. "South-East Asia since 1910." In *The New Cambridge History of Islam*, vol. 5: *The Islamic World in the Age of Western Dominance*, edited by Francis Robinson, 591–622. Cambridge: Cambridge University Press.

Hodgson, Marshall G. S. 1974. *The Venture of Islam: Conscience and History in a World Civilization*. 3 vols. Chicago: University of Chicago Press.

Ingrams, Doreen. 1949. *A Survey of Social and Economic Conditions in the Aden Protectorate*. Asmara, Eritrea.

Isa, Ab., Rashida Shuib, and M. Shukri Othman. 1999. Abstract for "The Practice of Female Circumcision among Muslims in Kelantan." *Reproductive Health Matters* 7 (13): 137.

Islamic Religious Council of Singapore. 2007. "Female Circumcision in Islam." http://muis.gov.sg/websites/rservices/opendocall.asp?type=1&sno=768.

Jaspan, Helen, and Lewis Hill. 1987. *The Child in the Family: A Study of Childbirth and Child-Rearing in Rural Central Java in the Late 1950s*. Hull, England: University of Hull.

Kahfi, Erni Harnyanti. 1997. "Islam and Indonesian Nationalism: The Political Thought of Haji Agus Salim." *Studia Islamika* 4 (3): 6–63.

Kassamali, Noor. 2006. "Genital Cutting." In *Encyclopedia of Women and Islamic Cultures*, edited by Suad Joseph, vol. 3: *Family, Body, Sexuality and Health*, 129–34. Leiden: Brill.

Koentjaraningrat. 1988. *Javanese Culture*. Singapore: Oxford University Press.

Laderman, Carol. 1983. *Wives and Midwives: Childbirth and Nutrition in Rural Ma-*

laysia. Berkeley: University of California Press.Low, Hugh. 1848/1968. *Sarawak: Its Inhabitants and Products*. Reprint. London: Frank Cass.

Mardiana, Abu Bakar. 1994. "Female Circumcision: A Viewpoint." *Singapore Sunday Times*, 30 October. www.themodernreligion.com/women/w_circumcision.htm.

Masry, Youssef el-. 1962. *Le drame sexuel de la femme dans l'orient arabe*. Paris: Robert Laffont.

Melayu, Hasnal Arifin. 2002. "Islam as Ideology: The Political Thought of Tjokroaminoto." *Studia Islamika* 9 (3): 37–81.

Merli, Claudia. 2008. *Bodily Practices and Medical Identities in Southern Thailand*. Uppsala, Sweden: Acta Universitatis Upsaliensis.

Moor, J. H., comp. 1837/1968. *Notices of the Indian Archipelago and Adjacent Countries*. Reprint. London: Frank Cass.

Moore, Ruth L. P. 1981. "Women and Warriors: Defending Islam in the Southern Philippines." PhD diss., University of California, San Diego.

Nagazumi, Akira. 1972. *The Dawn of Indonesian Nationalism: The Early Years of Budi Utomo, 1908–1918*. Tokyo: Institute of Developing Economies.

New Encyclopaedia Britannica. 1993. Chicago: Encyclopaedia Britannica.

Newbold, Thomas J. 1839/1971. *Political and Statistical Account of the British Settlements in the Straits of Malacca*. 2 vols. London: Oxford University Press.

Newland, Lynda. 2006. "Female Circumcision: Muslim Identities and Zero Tolerance Policies in Rural West Java." *Women's Studies International Forum* 29 (4): 394–404.

Noer, Deliar. 1973. *The Modernist Muslim Movement in Indonesia, 1900–1941*. Singapore: Oxford University Press.

Peacock, James L. 1978a. *Muslim Puritans: Reformist Psychology in Southeast Asian Islam*. Berkeley: University of California Press.

——. 1978b. *Purifying the Faith: The Muhammadijah Movement in Indonesian Islam*. Menlo Park (CA): Benjamin Cummings.

Peletz, Michael G. 1996. *Reason and Passion: Representations of Gender in a Malay Society*. Berkeley: University of California Press.

Putranti, Basilica D. 2008. "To Islamize, Becoming a Real Woman, or Commercialized Practices? Questioning Female Genital Cutting in Indonesia." *Finnish Journal of Ethnicity and Migration* 3 (2): 23–31.

——. Faturochman, Darwin Muhadjir, and Sri Purwatiningsih. 2003. *Male and Female Genital Cutting among Javanese and Madurese*. Yogyakarta, Indonesia: Gadjah Mada University, Center for Population and Policy Studies.

Reid, Anthony. 1988. *Southeast Asia in the Age of Commerce, 1450-1680*. Vol. 1: *The Lands below the Winds*. New Haven: Yale University Press.

Rodionov, Mikhail A. 2007. *The Western Hadramawt: Ethnographic Field Research, 1983-91*. Halle, Germany: Martin-Luther-Universität, Orientswissenschaftliches Zentrum.

Shiraishi, Takashi. 1990. *An Age in Motion: Popular Radicalism in Java, 1912-1926*. Ithaca, NY: Cornell University Press.

Siegel, James T. 1978. *The Rope of God*. Berkeley: University of California Press.

Snouck Hurgronje, Christiaan. 1906. *The Achehnese*. Translated by A. W. S. O'Sullivan. 2 vols. Leiden: E. J. Brill.

———. 1923-24. *Verspreide geschriften*. 6 vols. The Hague: Martinus Nijhoff.

———. 1931. *Mekka in the Latter Part of the Nineteenth Century: Daily Life, Customs and Learning*. Translated by J. H. Monahan. Leiden: E. J. Brill.

Strange, Heather. 1981. *Rural Malay Women in Tradition and Transition*. New York: Praeger.

Tsuchiya, Kenji. 1987. *Democracy and Leadership: The Rise of the Taman Siswa Movement in Indonesia*. Honolulu: University of Hawaii Press.

U.S. State Department. 2001. "Indonesia: Report on Female Genital Mutilation (FGM) or Female Genital Cutting (FGC)." Washington: State Department, Office of the Senior Coordinator for International Women's Issues. www.state.gov/g/wi/rls/rep/crfgm/101102.htm.

Wensinck, A. J. 1986. "Khitan." In *Encyclopaedia of Islam*, 5:20-22. 2nd ed. Leiden: E. J. Brill.

"Women in Indonesia (Clitoridectomy) Dialog." 1998. H-Net list for Asian History and Culture. H-ASIA@h-net.msu.edu.

Wulff, Inger. 1974. "Features of Yakan Culture." In *The Muslim Filipinos*, edited by Peter G. Gowing and Robert D. McAmis, 242-55. Manila: Solidaridad.

KATJA ZVAN ELLIOTT

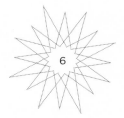

The Moudawana and Rural Marital Relationships

REFORMED OR RESOLUTE?

This chapter focuses on the changing marital relationships[1] in a rural Moroccan Berber community—which, like many other towns across the country, is of marginal importance to either officials in Rabat or academics. Drawing on the data collected during my fieldwork in this community from October 2009 to June 2010, this chapter addresses three related issues: what aspects of marital relationships are changing; whether the reformed Family Code played any significant role in influencing these changes; and people's attitudes toward both changes in marital relationships and the reform of the Family Code. This last issue is particularly salient because successful enhancement of women's rights in Morocco depends as much on the political and legal will as it does on the favorable attitude of the populace.

In 2004 Morocco's King Mohammed VI promulgated the much-anticipated reforms to the old Personal Status Code (PSC), which regulates marital relationships, child custody, and inheritance. With the reform, the largely urbanized political elite effectively determined the trajectory of future developments in the realm of women's rights and marital relationships and gave a strong message to the public: Moroccan society should make the status of wives more equitable, in harmony with the progressive reading of Islamic legal sources. However, despite the declarations of many foreign and domestic commentators and politicians that the new Family Code (Moudawanat al-Usra), as the law came to be called, institutionalized gender equality, a closer look at its clauses leads to a different perspective on the current state of gender relations in the country.

First, the Family Code deals with improving the situation of wives only, rather than women in general, and thus it would be more appropriate to speak of marital equality rather than gender equality. Incidentally, the status of unmarried women and their rights remain unchanged: they are still largely subjected to local traditions, according to which families treat their unmarried adult daughters as minors. Second, the word "equality" itself seems to be problematic, as there are many instances in the law where this word is used—but never in a way where it could be interpreted as gender equality. For instance, the law introduced the notion of mutuality of rights and obligations (*al-ḥuqūq wa al-wājibāt al-mutabādila*), in fact making both the wife and husband equally responsible for managing the household and bringing up children, but without making or calling them equal. Furthermore, the law sets the minimum legal age of marriage at eighteen years for both boys and girls and requires husbands to guarantee equality in their treatment of wives in a polygamous marriage. Therefore, the law gives the family a more democratic and women-friendly appearance, yet at the same time maintains its patriarchal character. Perhaps the most obvious manifestation of maintaining patriarchy is the law's oblique designation of the husband as the head of the family. One of the legal obligations of Moroccan husbands is providing financial maintenance for their wives. While wives are, at least in theory, thereby made financially secure, this entitlement also has a number of consequences for women's position in society. Jamal Nasir reports that the majority of Islamic jurists rule that wives lose their right to maintenance if they work outside the home without their husband's permission.[2] The clause on obeying the husband's orders, though removed from the PSC and replaced with the phrase "consultation on decisions concerning the management of family affairs" (article 51, section 4) in the reformed Family Code,[3] remains the basis of marital relationships in more rural communities, as will be shown below. Moreover, the entitlement of the wife to maintenance perpetuates women's financial dependency. In a more traditional milieu, such as the one discussed in this chapter, this deprives wives of the right of co-ownership of marital property.

The avoidance—quite possibly intentional—of the term "gender equality" is understandable, given the fact that the reform caused fierce public debates that lasted for more than a decade and divided the predominantly urbanized and informed Moroccans into two antagonistic blocs. Women's rights activists—many of whom participated in the One Million Signatures Campaign, which prompted the start of the reform process in the early 1990s—demanded these reforms to follow a Western model of women's rights. While they recognized the importance of religion in Moroccan society, they argued that laws should be governed by secular democratic principles. The other bloc, although recognizing the need to reform the ossified PSC, espoused a more culture-specific approach and thus a law based on reformed Islamic principles.

The new Moudawana, however, did introduce a few changes that have the potential to improve a woman's position in the marital relationship. It gives brides the option to add extra conditions to the marital contract and to conclude a prenuptial agreement. Unfortunately, there are many societal restrictions that prevent women, especially in more conservative environments, from using this right. Numerous reports,[4] as well as my interviews with local people, have shown that judges and 'dūl (public notaries) do not inform future wives of their rights, and that girls are not able to stipulate extra conditions lest they be branded as too demanding and thus jeopardize their chances of getting married.[5]

The value of the reformed Family Code, however, lies not in its stipulations but in the message it conveys. The king and the reformers desacralized the essence of family legislation and sanctioned further public debate and reforms in the realm of women's rights, something that had seemed implausible even two decades ago. Furthermore, the debate implicitly recognized that wives' status in Moroccan society is indeed poor and in need of being adapted to meet "modern" needs.

This chapter looks at how the debates and the law itself are influencing marital relationships within a rural Berber-speaking community and how people in this provincial area are responding to the enhancement of women's rights.

Community of Oued al-Ouliya:
Location, Socioeconomics, and Education

Nestled in an oasis on the southeastern side of Moroccan High Atlas Mountains lie a series of Berber-speaking fortified villages (*ksūr*) belonging to the rural commune (*baladiya*) of Tamazirt. This rural locale is divided into two administrative communities (each known as a *jāmiʻa*)—Oued al-Soufla (Lower Wadi) and Oued al-Ouliya (Upper Wadi), which is where I conducted my fieldwork.[6] Today, many of these fortifications are in ruins as villages have expanded beyond the old sun-dried adobe walls—either because floods ruined the original dwellings or because the influx of remittances and the general improvement in living standards have allowed people to build newer houses with more expensive and modern materials. Such developments culminated in various *ksūr* that form a continuous stretch of houses without clearly defined boundaries or uninhabited land between them.

My research and the more ethnographic part of my fieldwork was primarily conducted in one *ksar* (the singular of *ksū*) called Taddert. This *qsar* has many facilities not found in other *qsour*, such as the community's headquarters, a women's association, and a health center. Taddert serves as a sort of crossroad and a meeting center for many people of the surrounding *qsour*. I thus quickly realized that a case study based solely on one *qsar* was impossible. Indeed, many of the girls and women I socialized with were from different *qsour*. As mentioned above, there is no apparent border between some of the *qsour* such as between Taddert, Aït Ayyur, and Zagzaw, all of which I frequented on a daily basis. Many of the girls and women I visited and associated with were from these three nearby villages. Furthermore, most of the girls in the informal education program and my English students were from Qtaε al-Oued. On a more or less daily basis, they rode their bicycles to Taddert to attend afternoon classes in the women's association.

Part of the community and many of its *qsour*, including the ones mentioned above, lie on the main road connecting two of southeastern Morocco's main cities and tourist gateways: Ouarzazate and Errachidia. However, despite many tourist attractions situated close by and scenic roads such as the so-called Road of One Thousand Kasbahs passing through the area, life in this community in general remains unaffected by mass tourism. Economically and politically, the local people remain more or less isolated and unimportant. Unlike cotton production in Settat and tourism in Azrou, there is no industry or large firms that could employ the residents.

The main economic activities in the *qsour* I studied are raising livestock (mainly sheep and goats, and to a lesser extent cows) and agriculture (mainly dates, alfalfa, grains, some vegetables, and other fruit). There are also small, locally owned businesses such as grocery shops, mechanics' shops, tailors, and cafes, which employ mostly males. Many households survive on remittances from male family members residing and working abroad in such places as France and Spain, or in Morocco's more affluent and economically vibrant areas such as Marrakech or Casablanca.

As a consequence of the growing Western interest in Morocco as a tourist destination, many people nowadays associate Berber women with the weaving of carpets and making of other artisanal goods. Contrary to this stereotypical view, most women of Oued al-Ouliya do not weave. Married women in this community are to a large extent unemployed, working only at home, to care for the house and family. Some women do sew clothes and make small objects for home decoration, which they also sell, but most of them do so to earn pocket money rather than to contribute financially to the household budget. It should be emphasized that married women are, to a large extent, discouraged from working outside the home. The situation is slightly different for unmarried adult girls, although for them too the local job market is constrained. First, there are not enough jobs for men, who are legally and traditionally recognized as the family breadwinners; and second, many jobs are deemed as inappropriate for girls, such as working in cafes or even grocery stores. Yet despite this and due to economic hardships, many girls do significantly contribute to their families' earnings by working as teachers in the local kindergartens or women's association, or by sewing clothes and *taḥruyts* (a *taḥruyt* is a large black shawl worn by girls and women outside their homes, which they wrap around their bodies and heads).

Illiteracy in this community affects mostly middle-aged to older people; the majority of girls and boys today receive some kind of formal primary education. Ninety-nine percent of girls between six and eleven years of age attend school[7] — although, as the director of one of the four middle schools in the community stated, the dropout rate after finishing primary school (grades one to six) remains relatively high, particularly among girls. However, it is important to recognize that girls' finishing primary school is a great step forward in this community, when compared with the educational level of the girls' mothers and, in many cases, their fathers. The middle-aged to older generation of women rarely went to school, and those who did never went beyond primary school. People in general are becoming increasingly aware of the value and purpose that education holds, not just for children but also for adults. The number and consistent growth of literacy classes, which have been offered for the past decade to women and men, testify to what could be interpreted as successful consciousness raising. Furthermore, Taddert's local women's association is also carrying out the governmental initiative to increase the knowledge of people who left school at an early age or before finishing a certain level. Girls are thus encouraged to enroll in the informal education (*tarbiya ghair niḍāmiya*) program. In the school year 2009–10, about seventy-five girls and women up to their mid-thirties—of diverse educational levels, from the practically illiterate to those with up to ten years of formal education—attended afternoon classes in Arabic, French, and mathematics and participated in occasional weekend activities such as learning how to sew, bake, use a computer, and navigate the Internet.

Women's Social World

MULTIGENERATIONAL HOUSEHOLDS

Living conditions in this community have changed, compared to even twenty years ago. In the past, forty or more people belonging to the same extended family (*al-'ā'ila*) lived under one roof. Today, the number of family members in one household has decreased to less than ten on average. Yet it is still a common sight to see multiple generations living under the same roof, sharing not only the income of those who have a salaried job but also all other household responsibilities and decisions. As in many other regions in Morocco and the rest of the Middle East and North Africa, custom dictates that daughters will one day move out and take care of their husband's parents, but sons and their wives will stay at home and take care of his parents. In absence of a guaranteed pension or otherwise regular income, their sons' staying at home equals survival for the parents. It should be noted that reality suggests a different picture. In families with many children and hence also many daughters, it is almost inevitable that one of them will remain single and thus be designated to take care of her parents while living with her brother's family (or brothers' families). And in case of divorce, it is expected that the woman will return to her father's house; many divorced women take on the responsibility of caring for their aging parents.

An increasing number of couples live independently from their parents, but this is nonetheless still an exception rather than the rule. Most girls and women I discussed this issue with talked of living with their husband's parents' as the man and his family's right. As one woman put it, this is "because they were his parents before they've become my parents, and because they had sleepless nights because of him. They raised him to be a virtuous man." Some also believe that only by living with their parents-in-law can they be an example for their own sons, "so that one day when I have a son he wouldn't leave me, like when I wanted to live separately with my husband, even if that is the rule of life." Marriage, to a large degree, is an institution binding a wife to both her husband and his family; hence, many girls cannot imagine "monopolizing him [the husband] only for myself."

Furthermore, women are aware of the great influence that mothers have on their sons, and thus to earn the trust of the husband, they have to also earn the trust of his family—most important, of his mother. This can be done only by living with the family under the mother-in-law's authority. The narratives and personal observations I gathered of household life suggest that the relationship between the wife and her mother-in-law is proverbially burdened by the characteristics of a controlling and powerful mother-in-law on the one side, and those of an independent-thinking daughter-in-law on the other. Women report that the consequence of a strained relationship between the two women is a frequent cause for divorce. Moreover, there may also be tension between the newcomer and her sisters-in-law or other brides in the family, particularly if the new bride does household chores differently from the other women or, less commonly, if she works outside the home and thus does not fulfill her daily duties inside the house.

With such complex dynamics and economic constraints involved in family and marital relationships, it is no surprise that only a very few of the younger women and girls firmly expressed their desire to create a household independent from their in-laws. The new Moudawana gives brides the right to include additional stipulations in their marriage contracts. Creating an independent home could be one such enhancement of women's rights not otherwise guaranteed by the law, but—at least in the community I studied—this right is completely ignored. Living circumstances, such as local customs and ideals of female shyness and modesty, unemployment, and women not having a source of income of their own, ensure the perpetuation of, for example, multigenerational households and prevent brides from exercising their right to live independently. Such audacious thinking could have detrimental effects on their quality of life once they are old. Yet there is an apparent contradiction in what seems to be women's desire and what they know to be the reality of their living situation. Some women revealed in private that their dream is to live in a single-unit household because they feel that only through living independently will they be able to have a greater say in managing the household, gain a greater sense of self-worth, and relax.

Some men recognize the problem of large, multigenerational households, saying that husbands find themselves in a predicament. In the words of one middle-aged man: "If you go to a judge, he'd tell you that your wife has the right to live independently from her in-laws. [She wants this] because she wants her own house and to be free to spend the money as she wants to. . . But we should say that Aït [Ḥmed] and Casablanca are not the same. Aït [Ḥmed] says that if I separate from my parents, I'll be cursed by parents [*maskhūṭ al-wālidayn*]." Another man of similar age despairingly concluded that "if you follow your wife, you have a problem and if you follow your parents, you have a problem." Hsain Ilahiane describes the kind of power that the cursing of either the patriarch and the matriarch has over those who break away from the expected, customary trajectory. His explanation deserves to be quoted in length in order to show the great impact that such a curse has. Ilahiane reports that once individuals are cursed,

> wrath and misfortune await them ahead. A cursed son will always
> be a loser and unlucky, and in being a loser he is ostracized by the community.
> Any deals or activities involving a cursed person are believed to be imbued with
> *ssakht* [anger] and lack *baraka* [the blessing of God], a critical element for
> the blessing of human relationships and economic production. An old man, a
> patriarch himself, nicely and succinctly conveyed the essentials of *ssakht* to
> me, stating it is "like SIDA [the French word for AIDS], when thrown on
> someone they will wear it to the grave and the after-life." Only *tuba*
> (repentance) in the presence of a holy man and *ta'a* (obedience)
> of parents can expunge the curse.[8]

Most men, therefore, follow traditions and the wishes of their parents rather than consulting their future wives on signing the marital contract, but this behavior is something that not many brides or women in general would protest. Increasing numbers of women are aware of their rights emanating from the Family Code, including their right to stipulate extra conditions in their marital contract. However, the severity of the punishment, as described by Ilahiane, for violating the customary order prevents many from exercising their rights.

WOMEN'S DAILY LIVES

A typical day for most women starts with waking up around 7:00 in the morning to knead dough for bread so it has time to rise. Some women return to bed for another hour or so before finally getting up around 8:30 or 9:00 to prepare breakfast for the family. A day may start a lot earlier for those women who wake up for the first morning prayer or those who have livestock at home, such as cows, goats, and sheep, that need to be milked or otherwise taken care of.

Immediately after breakfast, girls and women disperse around the house to complete their morning chores: baking bread for lunch, washing dishes and tidying up the kitchen and living quarters, sweeping and mopping floors inside and outside the house, doing laundry—by hand, because washing machines are still a luxury rather than a necessity—and preparing lunch. These chores usually take up most of the morning, despite the fact that the work is divided among several women and girls.

The whole family gathers for lunch, which is the main meal of the day, and eats together after the midday prayer. If there are male guests who are not members of the family, men may eat separately from women. Following lunch one of the women washes the dishes, after which everyone takes a few hours off—to visit neighbors or family, watch TV, or take an afternoon nap. At around 5:30 afternoon *kaskrot* (snack) is served, after which women either continue watching TV or visiting, or sometimes read the Quran.

In the evening, one of the women prepares dinner, which is eaten at around 10:00 or later. After that, married couples retire to their rooms while the others bring their bedding to the living room and watch TV until the day finally comes to an end and they fall asleep on couches that serve as beds. Men's presence in the house is kept to a minimum,[9] which means that they normally only sleep and eat there, and perhaps watch TV in the late evening. When they are not working, many of them spend their free time relaxing with their male friends in cafes or shops.

The daily routine of women is often broken by one of many *munāsabāt* (occasions) such as engagements (*l-khūtuba*), weddings (*l-'ers*), birth celebrations (*s-sbū'*), ceremonies of mourning (*l-'zāl*), the month of Ramadan, sacrifice day holidays (*'id l-aḍḥa* or *'id l-kbīr*), or pre- and posthajj parties. Occasions such as weddings, mourning ceremonies, and parties before or after the hajj (the pilgrimage to Mecca) usually last at least three days—sometimes up to a week—depending on the family's financial capabilities, during which time the family receives numerous guests. Birth celebrations—or *s-sbū'*, which means "seven" and describes the seventh day after the birth of the child, when she or he is named and a sheep is slaughtered for the festivities—is the time when the mother and newly born child receive family members, neighbors, and friends, who come to congratulate her. This week culminates in the naming of the child, which takes place on the last, seventh day of the *munāsaba*. A majority of parents also have their sons circumcised (*khitān*) during this week.

An important part of these occasions, of course, is socializing. This means that when the family announces a celebration, it extends a more or less open invitation to the community. In other words, almost no one is directly invited, but everyone is welcomed, which can result in a family's hosting more than 500 people during a three-day occasion. Women of the family holding such an occasion are always helped by their female neighbors or female relatives not living in the same house. For the women of the family, organizing such an event causes quite a lot of stress and additional work, since they start each day much earlier than normal and only finish it around midnight or even much later, especially in the summer. Generally, however, these *munāsabāt* are a welcome break from the women's usual daily routine.

In summary, women's work is never finished. Compared to men, women do not take any days off or have free weekends, and when they travel to visit family members, they merely perform their usual work at a different house.

Gender Roles

Men's and women's responsibilities continue to be based on reciprocity rather than on equality. Their lives are significantly intertwined, as neither could survive without the other. Women, in the most basic interpretation of their responsibilities, need men to provide food and housing and to fulfill other basic obligations; men need women to take care of the house, prepare food, and rear children. Apart from these basic common interests and their interdependency, men and women in this community do not seem to share any other interests or responsibilities. This may be partly a consequence of the fact that there is usually a generational divide between husband and wife. The preferred age difference between spouses is at least ten years, though twenty years or more is not uncommon. More important, the society does not encourage the mixing of sexes and promotes the view that each one has its own duties.

Interaction between men and women is indeed rare and is usually based on discussing issues pertaining to family matters. Men's involvement in child rearing is quite marginal, particularly at the beginning of a child's life, compared to that of the mother or other women in the house. That this is the case is suggested by the following example. In mixed marriages, where one of the parents speaks Tachilhit (a Berber dialect) and the other speaks Darija (Moroccan Arabic), the children's mother tongue will always be that of their mother and not of their father. This means that in Tachilhit-speaking areas, such as in this community, if children learn Darija as their first language, it is not likely that they will ever learn more than a few words of Tachilhit. Later in a child's life, the role and importance of the father increase as he becomes the primary disciplinarian and authority figure. Young people often reported that their relationship with their father was based much more on fear and the utmost respect for his decisions, while their relationship with their mother tended to be more relaxed and affectionate.

Despite the Moudawana's declaring that both spouses should share household responsibilities and child rearing, in reality the work of the spouses remains intertwined at best. Women argued that the "European" style of sharing domestic chores makes them feel uncomfortable. They do not believe it is in their interest to step into men's territory, nor do they want men to take over their responsibilities. Each one of them is suited to perform her or his duties on the basis of their biological differences, which explains the laughter I inspired when I talked about the division of labor in my own household. Women often rebuked me for the fact that my husband did what they perceived as women's household work because in the context of Oued al-Ouliya, it is shameful for men to do women's work and vice versa. In a similar manner, when I discussed gender roles in Europe with a local man, he shook his head in disbelief at what he was hearing and finally asked: "And your husband is okay with cleaning the house?"

All the women I interviewed thus described women's role in society as more or less that of taking care "of her husband, home, and children." The responsibilities of men, in contrast, could be summed up in the answer of one of my younger female interviewees: "If he works outside the house and brings [home] food, what else do you want?" In other words, "[a husband] has responsibility outside the home and [a wife] inside the home."

It could be argued that at first sight, household life in this community is fundamentally organized by women, but it would be wrong to assume that the authority (*sulṭa*) of the man of the house is nonexistent or that his financial support is not vital for the survival of the household. Katherine Hoffman appropriately described this power of men, saying that "men's presence [is] constant despite their absence."[10] It is important to ask ourselves at this point: what effect do such gender roles have on women's status in society?

DOES STAYING AT HOME EQUAL WORKING OUTSIDE THE HOUSE?

When women are asked about their job, they either reply that they do not have a job or say that they are *gālsa f-dār*. This term literally means "sitting at home" or "staying at home" and is a sort of euphemism that people, both women and men, use to describe women's work inside the home. Thus, it does not indicate that women are being idle at home, as that is rarely the case. Instead, it is used to differentiate women's work at home from men's work outside the home (*khidma*). Thus, it also has an ideological connotation in the sense that women's work or "staying at home" is inferior to men's work outside the home, based on the latter's financial contribution to the household. This has important consequences for women's status in society, especially in their not being entitled to any division of property in case of divorce. This refers to what could be termed "marital property" or assets acquired during marriage, although in reality no such shared property exists.[11] I have not come across any couples who married after the reform of the Family Code who concluded a prenuptial agreement. This means that assets bought after the wedding are owned by the husband, as he is normally the one with a wage-paying job and thus has money to buy them. In case of divorce, women keep what they brought to the marriage—including their bride price, wedding gifts, and anything else they bought with their own money.

Some women and men recognize that those wives who work as *muḍḍafāt* (government employees) are not only much more independent from their husbands but also entitled to co-ownership of the house and other marital assets and sharing of household responsibilities. Being a government employee in a rural environment is considered an ideal job as it entails a steady income, social benefits, and a pension. It is also considered to be a respectable job for a woman and thus what seems to be the only job that a husband might consider as suitable for his wife, given the rare opportunity for such work. Unfortunately, with only a few government agencies there are not enough jobs for men, the main breadwinners, let alone for women, whose primary responsibility is to take care of the house rather than earn money.

Women recognize that when talking about property ownership, being a housewife is a disadvantage; yet this does not mean that they do not perceive their work as important, if not more important than that of men. Answers such as the following were quite common when I asked interviewees whether women's work at home is equal to that of their husbands: "Women's work at home is more than men's work outside. A wife has a big responsibility. She has to take care of her home and children. But her husband only has one job." Most interviewed men in fact shared this opinion. Despite this fact, when it comes to questions of marital property ownership and equal sharing of power in decision making, contribution to the welfare of the family seems to be measured in economic, material terms and not in the amount of work per se. In other words, men—defined ideologically and on the basis of biological differences as having more power than women, and thus also as the main providers of the family—are put into the positions of the family authority figure and of the main owner of marital property. Women's work in this sense is not acknowledged. Only one of my male interviewees, a former head of the local literacy classes, raised this issue of double standards, contending that "the problem here is that the associations that defend women have started to be aware [of the issue]. It is said that women's work as a housewife should be given value. For example, imagine that there's no wife and we hire a maid. We give her salary, which means that work inside the home is paid. We should give this work value and importance because it makes things easier for someone who works outside and it simplifies his conditions of work."

Should gender equality, as propounded by many Western aid organizations, really be the goal, or should women's rights associations and activists concentrate on sensitizing the society to the idea that women's household work is equal to men's work outside the home? Many women, in this community, and elsewhere in Morocco, prefer excelling at motherhood and in their role as a wife and homemaker to working outside the home. Such outside work is seen as liberating to a certain extent, only because women feel that if they earned money they would be entitled to equal status with men. At the same time, however, they argue that their priority as women is and should be striving toward becoming the best mother and wife possible. This carries much more weight and is also much more rewarding in societal terms than having a paid job for a woman. Furthermore, neither women nor men see how women could do both jobs equally well, simply because gender roles are viewed as reciprocal rather than equal. The problem appears to be the disconnect between the evaluation of women's work outside the home and their work inside the home. Women's waged work may indeed be devalued in people's minds, yet at the same time, in their opinion, it brings entitlement to power and expansion of rights. In contrast, housework and motherhood expands women's standing in society but does not bring them entitlement to extra rights, simply because of her nonfinancial contribution to the household and her being a woman. Arguably, if women's work inside the home were perceived as financially contributing to the household much like men's salaried work, the status of married women could improve. Such treatment could bring the society closer to the much-debated gender equity as mutual understanding, shared responsibility for managing the household, and shared marital property would not only be a theoretical and legal notion but a practiced reality.

MARITAL RELATIONS THEN AND NOW

The "past" was defined in my conversations with interviewees not as a distant past but rather as the period of the respondents' youth or that of their parents. What is interesting and may create confusion, if not a problem—especially for Europeans and other outsiders—is their almost complete disregard for time measured in years. Age does not seem to be defined by years, as many people either have to think hard about how old they are or give a rough estimate of their age. Instead, age to a large extent is gauged by maturity that a young person shows or the physical appearance of an older person. In other words, a girl is deemed ready for marriage not because she turned eighteen but because she completed her training in domestic chores. In this community, the most suitable age of marriage for girls remains fifteen, although several women reported that parents still engage or marry their daughters at a younger age. For older people, their age is defined by their having adult children and their physical appearance, such as wrinkles on their faces. They furthermore think of major events such as a floods or war in order to estimate their age. This is understandable given the fact that in the past births were not registered, and hence some people do not know their biological age. However, age measured in years is becoming more important, particularly for those girls in their twenties and older who are still unmarried—for them, their "old" age becomes a sort of race with time. Thus, the "past" referred to in this section pertains to a period approximately sixty to five years ago.

As with any society, the Tamazirt area is changing despite perhaps at first sight giving the impression of a static community. Both men and women discussed differences between marital relations in the past and today. The majority of them evaluated these changes as positive, but some looked back at the time of their parents or their own youth with nostalgia. In particular, men complained that wives nowadays are much more complicated and materialistic. According to one middle-aged man, "They want a TV, a DVD player, a satellite dish. And we have to fulfill their needs, but the problem is that there aren't any jobs in this region." To some women of all ages, life appeared much simpler in the past than it is now. One of the younger divorced women gave as evidence of such a simpler life the fact that in the past spouses did not quarrel and husbands respected their wives much more than today. Arguably, marital harmony was a consequence of the fact that spouses rarely talked to each other and that women never contradicted their husbands, or men in general. A middle-aged woman, a migrant to this community from the northern Moroccan city of Oujda, used the word ʿyb (shameful) to describe what was meant for a wife to contradict her husband, even if injustice had been done to her: "In the past, there were no problems (ṣdaʿ) between spouses, but now there are. In the past, when spouses had problems, the wife wouldn't return to her father's house even if her husband beat her, as it was shameful (ʿyb) to do so. Now, he only says one wrong thing, and the woman returns to her father's house."

In a similar manner, an older woman defended the marital relationship of the past, arguing that women nowadays have too much power, which even exceeds that of the husband: "Today wives control their husbands. The poor husbands are cornered. Wives do what they want to and control everything. They don't care about their husbands. If he wants to say anything, she corners him. He can't say anything. If he breaks up with her, she asks for their home and he has to rent a house. He's forced to do so even if he has children."

The belief that women get the house in case of divorce and men have to rent a house is based on the general misunderstanding of the new Family Code. I have heard it from a number of people all over Morocco, who complained that because of this clause and the Moudawana in general, men were reluctant to get married. In their opinion, women got married only in order to file for divorce and get the house. Moreover, two female Islamist activists, members of the censored Al-Adl wal Ihsan (the Justice and Spirituality Organization), claimed in an interview with me that when men had been told about this purported clause before the 2004 reform, many of them immediately filed for divorce in order not to be evicted from their houses.[12] Such statements, whether true or not, manifest deeper clefts within the Moroccan society, one of which is undoubtedly the movement's vilification of the Family Code as being out of touch with Moroccan reality and enabling easy-to-get divorces and promiscuity. It should be stressed at this point, however, that such a clause does not exist in the Moudawana, and that in order for marital property to be divided, the couple has to have concluded a prenuptial agreement.

Some of my interviewees perceived the relative improvement of women's status and the enhancement of their rights as necessarily decreasing the role and status of men, even making them inferior to those of women. The enhancement of women's rights, one of the main aims of the reformed Moudawana, is thus viewed as a zero-sum game and a disruption to the traditional order, something that many people in this community view negatively. Furthermore, in the discussion of whether men and women are *kif kif* (the same), as equality is interpreted by the local people, or whether men are more important than women, it should be emphasized that these are largely ideological, imported notions, which until recently did not exist in people's minds. To a certain extent, most people still do not think in these categories, as for them men and women are clearly different: "A man is a man. Look, they're called 'a man' and 'a woman.' And look at winter and summer—winter is female and summer is male."[13] Women and men are in charge of different aspects of life, but they are both equally essential for the survival of society, and this is where the local people felt that gender equality lies.

Traditions or Moving Away?

For some people, the reason why the current time and changes that have occurred since their youth are perceived as more or less negative is a consequence of the evolution of traditions, if not their diminishing importance. Moreover, my interviewees felt that any modification in traditions contradicted their parents' way of life. Ambiguity toward either following local traditions or what older people call the urban way of life is present especially among the younger people, who want to break away from the traditional way of living but are also aware of the fact that living in their father's house and in this region dictates specific rules that can be adjusted only to a certain, socially permissible degree. Girls, for example, see that the only way to live a different and more independent life from their parents' is to marry someone who either works in or is from a different community—preferably the city, where, in their opinion, their anonymity and hence freedom would be more or less guaranteed. In a small town or village such as Taddert and the surrounding *qsour*, constant and omnipresent social control forces people, especially girls, to defer to locally constructed norms of proper Islamic behavior, although even this sometimes proves not to be enough. One young woman claimed: "If you go out, people will talk about you, and if you stay in, people will talk about you. So what can we do?" Particularly young people explain this situation by saying that "people here have an old mentality . . . We're used to such life. It's like a habit."

Despite such unfavorable views of the current times and a rather negative evaluation of human and societal progress, most interviewed married women—including the young and the middle-aged—feel more empowered compared to their mothers. According to them, their husbands give them money to manage some daily household expenses—which, they argued, was unimaginable in the time of their mothers. Yet even today, adult men do the bulk if not all of the food shopping at the weekly *souq* (market), or buy daily provisions in small, locally owned grocery stores; they also deal with buying furniture and other large or more expensive items for the house. The majority of women still rely on men to bring home food and whatever else is needed for the household, whereas women are in charge of buying clothes and other small items they may come across while out of the house. Moreover, younger and middle-aged women often mentioned that their husbands consulted them about household matters — in their view, a welcome change compared to their mother's marital relationship. Words like "mutual agreement" (*tafāhum*) and "mutual consultation" (*tašāwur*) have become key words in describing present-day marital relationships. Women in particular take pride in the fact that they play a more active role in decision making, regardless of their husband's power to completely disregard their wishes or input. One such common instance of a contradiction in terms relates to the question of whether women should be allowed to finish their studies or work outside the home after they get married. The answer of one female interviewee was typical:

> "It's allowed if spouses agree on it [before the signing of the marital contract].
> If her husband wants it, it's possible. . . Even if she wants to [work outside the
> home or continue with education], if her husband doesn't want it she won't go
> [to work or school]. In Islam, if the husband doesn't approve [*al-riḍa*] of [his
> wife] going out, [she] shouldn't go out. . . When you go to your husband,[14] even
> if you had a job before, if he tells you to quit your work, you should quit it.
> But you have to agree on this before signing the marital contract."

Women mention this "agreement" between future spouses as one reason for not resorting to their right of stipulating extra conditions in the marriage contract. Hence, regardless of the fact that many Moroccan women's organizations urged women to state in their marriage contracts their desire to work outside the home after marriage,[15] in a rural environment with many social and economic constraints, the legal enhancement of women's rights has yet to translate into reality.

Some men also recognize that times are changing, but at the same time they reiterate that this change for the time being is more a theoretical (legal) notion than a lived fact. One middle-aged man admitted that the laws of the reformed Moudawana are not applied at home "because in my house there's still the authority of the man[16] even though the Moudawana came to fight against this authority of the man."

However, what is important in this context is not whether women seem empowered or not to an outsider, because this will always lead to distortions of what local people perceive as a reality. When discussing women's empowerment, it should be kept in mind that especially uneducated rural women's point of reference is the life of their mothers rather than that of a Western or educated urban woman. Hence, although women are still obliged to follow their husband's will, which may run contrary to their own desires, they emphasized that most husbands today consult them. This gives them a sense of agency and relative power over financial issues and their marital life and thus should be interpreted as a feeling of empowerment compared to their mother's situation.

Conclusion

Life in this community is not easy. Younger and unmarried people complain that there are no community clubs or places where they could spend their free time without the constant supervision of adults. Adults complain about the lack of jobs, which would guarantee their financial and social security and provide better access to health care, as well as the possibility of pensions. Unemployment, underemployment, and seasonal employment are, according to my observation, quite common. Both the young and the old criticize the current state of their society—young people perceive traditions as a prison preventing them from achieving their ambitions, which transcend the limits of the *qsour*; and their parents feel that the old values that functioned like glue to keep the society together are being eroded.

There are many economic and social problems in the community of Oued al-Ouliya in addition to local traditions that influence people's perceptions of issues such as the reform of the Family Code, and with it the enhancement of women's rights as secondary matters. To a certain degree, some women and men are uncomfortable with the idea of women's having a more prominent role outside and inside the home, arguing that such ideas only disturb the traditional order and, hence, normality. "Modernity," in the view of some younger and older interviewees, with the enhancement of women's rights and gender equality, only brings disorder and trouble to the already arduous lives of the local people. At the same time, most younger and middle-aged women positively evaluated the difference between their experience in marriage and that of their mothers. They enjoy having more freedom and control over their own lives and speak of mutual understanding and consultation between husband and wife as a basis for a successful marriage. Thus, despite the fact that the new

Moudawana has not had a significant impact on people's lives in this community, gender—or, rather, marital—relations seem to be moving toward a more just direction. Perhaps more than the Moudawana, education for both girls and boys, the media with numerous women's magazines and TV soap operas, the Internet, and the usage of mobile phones all have influenced gender and marital relationships to a larger degree than the Moudawana. Men certainly still have the authority, to which women admittedly are subordinated, but the prospects are not all bleak. The facts that women themselves feel empowered compared to their mothers and that some men recognize the need to enhance certain women's rights show that even small and relatively marginalized communities welcome and implement changes in the realm of marital relationships despite dictating their own pace for such changes. However, we must take into account the facts that people's bread-and-butter concerns come first, and that they view women's rights and gender equality, as defined in the West, as rights of secondary importance rather than as fundamental human rights.

Notes

1 I speak of "marital" rather than "gender" relationships because—at least in theory—outside their marital relationship, women and men should not have a relationship with someone of opposite sex. Most women do not associate with men outside their family, and contact between the sexes is kept to minimum and usually does not go beyond a fleeting greeting on the street or in the house during visiting.

2 Nasir 2002, 100.

3 Global Rights 2006.

4 See, for example, Global Rights 2008; Association Democratique des Femmes du Maroc 2007; Ligue Democratique des Droits des Femmes, unpublished.

5 For a more nuanced analysis of the reformed Moudawana, see Zoglin 2009; Zvan Elliott 2009; Zvan 2007.

6 All proper names for people and places in my fieldwork are pseudonyms. I first visited this site in December 2008, when I was researching the impact of literacy classes on participants' lives as part of my internship with the US Agency for International Development (USAID). I decided in 2009 to make this site my primary field site for my doctoral dissertation. All of the data contained in this chapter were gathered in the period from October 2009 to June 2010 and are based on participatory research—

semistructured recorded interviews with women and men, daily informal conversations with people, and participant observation.

7 "Monoghrafia Jamʿat [Oued] Al-ʿliya" 2004.

8 Ilahiane 2004, 96-97.

9 When I told the women in my host family that I wanted to interview men for my research project, one woman exclaimed: "Where are you going to find them? You should go to cafes!" She was doubtful that I would be able to interview any men because local cafes are a male-only environment, so any woman entering one would be trespassing all boundaries of appropriate behavior. I thus had to ask the president (*raʾīs*) of the community to arrange interviews for me, and even with his help, some men refused to grant me an interview.

10 Hoffman, *We Share Walls*, 27.

11 I do not include the marital house in this category because in most cases the bride moves into her husband's family house.

12 Names, date, and place of the interview withheld on the interviewees' request.

13 The interviewee said "*shita al-mra wa sajf al-rajul*," literally meaning that winter is a woman and summer is a man, which also corresponds to the grammatical gender of winter (female) and summer (male).

14 "Going to your husband" means getting married because a bride normally leaves the home of her father and moves to her husband's house or his father's house.

15 See Global Rights 2008.

16 The word the interviewee used was *irgez*, which can mean either "a man" or "a husband." I translated it as "the man" because it fits better into the context of a multi-generational family's living in the same house, where girls and women are under the authority of the father, the husband, the oldest brother, or all three. In fact, that was the situation of the interviewee.

References

Association Democratique des Femmes du Maroc. 2007. *Implementation of the CEDAW Convention: Non-Governmental Organizations' Shadow Report to the Third and Fourth Periodic Report of the Moroccan Government: Summary*. Rabat: Association Democratique des Femmes du Maroc.

Global Rights. 2006. "The Moroccan Family Code (Moudawana) of February 5, 2004: An Unofficial English Translation of the Original Arabic Text." Rabat: Global

Rights, December. www.globalrights.org/site/DocServer/Moudawana-English
_Translation.pdf?docID=3106.

——. 2008. *Conditions, Not Conflict: Promoting Women's Human Rights in the Maghreb through Strategic Use of the Marriage Contract*. Rabat: Global Rights.

Hoffman, Katherine E. *We Share Walls: Language, Land, and Gender in Berber Morocco*. Oxford: Blackwell, 2008.

Ilahiane, Hsain. *Ethnicities, Community Making, and Agrarian Change: The Political Ecology of a Moroccan Oasis*. Lanham (MD): University Press of America, 2004.

Ligue Democratique des Droits des Femmes. 2006. "Rapport Annuel 2006." Casablanca: Centre d'information et d'observation des femmes Marocaines.

"Monoghrafia Jam'at [Oued] Al-'liya." 2004. Unpublished manuscript.

Nasir, Jamal J. Ahmed. 2002. *The Islamic Law of Personal Status*. 3rd revised and updated ed. London: Kluwer Law International.

Zoglin, Katie. 2009. "Morocco's Family Code: Improving Equality for Women." *Human Rights Quarterly* 31 (4): 964–84.

Zvan, Katja. 2007. "The Politics of the Reform of the New Family Code (the Moudawana)." Unpublished manuscript. http://users.ox.ac.uk/~metheses/Zvan percent-20thesis.pdf.

Zvan Elliott, Katja. 2009. "Reforming the Moroccan Personal Status Code: A Revolution for Whom?" *Mediterranean Politics* 14 (2): 213–27.

CLAUDIA MERLI

Negotiating Female Genital Cutting (*Sunat*) in Southern Thailand

This chapter examines the performance of a mild form of female genital cutting (FGC) in southern Thailand (locally called *sunat*) and its embeddedness in situational social and family dynamics where religious education, seniority, and gender play a pivotal role in making decisions. The goal of this chapter is to call the reader's attention to the relevance of ethnographic investigation and microanalysis in detecting the existence of plural regional trends that need to be taken into account in planning public health policies. Analyzing selected case studies, this chapter will argue that in this region people following modernist, literalist interpretations of Islam usually reject the practice of FGC. Literalists pursue a direct reading and understanding of the scriptures rather than relying on the traditional interpretations of the Quran and hadiths offered by the major schools (*madhhab*) of Islamic jurisprudence (*fiqh*). These individuals can resort to different strategies to resist the requirement to circumcise girls maintained by the local traditionalist Shafii Muslims (the Shafii *madhhab* is the

Sunni school of *fiqh* followed by the majority of Muslims in Southeast Asia). The antagonism between different understandings of the practice manifests itself at times within a single family. Specifically, I will examine some of the dynamics I witnessed in Satun, a province of southern Thailand. Here, family dynamics are not isolated from the wider field of political and religious diversification, which has become almost palpable in the region in the last ten years, and should therefore be contextualized keeping in mind the increasing fragmentation of the Thai social and political cosmos. I will address issues that can provide valuable insights for government officials, health agencies, and nongovernmental organizations (NGOS) when designing policies for gathering information about the actual practice of FGC and eradicating it.

Female Genital Cutting in Southeast Asia

The practice of milder forms of FGC in Southeast Asia was traditionally underreported in comparison to the wealth of scholarly works on more invasive forms of cutting practiced in African regions. This trend has changed during the last ten years with works on Indonesia and Thailand (for Indonesia, see Budiharsana, Amaliah, Utomo, and Erwinia 2003; Feillard and Marcoes 1998; Newland 2006; Putranti, Faturochman, Muhadjir, and Purwatiningsih 2003; Putranti 2008; for Thailand, see Merli 2008a, 2008b, 2010a). The practice was previously mentioned in anthropological works on Malaysia (Strange 1981; Laderman 1983; Peletz 1996), Indonesia (Snouck Hurgronje 1923–24), and Thailand (Hanks 1963; Lamom 1994), but usually in the context of broader studies on traditional birthing practices or local customs, and not on its own. In Southeast Asia, the cutting is generally limited to an incision in or scratching of either the clitoris or the clitoral hood, what usually is described in the World Health Organization's classification of female genital mutilations as Type IV (any removal of tissue would fall into Type I).

The contentious issue of the possible pre-Islamic origin of FGC in Indonesia (Putranti, Faturochman, Muhadjir, and Purwatiningsih 2003; Putranti 2008) remains unsettled. On the other hand, historical sources as well as contemporary research in Southeast Asia provide evidence for the strong connection between the practice, the spreading of Islam in thirteenth century, and the prevalence of the Shafi *madhhab* (the only Sunni school of law to consider the cutting of the female genitalia obligatory) (Ali 2006; Clarence-Smith 2008 and chapter 5, this volume; Feillard and Marcoes 1998; Merli 2008a).

Thailand's Southern Region

The southern region of Thailand—consisting of the four majority-Muslim provinces of Pattani, Yala, Narathiwat, and Satun—has been characterized by constant political instability. Muslims constitute the largest minority group in Thailand, although there is much debate on their exact numbers. In 1988 Omar Farouk Bajunid (2005, 4) calculated the Muslim national population as between five and seven million, out of Thailand's total population of sixty-five million. Most estimates of the Muslim proportion are between 5 and 8 percent of the national population, although according to other estimates it would be 10 percent (Omar 2005, 4; Imtiyaz 2007, 323). In the four southern provinces bordering Malaysia, Malay-Muslims make up about 75 percent of the local population (quoted in Chaiwat 1987, 19).

Since the 1700s, the southern region of Thailand has been the target of, first, armies from Ayutthaya and the Siamese kingdom and, later, the assimilationist policies of the Thai state. The Malay-Muslims, who once belonged to the independent Patani kingdom (which comprised the contemporary provinces of Pattani, Yala, and Narathiwat), have historically resisted these attempts at assimilation and have organized separatist movements whose activity reached a peak between the end of World War II and the 1970s. When the Anglo-Siam treaty was signed in 1909, Satun territory, located on the southwestern coast and then part of the Kedah sultanate, was assigned to Siam. Satun is nowadays championed as an example of successful integration of a majority Muslim population into the Thai state with no insurgency activity recorded. A period of relative peace in the wider southern region started in the 1980s with effective programs of collaboration with the local population. Since 2000 the area has been in the headlines again with an escalation of violence that cannot be ascribed exclusively to separatist militants. The government of former Prime Minister Thaksin Shinawatra responded with tough repression and the enforcement of martial law and a curfew. The military coup of September 2006 that put an end to Shinawatra's mandate did not bring the much-hoped-for resolution of the conflict in the south. The entrenched instability of the region is paralleled by the deep division at the national level between support-ers of the ousted prime minister (called Red Shirts because of their apparel) and the loyalists (called Yellow Shirts).[1] Between 2009 and 2010, Bangkok, the capital city, was besieged by the Red Shirts' mass demonstrations and protests, demanding democratic elections. The situation became untenable and broke into urban guerrilla warfare between demonstrators and the army and police forces in April–May 2010. Although the situation has now returned to normalcy, the 3 July 2011 election which made Shinawatra's younger sister the new prime minister suggests that the calm surface hides an intractable division of opinions and loyalty between the two groups. In the south, the major political opposition overlaps with local fragmentations of the Islamic community, creating a sense of generalized insecurity and lack of trust among people within the local society, and a sort of self-censorship makes the issue a taboo topic in conversations. In the past, a major divide between the Kaum Tua (the Old Group, the traditionalists who follow the local Shafii *madhhab* and Sufi tradition) and the Kaum Muda (the Young Group, the reformists who follow more literalist interpretations) accounted for the major differences of interpretation of ritual activities and social life. Nowadays the proliferation of religious educational institutions and the presence of college graduates and clerics returning to Thailand after spending the years of their education in the Middle East or northern Africa (where they were influenced by Wahhabi and Salafist interpretations of the scriptures) render the situation more complex. This combination of factors explains the polarization of religious discourses and diatribes among local leaders, clerics, and congregations.

According to the latest census, from 2000, the population of Satun Prov-ince amounts to 247,900 people, of whom 67.8 percent are Muslims and 31.9 percent are Buddhists. Approximately 10 percent of the Muslims speak Thai and Malay (National Statistical Office 2001). Alongside modern medical prac-tices, literalist Islamic streams contribute to the criticism or neglect of ritual practices once considered uniform among local Muslims (Merli 2008a). The increasing medicalization of birth and the progressive marginalization of in-digenous midwives (called *mootamjae* in Thai and *bidan* in Malay) have also affected medical and ritual practices related to reproduction; female *sunat* is traditionally performed by Muslim *bidan* and is not undergoing the same process of medicalization as male ritual circumcision (Merli 2008a, 2010a, 2010b).

Methodology

I conducted anthropological research in Satun Province for a total of eighteen months since 2003. My fieldwork on reproductive health and traditional midwifery revealed that one of the practices performed by indigenous midwives was a mild form of female genital cutting locally called *sunat*, usually performed on newborn babies during the mother's postpartum seclusion period of forty days—therefore considered a perinatal practice because it was performed within the first year of the child's life.

Apart from the material accumulated during this time, in 2009–10 I started a series of more specific questionnaire-based interviews with both men and women investigating their experiences of and attitudes toward male and female genital cutting. This series complements my semi-structured interviews and informal conversations with local Islamic clerics and informants and is not yet completed. The material presented in this chapter is a first analysis of the data collected thus far. I selected cases from a sample of the semi-structured interviews that show how different opinions on the practice of FGC may coexist in the same region. They also illustrate the relevance of seniority in connection to gender for the process of making a decision about performing *sunat*. This kind of authoritativeness may be contested by individuals who can claim a distinct source of credibility. I conducted the interviews in Thai and Malay with the assistance of a local interpreter. There were fifty formal and semistructured interviews on male circumcision and FGC, and the analysis was conducted coding for the decision-making process, arrangement for celebration, season of performance, age of child, reasons for performing the cutting, and its optionality or obligatoriness.

Women at the Crossroad

The performance of female *sunat* is associated with postpartum practices for the mother, and women are responsible for negotiating and arranging it. Only women can be present during the cutting. If a Buddhist woman converts to Islam, for example to marry a Muslim man, whether or not she will be asked to be circumcised will depend on the view of the matter that the groom's family (especially his mother) holds. I have witnessed one female *sunat* performed on a baby by the same *bidan* who had taken care of the baby's mother during the gestation.[2] The women whose cases I discuss below communicated feelings of uncertainty concerning the status of the practice in the contemporary social context, as local religious knowledge on this matter is far from monolithic.

MARYAH

During a fieldwork sojourn in 2009–10 I met a woman I will call Maryah,[3] who had resisted female elders' questioning about her younger daughter's *sunat*. Our meeting was born from a coincidence. From my field notes:

> Wednesday 6 January 2010. While going for lunch my assistant received a telephone call from a friend in village A who [according to my assistant] sounded quite alarmed. Maryah had received the visit of a female relative who started questioning her about her daughter being already circumcised or not. She did not answer directly because she felt confused; in fact, another woman she knows had not circumcised her own baby girl but now Maryah's own relatives came to ask, implying that she should do it. She wants to talk to the Datok [Islamic judge] to ask what is the correct position to be held [on this issue]. I say I want to talk to her.

I asked my assistant to arrange a meeting for the following day. Maryah was then in her mid-thirties, educated (she had obtained an undergraduate degree), outspoken, and assertive. The day I met her she was dressed in blue jeans, a checked shirt with sleeves rolled up, and a black veil (*hijab*). When I arrived at her shop (in the front of her house), she was attending to some customers with two assistants working nearby. She led us through the shop's corridors into her house. Here, her eight-month-old daughter was sleeping in a fabric cradle hanging from a metal spring. A woman in black clothes sat on the tiled floor and looked after the baby. Maryah has another daughter who was then seven years old. When I asked Maryah what made her call the day before, she said that she was torn between the opposite local views about whether the cutting practice for girls, for which she used the Thai term *dtat* (literally, "to cut"), was *wadjib* (obligatory) or only *sunna* (customary). She added that she knows that *sunat* for the boy is *wadjib*. She was attempting to find a correct and incontrovertible answer based on Islamic law and jurisprudence to provide to those relatives who were questioning her in a rather pressuring way. Until that moment her strategy had been to avoid answering altogether, but this option was not tenable in the long term.

Maryah's first daughter had been cut at the age of one by Tok Moo (the Malay honorific term *tok* is followed by the general Thai term for medical practitioners, *moo*), who was then an elderly woman living in the village where Maryah had resided before marriage and whose name was suggested by a female neighbor. Maryah took her oldest daughter to Tok Moo's house, accompanied by her mother and the neighbor, and bringing along betel leaves (*bai phluu*), a gift often included in ritual exchanges both between people and between humans and the spiritual world. In performing *sunat*, Tok Moo passed one betel leaf over the girl's external genitalia, both the clitoris and the vaginal opening, while reciting a *doa* (or *dua*, meaning prayer in Arabic) in Arabic (to which Maryah referred to as "the *khaek* language").[4] Tok Moo then took a razor and scratched the skin of the clitoral hood, while pressing the clitoris over a piece of clean bamboo. Maryah described the extent of the area scratched as a triangle shape, one to three millimeters long. When some blood appeared, Tok Moo stopped reciting the *doa* and immediately applied a cotton swab soaked in iodine. At this point, the girl started crying louder. Maryah dressed her daughter in trousers and brought her home. The baby ate and slept regularly, but for two or three days following *sunat*, she cried every time she passed urine. After every urination, Maryah reapplied iodine on the scratch. No *nuri* (a shortened local form of the Malay term *kenduri*, a feast, which includes the accumulation of religious merit—locally referred to as "to make merit") was organized.

Since her younger daughter's birth, Maryah had received visits at regular intervals from her mother and her mother-in-law, who independently asked her whether *sunat* had been performed. Maryah was aware that in old women's opinion, *sunat* for girls is *wadjib* as it is for boys, and she contrasted this position with the presence of "new knowledge" (in Thai, *lakkan mai*: literally, "new principles"). In the beginning, her answer to the female relatives was "I will do it in the future," but the answer had recently shifted to "already done." I asked her what would happen if her mother or mother-in-law decided to check, and she replied that since there is no visible change to the appearance of the genitals, they could not detect the performance of the cutting. Her response is similar to other informants' testimonies, agreeing that there is no "real" cutting.

When talking about the practice in general terms, Maryah said that in the past "everyone must do it." Nevertheless, also in the past the female *sunat* was organized and performed very swiftly and no *nuri* was offered to guests. Under these circumstances, questions arise about the strategies to secure the performance of a practice which is done without any public acknowledgment in the form of celebration (such as the social meal provided to up to hundreds of guests on the occasion of a male circumcision) and performed without leaving any visible anatomical change. I asked Maryah how people would know that *sunat* had been performed and what consequences would have to be faced if a woman decided not to have it performed. She answered that people are informed "by talking [among women]." Of course, women do not talk of their own *sunat*, which they can usually neither remember nor physically assess, but they do talk about others' *sunat*. The decision about performing it rests primarily with a baby girl's maternal grandmother (often also with her paternal grandmother) and depends on residential arrangements. Because she can accompany the baby to the *bidan* or *mho*, she would be a witness, someone who can later report on and guarantee its completion. The practitioner is obviously another reliable source of information.

Maryah is convinced that people nowadays are very "confused" (*sapson*), a term that has a sense of insecurity, indecision) and that "if they can choose," they prefer not to perform it. This statement hinted at the possibility that some individuals' agency and decision-making power are limited. According to Maryah, they belong to families that "are not open-minded" and can impose their decision: "they are not modern."

ROZIAH

Originally from the Isaan region (in northeastern Thailand), Roziah is the woman who was looking after Maryah's little daughter. She was then in her mid-forties, and she had relocated to the southern region about ten years earlier, when she converted to Islam and married a man from Satun. She was circumcised in relation to her conversion. Roziah claimed that back then she did not know that the practice was not "necessary," and that to convert to Islam (*khao Islam*, literally, "to enter Islam") it is sufficient to pronounce the *shahadah*, the declaration of faith. This testifies to the presence in Satun of an established discourse that claims the performance of *sunat* is compulsory for women, especially in relation to becoming a Muslim. *Sunat* marks the entrance in the faith for both newborn girls and converting adult women. Retelling her story, Roziah described her experience of discomfort for two to three days following the cutting; but when I asked her to assess differences in tissues, feeling, and sensitivity, she said she could not otherwise perceive "any change."

In Roziah's story, it is evident that her recent acquisition of information about the requirements for conversion made her assess critically a practice that she had agreed to perform following local people's directives. The opposition between a traditional and a modern understanding of religious practice emerges.

KOMAL

Komal is a public health officer who was born in Patthalung Province (bordering Satun Province) but who has lived in Satun most of her life. In the Muslim community in Patthalung, not unlike the case in Satun, people do not organize a *nuri* for female *sunat*. Komal's position on the subject stands out from the others I collected, since she claimed that only women who convert to Islam (that is, who were not born Muslim) must be circumcised, not girls born into a Muslim family. Her story identifies regional differences in the performance. According to Komal, about twenty years ago in Patthalung the custom was that the indigenous midwife would use a betel leaf to touch the clitoris, whereby a cut was avoided altogether. As mentioned above, a betel leaf was used by the practitioner who scratched on Maryah's daughter with a razor. Komal contended that in Islam there is a difference between male *sunat*, which is *wadjib*, and female *sunat*, which is not, but there are variations depending on the region and local opinion and practice.

SUMMARY

Women in the cases presented above explained the existence of diverging opinions on the practice of female *sunat* as related to Islamic modernity, to the introduction of new knowledge or principles. In contrast, families and especially elderly women holding fast to the Old Group view try to exert control over younger women to secure their compliance with the practice. The open-mindedness that Maryah referred to can be backed with religious authority, as literalist interpretations of the scriptures contrast with interpretations of traditionalist schools.

Influential Men

From the interviews and conversations I collected, it was evident that men shared the opinion that female *sunat* was not necessary. Some even opposed it

as not belonging to Islam. They based this consideration on the lack of reference to female circumcision in the Quran and the lack of agreement on the
interpretation of hadiths among the schools of jurisprudence. The deeper a
man's knowledge of religious texts, the more likely he was to consider female
sunat unnecessary, even un-Islamic.

SULAIMAN

During a meeting with the chairman of the local Islamic committee to discuss
the practice and organization of group male circumcisions, he pointed at different views held by the four major Sunni *madhhab* on the matter of *sunat* for girls.
Deciding whether or not to perform the ritual on a daughter would primarily
depend on the specific *madhhab* followed by a family. This kind of awareness
is displayed by men who have a broader knowledge of the differences existing
among the various schools of jurisprudence. Another example is Sulaiman, a
man in his late thirties who studied Islamic law in the Middle East. He is a much
respected person, and his opinion is considered authoritative. His firm position
is that *sunat* is not *wadjib* for women and therefore does not need to be performed. During a conversation we had, I made reference to the famous scholar
Abu Zakariyya Yahya bin Sharaf al-Nawawi (1233–78) and his position on the
matter (from his work *Tahara*) that female *sunat* is obligatory, *wadjib*. Sulaiman
replied that al-Nawawi cannot be taken as representative of the Shafii *madhhab* in its entirety, since the school comprises different opinions. Moreover, he
emphasized that Muslims in Thailand are very influenced by Sufism and that it
would be reductive to consider them exclusively as Shafii. His position comes
across as not merely doctrinal. When the time arrived to circumcise his daughter, he refused to let *sunat* be arranged, defending this decision against his own
mother, who wanted to arrange for the ritual. His resolution became known in
the village; in fact, Wati, a female neighbor who was not certain about having
sunat performed on her own daughter, asked his opinion. Despite his reiteration
that female *sunat* was not obligatory, Wati yielded to the pressures exerted by
her relatives and decided that, since the practice was considered compulsory in
the village, she had to abide by the tradition. Wati finally organized the cutting
a few weeks after her daughter was born, summoning from another village an
indigenous midwife whom her family trusted. Although Sulaiman could stick to
his decision, in the same social context Wati could not. She was married to the
youngest son of the household and was living with her in-laws, so her position

was particularly weak.[5] Sulaiman's position was strong because it was based on his personal prestige and widely recognized knowledge of Islamic jurisprudence.

AHMAD

As I discovered during my research, individual doctrinal positions on the issue of female *sunat* are not immutable. Ahmad is a teacher in a local *madrasa*. He is fluent in Arabic and obtained a master's degree in Egypt. I have known him for several years, and in the course of our acquaintance, influenced by the public debate in Egypt, he has changed his position on the issue of female *sunat* and FGC. In April 2009, I visited Ahmad while he was finishing an Arabic language class with three female students, all wearing the *niqab* (a long veil covering a woman's face except her eyes, and locally worn by women who use a cloak to cover their body down the thighs, a sign of the increasing influence of more literalist streams in southern Thailand). Explaining my present research project to the students, he went on to explain that the Arabic term *khifaton* refers to female circumcision and *khitan* to the male procedure. Our conversation on the topic thus turned into a lesson for the students. He used the expression "girls must do it in secret and only a little bit" and specified that according to the Maliki *madhhab*, it is not compulsory but only *sunna*. However, immediately afterward he firmly stated that in his opinion women "must" do it, since it is *wadjib*.

Before 2009 whenever we had talked about this topic, he had claimed that the female *sunat* was not necessary, supporting his view by mentioning that there were authoritative legal opinions against it issued by influential Islamic clerics and academics in Al-Azhar University. To my great surprise during my fieldwork sojourn in 2009, I discovered that he had changed his mind and now deemed the procedure compulsory, *wadjib*. He had discovered other hadiths that he had not previously known and whose interpretation can support the practice. On theological grounds, he still opposed severe degrees of cutting (excision) such as the one performed in Egypt. He stated that the hadith Abu Dawud (the one most commonly referred to when disputing the requirement for female circumcision and one that he had mentioned on previous occasions) specifies that the cut should be limited.[6] He also claimed that there is no mention of female *sunat* in the Quran, whereas male circumcision is referred to in the form of Ibrahim's (Abraham's) sacrifice.[7] Local people do usually discuss female and male circumcision practices as associated topics by describing the differences between them, and for this reason I believe it is necessary to conduct research on both practices and related local discourses when both forms coexist (Merli 2010a). One hypothesis I have to explain Ahmad's change of opinion is that he had recently assumed a responsible role in one of the local mosques and therefore was strongly influenced by the doctrinal interpretations that were prevalent in that specific context. He had passed from a more literalist, modernist view to a more traditionalist one.

TOK IMAM MUSA

Another example I want to discuss concerns a Malay-speaking village that I visited in 2010 on the occasion of a group male circumcision organized under the banner of public health authorities. According to the village imam, female *sunat* is not compulsory and is a matter of choice for the family. He reported that a publication from Malaysia stated that uncircumcised girls would be more at risk of committing *zina* — having sexual relations out of wedlock. He stated that in his village, girls are usually circumcised between the age of two and five, and that if *sunat* is performed on the same day of *akikah* (the name-giving ceremony) there is a celebration with a *nuri*.[8] If performed on its own, no celebration follows female *sunat*. People in the village would not know when a girl is circumcised because there is no public celebration or discussion of it. Tok Imam Musa also claimed that male circumcision is not *wadjib* if it must be performed on an adult man converting to Islam and who fears the operation, whereas it is *wadjib* for Muslim boys. This description is the opposite of the one expressed by Komal and described above, according to which female *sunat* is compulsory only for converts.

PAK OSMAN

An episode that aptly illustrates the existence of complex familial dynamics on the subject of female *sunat* occurred in December 2009, when I went to visit an elderly Islamic scholar and teacher in a *madrasa*. He is recognized as a local authority on religious issues, highly respected, and considered a very pious man. He studied in the Middle East and still travels abroad on a regular basis. His children pursued higher education in the Middle East as well. He is a calm narrator, answering questions very clearly and plainly, using illustration and vivid metaphors. During our interviews, family members usually sat nearby and joined the conversations. In discussing *sunat* for girls, he thought we should start by sorting out the vocabulary used. He distinguished between:

(1) *sunnah* (the way of the Prophet), that which is considered preferable but not compulsory; (2) *sunahti*, literally, "my own way," which would not be as important as the way of the Prophet; (3) *wadjib*, that which is compulsory or obligatory; and (4) *sunat*, a term used locally for circumcision. "*Sunat* is *wadjib* for the boys but *sunnah* for the girls," he said, and for girls the cutting must be limited. Although he agreed that al-Nawawi considered it *wadjib* also for girls, he stated that there are different opinions about what is required for women and therefore there is the possibility to choose, whereas there is no choice concerning boys' circumcision. On both boys and girls, *sunat* would have the effect of lessening *nafsu* (passions), helping to control sexual desire.

During this conversation, his wife and daughter intervened, first by hindering my assistant's translation, then by making statements and interrupting the narration of the *alim* (cleric). The two women strongly contended that female *sunat* is also *wadjib*. Reiterating that I should convert to Islam, they added that if I converted and had *sunat* performed on the same day, all my past sins would be forgiven and my life would begin anew. With the intention of supporting the *alim*'s scholarly view, I observed that his opinion was in opposition to theirs. Since the young woman insisted on her position, her mother tried to dissuade her from being so vigorous in her argumentation, lest I be unnecessarily scared. The atmosphere was rather tense, and I had not anticipated ever witnessing this sort of open disagreement, which was very unusual in Thailand's social context. My assistant was addressed directly in Thai by the two women, who were aware that my understanding of Thai was very limited compared to my knowledge of Malay, the language of my dialogue with the *alim*. For the remainder of the interview, which I refocused on the topic of past ritual male circumcisions in the village, the two women maintained the same obtrusive pattern, managing to prevent our conversation. The situation proved difficult for me to manage, while the *alim* remained very still and aloof, observing. The *alim*'s wife even stated that her husband "was not saying the correct thing." The assertion left me dismayed, given Pak Osman's authoritativeness. In deciding to counter the two women's position, I championed the aged man's unique experience and knowledge of local history by saying "he is the memory of this land." I was implicitly saying that they should stop talking.

This taxing encounter gave me some insights. First, the exchange made it evident that the two women could effectively halt the interview process by obstructing the work of my assistant, a younger, educated woman from the area who was well acquainted with them and perceived her position in those circumstances as subaltern. On a subsequent visit my decision to be accompanied by a male assistant partially prevented the same pattern from being repeated. Second, the encounter led me to reconsider the degree of authoritativeness that women can derive from being related to respected male figures. As described in the stories above, women who searched for supportive legal or theological arguments were not able to use these if they occupied a weaker position in respect to other women in the household or family. Third, the episode with Pak Osman demonstrated the degree of control women can exert on conversation, openly challenging even authoritative male figures, and by way of these, a female anthropologist who is engaging local men in debates and scholarly research.[9]

Conclusion

Maryah's case is important because it raises a series of issues. The strategy she decided to adopt was to not tell the truth. This option was feasible only because the degree of cutting was unnoticeable. When Maryah needed an answer to the pressures of her mother and mother-in-law, she made two immediate resolutions: to find a good reason (and an appropriate way of communicating it) to refuse the insistence of her relatives and to make sure this reason was correct from a religious point of view—that is, incontrovertible. Her final choice was to let people believe that she had complied with the requirement, without presenting them with new knowledge (usually considered the position of the Young Group). She was initially looking for an authoritative source that would be accepted by her female relatives—specifically a male authority, educated and extremely respected at the local level, a kādī (doctor of the law or Islamic judge), rather than an alim or imam. Clerics and imams in the local social context may have very different views on religious and social issues depending on their congregations and mosques; a certain degree of internal division extends into political positions. The opinion of a man of Sharia would be above local disputes and is indeed the one authority people resort to have disputes settled and cases adjudicated.

Religious knowledge and authority are respected, but two problems need to be considered: first, knowledge of and expertise in Sharia are fragmented because of the plurality of jurisprudential interpretations available (in the four major Sunni *madhhab*); second, in facing conflicting opinions, women who want to avoid having *sunat* performed on their daughters run into other factors that have an impact on their final decision. The most relevant aspect is almost certainly the existing pattern of postmarital residence. Neolocality ensures a margin of autonomy in case like Maryah's, whereas patrilocality or matri-locality would give the elders of the household, especially the elderly women, a notable degree of authority. The arrangements to perform *sunat* at home rather than at the *bidan*'s house are equally pertinent in relation to residence.

During our conversation, Maryah asked my opinion of the performance of *sunat*, attributing to an anthropologist (specializing in the region and with extended fieldwork experience with indigenous midwives on the topic of re-productive health and perinatal practices) the required knowledge to influence local opinion, whether individual or collective. The anthropologist is required to assume a position in a situation similar to what Michael Peletz cogently de-scribed for Malaysia: "The key debates—and certainly the ones that are most intensely felt—in other words, bear on *intra*-civilizational clashes not those of an inter-civilizational variety" (2005, 243). The problem is therefore related to specific positions held by local groups on the more general understanding of sources of Islamic practices. I can very generally pose it as mapping onto the opposition between traditionalist Shafii and the literalists. This opposition is locally characterized as Kaum Tua versus Kaum Muda, respectively, and several informants referred to the people considering female *sunat* not to be obligatory as "young Muslims" (in Malay, "Islam *muda*").

People identifying themselves as Shafii would also consider changes in the local practice of *sunat* for girls as *bid'a* (unwarranted innovation).[10] But innova-tion with respect to which tradition? According to the *Encyclopedia of Islam*,

> Al-S͟hāiʿī laid down the principle that any innovation which runs
> contrary to the Ḳurʾān, the sunna, idjmāʿ, or at͟har (a tradition
> traced only to a Companion or a Follower) is an erring innovation, whereas any
> good thing introduced which does not run counter to any of these sources is
> praiseworthy. On this basis innovations have been classified according to
> the five categories (aḥkām) of Muslim law... But a number of traditions
> condemning innovations are found in the collections of Ḥadīt͟h
> as statements of the Prophet. (Robson 2010)

Since the interpretation of the hadith Sunan Abu Dawud is contentious, positions on female *sunat* are not homogeneous.

The point is that female circumcision is already a very controversial issue at the level of *sunna*; only a few hadiths mention the practice, and these are controversial at best. A male informant in 2009 told me that there is a reaction against the influence of other *madhhab* reaching southern Thailand through the experience of people who had studied abroad. To this trend corresponds a reaffirmation of the Shafii *maddhab*, with the growing number of supposedly traditional celebrations, even in mosques not previously known as associated with the Kaum Tua. The modernity Maryah referred to as linked to open-mindedness is also to be ascribed to the modern religious education pursued abroad, in countries where the scholarly traditions of other *madhhab* and literalist interpretations are prevalent. These new ideas can easily be perceived as unwarranted innovations by the more traditionalist Shafii. This opposition is partly generational.

In a social landscape characterized by oppositions between groups that go beyond the simply religious opinion and have consequences on affiliations to specific mosques and therefore also political activity, it is of paramount importance to identify local influential figures in the debate. Far from suggesting that women resort to male authority to influence female decision making, I recommend weighing the influence these men's opinions may have when solicited to address family disagreements on issues such as the performance of female *sunat*.

From the perspective of applied medical anthropology, four issues should be considered in designing policies to eradicate FGC. First, it is necessary to gather the results of up-to-date ethnography and deepen the understanding of local sociopolitical contexts and changes in attitudes in order to implement and achieve any durable change in the practices. Second, long-term fieldwork-based research will provide an insider's knowledge to identify key authoritative figures whose opinions can make a difference in the local community. Third, to design a successful policy it is necessary to endorse strategies leading to micro-projects that are focused and spatially limited. Fourth, it is of paramount importance to devote specific attention to established intrafamilial (gendered) dynamics. In Muslim southern Thailand where this research was conducted, one of the facts that surfaced was that women have decision-making power on internal family matters, a picture that is very different from the allegedly one-dimensional patriarchal myth of compliant Muslim women.

Notes

1 For an excellent political analysis of the southern situation, see McCargo 2008. For an appraisal of the national political crisis, see Funston 2009.

2 For a description of the ritual, see Merli 2008b.

3 All the names of informants in the text are pseudonyms.

4 In Thailand the term *khaek* (literally, 'guest' or foreigner) is used to identify the Muslims, who often resent it. It is also used by local Thai speakers to refer to both Malay and Arabic languages. In the case mentioned in the text, I asked Maryah to clarify the meaning.

5 In the region, it is customary for the youngest child (whether a son or a daughter) to remain in the paternal house to care for the parents as they become old.

6 Sunan Abu Dawud, book 41, number 5251, Narrated Umm Atiyyah al-Ansariyyah: "A woman used to perform circumcision in Medina. The Prophet (peace be upon him) said to her: Do not cut severely as that is better for a woman and more desirable for a husband."

7 There is no explicit reference to male circumcision in the Quran.

8 The *akikah* is usually performed shortly after birth, and in any case before the age of one.

9 I would not stretch this interpretation so far as to say that women can always challenge authority in public discourse (however useful the public-private dichotomy may be in this case), although I would be inclined to consider the conversation with a Western anthropologist as not a private domestic talk. I have mentioned elsewhere (Merli 2008b, 2010a) how outspoken elderly women may challenge male views on female *sunat* even in a public setting.

10 One example of a practice pointed to as *bid'a* in Satun is the use of beads to recite the names of Allah, which recent interpretations shun as opposing tradition (which uses fingers to reckon).

References

Ali, Kecia. 2006. *Sexual Ethics and Islam: Feminist Reflections on Qur'an, Hadith, and Jurisprudence*. Oxford: Oneworld.

Budiharsana, Meiwita, Lila Amaliah, Budi Utomo, and Erwinia. 2003. *Female Circumcision in Indonesia: Extent, Implications and Possible Interventions to Uphold Women's Health Rights*. Jakarta: Population Council.

Chaiwat, Satha-Anand. 1987. *Islam and Violence: A Case Study of Violent Events in the Four Southern Provinces, Thailand, 1976-1981*. Tampa: University of South Florida, Department of Religious Studies.

Clarence-Smith, William G. 2008. "Islam and Female Genital Cutting in Southeast Asia: The Weight of the Past." *Finnish Journal of Ethnicity and Migration* 3 (2): 14-22.

Feillard, Andrée and Lies Marcoes. 1998. "Female Circumcision in Indonesia: To 'Islamize' in Ceremony or Secrecy." *Archipel* 56:339-67.

Funston, John, ed. 2009. *Divided over Thaksin: Thailand's Coup and Problematic Transition*. Singapore: Institute of Southeast Asian Studies.

Hanks, Jane Richardson. 1963. *Maternity and Its Rituals in Bang Chan*. Ithaca, NY: Cornell University Press.

Imtiyaz, Yusuf. 2007. "The Southern Thailand Conflict and the Muslim world." *Journal of Muslim Minority Affairs* 27 (2): 319-39.

Laderman, Carol. 1983. *Wives and Midwives: Childbirth and Nutrition in Rural Malaysia*. Berkeley: University of California Press.

Lamom, Khommapat. 1994. "Folk Beliefs of Thai Muslims on Maternal and Child Health in Four Southern Border Provinces [in Thai]." Master's thesis, Mahidol University.

McCargo, Duncan. 2008. *Tearing the Land apart: Islam and Legitimacy in Southern Thailand*. Ithaca, NY: Cornell University Press.

Merli, Claudia. 2008a. *Bodily Practices and Medical Identities in Southern Thailand*. Uppsala, Sweden: Acta Universitatis Upsaliensis.

——. 2008b. "*Sunat* for Girls in Southern Thailand: Its Relation to Traditional Midwifery, Male Circumcision and Other Obstetrical Practices." *Finnish Journal of Ethnicity and Migration* 3 (2): 32-41.

——. 2010a. "Male and Female Genital Cutting among Southern Thailand's Muslims: Rituals, Biomedical Practices, and Local Discourses." *Culture, Health and Sexuality* 12 (7): 725-38.

——. 2010b. "Muslim Midwives between Traditions and Modernities: Being and Becoming a *Bidan Kampung* in Satun Province, Southern Thailand." In "La santé: miroir des sociétés d'Asie du Sud-Est," edited by Laurence Husson, special issue of *Moussons* 15: 121–35.

National Statistical Office, Office of the Prime Minister. 2001. *The 2000 Population and Housing Census, Changwat Satun.* Bangkok: National Statistical Office.

Newland, Lynda. 2006. "Female Circumcision: Muslim Identities and Zero Tolerance Policies in Rural West Java." *Women's Studies International Forum* 29 (4): 394–404.

Omar Farouk Bajunid. 1987. "The Origins and Evolution of Malay-Muslim Ethnic Nationalism in Southern Thailand." In *Islam and Society in Southeast Asia*, edited by Taufik Abdullah and Sharon Siddique, 250–81. Singapore: Institute of Southeast Asian Studies.

———. 2005. "Islam, Nationalism, and the Thai State." In *Dynamic Diversity in Southern Thailand*, edited by Wattana Sugunnasil, 1–19. Pattani, Thailand: Prince of Songkhla University.

Peletz, Michael G. 1996. *Reason and Passion: Representations of Gender in a Malay Society.* Berkeley: University of California Press.

———. 2005. "Islam and the Cultural Politics of Legitimacy: Malaysia in the Aftermath of September 11." In *Remaking Muslim Politics: Pluralism, Contestation, Democratization*, edited by Robert W. Hefner, 240–72. Princeton: Princeton University Press.

Putranti, Basilica D. 2008. "To Islamize, Becoming a Real Woman, or Commercialized Practices? Questioning Female Genital Cutting in Indonesia." *Finnish Journal of Ethnicity and Migration* 3 (2): 23–31.

Faturochman, Darwin Muhadjir, and Sri Purwatiningsih. 2003. *Male and Female Genital Cutting among Javanese and Madurese.* Yogyakarta, Indonesia: Gadjah Mada University, Center for Population and Policy Studies.

Robson, J. 2010. "Bid'a." In *Encyclopaedia of Islam*, edited by P. Bearman, Th. Bianquis, C. E. Bosworth, E. van Donzel, and W. P. Heinrichs 1:1199. 2nd ed. Leiden: Brill.

Snouck Hurgronje, Christiaan. 1923–24. *Verspreide geschriften.* 6 vols. The Hague: Martinus Nijhoff.

Strange, Heather. 1981. *Rural Malay Women in Tradition and Transition.* New York: Praeger.

PART THREE

The Law
in Action

STEPHANIE WILLMAN BORDAT WITH SAIDA KOUZZI

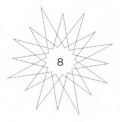

The Marriage Contract in the Maghreb

CHALLENGES AND OPPORTUNITIES FOR WOMEN'S RIGHTS

Detailed Marriage Contracts: Rationale and Justification

In Algeria, Morocco, and Tunisia, matters having to do with marriage, divorce, and property that affect women's rights are governed by family or personal status laws.[1] In contrast to other legislation governing contracts, torts, criminal matters, and commerce—which are derived from secular, European-style civil codes—family or personal status laws are based on Islamic precepts.[2] While this religious exceptionalism often prevents women from exercising their basic human rights, it also presents a unique opportunity to use common marriage contracts as a tool for promoting women's rights in the three countries of the Maghreb described here.

This chapter describes the first phases of an ongoing civil-society initiative to promote women's human and legal rights in the Maghreb through strategic use of the marriage contract. Lessons learned from action research at the grassroots level reveal changing legal and social ideas about the family as a biological, economic, and affective unit; current tensions between these different conceptions; and diverse practical obstacles to reconciling these when concluding a marriage contract. They also illustrate ways in which women in the Maghreb today understand their rights in the family and seek to articulate and exercise them within a dynamic context of legal reform and public debate on women's issues.

UNDER ISLAMIC LAW

According to Islamic legal theory, marriage is a civil contract between spouses—not a sacrament, as in some other religious traditions. The concept of marriage as a contract implies a negotiated agreement between two consenting parties that creates legally enforceable obligations. Spouses are free to define their respective rights and duties through detailed clauses introduced into the marriage contract. In addition, failing to respect such clauses is considered a breach of contract, for which the wronged spouse may seek a remedy such as compensation and divorce.

> Regarding contracts the Prophet (Peace be upon him) said:
> The rights are decided by the conditions.[3]

Academics and legal practitioners alike have examined the concept of marriage as a contract in Islamic law, illustrating its basis in classical jurisprudence as well as analyzing the varying degrees of its use in practice historically and currently as a tool to protect women's rights in marriage.[4] It is beyond the scope of this chapter to go into detail on the doctrinal basis for this principle. Instead, the authors focus on its application in reality in the contemporary Maghreb and examine current challenges to the use of the marriage contract as a strategy to promote women's rights.

IN NATIONAL LEGISLATION

The laws that are discussed here from all three countries of the Maghreb explicitly reaffirm the principle that marriage is a freely negotiated contract between two consenting parties that creates legally binding obligations.[5] The 2005 amendments to the Algerian Family Code refer specifically to the "marriage contract," in comparison to the 1984 code, which referred only to "marriage."

The Moroccan and Algerian Family Codes—even prior to the reforms of 2004 and 2005, respectively[6]—and the 1956 Tunisian Personal Status Code all provide that spouses may stipulate the addition of negotiated clauses to their marriage contract.[7] In addition, the laws give specific examples of written conditions protective of women's rights that may be added to the marriage contract, including those related to personal rights such as monogamy clauses (Morocco and Algeria), the delegation to the wife of the husband's right to repudiation (Morocco), and the wife's right to work (Algeria), as well as clauses related to property ownership and division (all three countries).[8] These articles essentially allow future spouses to stipulate any and all conditions they agree on to the marriage contract, provided the clauses are not in contradiction with the inherent nature of marriage.[9] The violation of a clause is considered a breach of contract for which the wronged party may seek a remedy, including compensation and divorce.[10]

UNDER CUSTOMARY LAW

Local customary laws in the Maghreb have also reflected the contractual nature of marriage and allowed stipulations designed to protect women's rights. In the southern Souss region of Morocco, brides prepare a written inventory listing and estimating all of their possessions and gifts they bring with them to the marital home, and this list is included in the marriage contract. In addition, the Souss customary law of *sukoun* provides that the husband must give his wife either a house or two plots of land.[11]

Traditional community property type systems known as *kad o saiya* in the Souss and *chka* (both may be loosely translated as "effort") in northern Morocco provide that on dissolution of a marriage by divorce or the husband's death, a woman is entitled to a share of the property he acquired during the marriage in compensation for her moral and physical efforts and work in the household.[12]

In Algeria, the practice of pronouncing *katie achart* (agreement on conditions) after the exchange of consent signifies consent to all negotiated—even only verbally—conditions before the official marriage ceremony at the city hall. According to this custom, lack of non respect of one of the conditions by one of the spouses can lead to the dissolution of the marriage.

Despite the fact that classical Islamic doctrine, national legislation, and local customary laws all affirm the contractual principle of marriage and provide for the stipulation of clauses protecting women's rights as described above, in practice such additional conditions are rarely included in the marriage contract. In the vast majority of marriages in the Maghreb, the written contract consists of a single page with the names and signatures of the parties and their witnesses, the amount of the dowry, and the date of the marriage, with no additional information or clauses.

In only 424 of the 289,821 marriages in Morocco in 2006 did couples draw up a separate marital property contract, and in 2007 there were just 900 marital property contracts out of 316,411 marriages.[13] A random survey of thirty-four marriage contracts filed at the Khemisset Family Court in the period August–October 2007 conducted by a local lawyers' association found that only one had an additional clause stipulated into it, in which the husband agreed not to be absent from the conjugal home for more than three months at a time. None had a separate marital property contract attached.[14] The Moroccan government has recognized that such contracts are rare, attributing this to romantic notions held by couples and their reluctance to think about divorce at the time of marriage.[15]

It is indisputable that women in the Maghreb, as elsewhere in the world, continue to suffer from inequality and discrimination in both laws and in practice. Under the existing Family and Personal Codes, for example, women have restricted access to divorce, polygamy is legal,[16] women have fewer rights than their husbands when it comes to child custody and guardianship, women are not guaranteed access to adequate housing during marriage or on its dissolution, alimony is not awarded on divorce, and women's unpaid work in the household is rarely taken into account when dividing up marital property. In addition, social and cultural norms can limit or deny women's rights to freedom of movement, to continue studies, to work outside of the home, to control their own reproduction, and to freedom from all forms of violence. Even laws that are positive on their face are often not applied by courts and those officials charged with enforcing them. There is thus a discrepancy between repeated positive perceptions of women's rights in the Maghreb in the current climate of family law reform and the realities of women's lives.[17]

Persisting inequality and discrimination against women could be addressed, and power relations between spouses rebalanced, by stipulating rights-protective clauses into detailed marriage contracts. Such clauses could reinforce and re-iterate rights specifically protected in current legislation, clarify areas of the law that are unclear or poorly written, and remedy existing discriminatory provisions.

Given the potentially beneficial legal arsenal that allows women to stipulate rights-protective clauses into their marriage contract, this chapter focuses on the reasons why women in the Maghreb so rarely take advantage of this opportunity in current practice. By examining women's knowledge of, opinions on, and experiences with the marriage contract, it identifies diverse personal, social, familial, and administrative obstacles to women concluding detailed marriage contracts. Finally, the chapter presents strategies offered by women themselves to overcome these identified challenges.

Project Strategy

The findings described in this chapter are from the first phase of a larger action research project on the marriage contract as a strategic tool for women's rights being carried out by the Global Rights Maghreb office in collaboration with local nongovernmental organizations (NGOS) in Morocco, Algeria, and Tunisia since 2007.[18] This multiyear project aims to empower individual women at the grassroots level to stipulate rights-protective clauses into their marriage contracts and promote the use and enforcement of such detailed marriage contracts by legal professionals and local authorities responsible for drawing up marriage contracts. The multifaceted set of project activities carried out to date includes a series of community consultations (a less formal type of focus group discussion) and legal rights education with women across the three countries, participatory legal research, and awareness raising and advocacy to local authorities and legal professionals.

The first stages of the action research were expressly designed to solicit grassroots-level participation from women at the very beginning of the long-term process of reforms to policies and practices on the marriage contract. The organizers hope that such a bottom-up approach will promote new content for the marriage contract and procedures that will respond to realities of women's lives and for which they have a sense of ownership. The widespread credibility and acceptance of such an initiative should ensure its future implementation, sustainability, and ultimate effectiveness.

The findings presented here come from the first phase of this initiative, describing input provided from participants in community consultations held from October 2007 to March 2008. During this time, fifteen local partner NGOS from diverse regions across Morocco, Algeria, and Tunisia held 119 four-hour sessions in seventy cities, towns, and villages across the three countries. A total of 1,474 women from a variety of different socioeconomic, educational, and ethnic backgrounds participated in these consultations, which were held in Arabic, French, or the local Tamazight (Berber) dialect.[19]

A significant component of the consultations focused on conditions women would like to stipulate in a marriage contract, with participants brainstorming to create an ideal list of rights-protective clauses. These ideas were then used to develop a detailed model marriage contract for future use by local NGOS as an awareness-raising and advocacy tool, as well as a practical resource for future spouses drawing up their own individual marriage contracts.

Another major part of the discussions centered on women's knowledge, opinions, and perceptions of, and personal experiences with, the marriage contract. Participants identified challenges to stipulating negotiated clauses into a marriage contract and suggested strategies on how to overcome them for potential future reform to marriage contract procedures that could better promote their rights. This chapter describes the lessons learned in this particular section of the consultations.[20]

The tangible, medium-term objectives of the consultations were to develop the content of an ideal marriage contract that would protect women's rights and to identify obstacles to negotiating such a contract. However, facilitators also described more immediate results, such as women's appreciation of participating in the consultations process. Participants were reluctant to bring the discussions to a close and asked many questions about follow-up to the meeting and when a detailed marriage contract would be made available and take effect.

In particular, facilitators noted that women appreciated the legal rights awareness-raising aspect of the consultations, on a topic they had never been informed of before: the self-expression aspect, which permitted them to exchange experiences and share their hardships; the consultation aspect, which enabled them to express their opinions and points of view on the subject; and the participation aspect, about which women expressed feelings of having contributed through their suggestions for an initiative that could have a positive impact on their lives and communities.

Action Research: Lessons Learned

WOMEN'S KNOWLEDGE OF THE MARRIAGE CONTRACT

Most of the women participating in the consultations knew that there is a document called a marriage contract, although they call it by different names—such as certificate, contract, or paper.

Knowledge of the Role of the Marriage Contract There was general consensus that the marriage contract serves two main purposes—making licit sexual relations between the spouses, and ensuring legitimate paternity to children born to the couple.[21] The women's understanding of the role of the marriage contract is thus quite limited. It is seen as protecting to some extent the rights of children to a name and to financial support and inheritance from their father, but not as a tool for protecting women's personal or financial rights in marriage.

Knowledge of the Content of the Marriage Contract A significant number of participants did not know the content of their own marriage contracts, citing various reasons including their illiteracy, the fact that their husbands had hidden the contract and they did not know where it was, and the failure of anyone to read the contract to them at the time of their marriage. According to a woman from Agadir, Morocco, "as long as it legitimizes the conjugal relationship, what is written inside it is unimportant since the person who drafted it knows the law better than we do."

Knowledge of Possible Additions to the Marriage Contract The vast majority of women were unaware that the law gives them the possibility to stipulate additional written clauses in the marriage contract, declaring that the community consultation was the first time anyone raised this issue with them. Facilitators noted in the meeting minutes that the question itself generated significant surprise and astonishment among the participants. The consultations also revealed women's lack of awareness of the legal option available in all three countries of drawing up a separate property contract. One might be tempted to attribute this ignorance to the recent nature of legal reforms or to high illiteracy rates among women that would prevent them from knowing their rights. However, even in Tunisia—where such a legal possibility has existed since 1998 and where literacy rates are among the highest in the region—women were very often unaware of the marital property contract options.[22]

On several occasions, participants cited other places such as France and communities in the Sahara Desert where, according to them, women could include rights-protective conditions in their marriage contract. Others said that they had heard of this possibility in their own country, but always to the benefit of men, and they cited examples of a husband imposing the wearing of the veil on his wife (in Morocco) or divorcing her when she cooked a specific dish proscribed in the marriage contract (in Tunisia).[23]

Frequently, participants did not distinguish between conditions agreed to orally by the two spouses (or their families) and written clauses recorded in the marriage contract. In numerous groups, women gave examples of verbal conditions. This suggests that it is not the idea of negotiating conditions when one gets married per se that is new, but rather the facts that that negotiating them is a right protected by law and that spouses may put these conditions in writing.

Areas of Confusion about the Marriage Contract Consultation facilitators remarked that participants frequently requested clarification on the substance of existing laws. This was particularly true in Morocco and Algeria, where reforms to the Family Code are relatively recent. Women were quite eager to verify information they had heard—for example, a group of rural women near Oran, Algeria, asked, "Is it true that women can now keep the family home when they get divorced?"

Confusion and misconceptions about the recent reforms were quite common, with women in Morocco frequently saying (incorrectly) that under the new law, women automatically have the right to half of all of their husband's property on divorce, and that men had completely lost the right to practice polygamy.[24]

Facilitators in all three countries also noticed that the law's provision for two contractual documents was also misleading. Women often confused the marriage contract per se, into which personal rights may be stipulated, with the separate marital property contract designating ownership of material possessions. They were frequently unaware of one of the two possibilities. In Tunisia, even those women who had themselves signed a separate community property contract said that they did not understand their rights under the system very well.

Opinions on the Importance of the Marriage Contract Women all agreed that the marriage contract per se is an extremely important document, but primarily for reasons directly linked to their understanding of the role of the marriage contract described above. Consequently, the significance of the marriage contract largely remains within the limited framework of legitimizing sexual relations and guaranteeing children's rights conferred by legitimate paternity.

Participants gave numerous examples to illustrate this point, explaining that without a marriage contract, the relationship between the man and woman is illegal and the woman is then "doomed." In many groups in Algeria and in Morocco, women who were married in the traditional way by the *fatiha*[25] described the problems they encountered when trying to prove their marriages and obtain civil status documents for their children, a process that took twenty years in some cases. These women described their suffering and how much time, effort, and money it took to prove their marriage in the absence of a written contract. Women married by the *fatiha* also declared that the marriage contract is a "form of protection when the husband is tempted to betray you," and that without it, women were "like single mothers."

It was interesting to note that in most groups, while women illustrated the importance of having a written marriage contract by giving concrete examples of children's rights, the participants were vaguer when it came to giving examples of women's rights protected by the contract. Apart from claims that the contract valorizes and preserves women's dignity by proving the legitimacy of the conjugal relationship, the consultation minutes do not note any example given by the participants of their own rights being protected by the marriage contract itself. Indeed, many of the discussions at this point turned to how women's rights are never respected anyway. As a participant in El Hajeb, Morocco, said, "the marriage contract does not guarantee our rights to financial support and the home." In Bogara, Algeria women said that the law is unjust to woman and does not give them any rights, and that the 2005 amendments changed nothing. Others contended that even if the law does guarantee certain rights, it is difficult to obtain them through the justice system.

> The marriage contract is important and yet at the same time is not
> important. Sometimes it turns out to be useless, particularly when we
> suffer from problems related to financial support or repudiation; at this
> moment this document has no importance. What's more, generally
> speaking, the law is never applied and is always on the man's side. Laws
> protecting women only exist in cities. In our valley, the law is never
> applied. Any woman who wants to obtain her rights has to go to the courts
> in Tangier or Casablanca. (A woman, Chefchaouen, Morocco)

Opinions on the Value of Adding to the Marriage Contract Once facilitators informed participants of the legal possibility to stipulate written rights-protective clauses into the marriage contract, discussions became quite dynamic, and many diverse opinions were shared.

The majority of participants strongly supported, at least in theory, the idea of stipulating written conditions into the marriage contract and agreed that this could be a useful and important tool that women should take advantage of. They offered a variety of reasons why, in their opinion, this practice could potentially protect women's rights during marriage and after its dissolution.

> This is an opportunity to be seized, because this way we can
> defend ourselves, not experience submission and humiliation anymore,
> and we shall no longer be thrown out like dirty laundry.
> (A woman, Tlemcen, Algeria)

The most vocal supporters of detailed stipulated clauses in the marriage contract included women currently experiencing problems with their husbands and divorced women, who wanted to prevent others from going through what they had and to avoid having the same experience should they remarry; young single women looking ahead to their own marriage; older women married for years, who expressed regret at not taking advantage of this opportunity when they got married and even asking the consultations facilitator if it was too late to rewrite their own marriage contracts; and mothers desiring a better future for their daughters and vowing that they would ensure the existence of written conditions in the marriage contracts for girls in their families.

> I accepted his [her husband's] conditions in order to preserve my house
> and my children. I am the victim and I don't dare say anything. But now
> that I understand things better, I will impose a marriage contract on
> marrying my daughters. I don't want them to suffer. (A woman, Oran)

A recurring theme was that this strategy would be useful given that laws are often not applied. Women frequently cited the need for wives to protect their personal property. Both traditional Islamic law and national legislation provide for separate marital property, in theory protecting women's right to their personal possessions. However, many participants described how their husband took their personal property (including money, inheritance, jewelry, and land) and used it to purchase or invest in something that was for his own use or registered in his own name. And women described being unable to seek legal recourse—because under the law there is no such thing as theft between spouses.

Some felt that a detailed contract could guarantee the stability and continuity of the marriage by preventing the husband from even thinking about divorce in order to avoid the (ideally severe and costly) consequences. Similarly, others thought that such a contract could play a preventive role by warding off a wife's conflicts with her husband and in-laws.

> When we asked participants for the reasons behind the elaboration
> of a detailed marriage contract, the same Berber proverb was repeated
> in four different groups, according to which "when we live in peace and
> harmony, we write, and when conflicts and quarrels start, then we
> read what we wrote." (A program facilitator, Agadir)

Others mentioned how a marriage contract drafted this way would provide clarity for the couple from the beginning of the marriage. If the two spouses have mutually agreed to certain conditions prior to the marriage, then the wife will not be not surprised afterward—for example, by a husband who prohibits her from finishing her studies, working outside the home, or visiting her family. Some women suggested that a detailed marriage contract would also encourage greater transparency and honesty between future spouses, and prevent them from hiding their weaknesses and flaws from each other.

Finally, participants considered that a detailed marriage contract would play an educational role by informing women about their rights in marriage. Others also said that with such a contract, women would have more confidence in themselves and be better able to work toward their family's fulfilment and development.

If I had included conditions that would have protected me in my marriage contract, I could have lived at ease. Without such clauses, women live in fear of divorce, or of another wife who will take everything away from her. (A woman, Agadir)

The significant minority of participants who did not support the idea of stipulating written clauses were no less vocal in their opposition. Women against the idea of stipulating conditions included those who claimed not to have any problems with their own husbands, and mothers who would soon be marrying off their sons and did not want to disadvantage them with a contract that would favor the future wife and her rights.

In all of the consultations, women raised and intensely debated the issue of trust between the two spouses, and whether or not merely talking about conditions demonstrates a "lack of confidence in the partner," which could lead to divorce. Some participants said that what counted most in marriage was good faith and mutual respect, and that if written clauses are imposed from the beginning of the relationship, this would prove the bride's bad faith toward the groom.

A similar debate ensued in one group when an older widow expressed her opinion that "if the wife is respectful of her husband and if she fulfils his needs, he will never deprive her of her rights." This idea was supported by some participants and contested by others. One woman from Tetouan, Morocco, declared: "Even if the wife is devoted body and soul to serving her husband, he will always find a way to turn his back on her and marry another woman. He can even become violent toward her and kick her out of the conjugal home at any time."

Opinions on the Feasibility of Adding to the Marriage Contract Most of the women were not opposed per se to stipulating clauses in the marriage contract, but many of them expressed significant reservations about the feasibility of putting the stipulations into practice. Some characterized the idea as utopian and gave their view that even if it was a reality in other countries, diverse personal, familial, social, legal, and administrative obstacles would make it difficult to implement in the Maghreb.

The major concern women expressed about the feasibility of stipulating rights-protective clauses was that potential husbands and their families would never agree to such a marriage contract. Many described their fear that a woman would never find a husband or that the fiancé or his family would cancel the engagement if she even talked about such conditions.

Even young, single participants who were enthusiastic about the idea of a detailed marriage contract were less excited by the prospect of actually applying it to their own future marriage. In several instances, participants declared that they would not include any conditions even though they now knew about this right; they felt that such private and personal matters could not be discussed before the consummation of the marriage, and they feared the reaction of their future husband. In their view, the main objective is to get married; other details could come later.

It must be emphasized, however, that this was a matter of debate and not consensus among women, as illustrated by the following opinions of two different participants:

> She finds someone who wants to marry her and then dares require conditions! And what else?! (A woman, Oran)

> I am scandalized by these young women who get married nowadays and accept all of the future husband's conditions, in what can only be described as a race to get a husband. (A woman, Tizi Ouzou, Algeria)

As prevailing beliefs are still that women exist primarily as wives and mothers and that marriage is a form of social and economic protection for them, the idea of a woman never getting married is unthinkable for most people.

In addition, some married women were skeptical about the value of clauses in the marriage contract, saying that if the law does not impose something, men will never agree to it voluntarily. "Men would rather divorce than share their property" was a commonly repeated opinion, and even discussing such issues once married was risky because it could "hurt the husband's pride and vanity as a man," which leads to conflict and divorce.

Even if a rights-protective clause is stipulated into the contract, women added, men will find a way to get around it. Women in Tunisia who had signed a community property contract gave examples of how their husbands just started registering acquired property in the name of their father or other relatives in order to prevent their wives from being entitled to a share.

Participants also said they felt that society would criticize women who stipulated conditions into their marriage contract, and that such women would become the target of gossip, judging them materialistic, arrogant, and capricious.

Finally, women wondered about the likelihood that local authorities responsible for marriage formalities would actually accept contracts with rights-protective clauses. Several said they thought it would be impossible to get such a contract validated in front of the pertinent official in their community. One woman asked, "What can we expect from the authorities concluding marriage contracts? They are all men, and they view women negatively and don't even respect their own female relatives." Others described not only the negative views of women that local officials may have, but also questioned their legal knowledge and competence to draw up proper rights-protective marriage contracts.

Opinions on the Content to be Added to the Marriage Contract Some of the women's concerns about the value or feasibility of stipulating clauses into the marriage contract came from the substance of a particular condition. These discussions arose during the part of the consultations when women brainstormed to create potential ideal clauses for inclusion in a model marriage contract. The debates on the content of such clauses reflect how the participants grappled with the challenges to crafting clauses, and the rich diversity in opinions about equality and justice—what they could look like in reality and how they could be achieved.

For example, although the proposal for a clause prohibiting domestic violence met with wide approval, a couple of participants suggested that such a stipulation could create problems between the spouses and have the opposite effect, provoking the husband to be violent toward his wife. Others thought that this condition wouldn't work because, in their view, men cannot control their behavior.

Although women agreed that it was important to stipulate into the marriage contract the right to work outside the home, they differed on the question of sanctions for failing to respect this condition. Some said that if the husband agreed to pay an amount of monthly compensation to the wife, then she should abandon outside employment. Others rejected this solution, saying that work outside the home valorizes women, and no amount of money could compensate the woman for losing that valorization. These women suggested divorce as the sanction for the husband's failure to respect this condition.

Participants questioned the reasonableness and feasibility of certain clauses due to current economic circumstances. Although the vast majority of women expressed their desire for a contractual guarantee of an independent conjugal home, separate from their in-laws, others pointed out that many men's financial situation does not allow this, and if women tried to impose this as a condition, many would-be husbands would give up on the idea of marriage altogether.

Women's misunderstandings about the substance of the applicable family laws described previously affected their suggestions for ideal clauses to include in a marriage contract. Sometimes they proposed conditions on rights already explicitly covered by the law or did not suggest clauses on rights that they mistakenly thought the law already protected.

In this sense, ironically, it is the laws themselves — or, rather, the positive public relations campaigns surrounding them — that often serve as an obstacle to women's stipulating rights-protective clauses into the marriage contract. Whether due to the recent family law reform dynamic in Morocco and Algeria, or the usual laurels historically attributed to the Tunisian Personal Status Code, women often voiced their belief that current laws protected their rights and that there was no need to stipulate additional conditions.[26]

The importance of mutual consent between the spouses on family planning matters was mentioned in the majority of consultations, the suggestion that such issues be addressed in the marriage contract generated heated debate. A significant number of women resisted the idea, stating that family planning is determined by destiny and arbitrary circumstances of life, and that one should not interfere with the will of God.

In only a couple of instances did participants raise the objection that a given clause would be against Islam — mainly in the cases of family planning issues and polygamy. A notable incident occurred on this issue in one of the groups during a discussion of a domestic violence clause:

It was also interesting to note participants' views on a clause stipulating the
power of *isma* in the marriage contract, by which the husband effectively delegates his right of repudiation to his wife. The vast majority of women were not
aware of this option, and several even opposed it by arguing that according
to customs, traditions, and religion, only the man should have the power of
divorce—despite the fact that this option comes from classical Islamic doctrine
and in Morocco is even provided for in the Family Code.[27]

WOMEN'S PERSONAL EXPERIENCES
WITH THE MARRIAGE CONTRACT

Social customs and administrative procedures related to the marriage process
itself contribute to women's general lack of awareness about their legal rights
and present significant practical obstacles to stipulating written clauses into
the marriage contract.

Experiences with the Marriage Process With the exception of many participants in Morocco, usually women over fifty years old whose marriages had
been concluded in their absence by their father or marital tutor,[28] all of the
women had been present at the signing of their marriage contracts. However,
without exception, women agreed that their presence at the conclusion of
the marriage contract was a mere formality and that they had in no way been
otherwise involved.

Some of the older women described how their marriages were arranged
by their fathers, and since they themselves did not even meet their husband
until the wedding day, they had no opportunity to discuss issues of concern
with their future husband. Other women testified that their fathers threatened
to kick them out of the house and disown them if they refused to agree to an
arranged marriage.

Women all described the omnipresence of families during the negotiations
prior to the conclusion of the contract, and indeed reported that these are conducted exclusively by the future spouses' male relatives. Even when couples

know each other and decide to get married out of love, once their engagement is announced, male relatives take over the negotiations and the future spouses have no say in the matter.

> Ignorance certainly exists, yes, that is a fact. But what is worse is men's domination and the prevalence of customs and traditions that prevent women from talking and speaking up even if we know very well that we have the right to participate. (A woman, Agadir)

Not only do male family members generally monopolize discussions surrounding the marriage contract, but the bride is marginalized and kept apart from the negotiation process until it is concluded. Families often do not give the bride the opportunity to discuss her contract and do not solicit her opinion or input.

In addition, participants in Morocco, Algeria, and Tunisia alike described how the official responsible for concluding the marriage (who could be a judge, *adoul*, or civil status officer)[29] only asked her consent to marry and then for her to sign the contract. No one explained the marriage contract content to the women or informed them that they could stipulate conditions into it.[30] Even participants married after the Family Code reforms in Morocco and Algeria in 2004 and 2005, respectively, said that they had not been informed of their new rights to stipulate clauses or conclude a separate marital property contract.[31]

One notable exception to this general failure by the relevant officials to inform spouses of their legal rights can be found in Tunisia. Women who got married at the city hall said that the civil status officer had reviewed the marriage contract content with them before asking for their signature. The majority made it clear, however, that although the contract's content was explained to them at the time of signature, it was not discussed between the spouses prior to the marriage.

In contrast, women in Tunisia who concluded their marriage in front of an *adoul*, in a ceremony where religious, customary, and traditional aspects prevail and that takes place either in the bride's parents' home or in the mosque, affirmed that the *adoul* asked them only the classical question about their consent. The bride often sat in a separate room, far from where the men met with the *adoul*, and she was given the document to be signed only after the contract was drawn up. Most women stated that the *adoul* not only did not notify them about the possibility of stipulating conditions in the contract but did not even read the marriage contract aloud.

Experiences with Negotiated Conditions With very few exceptions, none of the participants in any of the community consultations in the three countries had stipulated additional written conditions into their marriage contracts. Among the 466 married participants in Morocco, 3 did not have a written marriage contract, 4 had stipulated conditions in writing into their contracts, and none had concluded a separate martial property contract. Out of the 741 married participants in Algeria, 14 did not have a written contract, 1 had stipulated written conditions, and 6 had concluded a separate marital property contract. In Tunisia, all of the married participants had a written marriage contract, 2 had stipulated written conditions in their contracts, and 51 had concluded the separate community property contract.[32]

Among the examples of clauses given in the discussions, a mother in Marrakech, Morocco, described how her daughter stipulated a condition guaranteeing her right to work outside of the home; a participant in El Hajeb said that she put a monogamy clause into her contract (but that in return her husband required that she never leave the home); a woman in Oran stipulated a condition guaranteeing her right to pursue her studies; and in Zaghouan, Tunisia, a woman included a clause that she would not move with her future husband to his native region.

It is interesting to note that, although the vast majority of women had not stipulated any written clauses into the marriage contract, women very frequently referred to verbal conditions that they (or their families) had negotiated at the time of marriage.

> One woman explained that she was present at the conclusion of her
> marriage contract and insisted on having an independent home and
> keeping her job as an embroiderer, since she owned an embroidery shop.
> These conditions were not written down in the marriage contract because
> she did not know that such a possibility existed and that it was legal,
> so she just stated them verbally in front of the people present and the
> witnesses. According to her, her husband has always respected
> this condition. (A program facilitator, Agadir)

Likewise, women in all of the groups in Algeria described the verbal agreements reached between the future spouses' parents, and said the bride's marital tutor often places demands on the future husband prior to the marriage. Among these, women cited conditions such as stability and happiness; money or gifts such as gold jewelry or clothes; her right to continue working outside the home or to pursue her studies; an independent home; the children's upbringing; and the husband's honesty. A group of educated, working women in Oran described how they had reached a moral agreement directly with their husbands on their right to work outside the home, a condition that they claim was respected after the marriage.

As these conditions are only verbal, rather than being written down in the marriage contract, they remain at the level of principles to be respected by the two spouses in virtue of the moral agreement between the husband and the wife's marital tutor. They are not legally binding on the husband, and the wife has no recourse should he not respect the agreement later on. Participants mentioned numerous cases in which the families or spouses initially agreed on the wife's right to continue working or studying, but that after marriage the woman stopped working or studying due to pressure from her husband or in-laws. Others told stories of women they knew whose husbands had initially promised them the right to work, pursue their studies, or have an independent home but reneged on these promises after marriage.

Women concluded that even if conditions are discussed by the families and verbally consented to, the marriage contract itself remains a purely administrative formality. The spouses' parents, witnesses, and marital tutor are present when the negotiated conditions are discussed, yet they will never intervene if the conditions are not respected or when conflicts arise.

Marriages in the Maghreb historically have thus quite often included negotiated conditions potentially protective of women's personal and financial rights, just in the form of verbal agreements rather than contractual stipulations. Discussions in the community consultations suggest that it is not so much the substance of such conditions that is controversial, but rather the idea of putting them in writing. Since one's word is one's honor, requiring written stipulations is viewed as an insult, suggesting that the other party cannot be trusted.[33]

When the participants were asked why they had not stipulated any conditions in writing in their own marriage contracts, they gave a variety of reasons, relating to issues of knowledge, opinions, and experiences discussed above.

Many were simply not aware of this possibility. Others said that although they were aware of their rights, various personal feelings prevented them from taking advantage of those rights. These feelings included shame, embarrassment, lack of self-confidence, a sense that stipulating conditions was taboo, and compassion for their future husband and a desire to preserve his dignity. Several said that they were in love with their future husband and trusted him and his promises during the engagement period.

Others pointed out that society sends the message that the most important thing is that a girl get married and that she does not have the right to intervene in any of the details. It did not even occur to many of the women to raise the issue of stipulated conditions, given their male relatives' domination of the entire process. Their father's presence embarrassed and intimidated them and made them feel the weight of societal taboos in front of the future husband's family.

Many women also reported that prior to the marriage, they were busy with the preparations for the wedding ceremony and party—preoccupied with invitations, menus, gowns, and makeup—and did not give any importance to or take time to think about the contract or issues of their legal rights.

Finally, many women cited the fact that the official responsible for concluding the marriage did not explain the contract's content, inform them of their rights, or ask if they wanted to include any conditions in their marriage contract.

The *adoul* always arrive late, rush to write the contract in two minutes, eat quickly, and leave in a hurry so that they won't miss another marriage... We don't even understand what they are saying, they are just sputtering all the time. (A woman, Agadir)

In Marrakech, one participant explained that she knew she had the right to stipulate clauses into her contract and even raised the issue on the conclusion of her marriage. The *adoul* replied that she "should thank the good Lord and consider yourself lucky because others can't even find someone to marry," and as a result she said no more.

AREAS FOR FUTURE INQUIRY AND ACTION

In addition to conducting grassroots-level community consultations with women, from January through April 2008, partner lawyers in Morocco, Algeria, and Tunisia conducted participatory legal research that included a literature review of relevant laws and procedures, as well as individual interviews and round-table discussions with local authorities, legal practitioners, and other stakeholders involved in the drafting and conclusion of marriage contracts. Over 177 people attended the three national round-table discussions, and more than 100 participated in the individual focused interviews, with 15 of the latter local authorities directly responsible for officiating marriage contracts (*adouls*, notaries, and civil status officers).

Marriage Contract Procedures A significant obstacle to stipulating rights-protective clauses into the marriage contract is created by the marriage contract procedures themselves and the inadequacy of current laws and policies surrounding them. Reforms related to women's rights have not been accompanied by sufficient measures designed to guide, orient, monitor, and control their implementation by the authorities charged with applying them.

For example, spouses have the right to create a framework for their financial relations during marriage according to their individual circumstances. However, the few articles on this subject in the codes in the three countries of the Maghreb provide no examples or specific language that would help spouses choose a marital property regime or draft an effective contract to regulate their financial relationship. In general, there is no helpful guidance or orientation in the laws or procedures for either future spouses or the authorities to draft effective, rights-protective contractual clauses. In addition, there are few if any administrative mechanisms to compel local authorities to inform future spouses of their rights and insufficient sanctions for local authorities who do not comply with their legal obligations to do so.

It became clear during the action research that the outdated administrative procedures for concluding marriage are not conducive to women's exercising their legal right to stipulate clauses into their marriage contract, and indeed actively discourage women from doing so.

Personnel Responsible for Concluding Marriage Contracts Interviews with local authorities suggest that at least some of them lack knowledge of the national laws on the marriage contract. Civil status officers in Algeria stated that they were not aware of any specific laws on marital property, and that they had no knowledge of the laws and the amendments introduced concerning marriage contracts, or about the possibility of including conditions in the marriage contract.

Other local authorities openly declared their resistance to the idea of detailed negotiated marriage contracts and expressed their opinion that such a contract is incompatible with the relationship of trust presumed to exist between spouses and detrimental to the sanctity of the marital bond. When asked about the laws allowing women to include clauses in the marriage contract, one notary in Algeria replied: "There is no law more appropriate than that of Islamic Sharia, [under that] her [the wife's] conditions are preserved and guaranteed." Another said: "I am against this idea because I think there is no need to include conditions in a marriage contract. The idea just does not make sense." He added that there was no need to draw up a separate marital property contract "because the two spouses form one and the same indivisible entity," an idea that it must be noted contradicts classical Islamic law guaranteeing separate marital property.

None of the authorities interviewed had themselves actually seen or drawn up a marriage contract with stipulated rights-protective clauses. One civil status officer in Algeria said that he does not inform the spouses of their right to stipulate clauses into the marriage contract. However, this is understandable in light of the fact that substantial contradictions between the 2005 Family Code and the 1970 Civil Status Code mean that the officers basically do not have the legal authority to add anything to the marriage contract on their own initiative.

Local authorities also echo the concerns about social taboos and lack of sufficient understanding of the different options voiced by the women in the consultations. "We often have problems in informing the two spouses about their rights to include clauses in their marriage contracts," stated an *adoul* in Morocco. "We can't talk about money on the wedding day!" And in Tunisia a civil status officer acknowledged: "Spouses are reminded that they must choose a marital property regime but often without sufficient clarification, unless the two parties ask for it explicitly."

Conclusion and Next Steps

Despite the fact that the national laws of all three countries all explicitly state that spouses may stipulate conditions pertaining to their persons and property into the marriage contract, this action research reveals that these provisions are rarely applied or are misinterpreted in practice. Contributing factors include the lack of awareness and information about the laws, as well as prevailing views about women. Legislative reforms on women's rights in the Maghreb are frequently used for political propaganda and public relations purposes, rather than being accompanied by awareness-raising campaigns to mobilize the popular support around the reforms that is necessary to ensure their acceptance.

In order to address these personal and social challenges to concluding detailed marriage contracts, one element of the next phase of this project focuses on grassroots-level awareness raising. A primary tool is the model marriage contract with detailed clauses protecting women's personal and financial rights that was developed by women themselves during the community consultations. Participants identified the need for information campaigns and awareness raising among the population in general, to spread accurate information about the laws, break social taboos about the topic, and develop individual women's capacities to speak out for their rights in marriage. To achieve these goals, local NGOs are currently conducting popular education sessions on the marriage contract at the grassroots level, using a facilitator's pamphlet developed for this purpose. There is also a model marriage contract blog and a Facebook page for the initiative.

A second component of the next phase of this project addresses family and administrative obstacles to concluding detailed marriage contracts, through engagement with and advocacy to local authorities. When asked to suggest strategies to overcome the identified administrative challenges to stipulating rights-protective clauses into the marriage contract, women proposed that more competent and gender-sensitive officials be charged with concluding marriage contracts, and that they be more closely monitored. The women also suggested that brides be more involved in the process, with preliminary informational meetings held early in the process between just the two future spouses and the relevant authority. A compulsory marriage contract form that details all of the spouses' rights would also be useful, according to the women, to ensure standardized substance and procedures that would apply to everyone equally and take the burden of negotiation off the individual bride.

Local NGOs in the Maghreb have thus started advocating to authorities and legal professionals in their communities the use of the model marriage contract developed as a result of the community consultations. They also recently launched working groups among local authorities to draft concrete recommendations to policymakers for reforms to marriage contract procedures that reflect best practices and will enable women to protect their rights in reality.

Notes

The authors would like to thank Houda Benmbarek, program officer for Global Rights Maghreb, for her valuable research assistance, support, and helpful comments on this chapter. They also thank Chitra Raghavan and James Levine for their support and thoughtful comments on early drafts; Cassandra Balchin for her years of helpful technical assistance with this project; their local partner nongovernmental organizations in Morocco, Algeria, and Tunisia for their collaboration, energy, and creativity in promoting women's rights at the grassroots level in their local communities; and the donors who have so generously supported this project.

1 In Morocco, this is the Family Code, as reformed in February 2004; in Algeria, the Family Code of 1984, as amended in February 2005; and in Tunisia, the Personal Status Code of 1956, as amended in 1992.

2 In Morocco, Algeria, and Tunisia, the Malekite school of Sunni Islam is predominant.

3 Hadith, Abu Dawud and Al Hakim on the authority of Abi Hurairah, Sahih Al-Jami Al Sathir (No. 6714) (http://muttagun.com/marriage.html). Likewise, King Mohammed VI of Morocco—in his October 2003 speech to Parliament, later adopted as the preamble to the 2004 Family Code—declared, "Omar Ibn Al-Khattab, may God be pleased with him, is quoted as saying: 'The intersection of rights is in the conditions.'"

4 For a superb collection of essays examining the marriage contract as a tool for women's rights in legal doctrine, diverse historical practice, and current reform movements, see Asifa Quraishi and Frank E. Vogel, editors, *The Islamic Marriage Contract: Case Studies in Islamic Family Law* (Cambridge: Harvard University Press, 2008). For a discussion of classical religious doctrine and practice related to rights-protective clauses in the marriage contract in Ottoman Egypt, see Nelly Hanna, "Marriage among Merchant Families in Seventeenth-Century Cairo," in *Women, the Family and Divorce Laws in Islamic History*, edited by Amira El Azhary Sonbol (Syracuse, NY: Syracuse University Press, 1996), 143–54.

5 Algerian Family Code, Articles 4, 7, 9, 10, 13, 19, 53(9); Moroccan Family Code, Articles 4, 10(1), 11, 12, 57(3), 63; Tunisian Personal Status Code, Articles 3, 11, 21.

6 1993 Moroccan Family Code, Articles 30 and 31; 1984 Algerian Family Code Article 19.

7 Tunisian Personal Status Code, Article 11; Algerian Family Code, Article 19; Moroccan Family Code, Articles 47, 48.

8 Article 49 of the Moroccan Family Code and Article 37 of the Algerian Family Code introduced the possibility for spouses to conclude a separate marital property contract, and the Tunisian Law 98-91 of 11 September 1998 introduced an optional community property regime for married couples. Under traditional Islamic law, and in all national legislation in the Maghreb, the general rule is that of separate property, which deprives the wife from sharing her husband's income and any property acquired by him or registered under his name, even when she contributed to the development of the family assets through her work in the home.

9 Moroccan Family Code, Articles 47, 48; Algerian Family Code, Articles 19, 32; Tunisian Personal Status Code, Article 21.

10 Moroccan Family Code, Articles 98, 99; Algerian Family Code, Article 52; Tunisian Personal Status Code, Article 11.

11 Anecdotal evidence strongly suggests, however, that these practices have been progressively disappearing with codification of the Family Laws. Women from the Souss region participating in the community consultations described later in this chapter explained that these practices are no longer in widespread use.

12 *Kad o saiya* stills exists and has been applied by Moroccan courts. See Houssein Meelki, *The Kad o Saiya System: Examples from Moroccan Jurisprudence* [in Arabic] (Rabat: Dar es Salaam, 1999).

13 Official statistics from the Ministry of Justice (http://adala.justice.gov.ma/FR/Statistiques/Statistiques.aspx).

14 The survey was conducted by the Association des jeunes avocats de Khemisset during action research conducted during the Global Rights marriage contract initiative described in this chapter.

15 This was the response to a question posed to the Moroccan government delegation by the Committee on the Elimination of Discrimination against Women during its consideration of Morocco's third and fourth combined periodic reports, at the committee's 40th Session, held from 14 January 14 to 1 February 2008 (UN document CEDAW/C/SR.824 CEDAW/C/SR.825).

16 Tunisia is the only country in the Maghreb to prohibit polygamy.

17 For more details and sources for this assertion, see, for example, Ligue Démocratique des Droits des Femmes, *Rapports annuels sur l'application du Code de*

la Famille (Casablanca: Ligue Démocratique des Droits des Femmes, 2004, 2005, 2006, and 2007); *Le Code de la famille: Perceptions et pratique judiciaire* (Morocco: Friedrich Ebert Stiftung, January 2007); Association démocratique des femmes du Maroc, "Implementation of the CEDAW Convention: Non-Governmental Organisations' Shadow Report to the Third and the Fourth Periodic Report of the Moroccan Government," November 2007 (http://www2.ohchr.org/english/bodies/cedaw/cedaws40.htm).

18 Global Rights is an international human rights capacity-building NGO (www.globalrights.org).

19 Consultations were conducted by teams of local NGO members charged with leading focused discussions and taking notes (and video or audio recording when possible). Global Rights held a training session on organizing and facilitating community consultations (including general techniques, the role of the facilitator, ways to ask questions, and strategies for group management) for the fifteen partner NGOs during a start-up workshop for this project in September 2007. After returning to their respective communities, the partner organizations repeated the facilitator training workshop for 163 selected members of fifty-eight additional local organizations in their regions. Facilitators led discussions according to the structure and content set out in the community consultations protocol developed by Global Rights. The partner NGOs submitted detailed reports of the consultations, and the Global Rights Maghreb office then analyzed the findings.

20 The complete final report on the action research—Global Rights, *Conditions, Not Conflict: Promoting Women's Rights in the Maghreb through Strategic Use of the Marriage Contract* (Rabat: Global Rights, 2008)—and the model marriage contract, as well as additional information on this initiative, can be found in English, Arabic, and French at www.globalrights.org and http://globalrightsmaghreb.wordpress.com.

21 Sexual relations outside of marriage are illegal. "Illegitimate" biological paternity is not legally recognized at all in Morocco or Algeria. In all three countries, single mothers are stigmatized and have very limited legal protection for themselves or their children, although a 1998 Tunisian law as amended in 2003 allows for court-ordered paternity tests in a wide variety of circumstances, so that illegitimate children may benefit from the right to guardianship and a family name.

22 Law 98–91 of 11 September 1998. From 1995 to 2005 the adult literacy rate was 74.3 percent in Tunisia, 69.9 percent in Algeria, and 52.3 percent in Morocco (United Nations Development Program, *Arab Human Development Report 2009* [New York: United Nations Development Program, 2009; http://hdr.undp.org/en/statistics/]).

23 These examples are offered only to give an idea of the types of stories circulating, not to assert that such clauses have any legal validity or actually occurred.

24 Misconceptions about the content of the recent reforms to the Family Codes in Morocco are fairly common and can be attributed to, among other factors, the fact that too little time has yet passed for the laws to be understood, assimilated, or put into practice, either by the population or by the authorities charged with enforcing them. In addition, opposition to women's rights from diverse conservative Islamist groups has frequently taken the form of propaganda and misinformation about the Family Code reforms.

25 *Fatiha* marriage is a verbal marriage, concluded without a written contract.

26 This is similar to Mona Zulficar's description of the earlier experience in Egypt, where the practice of stipulating clauses into the marriage contract to protect women's rights fell out of use after the Personal Status Laws of 1920 and 1929 and the 1931 law on the organization of Sharia courts. At that point the marriage contract became a minimalist form, reflecting the (false) view that the reformed laws already protected women's rights and that there was no need for substantive conditions in the marriage contract. See Zulficar, "The Islamic Marriage Contract in Egypt," in *The Islamic Marriage Contract*, edited by Quraishi and Vogel, 234-35. This is also reflected in the current view of the Tunisian authorities, who encourage the use of stipulated conditions in marriage contracts concluded between Tunisian women and men from other Muslim countries—on the ground that other laws are not as protective of women's rights as Tunisian law is.

27 In classical doctrine *isma* is called *talaq tafwid*. The Moroccan Family Code provides for this in Article 89; the Algerian Family Code does not mention it; and the issue is irrelevant in Tunisia, where repudiation does not exist.

28 The marital tutor, or *wali*, is the bride's male relative—typically her father—who is charged with signing the marriage contract on her behalf. The use of a *wali* is still mandatory in Algeria, was made optional in Morocco with the 2004 Family Law reforms, and does not exist in Tunisia.

29 An *adoul* is a civil servant in Morocco and Tunisia, similar to a public notary but with a religious character. A civil status officer is a local government official who exercises authority over civil affairs, such as marriage, divorce, and birth and death certification.

30 It suffices for the *adoul* in Morocco and Tunisia to note in the marriage contract that the two spouses have been informed about article 49 of the Family Code or the 98-91 Tunisian law relative to community property, because the *adoul*'s legal obligation

of notification is not subject to any real control. In Algeria this responsibility to notify the spouses of their rights depends on the good will of the person officiating, who is under no legal obligation to do so. Only in Tunisia is it the official's legal obligation to notify spouses of their right to conclude a separate property contract subject to any real administrative control.

31 An additional obstacle to stipulating rights-protective clauses in Algeria is the continued practice of unregistered verbal *fatiha* marriages, often used to circumvent new restrictions on polygamy and, according to one participant in Tlemcen, more prevalent in rural areas than one might think.

32 Given the facts that the groups were made up of women from different age brackets and with different marital statuses, and that some women had been married before and some after legislative reforms in the three countries related to marriage, these statistics should not be interpreted as establishing accurate percentages overall or causal relationships. They are presented only as illustrations, to give a general idea of the current status of marriage contracts in the Maghreb.

33 Kecia Ali points out that classical Muslim jurists do not require marriage contracts to be written—a witnessed oral agreement is a valid contract ("Marriage in Classical Islamic Jurisprudence: A Survey of Doctrines," in *The Islamic Marriage Contract*, edited by Quraishi and Vogel, 17).

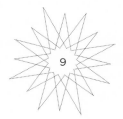

9

Unsatisfactory Aspects of Women's Rights to Property in Uganda and Proposals for Reform

This chapter examines women's rights to property in marriage, on divorce and on the death of a spouse in Uganda, highlighting the unsatisfactory aspects in both the state-made (statutory) and other (customary and religious) laws. It argues that with the exception of the 1995 Constitution, laws regulating the ownership of property during marriage, on divorce, and on the death of a spouse discriminate against women. It shows that even where the relevant statutory laws are protective of women's rights to property, their implementation is hindered by customary practices and the generally weak economic position of women. The chapter delves into the even weaker position of women's rights to matrimonial property under customary and religious laws. Under Islamic law regulating intestate succession to property, the entitlements for widows fall short of the constitutional standards for equality and nondiscrimination. Reform proposals including the adoption of an immediate community property regime are suggested.

Introduction

Except for Uganda's 1995 Constitution, laws regulating the ownership of property during marriage, on divorce, and on the death of a spouse, whether state-made (statutory laws) or not (customary and religious laws), discriminate against women. This chapter discusses the problematic aspects of these laws and practices and suggests reforms.

Owing to legal pluralism—a situation where many conflicting laws operate in the same jurisdiction—even where the relevant statutory laws are protective of women's rights to matrimonial property, their implementation is hindered by customary law practices (which are entirely tribal and vary from tribe to tribe), socialization, and the generally weak economic situation of many women. To address this situation, Uganda must reform both religious and customary laws regulating rights to matrimonial property besides the statutory laws.

Whereas customary and religious laws are theoretically subordinate to statutory laws, this is not always the case in practice. For example, for Ugandan Muslim women, discriminatory Islamic sexist norms regulate their rights in marriage, on divorce, and in widowhood. This state of affairs undermines the formal provisions granting women equal status with men and contradicts the Constitution and the UN Convention on the Elimination of All Forms of Discrimination against Women (CEDAW).[1]

In Uganda, pre-independence social stratification based on patriarchal values continues to exist. Worse still, although there is judicial review and courts on petition by aggrieved individuals strike down norms inconsistent with the Constitution, in practice access to courts is limited by high costs and judicial delays.

Given the foregoing, the CEDAW Committee, while considering the combined fourth, fifth, sixth, and seventh reports of Uganda at its 954th and 955th meetings, on 13 October 2010,[2] expressed concern over the country's laws that conflict with both its 1995 Constitution and CEDAW commitments. Concern was also expressed over Uganda's slow progress in removing provisions from its laws that discriminate against women. In particular, the committee expressed concern at the low priority given to comprehensive legal reform to eliminate sex-discriminatory provisions and bring the country's legal framework fully into compliance with the provisions of CEDAW and achieve women's de jure equality.[3] The committee was also concerned that legislation and customary practices that discriminate against women and are incompatible with the convention remain in force.

The committee noted that although rural women form the majority of women in Uganda, they are in a disadvantaged position, and their lives are characterized by, for example, lack of participation in decision-making processes. The committee reiterated its concern that customs and traditional practices that are prevalent in rural areas prevent women from inheriting or acquiring ownership of land and other property.[4]

The committee urged Uganda to eliminate all forms of discrimination with respect to the ownership, sharing, and inheritance of land. It further urged the introduction of measures to address customs and traditional practices, especially in rural areas, that affect the full enjoyment of the right to property by women. The committee expressed concern at the persistence of patriarchal attitudes and deep-rooted stereotypes regarding the roles, responsibilities, and identities of women and men in all spheres of life.[5]

Admittedly, it is difficult for the Ugandan government to improve women's rights to matrimonial property when state-made laws have no monopoly over people's lives. It is, nevertheless, incumbent on the government to ensure that all legal processes under its jurisdiction are fair to women. It is beyond the scope of this chapter to enumerate all of the benefits from reforming the various family and succession laws to enhance women's rights to property; in brief, it is one way of emancipating women from poverty. Recent studies on women's ownership of property and land, in particular, show that women in Uganda produce 60 percent of the country's cash crops and 80 percent of its food production, yet only 7 percent of registered landowners in the country are women.[6] A government study also reports that women "have limited economic opportunities due to their societal roles and responsibilities, their low social status, relationships with men, lack of ownership and access to productive assets, low participation in decision-making and high workload."[7] Granted, Uganda's pursuit of capitalist economic policies is exacerbating the poverty prevailing in the country, but the prevalence of discriminatory family laws is making the situation worse for women.

The above indicates the need to reform women's rights over matrimonial property in Uganda. It is not tenable for the government to remain complacent because the Constitution is protective of women's rights to property when the concrete reality for many is unsatisfactory. Clearly, the plural legal system contributes to the violation of women's rights to property. Although the Constitution prohibits customs and traditions that work against the welfare of women and the Judicature Act expressly provides that statutory laws prevail over customs and unwritten laws, the reality on the ground—where many women are marginalized by oppressive customes regarding property ownership—is different. There is still a gap between the law contained in the statute books and the law in practice. Worse still, even where the generally outdated written laws have been amended to become more progressive, the lives of the majority of women have hardly changed. For example, it is not uncommon for women to lose land and their homes because their husbands have sold or mortgaged land without obtaining the spousal consent that is obligatory under the Land Act of 1998.

Women's Rights to Property in Marriage and on Divorce

The Constitution, taking precedence over all other laws in Uganda, prescribes fundamental freedoms and rights of the individual. These rights include the right to property and protection from discrimination. Article 31 stipulates equal rights for men and women on marriage, during marriage, and at its dissolution, as well as equal rights to inherit property.

The Constitution has many other provisions designed to protect the rights of women. For example; Article 33(5) gives women the right to affirmative action for the purpose of redressing the imbalances created by history, traditions, or customs; Article 33(4) provides that women have a right to equal treatment with men, and that that right shall include equal opportunities in political, economic, and social activities; and Article 33(2) provides that the state shall provide the facilities and opportunities necessary to enhance the welfare of women to enable them realize their full potential and advancement. Concerning equality and freedom from discrimination, Article 21(2) provides that "a person shall not be discriminated against on the ground of sex, race, colour, ethnic origin, tribe, birth, creed or religion, or social or economic standing, political opinion or disability." To discriminate is defined in Article 21(3) as "to give different treatment to different persons attributable only or mainly to their respective descriptions by sex, race, colour, ethnic origin, tribe, birth, creed or religion, or social or economic standing, political opinion or disability."

The above constitutional protection notwithstanding, other laws regulating private rights continue to discriminate by gender. The flaw is that although the Constitution is protective of women's rights to property, it sets out rights only in general terms. To guarantee those rights, enabling laws are required, yet they have not been enacted. Uganda's present laws of marriage, divorce, and succession preceded the 1995 Constitution and, with regard to the rights of women, need to be reformed and be made fully compliant with it. For example, the present Marriage Act came into force on 1 April 1904, and because Britain was Uganda's colonial master between 1896 and 1962, the Ugandan law was modeled on English law of the time. Accordingly, interests in property are not acquired or lost by marriage. Section 3 of the Succession Act provides that "no person shall, by marriage acquire any interest in the property of the person whom he or she marries, nor become incapable of doing any act in respect of his or her own property which he could have done if unmarried." Consequently, valuable matrimonial properties, including land on which matrimonial houses are situated, are usually registered in the name of the wage-earning spouse—the husband.

There are several ways that a valid marriage can be contracted in Uganda, each of which involving its own legislation. There is the Marriage Act[8] to regulate secular marriages and the Marriage and Divorce of Mohammedans Act[9] for Muslim marriages. Customary marriages are registered under the Customary Marriages (Registration) Act,[10] and the Marriages of Africans Act[11] regulates African marriages. None of these archaic laws, however, is concerned with how property should be shared to benefit women in a manner consistent with the Constitution. Common among Uganda's disparate laws of marriage is their focus on procedural matters relating to how marriages are contracted, rather than on property sharing. Notwithstanding, alimony payments are provided for under sections 23–25 of the 1904 Divorce Act,[12] and maintenance for children is available under common law. Under section 26 of the Divorce Act, if a party's adultery has been the cause of a divorce, the court has the discretion to order that some property of the guilty party be forfeited for the benefit of the children of the marriage, the innocent spouse, or both.

It is on dissolution of a marriage that the issue of which spouse owns what arises. The power to vary settlements is provided for under section 27 of the Divorce Act, which enables courts to do so for the benefit of the wife, husband, or children as court may deem fit.

Overall, the separate property regime prevails during all recognized marriages, though under the Divorce Act, courts have discretionary powers to make orders for alimony[13] and vary property settlements as noted above. Predictably, neither the Marriage Act nor the Divorce Act sets out guidelines regulating property sharing at divorce or judicial separation. In practice, on divorce the parties share property acquired through joint efforts, but the courts must determine each party's contribution to the acquisition of the assets. The problem with such a separate matrimonial property regime[14] in both state-made and non-state-made laws of marriage and succession, and the reason why sustaining it makes women's rights to marital property weak, is because in many cases virtually all the valuable property belongs to the economically stronger party, usually the husband. There are no means, at least during the duration of the marriage, of enabling the economically weaker party, usually the homemaker wife, to buy an equal amount of property and exercise the same rights over it.

Furthermore, in Uganda not all divorce cases are entertained in the courts, given the disparate laws under which marriages can be contracted. It is rare for customary-law marriages or those contracted under practices inspired by Islam to end up in the high and magistrate courts.

Specific Proposed Reforms for Women's Rights to Property in Marriage and on Divorce

Recently proposed legislation affecting women's rights to property in marriage leaves much to be desired. The problem is the desire by the legislature to accommodate all views, interests, religions and vote-winning issues when enacting laws. This indeterminacy is perpetuating Uganda's inability to make the various laws of marriage and succession compliant with its constitution and CEDAW commitments. This is another problem faced by Ugandan women. One example will suffice to illustrate this view. While the laws regulating widows' rights of succession to property have not been a subject of reforms, in recent years, attempts have been made to address the injustices that women encounter when marriages disintegrate. Accordingly, based on research conducted by the Law Reform Commission, a Domestic Relations Bill (DRB) was proposed in

2003 to consolidate the laws pertaining to marriage, divorce, and separation and to establish and guarantee marital rights and duties. Since then rivalry between legislators who favor patriarchy and those who support gender equality, the paucity of women legislators in Parliament, and claims by Muslims that the DRB contradicts Sharia law on polygamy have led to its being watered down. Consequently, citing resistance from the Muslim community, the DRB was split in two in 2010: the Marriage and Divorce Bill, which caters to customary, Christian, Hindu, and Bahai marriages, and the Muslim Personal Law Bill specifically for Muslim marriages.

Concerning rights to property, it has been proposed in the Marriage and Divorce Bill that matrimonial property shall be owned in common by the spouses.[15]

The bill defines matrimonial property as the matrimonial home and household property in that home. It also includes any other property, immovable or movable, acquired before or during marriage and property that was separately owned by one spouse, but toward whose purchase the other spouse made a contribution. The couple has to agree to a sale of matrimonial property, especially the sale of family land and property from seed money provided by a spouse for the establishment of a business. The bill further proposes that two persons intending to marry or cohabit, or those already cohabiting or married, may make an oral or written agreement in respect of the ownership of the separate property of each spouse or property acquired during the marriage or while cohabiting. The agreement should include the settlement of any differences that may arise regarding property, defining the property to which each spouse is entitled to on separation, dissolution of marriage, or termination of cohabitation.

If the agreement is oral, a witness is needed to defend it in court if necessary. Written agreements must be signed by both parties and witnessed by two peoples chosen by the parties. A court can, however, dissolve the agreement if either party proves it was made under duress. A court has the jurisdiction to make an enquiry into any property agreement made during the cohabitation or marriage, or on the termination of cohabitation or dissolution of the marriage. So where there are reasonable grounds, a court may set aside the agreement. This would be after any of the interested persons applied for an inquiry or alleged fraud or misrepresentation, for example.

Either spouse can acquire separate property during the marriage. This is not matrimonial property, unless the other spouse proves that he or she made a contribution to its acquisition or maintenance. The bill defines separate property as that which is independently acquired, acquired before marriage, or acquired by inheritance or as a gift from a person other than the spouse even after the date of marriage.

If the bill were to become law in its present form, it would mean better access to matrimonial property by both parties in a marriage or cohabitation. The bill outlaws transactions related to matrimonial property unless there is written consent of the other spouse. In circumstances where one of the parties in the marriage acquired a liability relating to property before the marriage, the liability remains the responsibility of the spouse who incurred it, except when the property becomes matrimonial property.

Concerning polygamous marriages, the bill proposes that matrimonial property shall be owned in common by the husband and each of the wives. However, matrimonial property acquired by the husband and the first wife shall be owned in common by the husband and first wife, and the subsequent wives shall have an interest only in the husband's share of that property. Interestingly, the bill does not recognize cohabitation but provides that property acquired during cohabitation can be shared.

Although these proposals are an improvement on what currently prevails and are bound to influence practices and laws regulating rights of succession to property, they do not go far enough. For example, instead of abolishing legal pluralism and the attendant inequalities that adversely affect women, Uganda has opted to retain the status quo, albeit with some modifications. The retention of the Muslim Personal Law, moreover, contradicts gender equality between the sexes that the Constitution and CEDAW prescribe. It would have been more progressive to do away with polygamous marriages.

Although land is the most valuable property in Uganda, the laws regulating its ownership do not promote equality between the sexes. For example, the Land Act of 1998 provides that with regard to land held under customary tenure[16]—which is the most dominant form of land ownership, given that most land is not registered—the family is the legal person, represented by the head of the family. The law provides that matters to do with land titling can be pursued by the individual or the household.[17] This law is silent on who should be named on the certificate of title, if one is issued. With this lacuna in the law and patriarchal socialization in the country, the male who is head of the household usually gets the certificate issued in his name without much resistance from women in the family. Furthermore, Uganda's Land Act has no explicit provision to the effect that women's rights to land are equal to those of men.[18] Attempts to amend the Land Act of 1998, through the Land (Amendment) Bill of 2007, were also more geared at curbing rampart evictions from land than providing for equal rights to land ownership.

In 2004, amendments were effected to the Land Act; however, a co-ownership clause to have both spouses registered on the land title was not considered. Nonetheless, the Land Act includes a provision requiring the consent of either spouse or children of majority age[19] before mortgages or planned transfers of land on which the family lives and from which it derives its sustenance are effected. This is a progressive provision regarding access to and use of land, but it does not amount to an equal right to land ownership. Moreover, this provision protects only married women; those in cohabitation are not protected. Worse still, some Ugandan men move from one form of marriage to another: they marry wives under civil law, then add more wives under custom, or start with customary marriage and then marry another wife under civil law. The offense of bigamy exists largely on paper. Consequently, it is common for customary marriages to be contracted after monogamous marriages have been celebrated.[20] The law does not recognize the second marriage, although the woman involved may not know this. The effect of this situation is that such a subsequent wife's interest in land is not protected by the aforesaid consent clause. The other problem is that in some rural and urban settings, a family lives on one piece of land but derives sustenance from another. Inevitably in such cases, the consent clause protection is partial because, if a spouse is to be protected, the land on which the family lives must be the same as that from which it derives sustenance.

Unsatisfactory Aspects of the
Laws of Succession

Uganda's state-made laws regulating rights of intestate[21] succession to property are equally unsatisfactory. First, because of the implementation of the 1995 Constitution, other laws regulating rights of intestate succession to property have become outdated. The implication is that much of the state-made law of succession must be amended to advance women's rights, as set forth by the Constitution. The amendments are urgent, given that many men in Uganda die intestate.

Besides the above, there are so many laws governing rights of intestate succession to property that the applicable law in a particular case can be a combination of two or more pieces of legislation. It is not uncommon for two laws to confer different entitlements to widows. The effect is that in some cases, laws conferring superior rights on widows are never invoked in the courts.

Some laws relevant to the regulation of rights of succession to property are contained in other laws, such as chapter 162 of the Succession Act; chapter 157 of the Administrator General's Act; chapter 156 of the Administration of Estates (Small Estates) (Special Provisions) Act; Resistance Committee Judicial Powers Statute of 1988; and chapter 161 of the Public Trustee Act, which is relevant to succession only insofar as it empowers the administrator general[22] to administer legacies for infants and persons of unsound mind. The rationale is to protect persons of unsound mind, including women, from being cheated of their entitlements.

The statutory law of intestate succession ensures that those whom the deceased had a duty to support—primarily widows or widowers, children, and other dependent relatives—are provided for. However, some provisions of the law contradict Uganda's CEDAW commitments on women's rights. For example, under section 2(w) of the Succession Act, the definition of a wife is someone who, at the time of the intestate man's death, was validly married to the deceased according to the laws of Uganda. Given that some women are not legally married even under customary law, it means their rights of succession to property are precarious.

The maintenance of laws of succession that are not protective of women not legally married is a mistake, given that many people in Uganda are now cohabiting instead of marrying. Uganda ought to accept this reality and protect the rights of both married women and those in cohabitation. As discussed, CEDAW does not condone the distinctions between married and unmarried women.

When someone dies intestate, the law sets out the relevant percentages that entitled persons get from the estate—the deceased's movable or immovable property. Section 27(1) of the Succession Act states explicitly that, in a situation where an intestate is survived by a customary heir (the person recognized by the customs of the tribe or community of a deceased person as being the logical heir—typically the oldest son), a wife, lineal descendants (children, grandchildren, and so forth, one of whom might be the customary heir), and dependent relatives (a son or daughter under eighteen years of age, or an older child, parent, brother, sister, or grandchild who was wholly or substantially dependent on the deceased for the provisions of the ordinary necessaries of life), the customary heir shall receive 1 percent; the wife 15 percent; the dependent relatives 9 percent; and the lineal descendants 75 percent of the property of the deceased. The principal residence is the only exception. Section 27(2) states that nothing shall prevent the customary heir from taking a further share as a lineal descendant, if the heir is such a descendant.

Although lineal descendants, normally children of the deceased, receive the largest share, a widow with 15 percent of the estate, combined with what she holds in trust for her children, usually becomes the most suitable person to administer the estate of her late intestate husband, because under the Succession Act administration of an estate is granted to a person entitled to the greatest proportion of the estate.

The assumption that the widow would administer the deceased's estate would not hold, however, if the widow were not the mother of all the deceased's children, as often happens when the deceased male had been polygynous. Section 202 of the Succession Act provides that "subject to section 4 of the Administrator General's Act, administration shall be granted to the person entitled to the greatest proportion of the estate under section 27." Section 4(1) of the Administrator General's Act requires that all deaths that occur in Uganda be reported to the Administrator General with full particulars as to property.

Furthermore, section 4(3) requires the Administrator General to apply for letters of administration of the estate of the deceased, if the testator (someone who passed away after having executed a valid will) has left a will without appointing an executor (someone appointed in the last will of a deceased person to execute the terms of the will) or the named executors have predeceased the testator or renounced probate of the will (probate means the grant by court of competent jurisdiction authorizing the executor named in the testator's last will to administer the testator's estate).

Uganda's state-made law of intestate succession does not promote equality between men and women in accordance with the Constitution because it awards surviving spouses negligible shares in the deceased spouse's estate. For example, the law discriminates against a widow who makes various contributions to the development of her deceased spouse's estate by awarding her a mere 15 percent of the estate in her own right. Moreover, in situations where there is more than one widow, this 15 percent must be shared equally among them. It is, on the other hand, very rare to find more than multiple widowers sharing the said 15 percent equally among themselves because polyandry (the practice of a woman having more than one husband or male sexual partner at the same time), unlike polygyny (the practice of a man having more than one wife or female sexual partner at the same time), is not prevalent.

Under section 2(r) of the Succession Act, a personal representative is a person who is appointed by law to administer all or part of the estate of a deceased person, and who only holds the property in trust for the beneficiaries. Section 25 provides that "all property in an intestate estate devolves upon the personal representative of the deceased upon trust for those persons entitled to the property under this Act." Ideally this law is protects widows from being cheated of their entitlements by personal representatives. In practice, however, customary heirs—who are normally males—are chosen as representatives of the deceased and often abuse the confidence bestowed in them by wasting the property to the detriment of the widows and other beneficiaries. Although there are remedies to address this situation, in practice, the institutions involved in using these remedies are not easily accessible and generally costly and complicated procedures must be followed before a remedy is granted. A progressive law of succession would confer more rights on surviving spouses rather than on personal representatives.

Under section 27(1)(b) of the Succession Act, if an intestate person is survived by a customary heir, wife, and dependent relative but not a lineal descendant, with the exception of the principal residence, the customary heir receives 1 percent, the wife receives 50 percent, and the dependent relative receives 49 percent of the property of the deceased. Although the state-made law of succession restricts the entitlement of the customary heir to only 1 percent of the estate, in practice many families give these heirs more property than what the law offers in accordance with the traditional perception that customary heirs symbolize the deceased. The clan appoints the customary heir, but because all societies in Uganda are patriarchal, males are favored.[23]

In some situations, especially monogamous relationships where there are no children surviving the deceased, the law favors surviving spouses. Thus under section 27(1)(c) of the Succession Act, if an intestate person is survived by a customary heir and a wife or dependent relative but not a lineal descendant, the customary heir receives 1 percent and the wife or dependent relative receives 99 percent of the whole property. However, Uganda's population is growing rapidly, which suggests that it is unusual to find a married couple without children.[24]

There have been some reforms to the law, albeit through the courts rather than the legislature. On 5 April 2007, the Constitutional Court of Uganda declared sections of the Succession Act relating to occupancy rights of the matrimonial homes discriminatory and thus null and void.[25] The repealed law provided that a widower had an indefinite right to occupy the matrimonial home, whereas the widow's rights were conditional and ceased on her remarriage. Furthermore, the court found that section 27 (regulating the distribution of property on the death of a male intestate), section 29 (regulating the reservation of a principal residential holding from distribution), section 43 (regulating testamentary guardians—people appointed, usually through the will, by the parent of a minor child to take care of that child in case of the parent's death; testamentary guardians have no custody rights or financial responsibilities concerning the child), and section 44 (regulating statutory guardians—guardians appointed by statutory authority) were all inconsistent with the constitution and therefore null and void. Unfortunately, Parliament has yet to amend the law of succession to bring it in conformity with the Constitution.

Concerning the rights of separated spouses, section 30(1) of the Succession Act provides that "no wife or husband of an intestate shall take any interest in the estate of an intestate if, at death of the intestate, he or she was separated from the intestate as a member of the same household." Under section 30(3) however, on application by such a wife or husband, the court may declare that subsection (1) shall not apply to the applicant. The problem is that section 30(3) makes it possible for separated spouses to make claims and share in the intestate person's estate, which requires relying on the court's discretion rather than a basic set of guidelines and rules to resolve disputes. Ideally, the act of separation, as opposed to judicial separation or divorce, should not be a bar to any surviving spouse's sharing in the intestate's estate, especially if the relationship has lasted for a long time. It is possible for a spouse who is not aware of this law or lacks the money to afford legal representation to lose his or her entitlements to property that he or she helped to accumulate. Moreover, litigation — even if it is settled before trial — is often time-consuming and ruinously expensive to the parties involved in it.

Uganda's state-made law of intestate succession to property has a few strong points, as discussed above, but also many unsatisfactory aspects.

As regards testate succession, section 36(1) of the Succession Act provides that "every person of sound mind and not a minor may by will dispose of his or her property."

Testamentary freedom, however, is not absolute but is regulated to balance conflicting interests, principally related to the wishes of the individual testator and the well-being of his or her family and society. Consequently, under section 38 of the Succession Act, if a person dies testate but does not make reasonable provision for the maintenance of a dependent relative, the High Court may order that reasonable provision be made out of the deceased's estate for the maintenance of that relative. The term "dependent relative," which includes a spouse, is, however, given a very generous definition under section 2(g) of the Succession Act, to include a parent, brother, or sister wholly or substantially dependent on the deceased. The definition of "dependent relative" is unsatisfactory because the class of people who are qualified to claim entitlements from the deceased's estate is too large. It needs to be restricted to the immediate family.

As regards women's rights under Uganda's disparate customary laws, what is common to all of them is that males are given preference over females in terms of rights of succession to property. In one way or another, clans, in-laws, and extended families affect women's rights when they determine what is a fair distribution of property on the death of a husband. Moreover, in many cases, when state-made and other laws of succession conflict, the latter tend to prevail — to the prejudice of the women beneficiaries. For example, in some instances, wills may provide entitlements for widows on paper, but the clan distributes the property according to its own schemes under the umbrella of custom, to the detriment of such widows. Given that customary law regulates people's lives on a daily basis, challenging it is easier said than done.

Unsatisfactory Aspects
of Islamic Family Law

Whereas Muslim women appear to be marginalized in matters of inheritance, these reduced inheritance rights are compensated for by other means of wealth generation. These methods include a woman's equal ability to purchase items through earnings, endowments, and gifts and special supplements such as savings (from lack of financial obligations within the family), her dowry, and maintenance. Clearly, as regards property rights, Islam accords women a more egalitarian position than customary law or Christianity.

Nonetheless, some practices inspired by the Islamic religion—especially polygyny—continue to adversely affect women's rights to property in marriage, on divorce, and on the death of a spouse, regardless of what the Constitution prescribes to the contrary. There are various explanations for this defiance. One is that Islam is both a religion and a way of life, making separation of the two in the life of any individual believer difficult. Moreover, Islam predates Uganda's new constitutional standards for women's rights.

Concerning matrimonial property rights, marriages contracted under Islam involve a marriage agreement that imposes specific obligations on, and ensures rights for, each spouse. Among the significant rights and obligations are those that concern obedience and the regulation of the marriage agreement, dowry, and maintenance. There is cause for concern, however, because Islam requires maintenance for the woman only during *iddat* (a waiting period after divorce), during which time she is precluded from remarriage. There is, therefore, a very limited duty to maintain divorced wives under Islamic family law. Moreover, Islam is supportive of a separate property marital regime, in which neither spouse acquires interest in the property of the other because of the marriage. In addition, Islam accepts early marriages of girls, thus denying them the opportunity to pursue their studies and ultimately the ability to purchase their own property.

Islam allows polygyny. Several arguments have been advanced in support of polygyny among Muslims: It avoids a situation where a woman is kept as mistress with no right or legal claim on the man concerned. Islam forbids extramarital relationships.[26] The first wife is not abandoned when the husband marries a younger woman; he has an ongoing obligation to maintain and care for her. A second wife can help the first when the first is disabled by ill health or old age. Unless he is allowed to take a second wife, a man may be led into adultery to satisfy his natural biological needs. These and other arguments in favor of polygyny do not consider women's emotional needs and the complications the practice raises in terms of Uganda's compliance with its Constitution's commitments to equality. Ugandan law currently assumes that all marriages entered into by Muslims are governed by Sharia law and permit polygyny, whatever the couple's individual preference may be. Clearly, by tolerating Islam-inspired practices, Uganda is breaching its standards for equality between the sexes.

Although polygyny is permitted in Islam, it was never meant as an unrestricted licence for any man to marry as he wishes, contrary to the practices of many Ugandan Muslims. Before a man can take a second, third, or fourth wife, he should prove that he has sufficient income and assets to be able to make financial provision for them; is capable of treating all his wives equally and justly; has a good reason for wanting to take an additional wife, such as that the first wife is too old or ill to perform household duties or her marital obligations, or that she cannot have children or is of unsound mind; and obtain consent of his present wives.[27] These injunctions are followed more in theory than in practice in Uganda, with the result that when poor men marry more wives, the property available to the women on the husband's death is very meager.

Although Islam recognizes testamentary devolution of property, only one-third of the estate can be bequeathed by will. In effect, a testator does not have unrestricted authority over her or his property, which means that she or he cannot disinherit any beneficiaries. Accordingly, the bulk of the estate is distributed under intestacy rules—which direct the inheritance of property if the owner died without having made a valid will—as prescribed by the Quran, going to the widows or widowers, parents, and children of the deceased. According to the Quran (Surah An-Nisaa, 4:7, 11, and 12), the scheme of property distribution is based on the following principles: males and females are each entitled to a share of inheritance regardless of the size of the estate; a daughter's share is to be half that of a son's; if there are only daughters, two or more are to share two-thirds of the estate; if there is only one daughter, she receives half; both mother and father are each entitled to one-sixth if there are children, but if there are no children and the parents are the only heirs, the mother receives one-third. If the deceased left brothers and sisters, the mother receives one-sixth; the husband is entitled to a half if there are no children, and a quarter if there are children. A wife is entitled to one-quarter of her husband's estate if there are no children, and one-eighth if there are children. If the deceased has left neither ascendants or descendants but has a brother and sister who survive him, each sibling gets one-sixth; if there are more than two, they share a third of the estate.[28]

The problem, therefore, is that under Islamic law regulating intestate succession to property, the entitlements for widows are inadequate. The provision for a surviving widow falls short of the constitutional standards for equality and nondiscrimination between the sexes. The situation is compounded further if the deceased husband was polygnous and was survived by several children. Polygyny is widely practiced by Muslims in Uganda, which means that many wives jointly receive one-eighth of the estate when there are children and one-fourth when there are none.

It should be recognized, however, that under Islamic law, greater economic responsibility falls to men, whereas the women's role is economically lighter.[29] A female does not have social and family obligations to maintain other relatives. The obligation to support the women of the family is placed on males: fathers, sons, brothers, and even uncles. In theory, a wife, sister, or daughter would almost never have to support herself, and, therefore, the argument goes that she always has the right to call on a male relative to provide for her. What is unsatisfactory about this situation is that the widow is left dependent on the goodwill of her children and male relatives. In an ideal Muslim family, there would be no reluctance on the part of the children and relatives to contribute to the widow's support; however, in practice, many families fall short of this ideal.

The problem, therefore, is that the government is reluctant to make Islamic family law compliant with its CEDAW obligations, yet many Ugandan women profess the Islamic faith and Islamic law governs their marriages, divorce, and rights of succession to property. About 16 percent of Ugandans are Muslims, though the exact percentage of women who profess Islam is unknown.[30]

In conclusion, state-made, customary, and Islamic laws of marriage and succession do not award female spouses a substantial share in the estate consistent with equality of the sexes. Although each of Uganda's fifty-six ethnic groups has its own customary law, owing to patriarchy, in all cases men rather than women have superior rights to property during marriage, on divorce, and on the death of a spouse. The fact that customary law is not written, subject to variation, and largely enforced by men does not advance women's rights to property. As a general rule, division of matrimonial property under customary law for the benefit of estranged wives was, and still is, not recognized, nor is maintenance payable to a wife after divorce.[31]

The state-made laws of testate succession give courts power to protect widows against disinheritance by amending wills, but unfortunately, few people in Uganda write wills. Moreover, husbands can still give away whatever domestic property they want *inter vivos* (during the lifetime of the parties involved), and courts have no power to reverse such transactions, even if done with the purpose of defeating the interests of the surviving spouse. The courts' powers under the Succession Act are restricted to distributing the net estate of the deceased among all dependent relatives.

General Reform Proposals

Although judicial discretion under Uganda's state-made laws of marriage, divorce, and succession allows each judge to do justice in each individual case, it needs to be based on fixed rights to property so as to avoid unpredictability in the outcome of any particular case. It is, therefore, desirable for Uganda to adopt a matrimonial property regime that advances certainty and clarity in the laws regulating the sharing of the parties' resources on divorce. Certainty and clarity would enable the parties to know what to expect on divorce and, as well as reducing acrimony, would enable the parties to reach settlements more easily. Finally, it would promote consistency in the division of property throughout the country and between courts and individual judges. Given the unsatisfactory situation that prevails in Uganda, an immediate community property regime is worth adopting because under it, the spouses would own property equally, regardless of their respective contributions to its acquisition. This regime is justified by the notion that joint ownership recognizes the theoretically equal contributions of both spouses to the creation and operation of the family unit.

Under the immediate community property regime, marriage would creates a community, meaning that its property would automatically be jointly owned (regardless of apparent paper or registered ownership).[32] Both parties would have the power to manage and control the community property; in many cases, neither would be able to dispose of it without the other's consent.

Objectively, in function, there is no difference between a stable cohabitation and a stable marriage. Similarly, in both marriage and cohabitation it is difficult to prove contribution to property acquired in the relationship after a long period of time. Accordingly, section 2(w) of the Succession Act, which provides that a wife at the time of the intestate person's death has to be validly married to the deceased according to the laws of Uganda, should be amended to include cohabitants.

Proper interpretation and enforcement of Islamic law of marriage is long overdue. That would ensure that before a Muslim man takes an additional wife, he must prove that he has sufficient income and assets to make financial provision for his wives; and the same property should be available to all the women on divorce or the husband's death. Furthermore, the government should appoint a committee of judicial officers with representatives from the Uganda Muslim Supreme Council to ensure that Islamic law does not contravene principles of gender equality and nondiscrimination.

It is proposed that, at the very least, the overarching principle of a reformed customary law of succession is that if the deceased had more than one wife, all the surviving wives should share equally in his estate. The definition of "estate" should exclude the various matrimonial homes and their household properties, or the respective residences of each wife. To avoid competition over resources, before a man marries another wife, the law should, at the very least, ensure that he has acquired another furnished home for her.

Last but not least, the Uganda Law Reform Commission should seek ideas from members of the public and involve them in the debate about adopting a unified legal system. As shown above, there are many problems emanating from the legal pluralism presently in force. This chapter has proposed that customary and Islamic family law should be restructured to comply with the constitutional standards on equality; however, a better approach is a uniform legal system.

Conclusion

The archaic statutory laws and religious and traditional customary laws and practices currently in force in Uganda have resulted in women's being denied equal rights to property with men. A patriarchal culture, coupled with a paucity of women in politics, has enabled the government to move slowly when adopting comprehensive reforms, and to date there have been negligible advances in women's rights to property. Change will come only when women demand their rights, rather than expecting the government to grant them at its own pace.

Notes

1 Adopted by the United Nations General Assembly in 1979, CEDAW set international standards for the protection of women's human rights, including achieving equality between men and women. Uganda ratified CEDAW without any reservations on 22 July 1985. See www.un.org/womenwatch/daw/cedaw/states.htm.

2 "Concluding Observations of the Committee on the Elimination of All Forms of Discrimination Against Women, 47th Session, 4th-22nd October 2010" (http://www2.ohchr.org/english/bodies/cedaw/docs/co/CEDAW-C-UGA-CO-7.pdf).

3 Ibid.

4 Ibid.

5 Ibid.

6 Equality Now, "Uganda: Exclusion of Women from Land Ownership—The Lost Clause," www.equalitynow.org.

7 Uganda Ministry of Finance, "Plan for Modernization of Agriculture: Eradicating Poverty in Uganda,"www.finance.go.ug/documents.html.

8 The Marriage Act, Chapter 251, came into force on 1 April 1904.

9 Marriage and Divorce of Mohammedans Act, Chapter 252, came into force on 15 April 1906.

10 Customary Marriages (Registration) Act, Chapter 248, came into force on 1 October 1973.

11 Marriage of Africans Act, Chapter 253, came into force on 1 April 1904.

12 Divorce Act, Chapter 249, came into force on 1 October 1904.

13 Alimony is an allowance paid to a person by that person's spouse or former spouse for maintenance, granted by a court on a legal separation or a divorce, or while action is pending.

14 Section 3, Succession Act, Chapter 162 Laws of Uganda.

15 According to drafts of the legislation available to the author.

16 A form of land ownership where the owners need no documents to prove ownership. Their claims to the land, and the boundaries of the land, are locally recognized.

17 Section 5, Land Act of 1998.

18 Marjolein Benschop, *Rights and Reality: Are Women's Equal Rights to Land, Housing and Property Implemented in East Africa?* (Nairobi: United Nations Human Settlements Programme, 2002), 76.

19 Section 40, Land Act of 1998.

20 Esther Obaikol and Kamusiime Herbert, *Perspectives of the Legal Fraternity on the Adequacy of the 1998 Land Act in Protecting Land Rights of Women and Tenants* (Kampala: Uganda Land Alliance, 2003), 9.

21 Section 24 of the Succession Act declares that a person dies intestate in respect of all property that has not been disposed of by a valid testamentary disposition (a will).

22 The Office of the Administrator General is established under the Administrator General's Act to ensure that estates of deceased persons are administered in accordance with the laws of succession.

23 Tuhaise Percy, *The Law of Succession in Uganda: Women, Inheritance Laws and Practices* (Kampala: LDC Publishers, 2001), 299.

24 Uganda's population, which has been doubling every twenty years, was twenty-seven million people in 2005 (US Central Intelligence Agency, *The World Fact Book*, www.cia.gov/cia/publications/factbook/rankorder/2119rank.html).

25 See Law & Advocacy For Women in Uganda vs. Attorney General, Constitutional Petitions Nos 13/05& 05/06, [2007] UGCC 1.

26 Jamila Hussain, *Islamic Law and Society* (Sydney: Federation, 1999), 74.

27 Ibid., 34, 72.

28 Ibid., 34, 104.

29 Mai Yamani, *Feminism and Islam: Legal and Literacy Perspectives* (Reading Berkshire, England: Garnet, 1996), 69.

30 See US Central Intelligence Agency, *The World Facts and Figures* (www.worldfactsandfigures.com/religion.php).

31 Jennifer Okumu Wengi, *Weeding the Millet Field: Women's Law and Grassroots Justice in Uganda* (Kampala: Uganda Law Watch Centre, 1997), 42.

32 Elizabeth Cook, Tina Akoto, Anne Barlow and Therese Callus, "Community of Property—A Regime for England and Wales: Interim Report," in *International Family Law* 1 (September 2005), 133.

PART FOUR

Feminist Identities

YÜKSEL SEZGIN

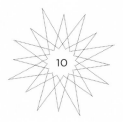

10

Triangulating Reform in Family Law

THE STATE, RELIGION, AND WOMEN'S RIGHTS IN COMPARATIVE PERSPECTIVE

In Israel, Egypt, and India, individuals who want to marry or get a divorce need to do that according to the rules of their ethno-religious communities: Muslims are subject to Sharia, Christians to canon law, Jews to Halakhah, Hindus to Hindu law, and so forth. In Israel, religious laws are applied directly by communal judges at religious courts,[1] whereas in Egypt and India they are implemented by civil judges at secular courts. To give an example, a Muslim woman who wants to get a divorce needs to bring her case to Sharia courts in Israel, but in Egypt and India she will go to civil courts, where secularly trained judges will decide her case according to Muslim laws. Neither Israel nor Egypt has a civil family code that is uniform and applicable to all citizens irrespective of communal affiliation. In other words, the only law in the field of personal status that these governments recognize is religious law. The Indian state, on the other hand, which claims to be a socialist, secular, and democratic republic, gives its citizens a secular alternative: the Special Marriage Act of 1954 permits individuals who do not want to be subject to religious laws to marry and divorce under civil laws.

Legal systems in which individuals are subject to the jurisdiction of their ethno-religious communities in matters of family law are widely known as personal status or personal law systems. Such systems have historically been employed by imperial powers to categorize their colonial subjects according to their racial, religious, and ethnic differences (Mamdani 1996; Mirow 2004). In other words, they were put in place to determine who was entitled to membership in the political community by regulating who could marry whom or who could have a child with whom. Yet personal status is not solely an antiquated legal or political system. On the contrary, many postcolonial nations that inherited such polycentric structures from their colonial predecessors still rely on these systems for regulating familial relations among their citizens.

In the process of nation and state building, nearly all postcolonial governments faced the same question: what were they going to do about the archaic institutions of personal status? Maintaining the old personal status regimes after independence would have not only resulted in further ossification of the colonial categories of race, gender, and ethnicity but would also have subverted the attempts of postcolonial leaders to redefine the terms of membership in the political community. Most governments have responded to the challenge by manipulating colonial institutions of personal law to impose a particular ideological vision and image of subjectivity on society, while ethno-religious communities fiercely resisted the government's meddling in attempts to preserve their juridical autonomy. In the end, governments' differing regime choices and varying ability to successfully impress their preferences on society, on the one hand, and the ethno-religious groups' varying capacity to resist government interventions, on the other hand, have given rise to differing forms of personal status across the postcolonial world. Here I will not indulge myself in the classification of different schemas of personal status; such an undertaking would be well beyond the scope of the present chapter. Elsewhere (Sezgin, n.d.), however, I have identified three ideal types of contemporary personal status systems: fragmented confessional, unified confessional, and unified semiconfessional.[2]

Although there are numerous analytical and heuristic benefits to categorizing personal status systems, there is not much difference among these models in terms of their impact on fundamental rights and liberties. Regardless of which ideal type they resemble, all personal status systems are invariably detrimental to fundamental human rights and liberties. This is because these systems institutionalize the discriminatory characteristics and gender inequalities of major religious traditions by giving them formal recognition and state-sanctioned backing. In countries where people are forcibly subjected to the jurisdiction of religious courts and norms without their consent, and where no alternative secular procedures are made available for dissenting individuals, the impact of personal laws on fundamental rights are particularly severe. Although personal status laws affect the rights of all individuals, they tend to have a harsher impact on women than on men. Nearly all religion-based personal status systems discriminate against women in familial matters such as marriage, divorce, inheritance, maintenance, and child custody. This is particularly true from the perspective of contemporary international human and women's rights law, which calls for absolute equality by eliminating all forms of gender-based discrimination against women and girls.[3]

In the rest of this chapter, therefore, I argue that although religion-based personal status laws discriminate against women, women do not sit silently on the sidelines and acquiesce in violation of their fundamental rights at the hands of male-dominated religious institutions. On the contrary, women's groups all over the world are spearheading a silent rights revolution that redefines women's role as rights-bearing individuals in familial and public spaces. In doing so, these groups contest the scriptural monopoly of state-sanctioned religious institutions, reinterpret religious laws, and reinvent religious tradition by vernacularizing international women's and human rights discourses. Against this background, the first part of the chapter demonstrates the implications of religion-based laws on rights and freedoms of women by looking at the Israeli, Egyptian, and Indian personal status systems. The second part of the chapter traces women-led reform movements that have emerged in the last two decades in these three countries and shows how women have responded to violations of their rights, and what tactics and strategies they have successfully employed to navigate the maze of religious law.

How Do Personal Status Systems Affect Women's Rights and Freedoms?

In personal status systems, religious authorities enjoy a nearly monopolistic control over their members' marital affairs. They get to decide on questions of who can marry whom; how much dowry is to be paid; what formalities are to be followed, such as the number of steps to be taken around the sacred fire, or the type of scribe and parchment to be used for the marriage contract; the minimum age for marriage; the duties and responsibilities of the husband and wife; rules of maintenance and succession; and many others. The so-called religious laws often relied upon to answer these questions are constructed by male-dominated religious institutions through selective readings of ancient texts and narratives, which subordinate women to men in almost every respect of law from marriage to child support. However, women's inferiority vis-à-vis men is most visible in divorce and, to a lesser degree, maintenance and succession laws (Madera 2009; Wegner 1982). Thus, I will next turn my attention to Israeli, Egyptian, and Indian personal status systems and show how gender-unequal divorce, maintenance, and succession laws impact women's fundamental rights.

ISRAEL: JEWISH MARRIAGE AND DIVORCE

Regardless of whether they are secular or members of non-Orthodox (that is, conservative or reform) congregations, all Israeli Jews are subject to the jurisdiction of rabbinical courts in regard to matters of personal status. These courts have exclusive jurisdiction over marriage and divorce, and concurrent jurisdiction with civil family courts in regard to all other matters of family law. Rabbinical courts apply only the Orthodox interpretation of Halakhah, as Orthodox Judaism enjoys a semi-official status in Israel. The courts have the monopoly on examining the Jewishness of every Jew, and determining whether he or she is suited for marrying another Jew. Halakhah forbids a union between a Jew and a non-Jew.[4] If a person fails the vetting, he would be permanently deemed unfit for marrying other Jews. In fact, the number of Israelis whose Jewishness is contested and who are banned from marriage by the rabbinical courts has reportedly reached about 400,000.[5]

Jewish divorce is an even more complicated matter, particularly for women. The act of divorce is finalized only when the husband grants his wife a *get* (a halachic bill of divorce). Issuance of a *get* is a must for dissolution of all Jewish marriages, not only those solemnized according to Halakhah in Israel or abroad, but also those contracted civilly outside of Israel (for example, Cyprus marriages[6]). A woman whose husband is either unable or unwilling to grant her a *get* is considered an *agunah*[7] and is thus chained to her husband.[8]

An *agunah* cannot marry another man or conceive a child with a man other than her husband until her *get* is properly issued. Otherwise, her relationship will be deemed adulterous, and her children will be stigmatized as *mamzerim* (a biblical term referring to the offspring of such relationships and their descendants),[9] whose offspring will not be allowed to marry other Jews for ten generations.

A recalcitrant husband has to be persuaded to grant a divorce of his own free will. In this game of persuasion, women usually bribe their way out of deadlocked marriages by paying the husband off or forgoing their claims to future child support and alimony (Bogoch and Halperin-Kaddari 2006). Bribing a husband to obtain a *get* has become such a common practice that the National Insurance Institute frequently allocates funds to help *agunot* pay their husbands off (Weiss 2002). In the face of growing *agunah* problem, the Knesset—the Israeli parliament—passed the Rabbinical Courts (Enforcement of Divorce Decrees) Law in 1995. The law established a mechanism to induce recalcitrant husbands to issue a *get* by imposing sanctions, including suspension of their credit cards, bank accounts, passports, and driver's and professional licenses and incarceration. However, the law is reported to have failed to produce most of its intended objectives, as the majority of *dayanim*, who believe that the new law openly violates the halachic principle of not coercing a man to divorce his wife against his will (Corinaldi 2002, 5–6), have opposed the law and effectively limited its application.[10]

The Jewish woman's ordeal of divorce may not be over even after the *get* is properly issued by the husband. In recent years, some activist *dayanim* were reported to have retroactively invalidated divorce decrees that they had granted earlier: "Such a scenario can arise when the husband claims that the divorce is contingent on the agreement to certain conditions (such as the size of alimony payments), and the wife tries to change these terms" (Raz and Neuman 2008). Nullification of divorce decrees may put the woman in a legal limbo. For example, if she has remarried, her new marriage will be deemed illegitimate, and if she has any children from this union, they will be considered *mamzerim*. Ruth Halperin-Kaddari calls the retroactive annulment of divorce decrees the ultimate "doomsday weapon" of rabbinical courts against the civil system and the women's rights in particular: "Nothing can be done against it. Even after the woman is divorced, she continues to be dominated by this sword hanging over her" (quoted in Raz and Neuman 2008).

Israeli Muslims are subject to the purview of Sharia courts, whose jurisdiction is exclusive over matters of marriage and divorce and concurrent with civil family courts in regard to all other matters of personal status (including child custody, maintenance, and succession). Like the Jewish women under rabbinical law, Muslim women have their fair share of problems under the Sharia law. However, for the most part, Muslim women have remained silent on issues of marriage and divorce, which are viewed as the pillars of Palestinian autonomy and identity in the Jewish state, and have confined their demands for change to procedural aspects of law and such issues as maintenance and custody.

Sharia courts apply the Ottoman Law of Family Rights (1917), according to which maintenance (*nafaqa*) that minimally includes food, clothing, and shelter is an indispensable aspect of Islamic marriage and an obligation of the husband. The amount of postnuptial maintenance is determined through negotiations between spouses. In the absence of consensus, however, the *qadi* (Islamic court judge), with the aid of informants (*mukhbirun*), determines the exact amount. As far as the amount is concerned, Sharia courts, like other religious courts in the country, have historically been very conservative. They "never ordered a man to pay child support in an amount higher than 500 shekels per child per month, while this amount was the minimum ordered in civil courts" (El-Taji T. 2008, 88). As I will show below, in order to increase the amount of maintenance that Muslim women receive, feminist activists campaigned throughout the 1990s for a legislative change that would transfer the Sharia courts' jurisdiction over maintenance to civil family courts, which they believed would be fairer and friendlier to women (Abou Ramadan 2006, 32).[11]

Divorce remains a major problem for women under the Egyptian personal status laws. All Muslim citizens of Egypt are subject to the Muslim personal law, which is implemented by civil family courts. Islamic law is also applied to Christian couples in case where spouses do not belong to the same sect (*ta'ifa*) and rite (*milla*). Under the law, a Muslim man has a right to a unilateral no-fault extrajudicial form of divorce known as *talaq*. The husband, who can have up to four wives, can divorce a wife—at any time and for any reason, and without needing to appear before a court—by pronouncing *talaq* three times. The Muslim wife, on the other hand, has been only given truncated rights to judicial divorce (*tatliq*), through which she can ask the court to dissolve the marriage on grounds of harm or injury (*darar*) (Esposito and DeLong-Bas 2001, 27-34, 49-61).[12] For example, under certain conditions (for example, the husband's sexual incompetence, prolonged absence, or imprisonment),[13] in which *darar* to the wife by the husband is satisfactorily established, the judge may dissolve the marriage at the request of the wife. However, unlike *talaq*, *tatliq* is a painful and costly process. It takes on average eight to ten years for a woman to obtain a divorce through the courts (Leila 2003; Sachs 2000; Singerman 2005, 165-66). The Egyptian women's predicament of divorce was somewhat eased with the enactment of Law No. 1 in 2000, under which the woman can initiate a no-fault divorce that does not require the husband's consent, provided that she forgoes all her financial claims on him including maintenance (*nafaqa*) and the deferred part of her dowry (*mu'akhar saddaq*) that the husband would normally pay his wife at divorce (Singerman 2005, 161). The question of whether this law has been able to fully remedy the Egyptian woman's predicament will be answered in greater detail below. At this point, it should suffice to note that the law has at least opened the door to no-fault divorce for an unlikely beneficiary: the Coptic Orthodox woman.

Personal status matters of Copts are subject to the jurisdiction of civil courts, which apply the 1938 Personal Status Ordinance of the Coptic Orthodox Community that was single-handedly promulgated by the liberal-minded laity without much input from the clergy. The ordinance, which had a very liberal attitude toward divorce, allowed it on nine different grounds,[14] including spousal incompatibility (Al-Banna 1984, 28-36; Atiya 1991, 1943; Salim 2004, 55). However, the church had repeatedly denounced the ordinance's liberal attitude and refused to recognize divorce decrees granted by civil courts for any reason other than adultery. The normative discrepancy between the views on divorce of the church and the 1938 ordinance has created a legal limbo for nearly 50,000 Copts whose marriages were dissolved by courts on grounds other than adultery. These people are practically banned from remarriage because in the eyes of the church they are still considered married (Ibrahim 2001). To avoid the likelihood of such a marriage ban, couples seeking divorce need to engage both ecclesiastical and civil authorities at once. All in all, this is a painstakingly long and complicated process.

Divorce for Coptic women is even more difficult and costlier, as they need to win the hearts and minds of unsympathetic judges and overcome their patriarchal attitudes. To ease their predicament, in recent years, some Coptic women have begun resorting to a backdoor approach to obtain *khul'* divorces by exploiting the aforementioned loophole that allows for the application of Sharia to non-Muslims. For example, Hala Sidqi, a famous actress, divorced her husband in 2002 through *khul'*. Both Sidqi and her husband were Orthodox Copts. In order to obtain a *khul'* divorce under Sharia, she had to belong to a church other than her husband's. Therefore, she converted to the Syrian Orthodox church, while her husband remained a Copt. By doing so, she was able not only to get a divorce under Islamic law, but also to obtain permission to remarry in the church, as her new faith allowed it. The exact number of Coptic women who followed in Sidqi's footsteps and applied for a *khul'* divorce is unknown. But, as observers indicate, not many Christian women have been granted such divorces because Egyptian judges remain deeply divided over the question of whether non-Muslims should be able to obtain them by resorting to deceitful conversions (Fouad 2002; Hasan 2003). Although it is debatable whether *khul'* is a feasible option for Coptic women, the very existence of this backdoor approach, according to Tadros (2009), has unmistakably strengthened the bargaining position of Coptic women vis-à-vis their husbands and communal institutions, as they can now threaten conversion to get a divorce.

INDIA: "TRIPLE *TALAQ*" AND MAINTENANCE

Divorce has been also a problem under the Indian personal law system, particularly for the Muslim women. The predicament that women suffer most from is "triple *talaq*," the practice of divorce by uttering *talaq* thrice in one single sitting. Even though triple *talaq* is the most frowned-on form of divorce under Sharia, it is the most common form among Indian Muslims. As exemplified by the *Shah Bano* case in 1985 (see chapter 3), Muslim men's unlimited power to divorce their wives instantly without needing to prove any grounds condemns Muslim divorcees to years of emotional suffering and destitution. According to the Muslim law in India, in the event of divorce the husband has to pay his wife the deferred part of her *mahr* (dowry or bridal gift) and provide her with maintenance (*nafaqa*) for three months—or until she gives birth, if she is pregnant. Other than that, he has no further financial obligations toward his wife. Even though Section 125 of the Criminal Procedure Code of 1973 requires all Indian husbands to continue providing for their divorcees, who would otherwise be destitute, Muslim men were excluded from the purview of Section 125 by virtue of the 1986 Muslim Women's (Protection of Rights on Divorce) Act. According to that law, a Muslim husband is under no obligation to pay any maintenance to his wife after the religiously sanctioned three-month period (*iddat*) (Agnes 2001; Menski 2001). That is to say, with the enactment of the 1986 law, the Indian government openly discriminated against Muslim women and denied them the financial guarantees that it had bestowed on Hindu, Parsi, and Christian women. As will be shown below, despite their recent successes in the battle for maintenance, Indian civil rights groups continue fighting to secure Muslim women's right to maintenance and put an end to gender discrimination perpetrated by religious and secular laws.

INDIA: SUCCESSION UNDER HINDU LAW

Nearly all religious traditions adopt a patriarchal attitude and favor agnatic heirs—those on the male side of family—in the distribution of the deceased's property (Radford 2000). Hindu law has been one of the religious legal systems that infamously discriminated against women and denied them the right to inherit or own property, especially before the enactment of the Hindu Succession Act of 1956 (HSA). Although the HSA, which reformed and codified the law relating to intestate succession among Hindus, unprecedentedly expanded women's right to property, it still was discriminatory legislation that denied women equal rights to agricultural land, joint family property, and the parental dwelling. The *Mitakshara* coparcenary (joint heirship) system that was adopted in the HSA divides a deceased father's property in two: individually owned and joint family property. As far as the former is concerned, both sons and first-class female heirs (daughters and widows) have equal rights to inherit. In respect to the latter, however, female heirs have only a right to sustenance while sons at their birth become co-owners with full control and ownership rights. Similarly, the HSA also denied Hindu women an equal share in agricultural land in the name of preventing the fragmentation of agricultural holdings. The gender-discriminatory succession laws had long been on the radar of women's rights organizations (Patel 2007; Saxena 2003). Their hard work finally paid off when they succeeded in getting the Indian Parliament to amend the HSA in 2005. Even though this amendment leaves much to be desired, it dealt a major blow to the traditional *Mitakshara* system and made a daughter's status equal to that of a son by removing some of her disabilities in respect to ancestral property and agricultural land. Below I will look at these changes at some greater detail.

How Do Women Respond to Violation of Their Rights and Freedoms under Religious Law?

As demonstrated above, religion-based personal status systems are detrimental to the rights and freedoms of women. This is because most governments have proved unable or unwilling to reform archaic systems of personal law and have failed to protect women against the encroachments of religious rules and authorities. Nevertheless, this does not mean that women just sit on the sidelines and silently accept persecution and violation of their fundamental rights. On the contrary, women are fighting fiercely to advance their rights and freedoms, and by doing so they continuously contest the hegemonic narratives of gender and subjectivity and redefine their roles as rights-bearing individuals in the familial and public space.

In religious systems, where women are systematically denied their fundamental rights in the name of obeying God's orders, the discussion always revolves around the question of whose interpretation of scripture shall be deemed authoritative (de Gaay Fortman et al. 2010). Hence, it is not surprising to see that in all three countries, women respond to violations of their rights by forming hermeneutic or interpretive communities that challenge the official interpretations of religious precepts and offer alternative, women-friendly readings of the law in the hope of advancing their rights and reforming the system from within. In the process, interpretive communities engage in An-Naimian "internal discourse" and vernacularize international standards of women's rights by meticulously grafting these imported ideas and practices onto the culture, tradition, and religious beliefs and teachings of their own societies (An-Naim 1992; Levitt and Merry 2009; Merry 2006a and 2006b; Rajaram and Zararia 2009). In this process of "owning" or "indigenization," the so-called alien discourses of rights and equality cease to be outside impositions and become the "own" value of the community, firmly grounded in its morals and traditions.

The hermeneutic groups are more than mere interlocutors that just engage in scriptural activity; rather, they function as agents of change who continuously define and redefine the place and role of women under the law. In doing so, they build alliances with like-minded groups, lobby for judicial and legislative change, mobilize courts, educate the public, and seek behavioral change by framing gender issues in terms that resonate with prevailing cultural norms. The particular strategy or tactic that a hermeneutic group eventually adopts is determined by a number of factors, including the objectives of the group, the political and legal culture of the country, institutional constraints, and opportunities for and the existence of a broader support structure (that is, allies, financial and legal resources, and so forth) or lack thereof. Furthermore, as will be demonstrated below, interpretive communities can be equally successful in democratic and nondemocratic countries. Although open societies normally offer far more opportunities for legal and political mobilization, it is not necessarily any easier to challenge the monopoly of religious law in a democracy than it is in an autocratic regime. For example, attempts at reforming religious laws of marriage and divorce in democratic Israel have repeatedly been defeated by Orthodox parties in the Knesset, while the democratically elected Indian government enacted the 1986 law to deny Muslim women equal rights to maintenance and to uphold discriminatory provisions of Muslim personal law. Thus, regardless of whether it is in democratic India or autocratic Egypt, when other venues of participation and reform are blocked, the hermeneutic path seems to become the choice of reform for groups seeking to alter religion-based personal status laws.

Although hermeneutic communities usually adopt moderate tactics and strive for incremental change, some of them may be gradually marginalized and adopt a more radical agenda, demanding complete abolition of existing personal status systems and even establishing alternative legal institutions. In other words, when authorities fail to respond to repeated calls for reform, some frustrated groups may cease to use state-run personal status institutions and steadily evolve into self-ruling communities, setting up their own judicial bodies that apply their own version of the law to members of their self-proclaimed communities. Examples of such self-ruling communities are the New Family in Israel, which offers an alternative, nonreligious mode of marriage and divorce to secular Jews, and the All India Muslim Women Personal Law Board (AIMWPLB), which—after long years of dissatisfaction with the particular version of Sharia promoted by the male-dominated All Indian Muslim Personal

Law Board (AIMPLB)—set up a *mahila adalat*[15] to offer religiously acceptable solutions to such problems as triple *talaq*. Against this background, the present section looks at activities of interpretive and rule-making communities in Israel, Egypt, and India and illustrates strategies and tactics successfully employed by these groups to advance women's rights under personal status systems.

EGYPT: THE KHUL' REVOLUTION

Hermeneutic communities have been particularly active in Egypt, where top-down approaches to reform have failed and the women's rights have diminished, especially since the Egyptian Supreme Constitutional Court's 1985 decision that struck down the 1979 Law No. 44 as unconstitutional. This law stipulated that taking a second wife without the consent of the first wife constituted an injury (*darar*) to the first wife, and therefore entitled her to seek divorce in the court.[16] Law No. 44, which had been unconstitutionally promulgated by a presidential decree, was a quantum leap in women's right to divorce. However, it did not take long for the opponents of the law—who viewed it as being in violation of Sharia for curbing Muslim men's God-given right to polygyny—to launch a judicial onslaught to stop its implementation.[17] In May 1985, their efforts finally came to fruition when the court declared Law No. 44 unconstitutional on technical grounds (Eldin, Hill, and Graham-Brown 1985). Two months later, a revised law (Law No. 100) was hastily put together by the Parliament as a replacement. It eliminated the controversial provision of Law No. 44 that "considered a second marriage by the husband as *ipso facto* a cause of harm to the first wife" (Najjar 1988, 341) and thereby a ground for divorce.

The failure of the 1979 law taught two invaluable lessons to Egyptian women's rights groups that wanted to reform the personal status laws. First, the reform had to be initiated by the women themselves through a combination of grassroots mobilization and government support, rather than for the women through unpopular top-down processes (Hatem 1992). Second, any change in the law had to be firmly rooted in historical sources and the tradition of Sharia. A solely liberal or secular approach was sure to backfire and do more harm than good to the cause of Egyptian women. As one prominent feminist put it, throughout the 1990s, Egyptian women's groups adopted the "strategy of engaging religious discourse, based on the women's reading of their rights under the principles of *Shari'a*" (Singerman 2005, 161). Hence, the setback experienced in 1985 led various women's groups to act collectively and campaign for equal rights for women in personal status by utilizing an Islamic framework.

During the next two decades, women's groups devoted their energy primarily to the so-called *khul'* law (Law No. 1 of 2000). This law allowed a woman to initiate a no-fault divorce even without the consent of her husband, provided that she renounced her claims to maintenance (*nafaqa*) and deferred dowry (*mu'akhar saddaq*, the part of the dowry paid by the husband to the wife at divorce) and returned the prompt dowry (*mahr al-muajjal*, the part of the dowry that is paid by the groom to the bride immediately after the solemnization of their marriage (*nikah*). Throughout the process that culminated in the enactment of Law No. 1, women's groups worked directly with government officials, lobbied members of the Parliament, and consulted with the members of *ulama* at al-Azhar. As Zeinab Redwan, a female member of the Egyptian Parliament and one of the architects of reform noted, during the entire process, "women repeatedly resorted to Islamic rhetoric and built their case around a hadith that reported Prophet Muhammad allowed a woman to divorce her husband by returning the orchard that she had received as dowry."[18]

The critics of the law argued that Sharia required the consent of the husband to divorce even in the case of *khul'*. Opponents also added that the law was meant only for rich women, as the poor could not afford to forgo their rights to maintenance and deferred dowry, nor could they pay back the prompt dowry. However, recent evidence shows that an increasing number of middle- and lower-class women are taking advantage of *khul'*, as its actual cost has not been as high as it was claimed to be by the critics of Law No. 1 (Sakr and Hakim 2001; Singerman 2005; Sonneveld 2007; Zulficar 2004). With this in mind, most of the problems that women have encountered seem to be of a social and institutional nature. Public opinion surveys point out that most Egyptians consider *khul'* as an option to be taken only by "loose," westernized women (Bahgory 1999; Fawzy 2004; Hassan 2001; Hill 2000; Sakr and Hakim 2001). In popular culture—movies, cartoons, and so forth—women who resort to *khul'* are often depicted as immoral persons in westernized garments who divorce their husbands for frivolous reasons so they can run into the arms of their secret lovers (Sonneveld 2006). In the early years of the reform, these negative images were also widespread among personal status court judges (Singerman 2005, 181–82). In fact, some attribute the vast discrepancy between the number of *khul'* petitions filed and the actual number of divorces granted by the courts to the unwillingness and obstructive practices of the judges.[19] During the first three years of the law, only about 5,000 *khul'* divorces (out of nearly 210,000 divorces) were granted by the Egyptian judges.[20]

ISRAEL: FEMALE REPRESENTATION AT RABBINICAL COURTS

While Egyptian women were fighting discriminatory divorce laws by producing women-friendly interpretations of Islamic law, Israeli women's organizations were taking an institutional approach instead and battling for more gender-balanced rabbinical courts. The first step in this direction was taken in 1990, when Orthodox women's groups succeeded in getting the rabbinical authorities to allow female advocates (*toanot*) in rabbinical courts (Shilo 2006). Today about half of the rabbinical advocates are women. Although this was a very important step in empowering Jewish women, it still was not a radical shift in gender balance of the courts, which continue to heavily favor men. Female advocates have been cautious not to openly challenge the male domination, which they fear might provoke the Orthodox establishment and undermine the limited gains women have made in the last two decades (Abramowitz 2004; Bak and Goldman 2000; Shamir, Shitrai, and Elias 1996). Some Israeli feminists who want to see a more conspicuous change in the gender composition of the courts advocate for female rabbinical judges, although according to the Israeli government's interpretation of Halakhah, women cannot serve as *dayanim*. However, some Orthodox women argue that there is nothing in Halakhah that bars a woman from becoming a *dayan*.[21] The problem, they say, is one of patriarchal interpretation rather than one of theological limitation. Although two women's organizations[22] have taken steps toward the realization of this dream, most feminists recognize that the time is not yet ripe for such a change. Hence, in the meantime, they have turned their attention to the committee that nominates rabbinical court judges. For example, in the last decade the International Coalition for *Agunah* Rights (ICAR), which brings together twenty-seven women's organizations to find a solution to the problem of *agunot*, has devoted its efforts to placing one of its members on the nomination committee. In fact, in December 2002, after an energetic lobbying campaign, Sharon Shenhav, an ICAR attorney, was elected as one of two representatives of the Israel Bar Association to the ten-person committee that appoints the rabbinical court judges (Shenhav 2004).[23] As one of the few female voices on the male-dominated Orthodox committee, Shenhav soon proved to be a force to reckon with in the appointment process. She played the role of a feminist watchdog and carefully scrutinized each candidate, making sure that only the ones who were in touch with mainstream Israeli society and sympathetic to the cause of women, were appointed as *dayanim*.[24]

ISRAEL: INTERNAL REFORM AT SHARIA COURTS

If Shenhav's election was a tremendous success for ICAR, the passage of the Law of Family Courts Amendment (No. 5) of 2001 was an equally iconic achievement for the Working Group for Equality in Personal Status Issues, a coalition of civil rights and women's groups representing Muslims, Jews, and Christians in Israel. This time, women's organizations worked together to make the legal status of Muslim and Christian women equal to that of Jewish and Druze women by granting the former "the option of recourse in maintenance suits to the new civil family courts" (Shahar 2006, 130). In 1997, the coalition initiated a bill to amend the Family Courts Law of 1995. Throughout the process, the Working Group members successfully publicized the inequalities that Palestinian women had to suffer by presenting statistics from the National Insurance Institute indicating that the alimony and child maintenance payments awarded to Muslim women by the Sharia courts were significantly lower than those awarded to Jewish and Druze women by the civil family courts (ibid.). After a successful public campaign and four years of negotiations in the Knesset, the amendment was finally passed in 2001 (El-Taji T. 2008).

Even though the passage of Law No. 5 of 2001 was an important achievement for Israeli Arab women, nearly ten years after its coming into force, it has not yet had much of its intended effect, for various institutional and political reasons. But there were some unintended and indirect changes that retrospectively made the Working Group's efforts a major success. Fearful of losing their jurisdiction and clients to the civil family courts, in 1995 the Israeli Sharia courts initiated a reform on their own by reviving a judicial mechanism that had been used a century earlier by the British in the Sudan: the legal circular, or *marsoum qadai*.[25] The circular, which was issued in the midst of calls for intervention by the Knesset, ordered *qadis* to rely on written evidence such as tax returns and insurance documents, instead of *mukhbirun* (informants), to set the amount of maintenance. In the months following the promulgation of the new circular, the amount of maintenance awards made to Muslim women by the Sharia court in West Jerusalem reportedly rose by about 50 percent

(Shahar 2006, 132). Despite this encouraging development, discrimination and unequal treatment of women remain a major problem under the Sharia system. Some Muslim women attribute this to the lack of female voices in the Sharia courts and advocate for appointment of female *qadis*. The current coordinator of the Working Group indicates that women's groups have already raised the issue with the nomination committee for Sharia judges and received the vocal support of several key members.[26] Muslim feminists remain hopeful that the Israeli authorities will follow the revolutionary example set by the Palestinian Authority[27] and appoint female judges to Sharia courts. However, women also recognize that the road to such a change will be long and thorny, as the idea of female *qadis* will be fiercely opposed by not only conservative Muslims but also orthodox Jewish parties, which will be fearful of the impact of such a drastic change on the rabbinical system.

INDIA: IMPACT LITIGATION AND MUSLIM WOMEN'S RIGHT TO MAINTENANCE

Indian women's organizations have historically adopted a secularist approach toward the personal law issue. From the 1950s on, it was the general belief among Indian feminists that the social uplifting of women could be achieved only by replacing religious laws with a Uniform Civil Code (ucc). However, ideological changes since the mid-1980s and the appropriation of the concept of the ucc by the Bharatiya Janata Party and other right-wing Hindu platforms have forced the women's organizations to reconsider their strategies and drop their earlier calls for a ucc (Agnes 2004, 5; Menon 1998, 252). Nowadays, they seem instead to rely on a mixture of legislative and judicial strategies and, whenever possible, to engage in interpretive activities to change personal laws from within.

In the last two decades, Indian women's groups have given some quintessential examples of ways to mobilize courts to challenge and reform gender-unequal personal laws. Especially in the aftermath of the infamous 1986 Muslim Women's (Protection of Rights on Divorce) Act, women launched a judicial onslaught to defeat the ill-famed legislation's minimalist interpretations that denied Muslim women's right to maintenance beyond the *iddat* period. Their campaign succeeded in 2001 with the Indian Supreme Court's decision in the *Danial Latifi* case, when the court overruled the restrictive interpretations of the 1986 act and extended Muslim women's right to post-

nuptial maintenance beyond the *iddat* period (Subramanian 2005). Thanks
to the court's upholding of their expansionist interpretations, Muslim women
are now reported to receive some of the highest maintenance awards in the
country (Menski 2006 and 2007).

INDIA: LEGISLATIVE REFORM AND HINDU SUCCESSION ACT

Legislative tactics have also been successfully used by some women's organizations. The amendment of HSA by the Indian Parliament in 2005 is a particularly good example of the ways Indian women's groups have approached bills
originally unfavorable to them and given the bills the shape that they desired
by engaging in constructive exchanges and building coalitions with numerous stakeholders. The resulting legislation in this case, the Hindu Succession
(Amendment) Act of 2005, was a remarkable step toward gender equality. Not
only did it make daughters coparceners (equal inheritors) of joint family property and recognize their right to inherit agricultural land, but it also gave them
the same right as sons to reside in or seek partition of the parental dwelling
(Agarwal 2005). Despite these remarkable gains, however, the law needs further
improvements in several areas. For complete gender equality, for instance, all
references to the archaic *Mitakshara* system need to be deleted from the law,
and restrictions need to be placed on parents' testamentary freedom to prevent
them from disinheriting daughters from their individually owned property by
establishing the principle of reserved shares (a portion of the estate, such as a
third, that cannot be willed away but must be reserved for a specific group of
heirs), as in Islamic law.

INDIA: ISLAMIC FEMINISM AND THE RISE OF WOMEN'S COURTS

Like their Egyptian and Israeli counterparts, Indian women's organizations have
also successfully used reinterpretative strategies to challenge the textual authority of religious institutions and advance women's rights under personal laws.
However, this strategy seems to be more commonly used by Muslim women's
groups than by Hindu ones, as Hinduism, due to its heterogeneity, avails itself
for scriptural analysis less readily than Islam (Sherma and Sharma 2008). Perhaps another reason why Muslim groups have been more active in the field of
hermeneutics is the political and ideological transformation the Muslim community has experienced in the last two decades. Since the *Shah Bano* case, the
community has grown increasingly resistant to the idea of change in its laws.

On the contrary, the community fell under the control of conservative elements such as the AIMPLB, which has set up independent Sharia courts (*Darul Qazas*) throughout the country and banned Muslims from taking their cases to state courts. The independent courts apply their own version of Islamic law and openly forbid women from claiming maintenance beyond the *iddat* period. Against this background, the demand for change had to come from within and be firmly grounded in the scripture and tradition. In fact, this is what Muslim women's organizations, like the AIMWPLB, did throughout the 1990s and 2000s (Vatuk 2008).

For example, the AIMWPLB, a splinter group that broke away from the male-dominated AIMPLB in a dispute over the issue of triple *talaq*, released a women-friendly *nikahnama* (Islamic marriage contract) in 2007 that prohibits triple *talaq* through text messaging, phone calls, e-mail messages, or video-conferencing and recognizes women's right to delegated (*talaq-e tawfiz*) and no-fault divorces (*khul'*). As Shaista Amber, the president of the AIMWPLB, reports, the new *nikahnama* is steadily gaining acceptance in the community and about fifty couples so far have married under the relatively gender-balanced contract.[28] In addition, the women's board has set up its own court structure (*mahila adalat*) in Lucknow (Awasthi 2006), which currently decides about 200 divorce cases per year. Male and female judges (*qazis*) sit together in court. The law they apply, Amber says, is not substantively different from the Islamic law applied by AIMPLB courts, but *qazis* at the *mahila adalat* implement it in light of international standards of human and women's rights.[29] The Bharatiya Muslim Mahila Andolan (BMMA), another organization working to secure the rights of women through feminist and humanist interpretations of Islam, has taken the women's cause one step further and made the history by allowing a female *qazi*, Sayeda Hamid, for the first time ever, to solemnize a *nikah* ceremony—at which the wedding contract is signed—where all four witnesses were also women. While the members of the mainstream *ulama* were busy questioning whether a woman could solemnize a marriage under Islamic law, the BMMA silently broke with tradition and opened a new page for the Muslim women in India—who had to rely on their own initiative, rather than the secular state or the male-dominated communal institutions, to put end to the discrimination they suffered under the Indian personal laws.

Conclusion

As noted earlier, governments' differing regime choices and ability to impose a particular image of citizenship on society, on the one hand, and ethno-religious groups' varying capacity to resist the state's interventions into religious jurisdictions, on the other hand, have given rise to different forms of personal status throughout the postcolonial world. Yet, as this chapter has shown, regardless of their form, personal status systems are invariably detrimental to the rights and freedoms of women. Put this way, as far as the impact of religion-based personal laws on human and women's rights is concerned, there is not much difference between an exclusionary theocratically inclined regime and an inclusionary secular regime, as exemplified by the cases of Israel and India.

However, this should not come as a surprise, as no society seems to have found an answer to the questions of how to best protect the rights of individuals under personal status systems; and to what extent a democratic regime should tolerate communal norms and institutions that impose illiberal sanctions and restrictions on female citizens. In search of answers, some scholars have emphasized the importance of individuals' freedom of association and right to exit from their cultural communities. In plain language, they have argued that if international human and women's rights standards are to prevail, then people must be completely free to leave the communal track and transfer their disputes to civil institutions (Barzilai 2003 and 2004; Benhabib 2002; Gutmann 2003; Kymlicka 1995 and 1996; Rawls 1999; Shachar 2001; Young 2000). However, like Chandran Kukathas (1992), I am of the opinion that an individual's right to exit is usually a hollow right, which exists merely on paper. The right to exit can be meaningful only if the community in question grants such freedom willingly to its individual members—without ramifications related to property—and if there is a larger society outside that embraces liberal values and is ready to welcome and protect the person after she has left her own community. What would happen to an Israeli Muslim woman who renounced Sharia courts and instead sought justice from the Jewish-dominated family courts? Would the community respect her decision and let her "forum shop" freely? Would the Jewish majority stand by her and protect her against possible retaliation by the community? It is not really difficult to guess, for we very well know what happened to seventy-five-year-old Shah Bano when she stepped out of her communal boundaries and tried to take advantage of civil remedies made available to her by the secular Indian state (Engineer 1987; see also chapter 3 in this volume).

This is a dire picture. But there is still much to be hopeful about. As shown throughout the chapter, a silent revolution, spearheaded by hermeneutic and rule-making communities, is taking place across the personal status systems of many nations, from Egypt to India. Religious laws have been products of human agency, which—through androcentric readings of the tradition—have denied women equal representation in the construction of religious legality. In this revolution, hermeneutic and rule-making communities are altering the way we understand the legality of sacred laws that define women's role in the familial and public space by deconstructing the meaning of texts, historical narratives, and tradition. The pace of the reform introduced through interpretive activity may be criticized for being too slow. Furthermore, as noted by Human Rights Watch in its critique of Law No. 1 of 2000 in Egypt (Deif 2004), it may also fall short of international and secular standards of women's rights. However, these limited and gradual changes may be more likely to affect women's rights positively than secular top-down remedies, which—as seen in the case of Law No. 44—may cause more harm than good in the long run by diminishing chances of ever implementing international women's rights standards in religious legal systems. Reform from within stands a better chance of acceptance and success, as it not only better reflects the sociolegal and political realities of nonwestern societies, but it also symbolizes a hard-won consensus on gender roles and the place of women in the society.

Nowadays any discussion of human rights under religio-legal systems inexorably revolves around the axis of universalism and cultural relativism. However, it is imperative to transcend this false and counterproductive dichotomy to reach a cross-cultural understanding of human rights (Santos 2002; Twining 2009). In this regard, international human or women's rights should not be treated as products of a particular civilization or culture. On the contrary, they belong to all humanity. Rights and liberties should be equally enjoyed by every human being, regardless of race, gender, religion, ethnicity, age, culture, or any other consideration. However, how one attains them may change from one society to another. In this regard, the hermeneutic approach to reform may be instrumental in importing international rights discourses and values into local cultures by firmly grounding them in the traditions and institutions of local communities. At the same time, one must also understand that there are some fundamental inequalities or discriminations inherent to all religious traditions that cannot be simply washed away by reinterpreting the tradition through liberal or feminist lenses. Hence, an interpretive approach should be employed as part of a multi-pronged program that views it only as an interim strategy for full integration of international women's rights standards into religion-based personal status systems.

Notes

1 For example, *qudah* (Islamic court judges; the singular is *qadi*) at *mahakim shar'iyya* (Islamic courts with jurisdiction over personal status matters) or *dayanim* (rabbinical court judges; the singular is *dayan*) at *battei din* (rabbinical courts that exercise jurisdiction over personal status matters; the singular is *beith din*).

2 Unified semiconfessional personal status systems are usually found in countries with strong inclusionary or secular inclinations (for example, regimes that are committed to the ideal of building an egalitarian, civic citizenry and a secular society) that have already achieved considerable levels of unification and secularization in their systems, but whose attempts at further reform are hindered by the opposition of some ethno-religious groups (for example, India). Fragmented confessional systems, in contrast, are often observed in regimes with theocratic or exclusionary proclivities (for example, regimes that promote the supremacy of a particular race, ethnicity, or religion over others in the society) and that exploit archaic personal status laws to realize their vision of building ethno-religiously stratified societies and augmenting the role of religious norms and institutions in public life (for example, Israel). Unified confessional systems are mostly found in bureaucratic authoritarian regimes that intervene in the field of personal status with the sole purpose of achieving bureaucratic efficiency through rationalization and unification of communal jurisdictions under an overarching administration of law and courts (for example, Egypt).

3 At this point, an explanatory remark is in order. I argue that religion-based personal status laws should be deemed harmful to women's rights when they do not comply with international standards enshrined in various human and women's rights treaties, such as the UN Convention on the Elimination of Discrimination against Women (CEDAW). Otherwise, religious laws by no means should be viewed as inherently antiwomen or misogynistic. On the contrary, as many scholars have shown, some religious traditions (for example, Islam), when they were first revealed, significantly advanced women's rights by granting them revolutionary rights and freedoms that had not previously

existed in their respective societies (Esposito and DeLong-Bas 2001; Tucker 2008). Moreover, as some suggest, particularly in legally pluralistic settings, religious laws may be more favorable and accessible to women than other legal systems, as they may better fit women's immediate needs and interests. In other words, religious laws are not always the least preferable option for women. For example, both Layish (2006) and Menski (2001) show that for various socioeconomic and cultural reasons, some women in Islamic societies may prefer and willingly enter into polygynous marriages. And in some cases — as Ezeilo (2000) demonstrates in the context of Nigeria, where widows prefer Islamic law over customary law because the former gives them a fixed share in the deceased husband's estate, while the latter completely disinherits them — women's rights and interests may be better protected under religious law.

4 Halakhah defines a Jew as a person whose mother was Jewish at the time of his birth, or a person who was converted to Judaism by a recognized rabbinical court (Biale 1984, 70–101).

5 Interview with Ronny Brison, former member of the Knesset from the Shinui Party, Jerusalem, February 2005.

6 Since civil ceremonies performed abroad are recognized by the Israeli government under private international law, individuals who are unable to wed in Israel or resent the power of the Orthodox establishment often fly to Cyprus to marry civilly. However, the recognition of these marriages does not solve the couple's problem entirely. Their children may still not be recognized as Jewish if it is an interfaith marriage or if the parents' Jewishness is contested. And in the case of divorce, the marriage still needs to be dissolved according to religious law (that is, by issuing a *get*). Moreover, even if the couple goes abroad and obtains a civil divorce, the man and woman will still be considered married in the eyes of the rabbinical authorities.

7 A woman denied a *get* by her husband is technically called *mesorevet get* in Jewish law, but the term *agunah* — a woman whose husband disappeared or went missing without issuing a proper *get* — is much more commonly, albeit wrongly, used.

8 According to the rabbinical authorities, as of 2007 there were sixty-nine *agunot* (the plural of *agunah*), and only twenty-five of them were living in Israel (Ratzlav-Katz 2007). Israeli women's rights activists, however, argue that rabbinical authorities deliberately reduce the number of *agunot* by using a very narrow and technical definition, according to which they count only women who have waited over two years for their husband's consent to divorce, and women whose husbands have disappeared and cannot be located. The actual number of women who are denied a *get* by their husbands is estimated to be around 8,000–10,000.

9 The Ministry of Interior Affairs maintains a list of certified *mamzerim* in Israel. As of 2004, the list contained the names of ninety-two Israeli citizens (Rosenblum and Tal 2004, 39). For further information on the legal consequences of bastardy in Israel, see Gross (2001) and Feldblum (1997–98).

10 Halperin-Kaddari reports that from 1995 to 1999, only 163 restraining orders were issued against recalcitrant husbands by the rabbinical courts. Of these, 76 came from a single rabbinical court (2004, 239). In 2006, judges issued compulsion decrees against recalcitrant husbands in only 41 of 942 unresolved *get* cases (Ratzlav-Katz 2007). Sanctions against husbands were imposed in 44 cases in 2009 and in 73 cases in 2008. "Only six of the verdicts handed down in 2009 included arrest warrants for the husbands, as compared to 23 cases in 2008" (Ettinger 2010).

11 Civil family courts would still need to adjudicate maintenance cases according to rules set out in the 1917 Ottoman law. However, as is the case with the laws of other religious communities, Sharia law applied by secularly trained civil court judges, most of them are Jews, would not be the same Islamic law as that applied by *qadis* at Sharia courts. Civil courts, which operate on principles of a different legal culture than do Sharia courts, would employ their own rules of evidence and procedure and would abide by standards of private international law while implementing Sharia (Abou Ramadan 2006, 43).

12 See Law No. 25 of 1920, Law No. 25 of 1929, and Law No. 100 of 1985.

13 Other grounds for divorce are the husband's failure to provide maintenance (*nafaqa*), his having a contagious or dangerous disease, and his maltreatment of the wife (Esposito and DeLong-Bas 2001, 51; Karam 1998, 148; Nassar 1999, 198–202).

14 These are adultery; the conversion of one spouse to another religion; one spouse's five-year absence with no news of his or her whereabouts; a spouse's imprisonment for at least seven years; a spouse's mental illness lasting more than three years with no hope of a cure, a spouse's contagious disease that threatens the partner's health, or the husband's sexual impotence for a period of three years; domestic violence; a spouse's immoral or incorrigible behavior (for example, homosexuality); spousal incompatibility for over a period of three years; and a spouse's joining a monastic order (for further details, see Articles 50–58 of the 1938 ordinance).

15 A women-friendly alternative dispute-resolution or court system in India that addresses issues specifically related to violence against women and other family matters such as divorce and maintenance.

16 For further information on matters of polygyny in Egypt, see Shahd 2003, Gupta 1992, and Fargues 2003.

17 In this campaign, the Islamist groups found an unexpected ally: the judges of the personal status courts. A. Shmais, who surveyed the attitudes of the Egyptian judges towards Law No. 44, reports that "twenty out of twenty-seven judges" considered women's right to divorce if their husband took a second wife "an explicit violation of the Qur'an, giving scope to women to seek divorce and constraining men's right to marry polygynously" (quoted in Fawzy 2004, 37). For similar comments as well as the personal status court judges' attitudes toward female litigants in general, see Najjar 1988 (337), Zaalouk 1975 (142–46) and Talhami 1996 (115).

18 Interview with Zeinab Radwan, Cairo, May 2004.

19 For example, it is reported that in the Cairo Governorate, only 4.5 percent of the *khul'* applications filed between March 2000 and March 2001 were actually ruled on by the personal status courts. The rate in the same period in the Gaza Governorate was 6.9 percent (Al-Sawi 2002, 20, 24).

20 Divorce statistics come from the Arab Republic of Egypt, Central Agency for Public Mobilization and Statistics (www.msrintranet.capmas.gov.eg/pls/census/spart_all_e?lname=FREE&lang=o). The agency does not provide any information on the number of *khul'* divorces awarded by the courts. Unfortunately, nearly all the information about the number of these divorces is based on anecdotal evidence offered by judges, lawyers, and activists.

21 Telephone interviews with Deborah Weissman, March 2010; Hannah Kehat, April 2010; and Sharon Shenhav, March 2010.

22 These two organizations are Kolech and Mavoi Satum. The former is in the process of establishing a new institute that will train both female and male *dayanim*, while the latter is undertaking a multistage project to set up an independent *beith din* to resolve the problem of *agunot* once and for all.

23 Shenhav was elected for a second term in December 2005.

24 In-person and telephone interviews with Sharon Shenhav, Jerusalem, January 2005, and New York, April 2010.

25 For further information on *marsoum qadai*, see Reiter 1997 and Abou Ramadan 2003, 2005, and 2006.

26 Telephone interview with Heba Yazbak, April 2010.

27 The Palestinian government in the West Bank appointed two female *qadis*, Khul'oud Faqih and Asmahan Wuheidi, to Islamic courts in February 2009.

28 Telephone interview with Shaista Amber, May 2010.

29 Ibid.

References

Abou Ramadan, M. 2003. "Judicial Activism of the Shari'ah Appeals Court in Israel (1994–2001): Rise and Crisis." *Fordham International Law Journal* 27: 254–98.

——. 2005. "Divorce Reform in the Shari'a Court of Appeals in Israel (1992–2003)." *Islamic Law and Society* 13 (2): 242–74.

——. 2006. "Islamic Legal Reform: Shari'a Court of Appeals and Maintenance for Muslim wives in Israel." *Hawwa* 4 (1): 29–75.

Abramowitz, L. 2004. "Women Advocates Make Their Mark." *Jewish Action Online* 65 (2), www.ou.org/publications/ja/5765/5765winter/WOmenaDV.PDF.

Agarwal, B. 2005. "Landmark Step to Gender Equality." *Hindu Online*. 25 September, www.hindu.com/thehindu/mag/2005/09/25/stories/2005092500050100.htm.

Agnes, F. 2001. *Law and Gender Inequality: The Politics of Women's Rights in India.* New Delhi: Oxford University Press.

——. 2004. "Constitutional Challenges, Communal Hues and Reforms within Personal Laws." *Combat Law* 3 (4): 4–10.

Al-Banna, K. S. 1984. *Al-ahwal al-shakhsiyya lil Aqbat al-Orthodox fi daawa al-fiqh wa ahkam al-Naqd* [The personal status of Orthodox Copts in the light of jurisdprudence and the Court of Cassation]. Al-Qahira, Egypt: Alam al-Kotob.

Al-Sawi, A. 2002. *Al-Hasaad: a'amaan 'aala al khul': Dirasah Tahliliyah* [The harvest: two years after *khul'*]. Al-Qahira, Egypt: Markaz Qadaia al-Mara al-Masriyya.

An-Naim, A. A. 1992. "Toward a Cross-Cultural Approach to Defining International Standards of Human Rights: The Meaning of Cruel, Inhuman or Degrading Treatment or Punishment." In A. A. An-Naim, *Rights in Cross-Cultural Perspectives: A Quest for Consensus* 19–43. Philadelphia: University of Pennsylvania Press.

Atiya, A. S., ed. 1991. *The Coptic Encyclopedia.* New York: Macmillan.

Awasthi, P. 2006. "Our Own Personal Law Board." www.indiatogether.org/2006/sep/wom-aimwplb.htm#continue.

Bahgory, G. 1999. "Train of Thought." *Al-Ahram Weekly Online*, 12–18 August. http://weekly.ahram.org.eg/1999/442/feature.htm.

Bak, N., and Y. Goldman. 2000. "Resting Our Case: Toanot Beit Din." *Amit* 72 (1): 38–40.

Barzilai, G. 2003. *Communities and Law: Politics and Cultures of Legal Identities.* Ann Arbor: University of Michigan Press.

——. 2004. "Culture of Patriarchy in Law: Violence from Antiquity to Modernity." *Law and Society Review* 38 (4): 867–83.

Benhabib, S. 2002. *The Claims of Culture*. Princeton: Princeton University Press.

Bogoch, B., and R. Halperin-Kaddari. 2006. "Divorce Israeli Style: Professional Perceptions of Gender and Power in Mediated and Lawyer-Negotiated Divorces." *Law and Policy* 28 (2): 137–63.

Corinaldi, M. 2002. "A Halakhic Solution for Women Whose Husbands Refuse to Grant a Divorce: The Shunning Measure of Rabbeinu Tam." *Jewish Law Watch* (5): 5–16.

De Gaay Fortman, B., et al. 2010. *Hermeneutics, Scriptural Politics, and Human Rights: Between Text and Context*. Basingstoke, England: Palgrave Macmillan.

Deif, F. 2004. "Divorced from Justice: Women's Unequal Access to Divorce in Egypt." N.p.: Human Rights Watch.

Eldin, Kamal Amany, Enid Hill, and Sarah Graham-Brown. 1985. "After Jihan's Law: A New Battle over Women's Rights." *Middle East* 129 (June): 17–20.

El-Taji T., M. 2008. "Arab Local Authorities in Israel: Hamulas, Nationalism and Dilemmas of Social Change." PhD diss., University of Washington.

Engineer, A. 1987. *The Shah Bano Controversy*. Bombay: Orient Longman.

Esposito, J. L., and N. J. DeLong-Bas. 2001. *Women in Muslim Family Law*. Syracuse, NY: Syracuse University Press.

Ettinger, Y. 2010. "Rabbinical Courts Softened Stance on Husbands Refusing Their Wives Divorce." *Haaretz*, 27 January. www.haaretz.com/hasen/spages/1145446.html.

Ezeilo, J. N. 2000. "Laws and Practices Relating to Women's Inheritance Rights in Nigeria." Enugu: Women's Aid Collective.

Fargues, P. 2003. "Terminating Marriage." In *The New Arab Family*, edited by N. S. Hopkins. Cairo: American University in Cairo Press.

Fawzy, E. 2004. "Muslim Personal Status Law in Egypt: The Current Situation and Possibilities of Reform through Internal Initiatives." In *Women's Rights and Islamic Family Law: Perspectives on Reform*, edited by L. Welchman, 15–94. London: Zed.

Feldblum, M. S. 1997–98. "Baiyot Agunah ve-mamzerim—Ha-tsat pikaron makifa ve-kolelet" [A proposal for a comprehensive solution to the *Agunah-Mamzer* problem]. *Diné Israel* 19:203–17.

Fouad, H. 2002. *Al Khul' ind al-Aqbat . . . qadaya maftouha lel munaqasha* [Khul' for Copts... an issue open tor debate]. *Akhir Sa'ah*, 3 April.

Gross, C. N. 2001. "Fighting the Curse." *Jerusalem Report*, 13 August.

Gupta, Kiran. 1992. "Polygamy—Law Reform in Modern Muslim States: A Study in Comparative Law." *Islamic and Comparative Law Quarterly* 12:114–54.

Gutmann, A. 2003. *Identity in Democracy*. Princeton: Princeton University Press.

Halperin-Kaddari, R. 2004. *Women in Israel: A State of Their Own*. Philadelphia: University of Pennsylvania Press.

Hasan, A. 2003. "Granting Khul' for a Non-Muslim Couple in Egyptian Personal Status Law: Generosity or Laxity?" *Arab Law Quarterly* 18 (1): 81–89.

Hassan, F. 2001. "The Meaning of Emancipation." *Al-Ahram Weekly Online*, 1–7 March.

Hatem, M. F. 1992. "Economic and Political Liberation in Egypt and the Demise of State Feminism." *International Journal of Middle East Studies* 24 (2): 231–51.

Hill, E. 2000. "Legal Cultures and Controversies in Egypt Surrounding Marriage and Divorce." Unpublished manuscript.

Ibrahim, A. 2001. "Hope on the Horizon?" *Al-Ahram Weekly Online*, 11–17 March.

Karam, A. M. 1998. *Women, Islamisms, and the State: Contemporary Feminisms in Egypt*. New York: St. Martin's.

Kukathas, C. 1992. "Are There Any Cultural Rights?" *Political Theory* 20 (1): 105–39.

Kymlicka, W. 1995. *The Rights of Minority Cultures*. Oxford: Oxford University Press.

———. 1996. "Two Models of Pluralism and Tolerance." In *Toleration: An Elusive Virtue*, edited by D. Heyd, 81–113. Princeton: Princeton University Press.

Layish, A. 2006. *Women and Islamic Law in a Non-Muslim state: A Study Based on Decisions of the Shari'a Courts in Israel*. New Brunswick, NJ: Transaction.

Leila, R. 2003. "A Family Affair." *Al-Ahram Weekly Online*, 16–22 January.

Levitt, P., and S. E. Merry. 2009. "Vernacularization on the Ground: Local Uses of Global Women's Rights in Peru, China, India and the United States." *Global Networks* 9 (4): 441–61.

Madera, A. 2009. "Juridical Bonds of Marriage for Jewish and Islamic Women." *Ecclesiastical Law Journal* 11 (1): 51–64.

Menon, N. 1998. "Women and Citizenship." In *Wages of Freedom: Fifty Years of the Indian Nation-State*, edited by P. Chatterjee, 241–66. Delhi: Oxford University Press.

Menski, W. 2001. *Modern Indian Family Law*. Surrey, England: Curzon.

———. 2006. "Asking for the Moon: Legal Uniformity in India from a Kerala Perspective." *Kerala Law Times*, no. 2: 52–78.

———. 2007. "Double Benefits and Muslim Women's Postnuptial Rights." *Kerala Law Times*, no. 2: 21–34.

Mirow, Matthew C. 2004. *Latin American Law: A History of Private Law and Institutions in Spanish America*. Austin: University of Texas Press.

Merry, S. E. 2006a. *Human Rights and Gender Violence: Translating International Law into Local Justice*. Chicago: University of Chicago Press.

——. 2006b. "Transnational Human Rights and Local Activism: Mapping the Middle." *American Anthropologist* 108 (1): 38–51.

Najjar, F. M. 1988. "Egypt's Laws of Personal Status." *Arab Studies Quarterly* 10 (3): 319–44.

Nassar, N. 1999. "Legal Plurality: Reflection on the Status of Women in Egypt." In *Legal Pluralism in the Arab World*, edited by B. Dupret, M. Berger, and L. Al-Zwaini, 191–204. The Hague: Kluwer Law International.

Patel, R. 2007. *Hindu Women's Property Rights in Rural India: Law, Labour and Culture in Action*. Aldershot, England: Ashgate.

Radford, M. F. 2000. "The Inheritance Rights of Women under Jewish and Islamic Law." *Boston College International and Comparative Law Review* 23 (2): 135–84.

Rajaram, N., and V. Zararia. 2009. "Translating Women's Human Rights in a Globalizing World: The Spiral Process in Reducing Gender Injustice in Baroda, India." *Global Networks* 9 (4): 462–84.

Ratzlav-Katz, N. 2007. "Statistics Dispel Claims of 'Thousands of Israeli Agunot.'" www.israelnationalnews.com/News/News.aspx/122884.

Rawls, J. 1999. *A Theory of Justice*. Cambridge: Belknap Press of Harvard University Press.

Raz, H., and E. Neuman. 2008. "Two Steps Backward." www.haaretz.com/hasen/spages/964122.html.

Reiter, Y. 1997. "Qadis and the Implementation of Islamic Law in Present Day Israel." In *Islamic Law: Theory and Practice*, edited by R. Gleave and E. Kermeli, 205–31. London: I. B. Tauris.

Rosenblum, I., and E. Tal. 2004. "Report on the Status of the Israeli Family 2004." Tel Aviv: New Family Organization.

Sachs, S. 2000. "Egypt's Women Win Equal Rights to Divorce." *New York Times*, 1 March.

Sakr, H., and M. Hakim. 2001. "One Law for All." *Al-Ahram Weekly Online*, 1–7 March.

Salim, A. S. A. 2004. *Usul al-ahwal al-shakhsiyya lil ghair al-Muslimin* [Principles of non-Muslims' personal status]. Iskandariya, Egypt: Dar al-Matba'at al-Jamia.

Santos, B. D. S. 2002. "Toward a Multicultural Conception of Human Rights." *Beyond Law* 9 (25): 9–32.

Saxena, P. P. 2003. *"Family Law Lectures: Family Law-II*. New Delhi: LexisNexis.

Sezgin, Yüksel. N.d. "God v. Adam & Eve: Human Rights under Religious Law in Israel, Egypt and India." Unpublished manuscript.

Shachar, A. 2001. *Multicultural Jurisdictions:Cultural Differences and Women's Rights.* Cambridge: Cambridge University Press.

Shahar, I. 2006. "Practicing Islamic Law in a Legal Pluralistic Environment: The Changing Face of a Muslim Court in Present-Day Jerusalem." PhD diss., Ben-Gurion University of the Negev.

Shahd, Laila S. 2003. *An Investigation of the Phenomenon of Polygyny in Rural Egypt.* Cairo: American University in Cairo Press.

Shamir, R., M. Shitrai, and N. Elias. 1996. "Religion, Feminism and Professionalism: The Case of Rabbinical Advocates." *Jewish Journal of Sociology* 38 (2): 73–88.

Shenhav, S. 2004. "Busting the Old Boys' Club. *Jerusalem Post,* 1 December.

Sherma, R. D., and A. Sharma 2008. *Hermeneutics and Hindu Thought: Toward a Fusion of Horizons.* New York: Springer.

Shilo, M. 2006. "A Religious Orthodox Women's Revolution: The Case of Kolech (1998–2005)." *Israel Studies Forum* 21 (1): 81–95.

Singerman, D. 2005. "Rewriting Divorce in Egypt: Reclaiming Islam, Legal Activism, and Coalition Politics." In *Remaking Muslim Politics: Pluralism, Contestation, Democratization,* edited by R. W. Hefner, 161–88. Princeton: Princeton University Press.

Sonneveld, N. 2006. "If Only There Was *Khul'* . . ." *ISIM Review* 17:50–51.

——. 2007. "Reinterpretation of Khul' in Egypt: Intellectual Disputes, the Practice of the Courts, and Everyday Life." PhD diss., Leiden University.

Subramanian, N. 2005. "Legal Pluralism, Legal Change and Gender Inequality: Changes in Muslim Family Law in India." Paper presented at the annual meeting of the American Sociological Association, Philadelphia, 12 August.

Tadros, M. 2009. "The Non-Muslim 'Other': Gender and Contestations of Hierarchy of Rights." *Hawwa* 7 (2): 111–43.

Talhami, G. H. 1996. *The Mobilization of Muslim Women in Egypt.* Gainesville: University Press of Florida.

Twining, W. L. 2009. *Human Rights, Southern Voices: Francis Deng, Abdullahi An-Na'im, Yash Ghai and Upendra Baxi.* Cambridge: Cambridge University Press.

Vatuk, S. 2008. "Islamic Feminism in India: Indian Muslim Women Activists and the Reform of Muslim Personal Law." *Modern Asian Studies* 42 (2–3): 489–518.

Wegner, J. R. 1982. "The Status of Women in Jewish and Islamic Marriage and Divorce Law." *Harvard Women's Law Journal* 5:1–33.

Weiss, S. 2002. "Loud Talk, Small Stick." *Jerusalem Report,* 12 August.

Young, I. M. 2000. *Inclusion and Democracy*. Oxford: Oxford University Press.

Zaalouk, M. E. H. 1975. "The Social Structure of Divorce Adjudication in Egypt." Master's thesis, American University in Cairo.

Zulficar, M. 2004. "Egypt: New Signs of Progress for Women in Egypt." http://www/wluml.org/node/1774.

ROJA FAZAELI

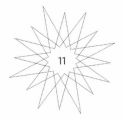

Contemporary Iranian Feminisms

DEFINITIONS, NARRATIVES, AND IDENTITY

This study, apart from being an academic project, has also been a personal journey. In contrast to feminist writers such as Mehrangiz Kar, Azadeh Kian, Shirin Ebadi, Ziba Mir-Hosseini, and Nayereh Tohidi, whose feminist consciousness is at times simultaneously linked to moments before, during, and after the Iranian Islamic Revolution, I am a child of the revolution. I grew up in the Islamic Republic of Iran during the Iran-Iraq War (1980-88). At the age of three I became a martyr's daughter,[1] having lost my father during the war. I grew up in an all-female family, consisting of my mother, my sister, and me. I grew accustomed to my mother's fights for our rights. She fought her family for an independent life. She fought my paternal grandfather for the guardianship of my sister and me.[2] She fought male colleagues for her rights at work, and, above all, she fought her status as a war widow. She was one of a very few female university lecturers on horticulture at a time (1989-92) when horticulture was still an almost exclusively male subject.[3] My mother personified the paradox that is the Islamic Republic. Veiled in a dark *maghnae*[4] and wearing a long, dark *manteau*,[5] she taught all-male classes. In one incident she had to ask a student's armed bodyguard to leave the class. Later, the head of the faculty called her to let her know that she had literally disarmed one of the heads of Gilan Province's[6] *sepah-e pasdaran*.[7] I was always fascinated with the clothes worn by my mother in photos from before the revolution, in contrast to her attire after it. Before, she wore seventies-style corduroy pants and even short skirts. After, a war widow, she veiled herself. She fought for a scholarship to Ireland, only to be informed six months after our arrival in Dublin that it was to be discontinued because Iranian law would not allow a single woman (whether widowed, unmarried, or divorced) to study abroad on government funds.[8] Although I saw my mother as a powerful woman, I also became aware at an early age of the power dynamics that existed in the public institutions of Iran and the dependencies that they created and fostered.

In the summer of 2003, I went back to Iran after eleven years to research my master's thesis on family honor and women's rights in Iran. We had left Iran for Ireland in October 1992 in order for my mother to pursue her PhD studies. On my return to Iran, I found that the country had changed considerably from the place I recalled eleven years before. The chador-enveloped women of my memories, emblems of 1979 Islamic revolution, had been replaced by young women whose faces were painted with makeup and who wore tight *manteaux* with ornamental scarves that spoke more of a desire for beauty than of propriety. War and moral slogans such as *marg bar bi hejab* (death to the hijab-less),[9] and *khaharam hejabe toe sangar ast* (my sister, your hijab is a shelter from war),[10] which were plentiful when I left Iran, had been replaced by billboards featuring advertisements for Sony, L.G., Casio, and more. That summer I attended courses on women's studies in Tehran and interviewed an array of civil and women's rights activists. Fascinated by the reform dynamics alive among women's and youths' networks, I returned to Iran again in the spring of 2004 for more research.

I became engrossed in the Iranian women's rights movement and wrote a paper dividing the movement into feminist subcategories: Islamic state feminists, Islamic nonstate feminists, Muslim feminists, and secular feminists. That paper was published in the *Muslim World Journal of Human Rights* in 2007.[11] I have continued to expand on the research contained in that paper, and in this chapter I build on those early arguments and observations. I also expand the earlier research with interviews conducted with Iranian women's rights activists in 2010. Although I have not been back to Iran since 2004, I have followed the Iranian women's movement closely and started deeper—and at times, more personal—conversations with some of the activists and academics. In the summer of 2010, when speaking about different feminist categories in Iran to a friend, the Iranian journalist and women's rights activist Maryam Hosseinkhah, I was convinced that it was necessary and timely to revisit the same questions that I had posed six years earlier, this time taking into greater account of how the transitional nature of the movement's identities affected its multiple dependencies.

Maryam helped me identify and interview an array of women's rights activists and academics inside and outside of Iran. We conducted thirty interviews in all.[12] We used written questionnaires for interviewees living in Iran (phone conversations would have posed a threat to their personal security). The communications were mainly by e-mail. Other interviews were conducted by phone or Skype and were recorded, or were carried out in person. We chose our interviewees carefully to represent different cities (Tehran, Tabriz, Kermanshah, Rasht, Gorgan, Shiraz, and Karaj) and ages (twenty-five to fifty-five). As well as interviewing well-known women's rights activists who are featured regularly in Western academic writing, we also interviewed younger women and men who have transformed the face of the women's movement in the last five years, both ideologically and demographically.

The Struggle to Define
"Islamic Feminism"

In Muslim majority countries, the term "feminism" often has a negative connotation and is at times regarded as a Western import. In Iran, some of the confusion arises from the fact that the word "feminism" does not have a Farsi equivalent and is widely used "as a Western import into Farsi."[13] Much of the literature on Islamic feminism portrays it as newly invented. However, I argue that its underlying notions have existed for centuries, and that it is simply the term "Islamic feminism" that is recent.[14]

Since it became a common term in the 1990s,[15] "Islamic feminism" has been defined in various ways according to context. I contend that no single definition of the term can be applied to all contexts. As Ziba Mir-Hosseini notes, "the problem lies both in the explicit issue of how the term is defined and in the implicit meanings it has acquired in its usage."[16] Margot Badran defines Islamic feminism as "a feminist discourse and practice articulated within an Islamic paradigm . . . which derives its understanding and mandate from the Qur'an, seeks rights and justice for women, and for men, in the totality of their existence."[17] According to Badran, Islamic feminist discourse is "grounded in the Qur'an and other religious texts."[18] Badran's definition of Islamic feminism is predicated on the engagement of the scholar with a sacred text.[19] This is the common understanding of the term that has been conveyed in the literature produced in the last ten years.[20] However, I argue in this chapter that the Iranian version of Islamic feminism differs from Badran's definition. While the discourse of Islamic feminism in Iran is certainly articulated within the framework of Islam, it is grounded more in political Islam than in any attempt to exegete the Quran through an egalitarian lens. If we accept Badran's definition of "Islamic feminism," then Islamic feminism in Iran would not be a significant category. Although historically there have been a number of *mujtahidas*—female *mujtahids* or *Shii* jurists who have received permission to practice *ijtihad* (the use of independent reasoning to form an opinion or to deduce a rule)—in Iran, their works remain largely unknown and their exegetical works—that is, works that perform detailed analyses of sacred texts within a faith framework—do not always represent an egalitarian or a feminist interpretation of the Quran and the Sunnah.[21] Furthermore, observing the women's rights movement in Iran, it is clear that women activists and lobbyists depend more on male religious authorities' views of women's issues than on the views of the women *mujtahidas*.[22]

The Iranian feminist journal *Zanan*[23] has been credited by some as being the publication in which Islamic feminism in Iran was born and where Islamic feminists "offered Islamic readings of gender equality and justice."[24] Having gone through most of *Zanan*'s articles from 1992 until its closure in 2008, I was interested to observe that the main authors who offered egalitarian readings of the Islamic text were men.

One male cleric in particular played an important role in giving *Zanan* an Islamic feminist brand. Hujjat ul-Islam Seyed Mohsen Saidzadeh, a religious scholar educated in a *hawza* (a school of Shi'a religious learning) before the Islamic revolution,[25] began writing for *Zanan* under his wife's name, Mina Yadegar Azadi, then under his own name and later under a female pseudonym, Zinat ul-Sadat Kermanshahi. Saidzadeh was arrested and defrocked in 1998 after publishing an article in a daily newspaper that year where "he criticize[d] the religious sayings and traditions that rationalize discrimination against women."[26] Since his release from prison, Saidzadeh has withdrawn from intellectual public life and no longer writes.[27]

Another journal, the quarterly *Farzaneh*, was established in 1993, a year after *Zanan*. *Farzaneh* did not reach as wide an audience as *Zanan*, which enjoyed a wide readership both inside and outside of Iran.[28] Women such as Monir Gorji, an interpreter of the Quran and the sole female member of the Assembly of Experts for the Constitution (the body that revised the Iranian Constitution at the inception of the 1979 Islamic Revolution), and Massoumeh Ebtekar (the editor and the license holder of the journal), an academic and a former vice president in charge of environmental affairs, wrote regularly for the journal. Gorji in particular is identified both in the published literature and our interviews as an example of an Islamic feminist in Iran, although she might not identify herself as such. Yet after having spoken to her, attended her lectures, and read some of her writings, I cannot say that she supports gender equality in all aspects. Gorji works within a traditional Islamic framework, although her disillusionment with the Islamic Republic's practices of misogyny and abuses of power led her to change her views considerably since the 1979 revolution.

In my first research visit to Iran in 2003, I met Mahboubeh Abbasgholizadeh, a women's rights activist, when I attended her introductory course on Islamic and Muslim feminisms. She explained to the students that she had affiliated herself with Islamic feminism, an identity that she acquired immediately following the revolution of 1979. The identity, she told us, was closely linked to her utter devotion to Ayatollah Khomeini at the time. Later, however, the way she identified herself began to shift along with her understanding of women's rights and reinterpretation of Islam.

When we met again, in 2006, to my surprise she said that she was now a secular feminist. Maryam Hosseinkhah and I interviewed her in 2010. I asked her to elaborate on the shifts in her feminist identity over the past thirty-one years. Mahboubeh told us that when she looks back, she realizes that these labels were no more than academic terms used to describe the change that religious or nonreligious women went through during the revolution and in the years following the establishment of the Islamic Republic. She added that she does not agree with these labels, given Iran's present political situation. However, she told us about her own experience.

In her narrative, it is clear that Mahboubeh's feminist identity formation was intertwined with the Islamic revolution and influenced by revolutionary Islam, as articulated by the thinker Ali Shari'ati and by Ayatollah Khomeini. According to Mahboubeh, it was Shari'ati's book *Fatemeh Fatemeh Ast* (Fatima is Fatima) that created a strong identity for her. Wearing the hijab, Mahboubeh explained, gave her a feeling of belonging, a sense of having entered into the domain of power. Women like Mahboubeh took part in the revolution to be part of the masses, not to address gender discrimination. They believed that once the monarchy was abolished, the rest would work itself out. However, soon after the inception of the Islamic Revolution, they began to sense a change and became disillusioned. Mahboubeh talked about this change in her interview: "For example, segregation started. At the start of the revolution, meetings were mixed but eventually they became segregated. Women were going to another room, chatting and breastfeeding their babies, while the men held meetings in another room. During the revolution, one would not order the other to cook. Wife and husband treated each other equally. A year or two years later, everything changed."[29]

Mahboubeh tells us about how Fatima (Prophet Muhammad's daughter), who was portrayed during the revolution as a strong revolutionary role model, became Fatima the good wife and mother during the Islamic Republic. Women were politically sidelined and lost some of their public and private rights. Slowly these women came to think that although the state called itself an Islamic Republic, its legislation and mores were not really Islamic. The laws reflected the male clerics' interpretation of religious texts and consequently favored men. Some of these women began to question their change of status from revolutionary women to good wives and mothers. This questioning brought a number of women to ask what their duties were in the family and public realms.

Mahboubeh recalled that in the first few years, only small groups of women would gather and study to try to understand their gendered duties by reading Islamic texts (the Quran and Nahjul Balagheh[30]) and Khomeini's writings (such as *Tahrir al-Vasileye Khomeini*).[31] In 1985, a group of women led by Gorji traveled to the UN Women's Conference in Nairobi.[32] In Nairobi, when they were faced with criticism in regards to women's rights in Islam by other international participants, they realized that they had no argument with which to defend themselves. This group was the first and perhaps one of the most important groups to set out to reread the Quran in order to be able to answer the international community's questions about the legitimacy of the Quran and of Islam itself. None of these women, according to Mahboubeh, had studied classical religious texts or had any *hawza* training. One could say that this was the beginning of the Islamic feminist discourse in Iran.

However, as Afsaneh Najmabadi notes, "one of the problems with current discussions of Islam and feminism is ahistorical generalizations."[33] Mahboubeh elaborated on this point, stating: "It is a mistake to look at Islamic feminists in Iran outside a historical context."[34] It is important to be clear not only about the context of and the history in which we theorize the meaning of Islamic feminism, but also about the role that Iranian politics—and, in particular, revolutionary ideals—has played in forming identities of the women and men who make up the body of the feminists in Iran. These women, labeled Islamic feminists in Mahboubeh's narrative, are, according to her, the women who attempt a rereading of the Quran within the framework of Shari'a. However, their critique of male-centric views does not go beyond the framework of political Islamism (*eslamgariy-e dini*). In short, Mahboubeh defined Islamic feminism in this context as "a group who in the framework of Islam and the Quran question their duties." She also defined "Islamic feminism" as "a group who question their duties within the framework of Islam and the Quran." This is juxtaposed to Muslim feminists[35] who, in addition to reaching outside the Islamic framework, also take into consideration debates on cultural and social realities. They ask questions not only about their duties but also about their rights. Both of these categories are expanded on in the sections below.

Thus far it is clear that the current definition of "Islamic feminism" in Iran is not predicated solely on primary engagement with religious texts. Nayereh Tohidi writes that Islamic feminism has emerged "primarily in cities among highly educated middle-class Muslim women who . . . are unwilling to break away from their religious orientation and hold Islam as a significant component of their ethnic, cultural, or even national identity."[36] Fatemeh Haghighatjoo, a member of sixth parliament (1999–2003) and one of our interviewees, serves as an example of this definition. Haghighatjoo explains her Islamic feminist identity as being that of a Muslim woman who believes in legal gender equality. She does not regard Islam to be the sole factor in the creation of gender hierarchy and patriarchy. Haghighatjoo, like Mahboubeh, refers to the influence of Islamic modern thinkers and reformists on Islamic feminist ideologies, which I will elaborate on in the section on dependencies.

To return to the question of whether only those who engage in *ijtihad* in an egalitarian way can be referred to as Muslim or Islamic feminists, I would note that both Haleh Afshar and Ziba Mir-Hosseini write on Islamic feminism in Iran, but that neither of them claim that Islamic feminists are religious scholars. Afshar writes that women in Islamic countries have been fighting on different fronts and for different causes, but that none have been as successful as "those who have located their political action in the context of Islam and its teachings."[37] She reasons that since the Islamic Republic prides itself on its adherence to what it defines as Islamic values, "the believers have been better able to engage in positive discussion and extract 'Islamic' measures which are liberating."[38] According to Mir-Hosseini, after the 1979 revolution, Muslim women acquired a new consciousness and "a gender discourse that is 'feminist' in its aspiration and demands, yet is 'Islamic' in its language and source of legitimacy emerged."[39] The new discourse has become known as Islamic feminism.

When we asked our interviewees to define "Islamic feminism," they gave us a number of different responses, all of which further emphasised the diversity of ways in which the term is understood. Apart from the definition presented above, some stated that Islamic feminism as defined by Badran never existed in Iran. Kaveh Mozafari, an active member of the One Million Signatures Campaign Demanding Changes to Discriminatory Laws,[40] responded to the question as follows:

> In reality, one can say no one with such a label is active in Iran, those who may be known as Islamic feminists do not use this title themselves. Certainly, there are those who pay attention to the fabric of an Islamic society [in their activism] and, for example, call themselves Muslim feminists. However, the use of this title is not common in Iran. . . Those referred to are in general reformist women who themselves believe in Islam, and who attempt to interpret Islam in a way that would help the equality of men and women.[41]

This link between Islamic feminism and reformist women, or even more generally reformist thought, was also elaborated on by Mahboubeh not only in her interview but also in her writing: "Islamic feminism in Iran is based on contemporary religious renewal."[42] Negar Rahbar, a twenty-four-year-old mechanical engineer and an active member of the One Million Signature Campaign in the north of Iran stated: "The Islamic feminists I know in Iran are either women who are close to the [reformist] government (*hokumat*) or are feminists who, although they have secular outlooks, believe that the way for obtaining [gender] equality in Iran is through the use of dynamic jurisprudence (*fiqh pooya*)."[43] Jelveh Javaheri's discussion on Islamic feminism is also worth noting:

> In my opinion this view [Islamic feminism] found potency in Iran in the 1990s when attention to difficulties faced by women in their daily lives prompted some women's rights activists and publications [with such inclinations], to turn to clearer interpretations (*tafasir-e roshantar*) of Islam for solving women's actual problems. Therefore, with presenting such interpretations, they challenged the discriminatory laws against women that have caused extensive damage to the lives of women and many social ills. And they demanded amelioration of women's status and a change in laws with reliance on these interpretations. Gradually, the rhetoric of "reform" (*eslah gari*) or "religious modern thinking" (*no anidishi-e dini*) found currency in the women's realm. . .
> Some researchers regard such outlooks as "Islamic feminism."[44]

Jelveh adds that the term "Islamic feminism" has been a contentious one in Iran and that there is no consensus on its definition. Moreover, some women's rights activists have been vehemently opposed to using the term. She asserts that among those who have used the rhetoric of "Islamic feminism," some accept the label whereas others have rejected it.

The interviewees emphasized repeatedly that Islamic feminists do not constitute a homogeneous group. Rather, they come from a variety of cultural, regional, socioeconomic, and educational backgrounds. As Mir-Hosseini states, "like other feminists, their positions are local, diverse, multiple and evolving."[45] In the case of Iran, certain groups that were identified as Islamic feminists now call themselves Muslim feminists, and some who regarded themselves as Muslim feminists now call themselves secular feminists, reaffirming the transitional nature of their identities. It is noteworthy that the changes in the identity of these women are contingent on their responses to the structures of power.

Feminists Categorized

As noted above, in a previous study, I had concluded that there are four categories of feminists in Iran: Islamic state feminists, Islamic nonstate feminists, Muslim feminists, and secular feminists. In the interviews I conducted in 2010, some of the interviewees happily identified themselves as either Islamic or secular feminists. Others disagreed with such categorizations, stating that these were labels primarily used by academics that have now become politicized.[46] Some of the interviewees offered other labels, such as radical, socialist, liberal, modern thinker (*no andish*), and pragmatist (*amalgara*) feminist.[47] Although I realize that the categories below are only four of many other possible groupings, they remain important in their recognition of power dynamics and dependencies, as explained below.

ISLAMIC STATE FEMINISTS

The aftermath of the Islamic revolution was followed by the enactment of state-interpreted Islamic laws. Many of the female *khat-e imamis* (supporters of Khomeini had developed a unique gender perspective even before the revolution. They had fought in the war and demanded their "rightful place in the postwar society."[48] Some of these women became active in politics, either through their affiliation with males in power or through their rigorous support of the regime.

These Islamic state feminists were involved from the beginning in state politics. As Azadeh Kian states, "they attempted to present a different reading of Islam and Islamic laws which would be more attentive to the condition of women."[49] They realized that the state's adherence to traditional Islam was rooted in the male-dominated state apparatus. However, these women's dependence on the state and traditional Islamic ideology made their attempts both less credible in some circles and more credible in others. Another part of this failure was that women's issues did not take priority in the government agenda during the Iran-Iraq War. Regardless of women's right to be elected to Parliament, only a handful of women had seats in the first, second, and third parliaments, and these women were all from conservative religious backgrounds. As Marziyyeh Dabbagh explained, for women to try to pass any motion in Parliament, first they had to persuade their male colleagues of the validity of their argument, and most times they failed at this.[50] Haghighatjoo had a similar experience in the sixth parliament: "We used to refer to social realities, but also we conveyed [the idea] that these issues were not against Islam. For each of our projects, we used to speak to the clerics to gain their supports."[51] Although these women supported some women's causes, they were part of the conservative religious network that lent its support to the *vilayat-i-faqih*.[52] Furthermore, although they did not oppose women's presence in the public sphere, they still viewed a woman's main role as that of mother and housewife.[53]

These women remained loyal to the traditional Islamic framework, but some of them came to the realization that the revolutionary promises of social justice were not being carried forward in the legal framwork. During the reform era, some amendments were made to the advantage of women, but women members of Parliament were not always successful in preventing hardliners from passing discriminatory laws against women. However, it is certain that "no positive laws have been passed without women members of parliament initiating them."[54] Early state feminists worked to advance the cause of the state as well as their own. Religious fundamentalist regimes, as Afary points out, often have a number of women in prominent positions in order to popularize and develop the regime's gender ideology.[55]

A new generation of Islamic state feminists has emerged in the postwar era, when—due to new economic, social, and demographic realities—the government saw the need to adopt new strategies. This resulted in a rise in the number of women professionals. In 1992, the number of women members of Parliament tripled, from three to nine. Nine women were also elected to the 1995 parliament.[56] In the same year, women's affairs offices were established in each ministry and other government agency, and numerous nongovernmental or quasi-governmental organizations dealing with women's issues were created. The new women members of Parliament were more vocal on women's issues. They called for an end to patriarchy and antiwomen attitudes.[57] In the latter part of the 1990s, a reform movement emerged that was comprised largely of students and women. Women's rights became one of the most debated issues in government circles. A new wave of more powerful state feminists was appointed to top governmental positions. Massoumeh Ebtekar was named as Khatami's vice president in charge of environmental affairs. Azam Nouri was appointed by Ayatollah Mohajerani as deputy culture minister for legal and parliamentary affairs. Zahra Shojaee was named Iran's first director general for women's affairs and the advisor on women at the Markaz Mosharekate Zanan

(Center for Women's Participation).[58] These women are gender-conscious and have discovered politics as a way to bring about radical change in women's status. They are a paradoxical byproduct of the revolution.[59] They are attempting "to adapt Islam to the realities of a society in which women's social, economic and political activities have become an integral part."[60]

In talking to some of these state feminists, I realized that they paint a much idealized picture of Muslim women's lives. Their ideal is the veiled woman of the revolution, liberated from the fetters of Western consumerism and capitalism. She is the mother, wife, sister, or child of a martyr who lives her life according to the Islamic creed, using Fatima as her role model. Women's rights, as conceived by them, are complementary to men's rather than equal.

ISLAMIC NONSTATE FEMINISTS

As defined in my previous study, Islamic state and nonstate feminists seek justice and equality for women in an Islamic framework by trying to reinterpret Islamic laws in order to reform existing discriminatory legislation and *urf* (custom or customary law). According to this definition, which is similar to that of Badran, Islamic feminists "challenge *ulamas'* monolithic interpretational power"[61] as a way to liberate women from a patriarchal Islam based on their interpretations of the Qur'an, the *sunna*.[62] They hope that a gender-sensitive reinterpretation of Islamic law will lead to desirable reforms in laws that discriminate against women. According to them, these reforms are better suited for women living in Islamic societies than Western feminism is. However, I have argued that these women's interpretations of religious texts do not carry the same weight as their male counterparts when it comes to the actual reform of laws. Therefore, the two categories of state and nonstate feminists are better described in relation to political and religious power structures than in terms of their roles as reinterpreters of text.

The majority of the nonstate Islamic feminists also supported Khomeini at the start of the revolution, and some took part in the Iran-Iraq War. Some of these women entered politics. However, as in the case of Azam Taleghani, some withdrew and became active in civil society instead. I worked for Azam Taleghani, who is a good example of an Islamic nonstate feminist. The daughter of the late Ayatollah Mahmoud Taleghani, she was a political prisoner during the shah's reign, a member of the Women's Association of the Islamic Revolution,[63] and a member of the interim (first) parliament. Taleghani's work on women's issues began after she served in Parliament. Although still involved in politics, her women's rights activism is not confined to the state apparatus, as would be the case with an Islamic state feminist. Taleghani was the founder and editor of *Payam-e Hajar*, the first postrevolutionary magazine that worked within the framework of Islam to raise questions concerning the need to re-interpret Islamic laws.[64] Taleghani used Ayatollah Taleghani's teachings both in the reinterpretations published in *Payam-e Hajar* and in the weekly meet-ings she held to study and reinterpret the Quran.[65] Her organization depended on voluntarism due to inadequate funding, and Taleghani was eager to tap into foreign funds and network with like-minded national and international orga-nizations. However, the lack of initial funds also meant an inability to recruit people with specialized skills. During a round of arrests in the summer of 2004, Taleghani's passport was confiscated. She and many of the people working for her were interrogated and harassed. Taleghani was placed under constant sur-veillance by government agents and at times has been prohibited from leaving the country to attend conferences.[66] While working with Taleghani, I realized how difficult it was for her and other women's rights activists to be agents of positive change when trapped in a web of multiple dependencies.

MUSLIM FEMINISTS

The term "Muslim feminism" is at times used interchangeably with "Islamic feminism."[67] However, some make a clear distinction between the two terms. The term "Muslim feminism" is used by some feminists in Iran who previously identified themselves as Islamic feminists but who now wish to separate them-selves from that category.

According to a self-indentified Muslim feminist whom I met in Iran in 2004, Muslim feminists, like Islamic feminists, seek to reform Islamic law using *ijti-had*. However, Islamic feminists' use of dynamic *ijtihad* as a tool for reform is confined to the framework of traditional Islamic *fiqh*, whereas Muslim femi-nists look for answers outside this framework. For Muslim feminists, time and context are crucial elements to consider when participating in debates con-cerning dynamic *ijtihad*. She added that "one has to take into account some principle rules such as justice and equality, both of which are the essence of [the] Quran."[68]

The few Muslim feminists I met in Iran were among the supporters of Kho-meini (*khat-e imamis*) before and after the revolution. However, in the last few years they have chosen a separate identity. They criticize Islamic state and nonstate feminists for not seeking reform outside the framework of Islam. As Mahboubeh explained in her interview, the main point that sets these two categories apart is their stance on rights and duties. Islamic feminists question their duties within the framework of Islam, whereas Muslim feminists look for their rights both within that framework and outside it. Mahboubeh added that Muslim feminists and secular feminists concur on most issues in regard to gender equality and the need to reform discriminatory laws. However, there are four main points of contention: the first revolves around debates about the Convention on the Elimination of All Forms of Discrimination against Women (CEDAW); the second deals with changes to the Constitution; the third is the wearing of the hijab; and fourth focuses on sexuality.

On the first two, CEDAW and the Constitution, secular feminists demand that Iran ratify CEDAW without any reservations and reform the Constitution so that gender equality will not be contingent on Islamic law. Muslim feminists support CEDAW with reservations, and due to ideological links with the Islamic republic, they support the current constitution. On the question of the hijab, while most Muslim feminists wear it themselves, they do not seek to impose it on others. Muslim feminists to date have not addressed sexuality in any detail. Muslim feminists, therefore, regard themselves as a new category of feminists situated between Islamic and secular feminists.

SECULAR FEMINISTS

Secular feminists, as their name suggests, are proponents of the separation of the state from religious institutions.[69] They see such separation as the ideal condition for women to achieve gender equality. Given the current situation and the historical relations between the state and the clergy in Iran, many secular feminists have come to realize that even if Iran is secularized, the clergy will wield and exercise substantial social power. Therefore, some secular feminists support dynamic *ijtihad*.[70]

In my previous study, I suggested that the majority of secular feminists went into exile after the revolution, and only a few secular feminist scholars remained in the country. Although this is true to a certain extent, the 2010 interviews show a general trend of the feminist movement toward secularism. These women, although not all vocal at the beginning of the Islamicization of the country, became more and more outspoken during the reform era, using new women's magazines such as *Zanan* as a platform to voice their concerns. It is also imperative to note that the younger generation of feminist activists, who some refer to as the fifth generation of Iranian feminists,[71] lean more and more toward secularism both in their activism and their advocacy.

The above categories of feminists all work within a web of dependencies, some positive and some negative, which are described in the section below.

Feminist Dependency Paradigm

The feminist dependency paradigm for developing countries[72] is defined in this chapter as the economic, social, and ideological dependence of feminists (in Islamic countries, for the purposes of this chapter) on one or more of the following institutions: state, family, funders (state or foreign) or Western scholars. The paradigm refers, in particular, to the multiple dependencies of feminist activists in Islamic countries who use civil society as the main platform for their actions. These dependencies are divided into negative and positive dependencies.

A PERSONAL EXPERIENCE AND NEGATIVE STATE DEPENDENCY

While I was being interrogated by a representative of one of the many branches of the Iranian intelligence services, the full implication of feminist dependency hit me. It was in the basement of a morality police station (*Amaken*) at the junction of Mirdamad and Motahari Streets on October 2004, during Ramedan (the holy month of fasting in the Islamic calendar). I felt helpless, my voice smothered by a web of paradoxes and the lies being spun about me. The *hajagha*[73] started his interrogation:

> So I hear that you are a martyr's daughter. They say that you research
> human rights. Did you not know that what you [Westerners] call human rights
> is against our religion? That woman who won the Nobel Peace Prize [Shirin
> Ebadi] ... do you work with her? Did you know that she is a dirty bitch? Did
> you know that she is a sinner? She goes abroad and takes off her scarf and
> shakes hands with men. You bitches are all the same! You say that you work
> for women's rights, but this is only a pretext for all of you feminists to do
> dirty deeds, to sin and be immoral, and then you call it rights.
> We expect more from a martyr's daughter!

He continued to denigrate Shirin Ebadi, whom I had met for a brief moment at one of her talks in Tehran: "Do you not think that she is a sinner? What has she done for her country after receiving so much money?" My responses were cut short by the *hajagha*'s shouts and the sound of his fists hammering on the table. As if his accusation that all feminists were immoral bitches was not enough, the *hajagha* had to prove that I was a certified immoral Western bitch, even though, as he stated, I was also a martyr's daughter and therefore apparently entitled to more respect than others. While shouting at me to cover my neck, he asked me to describe in detail my relations with all the males I was friends with or worked with during my stay in Iran. He accused me of *zena*[74] and demanded a written confession. He also wanted me to tell him what one of my American roommates did when she was alone with her boyfriend. He indicated a few times that he wanted the details (as if I looked through the peephole every time the couple was alone).

What I relate above is but a fragment of what some women's rights activist go through in Iran on a frequent basis. During the three months that I was interrogated, a number of women's rights activists were in jail. Why should Iranian feminists be dependent both financially and ideologically on a system where *hajaghas* abuse their power to humiliate women and women's rights defenders? Later, in an interview with another branch of the Iranian intelligence, I was able to debate the un-Islamic action of the *hajagha* who wanted to know personal details of my relationships with others and who wanted me to tell him in detail what went on in the intimate affairs of others behind closed doors. What would a self-professed righteous Muslim man, an "officer of Islam" (*pasdar-e Islam*), as he put it, want with such a detailed confession? If we are to talk in terms of righteousness and propriety, I wondered, is it not *haram* (prohibited) for two men to be alone in an interrogation room with a woman half their age, especially during Ramedan when everyone else in the station had gone to have *eftar* (the evening meal during Ramadan)? Was this their interpretation of Islam? And if so, why was it then okay for them to be alone with me and not for me to be alone with any other man? The *hajagha* had said, "We know that you were alone in a room with this male" and continued, "things happen when males and females are alone together." But I protested at the irony of this ugly insinuation being made when I was in fact alone with two men who were pressuring me to confess that I was immoral. As Kar points out, the principle of *Amre be maroof va nahy az monker* (the promotion of virtue and the prevention of vice), as enshrined in article 8 of the Iranian Constitution, has become a tool in the hands of extremists to undermine individual rights and freedoms and terrorize the population.[75] Was it this law that the supposedly virtuous *hajagha* was implementing?

Gender is often used by fundamentalist leaders as a category for mobilizing their supporters and discrediting their opponents.[76] For the *hajagha*, as a woman, I represented the opposition. But some other women with close ties to the state remained untouched and unthreatened. In fact, they occupied the largest offices in the most luxurious locations in north Tehran.

FOREIGN DEPENDENCE

As Leila Ahmed suggests, the early dominant voice of feminism in Muslim majority countries in the early 1900s was intertwined with societal tendencies of westernization and secularization. These tendencies, according to Ahmed, are located mainly in "the upper, upper-middle, and middle-middle classes," which "promoted a feminism that assumed the desirability of progress toward Western-type societies."[77] These feminists' ideologies depended largely on Western feminist ideology.[78] The first women college graduates in Egypt, for example, had matriculated in France, England, and the United States.[79] The same held true for Iran.

All categories of Iranian feminists—but particularly Muslim and secular feminists—are dependent on foreign funding and are often subject to ideological dependency. Due to their dependence on Western funding, protection, and publicity, some of these feminists are labeled by the state as Western implants, or the immoral imports of the West, and hence their legitimacy is called into question.[80] However, it is crucial to note that all categories of feminists, and Iranian women's movements in general, are less and less inclined to accept foreign funding. In the last seven years, campaigns such as the One Million Signatures Campaign to End Legal Discrimination against Women have chosen not to accept any outside or government funding, precisely so that they could stay autonomous and independent. Muslim and secular feminists are less likely to seek funding from the government for their projects, and hence their goals are more likely to be painted as antigovernmental. Therefore, they have become targets of state crackdowns.[81]

Some secular feminists also argue that Islamic feminists and their expatriate academic supporters either consciously or unintentionally delegitimize secular trends and social forces. Moghadam writes that those who oppose Islamic feminists and their expatriate supporters "maintain that the activities and goals of 'Islamic Feminism' are circumscribed and compromised, and that there cannot be improvements in women's status as long as [the] Islamic Republic is in place."[82] Iran's ratification of international human rights treaties and conventions such as the International Covenant on Civil and Political Right and the International Covenant on Economic, Social and Cultural Rights,[83] the International Convention on the Elimination of All Forms of Racial Discrimination,[84] and the International Convention on the Rights of the Child[85] has brought the state under pressure to defend its record of human rights. The pressure, although positive and necessary, at times creates problems for women activists. During my encounter with the *hajaghas*, I was both fortunate and unfortunate to have worked for organizations such as Amnesty International. It meant that I was at once protected and simultaneously classified as a foreign agent.[86]

Another point to take into account is the murkiness of the boundaries between civil society and the state in Iran. Iranian feminist organizations, or ones labeled as women's rights organizations, face multifaceted constraints when they attempt to pursue their work outside of the government's purview, as do other nongovernmental organizations (NGOS). These include inadequate legal and regulatory protections that lead to internal management problems, lack of professionalism, weak technical and financial capacities, and insufficient transparency. Most women's rights organizations I worked with in Iran, if truly nongovernmental, were incapable of tapping into international funds, not only due to lack of skills but also due to a fear of prosecution by the government. These organizations' dependency on the government is based on the amount of funding and support they are willing to accept from it or that it is willing to give to them. It is well known that if women's rights organizations (or other NGOS) wish to be independent, they face scrutiny and persecution from the government.[87] The irony remains that the government-organized NGOS, which have links to the government, are able to get funding from both the government and foreign donors. Their dependence on the state makes them less likely to be a target of scrutiny, and they are free to use foreign funds as long as they remain subordinate to the state.

Family Dependence All the feminists mentioned above are entangled in some sort of family dependency. The patriarchal model of the family still prevails in Iran. Certain articles of the Iranian civil law—coupled with the sociocultural, religious, and historical backgrounds of the patriarchal model—legitimize the second-class status of women within the family. For example, article 1105 of the Iranian civil code designates the husband as the head of the household. Article 1114 of the civil code asserts that a wife is to live in the residence that her husband provides, unless the choice of selecting a residence is given to the woman. Immigration and passport regulations make it necessary for a married woman to have her husband's written permission in order for her to obtain a passport or travel outside the country. According to article 1169 of the civil code, the mother of a child has priority in looking after her son until he reaches the age of two, and her daughter until she reaches the age of seven. When the children are older, their custody of the child shall go to the father. Taking into account these laws, one can only imagine the difficulties that some feminists (and women in general) face if they wish to work and live in a city other than their husband's, or if they wish to travel abroad to attend international conferences.

Iranian feminists are fighting to end these discriminatory laws and consequently to end these sorts of dependencies. The One Million Signatures Campaign is one such example. Initiated by the younger generation of Iranian feminists, it has become a channel through which feminists from all camps have come together. Although the campaign's activists have attempted to maintain their autonomy, they have also sought international support that, on the one hand, strengthens them and, on the other hand, gives the state an excuse to harass them.[88]

POSITIVE DEPENDENCY: THE OTHER SIDE OF THE COIN

As Deniz Kandiyoti writes, a certain kind of strategic patriarchal bargaining process has to be negotiated by women trying to gain their rights.[89] Such strategies have led to the formulation of an Islamic gender discourse. Shahin Gerami and Melody Lehnerer identify four strategies used by women to transform a fundamentalist framework: collaboration, meaning actively supporting state policies that are designed to reinstitute women's primary role as domestic workers, using formal and oppressive tactics; acquiescence, meaning submission to the state policies; co-optation, meaning manipulating these state policies; and subversion, meaning undermining these policies.[90] Some of the women mentioned above have "collaborated with the regime by aligning their interest with the state's agenda, whereas others submitted to family demands and state authority.

In contrast, there were women who manipulated both of these forces or played one against the other."[91] And, finally, some of the women have used subversion as a strategy to undermine these patriarchal forces. Some women, particularly Islamic state feminists, fared well after the revolution by collaborating with the state. Afary uses Erich Fromm's analysis and theories of fundamentalism to describe a collaborative strategy that certain women use:

> A decision to join these movements stems from a desire to both "escape from tradition" and "escape from freedom." Women who join right-wing Islamist movements gain a number of rights that the traditional patriarchal society does not offer them. These privileges, however, come at a heavy cost to others, especially secular advocates of women's rights who have suffered immensely under the Islamic theocracy of Iran.[92]

In present-day Iran, invocations of colonialism and Western imperialism are ritually used by the state to oppress feminists and others. Muslim and secular feminists believe that the Islamic state has created an unjust society along gender lines. These women constantly challenge this division, but pressures from family and state hinder their efforts.

Conclusion

The definition of "Islamic feminism" remains contested. Feminists of all sorts work within a larger domestic and global structure, where multilayered dependencies complicate their efforts. In the context of Iran, Islamic state feminists dependent on the powerful male elite look for women's equal rights not simply within an Islamic framework, but within an Islamic framework that has been shaped by the state. Islamic nonstate and Muslim feminists also look to an Islamic framework and try to extract notions of equality from alternative interpretations of Islamic texts. Some of these reinterpretations are made by women, but nonetheless a sense of dependency exists, if only because their purpose is to convince the dominant male clerics to adopt these new feminized interpretations. Secular feminists rely heavily on Western understandings of feminism and also rely on the West for financial support. However, after talking to feminist activists, I realized that such categorizations are an academic practice that interprets, but does not confine, the feminist movement.

Many of the feminists mentioned above are now in exile from Iran following the crackdown on the women's movement, in particular actions taken after the June 2009 presidential elections. Wherever they are, and despite their ideological differences, these feminists have come to recognize that their common goal is women's emancipation. Each of these groups of women believes in a woman's right to nondiscrimination. While I was in Iran in 2004, I attended monthly meetings of women's rights activists. Feminists from most of the categories mentioned above were present at these meetings. They did not always agree on matters of theory, but their practical collaboration was always guaranteed.

Notes

Many thanks to the *Muslim World Journal of Human Rights* and the Berkeley Electronic Press for allowing the reprint of portions of this paper, Berkeley Electronic Press © 2007.

1 My father died when he was thirty years old. He had recently finished his medical degree and had been posted as the chief of a hospital in Sardasht, a majority Kurdish city in Iran's West Azerbaijan Province, on the border of Iran and Iraq. The circumstances of his death were highly suspicious, as he was shot in the head by an Iranian soldier. When I went back to Iran in 2003, I found out that his gravestone had been removed. He is buried in the martyr's cemetery in Noor, but it is probable that due to his socialist political leanings and associations prior to his death, he was not worthy of the title "martyr." It was therefore surprising that an interrogator referred to me as a martyr's daughter in 2004.

2 According to article 1181 of the Iranian civil code, the father or the paternal grandfather is deemed to be the legal guardian of a child.

3 As education became segregated, certain subjects such as horticulture and legal studies leading to becoming a judge were prohibited to women. Some of these were again opened to women in the second decade after the revolution.

4 A scarf-like veil that can be described as a tube top for the hair.

5 In Iran *manteaux* (a word that means "coats" in French) are usually below the knee and, although they come in different styles and colors, at work and school darker shades of black, navy, brown, and gray are preferred. In some workplaces and universities, women are required to wear a black chador (literally meaning "tent"), which is a body-enveloping cloth that covers the whole body except for the face and hands.

6 A northern province of Iran, situated on the coast of the Caspian Sea.

7 The revolutionary guards.

8 The regulations for academic scholarships and sending students abroad of 3 March 1990 set out in sixty articles the general requirements for applying for government scholarships to study aboard. Article 13 of these regulations states, in part, that only women applicants who are married will be considered for scholarships, and that those chosen should be accompanied by their husbands. See "Ayeen Namey-e Etay-e Boors-e Tahsili va Ezam Daneshjoyan Be Kharej az Keshvar" [Regulations granting academic scholarships and sending of students abroad] (www.um.ac.ir/Education -laws-9.htm).

9 Hijab is an Arabic word commonly translated as veiling or covering of the hair (mainly of women). The *Encyclopaedia of Islam* traces the word to the verb *hadjaba*, "to hide from view, conceal." *Hidjāb* connotes "any veil placed in front of a person or an object to conceal it from view or to isolate it." See Joseph Chelhod "*Hidjāb*," in *Encyclopaedia of Islam*, edited by P. Bearman, T. Bianquis, C. E. Bosworth, E. van Donzel, and W. P. Heinrichs, 2nd ed. (Leiden: Brill, 2011), 3:359.

10 Another slogan was *arzandetarin zinate zan hefze hejab ast* (a woman's most valuable asset is her hijab).

11 Roja Fazaeli, "Contemporary Iranian Feminism: Identity, Rights and Interpretations," *Muslim World Journal of Human Rights* 4, no. 1 (2007): Article 8.

12 In 2003 and 2004 I conducted over twenty interviews, but these were not as focused on questions about feminism as were the interviews conducted in 2010. The interviews were all conducted in Persian. The translations are all mine.

13 Parvin Paidar, "Gender of Democracy: The Encounter between Feminism and Reformism in Contemporary Iran" (Geneva: United Nations Research Institute for Social Development, October 2001, www.onlinewomeninpolitics.org/beijing12/paidar .pdf), 2. Shalah Sherkat also noted in the early 1990s that the term "feminism" was misunderstood by some parts of Iranian society and references to the word were "mixed with negative convictions" (quoted in Hammed Shahidian, "'Islamic Feminism' Encounters 'Western Feminism': Towards An Indigenous Alternative?" (paper presented to the Feminism and Globalization Seminar, Illinois State University, Springfield, 12 February 1998), 3. Shahidian himself states that "a major obstacle before Iranian women has been the absence of a general knowledge of feminism and [the] women's movement around the world" (ibid.).

14 See, for example Shahrzad Mojab, "Theorizing the Politics of 'Islamic Feminism,'" *Feminist Review* (Winter 2001): 124–46

15 Ibid., 124.

16 Ziba Mir-Hosseini, "Beyond 'Islam' vs. 'Feminism,'" *IDS Bulletin* 42, no. 1 (2001): 67.

17 Margot Badran, "Islamic Feminism: What's in a Name?" *Al-Ahram Weekly Online*, 17–23 January 2002 ,http://weekly.ahram.org.eg/2002/569/cu1.htm.

18 Yoginder Sikand, "Islamic Feminism Is a Universal Discourse: Interview with Margot Badran." 15 September 2009, www.qantara.de/webcom/show_article.php/_c-307/_nr-26/i.html).

19 Scholars who directly engage with sacred texts include Amina Wadud, Monir Gorji, Mohsen Saidzadeh, and Asma Balras. However, not all these scholars consider themselves feminist. See, for example, Mina Yadegar Azadi [Mohsen Saidzadeh], "Ejtehad va Marja'iyate Zanan" [*Ijtihad* and *marja'iyat* of women], *Zanan* 8 (1992): 24–33; Amina Wadud, *Qur'an and Woman: Rereading the Sacred Text from a Woman's Perspective* (New York: Oxford University Press, 1999); Asma Balras, "*Believing Women" in Islam: Unreading Patriarchal Interpretations of the Qur'an* (Austin: University of Texas Press, 2004).

20 Freshteh Ahmadi, for example, writes that the basic methodologies of Islamic feminism are *ijtihad* and *tafsir* ("Islamic Feminism in Iran: Feminism in a New Islamic Context," *Journal of Feminist Studies in Religion* 22, no. 2 [2006]: 36).

21 See Mirjam Künkler and Roja Fazaeli, "The Life of Two Mujtahidas: Female Religious Authority in 20th Century Iran," in *Women, Leadership and Mosques: Changes in Contemporary Islamic Authority*, edited by Masooda Banoo and Hilary Kalmbach (Leiden: Brill, forthcoming).

22 In recent years, there is evidence of consultation only with the *mujtahida* Zohreh Sefati about reforming the age of marriage for boys and girls. See Mohammad Badiee, "Goftegu ba Faqih Pajuhandeh Banu Zohereh Sefāti" [Interview with the researcher jurist Lady Zohreh Sefati], *Keyhan Farhangi*, no. 199 (2003): 5-30, (www.noormags.com/View/Magazine/ViewPages.aspx?numberId=1131&ViewType=1&PageNo=8).

23 *Zanan*'s license to publish was revoked in 2008 after sixteen years. According to news articles cited in a report by Amnesty International, the following accusations had been made against *Zanan*: it "endangered the spiritual, mental and intellectual health of its readers, gave the impression of insecurity in society, and drew a dark image of the situation of women in Islamic society by publishing certain articles" (Amnesty International, "Iran: Women's Rights Defenders Defy Repression," [London: Amnesty International, 2008], 3; www.amnesty.org/en/library/asset/MDE13/018/2008/63dd8933-e16d-11dc-9135-058f98b1fb80/mde130182008eng.pdf). Also see M. Nissimov, Y. Man-

sharof, and A. Savyon, "Iranian Women's Magazine Shut Down for Publishing Investigative Article on Martyrdom Movement," Middle East Media Research Institute, Inquiry and Analysis Series Report, No. 439, May 2009, 4.

24 Margot Badran, "Engaging Islamic Feminism," in *Islamic Feminism: Current Perspectives*, edited by Anitta Kynsilheto (Kynsilehto, Finland: Tampere Peace Research Institute, 2008), 30. Also see Roza Eftekhari, "Zanan: Trials and Successes of a Feminist Magazine in Iran," in ibid., 19.

25 Saidzadeh began his religious education at the age of ten at Qa'in Seminary in Khurasan. At the age of fifteen, he went to the seminary in Mashahad, and at the age of twenty he left Mashhad for the *hawza* in Qom. A *hawza*-educated Islamic scholar, Saidzadeh served as a judge from 1983 to 1986 in Kermanshash. He began writing on women's rights in Islam in 1988 for *Payam-e zan* (a right-wing journal linked to the *hawza*) and in 1992 for *Zanan*. (The title Hujjat ul-Islam literally means "proof of Islam." In modern-day Iran the word refers to a mid-ranking cleric.)

26 Mehrangiz Kar, "Women's Strategies in Iran from the 1979 Revolution to 1999" in *Globalization, Gender, and Religion: The Politics of Women's Rights in Catholic and Muslim Contexts*, edited by Jane H. Bayes and Esfahlano Tohidi (New York: Palgrave, 2001), 194.

27 Ziba Mir-Hosseini, *Islam and Gender: The Religious Debate in Contemporary Iran* (Princeton: Princeton University Press, 1999), 274.

28 In her interview with me, Mahboubeh Abbasgholizadeh asserted that *Farzaneh* was more of an academic journal than *Zanan* was and had a more intellectual readership, as well as Islamic feminist backing.

29 Skype interview with Mahboubeh Abbasgholizadeh, 20 August 2010. I also spoke to Mahboubeh in various occasions in Tehran during the summer of 2004.

30 Sermons, letters, and sayings of Ali ibn Abi Tablib (the first Shi'a imam). Translations of *Nahjul Balagheh* (literally, "peak of eloquence") are available in English online; see, for example, a translation by Sayed Ali Reza (http://arthursclassicnovels.com/islam/nahjul10.html).

31 Ruhollah Khomeini, *Tahrir al-Vasileye Khomeini* [Commentary on the Vehicle] (Tehran: Entesharat-e Kazemeini, 1987).

32 The other delegates were Ashraf Broujerdi (deputy minister of justice, 1997–2005), Masoumeh Ebtekar (the first woman cabinet member during Khatami's government, 1997–2005, who was known for her involvement in the Iran hostage crisis of 1979 as the spokesperson for the hostage takers), and Azam Taleghani (the daughter of the late Ayatollah Taleghani and the only nongovernmental organization representative from

Iran at the conference, she was a member of the first parliament, formed in 1979, and now heads *Jame-e Zanan Enghelab Eslami*, a nongovernmental organization based in Tehran).

33 Afsaneh Najmabadi, "(Un)Veiling Feminism," *Social Text* 18, no. 3 (Fall 2000): 29.

34 Skype interview with Mahboubeh Abbasgholizadeh, 20 August 2010.

35 The term "Muslim feminist" in this paper is distinct from the term "Islamic feminist."

36 Nayereh Tohidi, " 'Islamic Feminism': Perils and Promises," in *Middle Eastern Women on the Move* (Washington: Woodrow Wilson International Center for Scholars, 2003), 136.

37 Haleh Afshar, "Islam and Feminism: An Analysis of Political Strategies" in *Feminism and Islam, Legal and Literary Perspectives*, edited by Mai Yamani, (New York: New York University Press, 1996), 200.

38 Ibid., 197.

39 Ziba Mir-Hosseini, "The Quest for Gender Justice: Emerging Feminist Voices in Islam" (paper presented at the conference "Reframing Islam," Irish Centre for Human Rights, National University of Ireland, Galway, 10–11 September 2005, 2 (www .nuigalway.ie/human_rights/reframing_Islam/Docs/Papers/Mir-Hosseini.pdf).

40 Sussan Tahmasebi writes: "The One Million Signatures Campaign officially launched on August 27, 2006, aims to collect one million signatures in support of a petition addressed to the Iranian Parliament asking for the revision and reform of current laws which discriminate against women" ("One Million Signatures Campaign: Answers to Your Most Frequently Asked Questions," 24 February 2008, http://1millionchange .info/english/spip.php?article226).

41 E-mail interview with Kaveh Mozafari, 23 July 2010, conducted in collaboration with Maryam Hosseinkhah.

42 Mahboubeh Abbasgholizadeh, "The Experience of Islamic Feminism in Iran," translated by Haleh Ghorayshi, *Farzaneh* 5, no. 10 (2000), http://en.farzanehjournal .com/index.php/articles/no-10/36-no-10-2-the-experience-of-islamic-femenism-in-iran.

43 E-mail interview with Negar Rahbar, 13 July 2010, conducted in collaboration with Maryam Hosseinkhah.

44 Interview with Jelveh Javaheri, Tehran, 2 August 2010, conducted in collaboration with Maryam Hosseinkhah.

45 Mir-Hosseini, "The Quest for Gender Justice," 3.

46 For a description of the divide between secular and religious that has been politicized by the Islamic government, see Najmabadi, "(Un)Veiling Feminism," 32.

47 In her interview, Javaheri defines a "pragmatist (*amalgara*) feminist" as a person who does not use just one ideology but instead chooses from a collection of views and thoughts that are useful depending on the time and the context we work in.

48 Javaheri interview.

49 Azadeh Kian, "Women and Politics in Post-Islamist Iran: the Gender Conscious Drive to Change," *British Journal of Middle Eastern Studies* 24, no. 1 (1997): 75.

50 Cited in ibid., 79.

51 Skype interview with Fatemeh Haghighatjoo, August 2010, conducted in collaboration with Maryam Hosseinkhah.

52 According to Ahmad Vaezi, the *vilayat-i-faqih* "advocates a guardianship-based political system, which relies upon a just and capable jurist (*faqih*) to assume the leadership of the government in the absence of an infallible Imam" (*Shia Political Thought* [London: Islamic Centre of England, 2004], 53). I would no longer put Haghighatjoo in this category. See also Ibrahim A. Karawan, "Monarchs, Mullas and Marshals: Islamic Regimes?," *Annals of the American Academy of Political Science* 524, no. 1 (1993): 103–19.

53 Kian, "Women and Politics in Post-Islamist Iran."

54 Paidar, "Gender and Democracy," 23.

55 Janet Afary, "Portraits of Two Islamist Women: Escape from Freedom or from Tradition?" (Women Living under Muslim Laws, 2001, www.wluml.org/node/466), 3.

56 Valentine M. Moghadam, "Islamic Feminism and Its Discontents: Towards a Resolution of the Debate," *Signs* 27, no. 4 (2002): 1141.

57 Ibid.

58 Ibid. See also interview with Zahra Shojaee, Tehran, June 2003. It is important to note that not all these women would accept being categorized as feminists. However, as noted by Abbasgholizadeh in her interview, this is no more than an academic practice.

59 Ziba Mir-Hosseini, "Women and Politics in Post Khomeini Iran: Divorce, Veiling and Emerging Feminist Voices," in *Women and Politics in the Third World*, edited by Haleh Afshar (London: Routledge, 1996), 142–69.

60 Kian, "Women and Politics in Post-Islamist Iran," 76.

61 Haideh Moghissi, *Feminism and Islamic Fundamentalism: The Limits of Postmodern Analysis* (London: Zed, 1999), 40.

62 Ibid.

63 Other members of the association included Fereshte Hashemi, Shahin Tabatabaii, Zahra Rahnavard, and Gawhar Dastgheib. See Asef Bayat, "A Women's Non-Movement: What It Means to Be a Woman Activist in an Islamic State," *Comparative Studies of South Asia, Africa and the Middle East* 27, no. 1 (2007): 162.

64 Kian, "Women and Politics in Post-Islamist Iran," 81. See also interviews and work experiences with Azam Taleghani, 2003 and 2004.

65 While working for Taleghani, I attended some of these meetings, which were frequented by a very mixed audience: young and old, wealthy and poor, educated and uneducated.

66 It was later revealed that one of the government informants was a young woman who attended Taleghani's Quran classes before the 2004 harassments.

67 See, for example, Azza M. Karam, *Women, Islamism and the State: Contemporary Feminism in Egypt* (London: MacMillan, 1998).

68 Mahboubeh Abbasgholizadeh in a group interview as part of the International Course on Islam and Human Rights, Tehran, June 2004. See also Maryam Hosseinkhah, "Goftegoo va Shonudhayee darbareye Taarozat huquqe Zan dar Islam ba Hughoghe Bashar [Dialogue on the conflicts between Islam and human rights concerning women's rights]," *Iranian Feminist Tribune*, 9 October 2004 (www.iftribune .com/news.asp?id=7&pass=19), 1-4.

69 The definition of "secularism" used here is simplified for the purposes of this chapter. For more on the relationship between the state and religion, see Jeroen Temperman, "The Neutral State: Optional or Necessary? A Triangular Analysis of State-Religion Identification, Democratization and Human Rights Compliance," *Religion and Human Rights* 1, no. 3 (2006): 269-305.

70 Secular feminists such as Mehrangiz Kar published numerous articles in *Zanan* on the subject.

71 The term "fifth-generation Iranian feminist" was first used by Noushin Ahmadi Khorasani in "The 'One Million Signature Campaign': Face-to-Face, Street-to-Street," translated by Shole Irani, *Change for Equality*, 29 March 2007 (www.we change.org/english/spip.php?article52).

72 This notion is comparable to Abdullahi A. An-Na'im's definition of "human rights dependency" ("Human Rights in the Arab World: A Regional Perspective," *Human Rights Quarterly* 23, no. 3 [2001]: 702).

73 *Hajagha* (meaning a man who has gone to *haj*—that is, who has made his pilgrimage to Mecca, one of the five pillars of Islam) is an alias used by many interrogators. I had two different interrogators during my detainment in Iran, both of whom were referred to *hajagha*. See also Habibola Doran, *Dar Mehmaniy-e Hajagha* [In the party of *Hajagha*] (Tehran: Entesharate Omide Farda, 2003).

74 *Zena* has almost the same meaning as adultery. According to the definition in Article 63 of the Iranian penal code, it includes the act of intercourse, including anal

intercourse, between a man and a woman who are forbidden to each other, unless the act is committed unwittingly. The punishment for *zena* extends from a hundred lashes to death by stoning.

75 Mehrangiz Kar, "Shari'a Law in Iran," in *Radical Islam's Rule: The Worldwide Spread of Shari'a Law*, edited by Paul Marshal (Lanham, MD: Rowman and Little-field, 2005), 41.

76 Sucheta Mazumdar, "Moving Away From a Secular Vision? Women, Nation, and the Cultural Construction of Hindu India," in *Identity Politics and Women: Cultural Reassertions and Feminism in International Perspective*, edited by Valentine Moghaddam (Boulder, CO: Westview, 1994), 243-73. See also Khawar Mumtaz, "Identity Politics and Women: 'Fundamentalism' and Women in Pakistan," in *Identity Politics and Women*, 228-42.

77 Leila Ahmed, *Women and Gender in Islam: Historical Roots of a Modern Debate* (New Haven: Yale University Press, 1992), 174.

78 It is important to note that "Western feminism" is a generalized term and that it represents a broad range of feminist ideologies. Like "Islamic feminism," the definition of this term depends on its context, including its time.

79 Ahmed, *Women and Gender in Islam*, 174.

80 Iranian women activists are becoming more and more careful about the sources of their funding, because the government tends to use feminists' use of foreign funds to clamp down on them and to delegitimize their goals.

81 The crackdown on women's rights activists and the civil society in general has been more acute since the contested presidential elections of 12 June 2009. Many women's rights activists have been exiled, and a number of those who have remained in Iran have been imprisoned.

82 Moghadam, "Islamic Feminism and Its Discontents," *Signs*, 1142.

83 Both signed on 4 April 1968 and ratified on 24 June 1975.

84 Signed on 8 March 1967 and ratified on 29 August 1968.

85 Signed on 5 September 1991 and ratified on 13 July 1994.

86 The death of the Canadian-Iranian journalist Zahra Kazemi under interrogation in Iran caused much international outcry. Since then, although the government still harasses Iranian dual citizens, it does not dare to physically harm them.

87 The extent of the scrutiny, however, is dependent on those in positions of power. For example, during Khatami's presidential term (1997-2005), civil society organizations in general enjoyed more independence, and the number of NGOs mushroomed throughout Iran. It was toward the end of Khatami's reign that the civil society came

under attack. The backlash against the civil society increased during Ahmadinejad's first term in power (2005–2009) and has increased even more during his second term in office.

88 For more on the campaign, see its official website (www.weforchange.info/english/).

89 Deniz Kandiyoti, "Bargaining with Patriarchy," *Gender and Society* 2, no. 3 (1988): 274–90.

90 Shahin Gerami and Melody Lehnerer, "Women's Agency and Household Diplomacy: Negotiating Fundamentalism," *Gender and Society* 15, no. 4 (2001): 558–60.

91 Ibid, 558.

92 Afary, "Portraits of Two Islamist Women," 4.

EPILOGUE

As this volume was being completed in early 2011, a series of remarkable events happened in a number of Muslim countries in North Africa and the Middle East—what has been colloquially dubbed "the Arab spring." In a short period of time, nation after nation witnessed popular upheavals and political turbulence that had previously been almost unthinkable. Protests demanding the ousters of heads of state, constitutional changes, and social reform spread throughout the region. As of this writing, in November 2011, the authoritarian governments of Zine el-Abidine Ben-Ali in Tunisia and Hosni Mubarak in Egypt have been toppled; strongman President Ali Abdullah Seleh of Yemen, having survived serious burns after his palace was attacked early in 2011, is negotiating a resignation; the repressive regime of Muammar El-Qaddafi in Libya has been swept aside by rebels supported by NATO forces and Qaddafi himself has been executed; Syria is awash in mass demonstrations against its president, Bashar el-Assad; and Bahrain has likewise experienced widespread demands for change.

While these movements have much in common—in large part because they all stem from deep-seated anger about the tyrannical and ruthless nature of national leaders—there are multiple and competing agendas at work. On the one hand, many insurgents are eager for democratization, modernization, and the protection of human rights. On the other hand, sectarian divisions now reappearing after repression have pitted group against group, posing the prospect of civil strife. Furthermore, many people who have embraced the calls for change have a fundamentalist mission that seeks greater adherence to religious codes, more social control, and additional restrictions on freedom.

So what do all these exciting yet confusing developments mean for the future of women in Muslim societies? Women have been at the forefront of many of the uprisings, using electronic methods of communication such as Facebook and Twitter to spur popular mobilization. They have precipitated extensive consciousness raising among women, in particular an eagerness for self-determination. The activism of women in pursuit of political change has unquestionably fostered a questioning of subordinate and submissive roles based on gender and awakened yearnings for a new era.

Even Muslim nations that have not witnessed social unrest and challenges to those in power have of late made adjustments to prevailing practices that benefit women. Most notably Saudi Arabia, which is widely known for its staunch resistance to feminist agendas, has seen changes, such as the decision by King Abdullah in September 2011 to grant women the right to vote in municipal elections. The significance of this reform was captured by Hatoon al-Fassi, a Saudi history professor and activist quoted by Neil MacFarquhar in the *New York Times* on 26 September 2011: "There is the element of the Arab Spring, there is the element of the strength of Saudi social media, and there is the element of Saudi women themselves, who are not silent."

Notably, few of the women taking part in revolutionary movements are calling for secularism. Rather, they desire social change that merges Islam and feminism—a furthering of women's rights that draws on and preserves religious tradition. In short, the new identities being fashioned are simultaneously radical and conservative. Such a melding of the old and the new has the potential to liberate women without threating to unravel the entire social fabric.

But as events continue to unfold and the future reveals itself, there is a counterpoint to the social transformations being envisioned: the abiding strength of the status quo. A classic French aphorism bears repeating: *plus ça change, plus c'est la même chose* ("the more things change, the more they stay the same"). There are a number of signs that the very women who were instigators and planners of the revolts have been relegated to subservient roles and excluded from the new social orders that are emerging. This prompted a Libyan woman to resign her post on the national council created by the rebels, giving an explanation that was quoted in the *New York Times* by Kareem Fahim on 20 May 20 2011: "When the revolution started, women had a big role. Now it's dissolved, it's disappeared. I don't know why." It is much too early to predict ultimate outcomes, but a certain caution is in order about prophesying the long-term impact on women of the dramatic political developments sweeping a good part of the Muslim world. From a feminist perspective, euphoria is premature.

As editors of this volume, we have resisted the temptation to inject our own views lest we engage in polemics and compromise our objectivity. But in these final two paragraphs we do dare to set forth our personal convictions. We heartily endorse the words of Boston College Professor Natana J. DeLong-Bas, editor-in-chief of the *Oxford Encyclopedia of Islam and Women*, in "Women of the Arab Spring," published by Common Ground News Service on 14 June 14 2011: "The inclusion or exclusion of women from the corridors of power and decision-making is, at heart, nothing less than a litmus test of the authenticity of any democracy."

Although the road ahead will have many twists and turns, it is our wish that women's rights become a centerpiece of the reordering of Muslim societies. We hope that the inspiring events of 2011 herald an enhanced quality of life and optimism about future possibilities for those who have been held back for so long because of gender. Muslim women deserve no less.

Chitra Raghavan

James P. Levine

GLOSSARY

Abangan Javanese. One who is not a strict follower of Islam in Java; a syncretist.

Agnatic Related through a father's or male's side of family.

Agunah Hebrew. Strictly speaking, a woman whose husband died or went missing without issuing a proper bill of divorce; also used to describe a woman denied a bill of divorce by her husband. *See also* get.

Al-Adl wal Ihsan movement The Justice and Benevolence Movement (also known as the Justice and Spirituality Movement); established by Abdessalam Yassine in the 1970s, and today Morocco's largest Islamist movement.

ALGA (Rural Women's Union) A nongovernmental organization focusing on increasing the quality of life of rural women in Kyrgyzstan.

Al-ḥuqūq wa al-wājibāt al-mutabādila Arabic. Literally, "mutuality of rights and obligations." In context of the Moroccan Family Code, refers to husband and wife both possessing equal rights and responsibilities with regard to management of household and rearing of children.

Amalgara Persian. Pragmatist.

Amazigh The indigenous (pre-Arab) peoples of North Africa. *See also* Berber.

Ayatollah Persian of Arabic origin. Literally, "sign of God." Title given to the highest ranking male Shi'a cleric.

Berber Refers to the North African indigenous people who reside west of the Nile River. Considered demeaning by some who prefer the term Amazigh.

Canon law In Christianity, an ecclesiastical law or code of laws established by a church council.

Civil status officer A local government official who exercises authority over civil affairs, such as marriage, divorce, and certification of birth and death.

Chador Persian. A large piece of material worn as a long shawl or cloak by Iranian women and sometimes by Hindu or other women.

Customary tenure A form of land ownership in which owners need no documents to prove ownership. Claims to the land, and the boundaries of the land, are locally recognized.

Dayan/Dayanim (sing/plural) Hebrew. Rabbinical court judges who oversee personal status matters such as marriage and divorce.

Dawoodi Bohra A subsect of Ismāīlī Shīa Islam now based in India. The belief system originated in Yemen, where it evolved from the Fatimid Caliphate and where proponents were persecuted due to their differences from mainstream Sunni Islam.

De jure equality Equality guaranteed or prescribed by law.

Desacralization Personal Status Codes are deemed sacred because of their rootedness in the Islamic law. Reforming the Moroccan Personal Status Code in the early 1990s meant desacralizing the law and was perceived by many women's rights activists as a step forward.

Domestic Relations Bill In Uganda, a bill that consolidates laws pertaining to marriage, divorce, and separation, aimed at establishing and guaranteeing marital rights and duties; the bill is based on the results of research conducted by the Uganda Law Reform Commission.

Eftar Arabic. The evening meal during which Muslims break their fast during the month of Ramadan.

Eslamgariy-e dini Persian. Political Islamism.

Family Code Also known as Moudawanat al-Usra or Moudawana; a revised Moroccan Personal Status Code, passed in 2004, that regulates marital relationships, child custody, and inheritance.

Fatwa/fatawa (sing/plural) Arabic. In Islam, a legal pronouncement on a specific issue, normally issued by a mufti, a religious law specialist.

Female circumcision A term that refers broadly to a set of practices ranging from the surgical removal of the clitoris to symbolic rituals that draw no blood.

Female genital cutting, female genital mutilation Any procedure that involves partial or total removal of the external female genitalia, or other injury to the female genital organs for nonmedical purposes. "Cutting" and "mutilation" evoke different emotive responses. *See also* female circumcision, pricking.

Fiqh Arabic. The process of understanding and codifying sacred Islamic texts into jurisprudence. *Fiqh pooya* is innovative or dynamic jurisprudence, used by modernist Islamic scholars to revise the traditional interpretation of Islamic law.

Get Hebrew. Under Jewish Law, the bill of divorce presented by a husband to his wife and necessary to effect the divorce.

Global Rights An international human rights capacity-building organization that for over thirty years has worked with local activists in Africa, Asia, and Latin America. At the core of its programming is a commitment to increasing access to justice for poor and marginalized groups. The Rabat-based Maghreb field office partners with local nongovernmental organizations and lawyers in Algeria, Morocco, and Tunisia.

Hadith Arabic. Statements and actions ascribed to or described as approved by the Prophet Muhammad.

Hajagha Persian. A man who has been to *hajj* (pilgrimage to Mecca, one of the five pillars of Islam). In the context of chapter 11, it is an honorific pseudo-name used to refer to interrogators whose actual names are not disclosed.

Halakhah Hebrew. Jewish religious law whose main sources traditionally include the Torah, Talmud, *takkanot* (rabbinical enactments), *she'elot u-teshuvot* (response) and *minhag* (custom).

Halal Arabic. Literally, "allowed" or "permitted," "rightful," "legal"; used by Muslims to refer to that which is permitted by the faith.

Hanafi One of the four *madhhab* (schools of law) in jurisprudence (*fiqh*) within Sunni Islam; the other three are Hanbali, Maliki, and Shafii.

Hanbali One the four *madhhab* (schools of law) in jurisprudence (*fiqh*) within Sunni Islam; the other three are Hanafi, Maliki, and Shafii. Hanbali traces its origins back to Imam Ahmad ibn Hanbal (d. 855) and was institutionalized by his students.

Haram Arabic. Literally, "forbidden"; used by Muslims to refer to anything that is prohibited by the faith.

Hawza (full term *hawza 'ilmiyya*) Arabic. An institution of Shi'a religious learning; a seminary or theological college.

Hijab Arabic. Literally, "curtain" or "cover." Used to describe the head covering traditionally worn by Muslim women and modest Muslim styles of dress in general.

Hokumat Persian of Arabic origin. Government.

Hujjat ul-Islam Persian of Arabic origin. Literally, "proof of Islam"; in modern-day Iran the word depicts a middle-ranking cleric.

Iddat Arabic. The period of time after divorce or the death of a spouse, during which an Islamic woman may not marry another man.

Ijtihad Arabic. Literally, "exertion of oneself." The making of a decision in Islamic law (Sharia) by personal effort (*jihad*), independently of any school (*madhhab*) of jurisprudence (*fiqh*)—as opposed to *taqlid*, copying or obeying without question. *See also* fiqh, sharia.

Intestacy rules A set of rules/laws guiding the succession to property in cases where an owner dies without a valid will.

Islamic Consultative Assembly Also called the Iranian Parliament or People's House; established after the Iranian Constitutional Revolution in 1907 to limit the power of the Shah. This assembly is the national legislative body of Iran. Before the revision of the constitution in 1989, this organism was called National Consultative Assembly.

Islamic Personal Law or Personal Status Code A body of laws based on the Islamic law governing issues pertaining to marriage and family in many Muslim-majority countries.

Isma Arabic. A term used in Morocco to designate a form of divorce by which the husband delegates his right of repudiation to his wife, thus allowing her to initiate divorce herself.

Ismaili The second largest branch of Shi'a Islam, after the mainstream Twelvers. *See* Shi'a.

Istihsan Arabic. Literally, juristic "preference." Muslim scholars may use the term to express preference for particular judgments in Islamic law over other possibilities; one of the principles of legal thought underlying personal interpretation, or *ijtihad*.

Judicature Act A 1996 law that specifies laws applicable in Uganda, including statutory law, common law, doctrines of equity, and customary law inconsistent with statutory laws.

Kebersihan Malay or Indonesian. Refers literally to cleanliness, purity.

Khafd/Khifad Arabic. Female circumcision.

Khitān Arabic. Translates as "circumcision" and refers to the circumcision of baby boys.

Khitan perempuan or *khitan wanita* Malay, Indonesian. Refers to female circumcision.

Khula The right of a woman in Islam to divorce or separate from her husband.

Land Act of 1998 A set of provisions aimed at regulating and securing the ownership, tenure, and management of land in Uganda.

Law of intestate succession A law that determines who will inherit the estate in case the owner dies without having made a valid will.

Mabaraat Mutual release.

Mahakim shar'iyya (plural) Arabic. Islamic courts that exercise jurisdiction over personal status matters.

Mahila adalat Hindi. A women-friendly alternative dispute-resolution or court system in India that addresses issues specifically related to violence against women and other family matters, such as divorce and maintenance.

Mahr al-muajjal Arabic. Prompt dowry or money paid by the groom to the bride immediately after solemnization of the marriage.

Maliki /Malekite One of the four *madhhab* (schools of law) in jurisprudence (*fiqh*) within Sunni Islam; the other three are Hanafi, Hanbali, and Shafi. Maliki is the second largest of the four schools, followed by approximately 25 percent of Muslims— mostly in North Africa, West Africa, the United Arab Emirates, Kuwait, and some parts of Saudi Arabia. Maliki doctrine is based on the works of Mālik ibn Anas and the Medinan tradition. It is the most prevalent school of Islam in the Maghreb.

Mamzerim Hebrew. Plural of *mamzer*; children of *agunah* with a new partner.

Matrimonial property regime A set of Ugandan guidelines regulating the property ownership between spouses by outlining how property is acquired, by whom it is managed, and other related issues.

MENA Region MENA is an acronym for the Middle East and North African regions, home to 6 percent of the total world population. It includes Algeria, Bahrain, Djibouti, Egypt, Iran, Iraq, Israel, Jordan, Kuwait, Lebanon, Libya, Malta, Morocco, Oman, Qatar, Saudi Arabia, Syria, Tunisia, the United Arab Emirates, the West Bank and Gaza, and Yemen.

Menstrual regulation A practice defined as an early uterine evacuation that restores the menstrual circle and impedes pregnancy either by preventing embryonic implantation or by preventing the maintenance of embryonic implantation.

Mu'akhar saddaq Arabic. Deferred dowry; money paid by the husband to wife at divorce. In contrast to prompt dowry, which is paid before the marriage is consummated, the deferred dowry is due at the time of the dissolution of marriage.

Muddafat Arabic. Literally, "female government employees," white-collar female workers.

Mufti Arabic. In Islam, a regional advisor on religious law who usually outranks the *qadi*, or religious court judge.

Mujtahidas Arabic. Plural of *mujtahida* or a female *mujtahid*—a Shi'a jurist who possesses the aptitude to or who has been given permission to practice *ijtihad*.

Nahjul balagheh Persian. Literally, "peak of eloquence"; letters and sermons of the first Shi'a imam, Ali ibn Abi Talib.

Nikah Arabic. Islamic marriage.

Oued Arabic. *See* wadi.

Personal Status Code The 1956 Tunisian law governing marriage, divorce, child custody and guardianship, parentage, inheritance, and marital property, with significant
implications for women's rights in the family. The Tunisian law is unique in the
region in that it outlaws polygamy and provides equal access to divorce for both
men and women.

Pesantren Javanese. In Java, a school of Koranic studies for children and young people,
most of whom are boarders.

Pre- and post-ḥajj parties Parties to celebrate the embarking and return of Muslim family members and friends prior to and following their religious pilgrimage to Mecca.

Pricking Nicking of the clitoris; classified as Type 4 Female Genital Mutilation by the
World Health Organization. *See also* female genital cutting.

Qadi/qudah (sing/plural) Arabic. Islamic court judges.

Qsar/qsour (sing/plural) Arabic. A fortified village usually in the South of Morocco.

Road of One Thousand Kasbahs Ancient road traversing the Sahara Desert and the
Atlas Mountains.

Rule of law A legal tenet that provides that no person is above the law, that no one
can be punished by the state unless they have violated the law, and that no one can
be convicted of breaching the law except in the manner set forth by the law itself.

Shafii One of the four *madhhab* (schools of law) in jurisprudence (*fiqh*) within Sunni
Islam; the other three are Hanafi, Hanbali, and Maliki. The Shafii school is named
after Imām ash-Shafii.

Shah Persian. Literally, "king." "Shahanshah" means king of kings. Until the Islamic
Revolution, this title had been given to the monarch of Iran since the Persian
Empire.

Shah Bano The plaintiff in *Mohd. Ahmed Khan vs. Shah Bano Begum & Ors* (1985).
Shah Bano, an elderly Muslim woman in India, was unilaterally divorced and initially denied alimony by her husband. Her case created heated controversy over
the conflict between religious personal laws and Article 44 of the 1950 constitution
that directs the government to apply a uniform civil code to all citizens irrespective
of religion.

Sharia The code of conduct or religious law of Islam. Most Muslims believe Sharia is
derived from two primary sources of Islamic law: the precepts set forth in the Quran,
and the sayings and actions of the Prophet Muhammad. *See also* hadith.

Shi'a The second largest denomination of Islam. Shi'a is a shorter form of the sentence "followers of Ali." The Shi'a believe 'Ali ibn Abi-Talib, Muhammad's son-in-law, is the Prophet's legitimate successor. There are three different branches of Shi'a: the Twelvers, the Ismaili, and the Ziadi. The majority of modern Shi'is are Twelver Shi'is, the branch of Shi'ism that accepted a line of twelve hereditary successors called imams. The Babi and Baha'i faiths arose in the Twelver Shi'i milieu in Iran and their beliefs and practices are related in many ways to those of the Twelvers.

Statutory guardian In Uganda, a guardian appointed by statutory authority.

Sukoun Tamazight. Customary marriage law in the Souss region of southern Morocco that provides that a husband must give his new wife a house or two plots of land, one plot to be sold with proceeds used to build a home on the other plot.

Sunat perempuan Malay, Indonesian. The tradition of female circumcision.

Sunnah Arabic. Literally, "habit, custom." Refers to the life and traditions of the Prophet Muhammad. Compare to *hadith*—traditions of the Prophet Muhammad or an account of his deeds or sayings. For the Twelver Shi'as, the word also means the traditions and sayings of the twelve imams. *See also* hadith, Shi'a.

Sunni The largest branch of Islam. Sunni is a term derived from *Sunnah*. About 80 percent of Muslims today are Sunni Muslims.

Sura An-Nisaa The fourth chapter of the Quran that discusses the position of women within the family and society, proscribing their duties, obligations, and rights.

Tafsir Arabic. Quranic interpretation and commentary.

Talaq Arabic. The unilateral and extrajudicial right of the husband under classical Islamic law to end his marriage by saying *talaq* ("I divorce you").

Tamazight The Tamazight language and its dialects are spoken in North Africa among the Amazigh population.

Testamentary freedom A freedom to dispose of one's property at one's desire through one's will.

Testamentary guardian In Uganda, a person who is appointed, usually through the will, by a mother and/or father of a minor child to take care of that child in a case of parents' death; testamentary guardians have no custody rights or financial responsibilities over the child.

Testate The state or condition of having a valid will; to die testate.

Testator Someone who has made a will or legacy.

Ulama (plural of *alim*) Arabic. Literally, "scholars." The *ulama* are legal scholars in Islamic studies, such as Muslim laws or religion. A Council of Ulama is a group of *ulama*; in the case of Saudi Arabia, the Council of Ulama plays a major role in government.

Ummah Arabic. Community or nation; usually used to refer to Muslims of different backgrounds and nationalities as one community.

Wadi Arabic. Valley or ravine.

Wadjib Arabic. Literally, "obligation," "duty"; generally refers to a Muslim law or custom that must be adhered to.

Yogyakarta Principles In India, a set of principles that address a broad range of human rights standards and their application to issues of sexual orientation and gender identity.

Zahiri A school of thought in Islamic jurisprudence and *aqida* (creed or belief). The founder of this school was Dawud ibn Khalaf (d. 883), also known as Daud al-Zahiri because of his insistence on sticking to the manifest (*zahir*) or literal meaning of expressions in the Quran and the Sunnah. The school and its followers collectively are called *Zahiriyah*.

Zena Arabic. Adultery.

Zihar Arabic. A form of imprecation (curse) that involves the separation of husband and wife by declaring the wife similar to the mother until expiation is made.

CONTRIBUTORS

Editors

CHITRA RAGHAVAN was raised in Malaysia. She is a professor of psychology at John Jay College of Criminal Justice, City University of New York. Her research focuses broadly on gender and intimate partner violence. In addition to researching and teaching gender victimization, she is a practicing clinical psychologist.

JAMES P. LEVINE received his PhD in political science from Northwestern University in 1967. Thereafter he was a faculty member at Michigan State University, the University of Oregon, and Brooklyn College. From 1993 to 2010, he served successively as executive officer of the doctoral program in criminal justice, dean of graduate studies, and dean of research at John Jay College of Criminal Justice, City University of New York.

Authors

AZIZA AHMED is an assistant professor of law at Northeastern University School of Law, where she teaches courses on reproductive and sexual health and rights, international health law, and property. In addition to being a scholar of health law, she writes on Islam, gender, sexuality, and the treatment of Muslim minorities after 9/11.

STEPHANIE WILLMAN BORDAT is director of the Maghreb Regional Office of Global Rights, an international human rights capacity-building NGO, where for over twelve years she has collaborated with local NGOs to promote women's legal rights. She was a Fulbright Fellow in Morocco and has law degrees from Columbia University and Paris I-Sorbonne.

WILLIAM G. CLARENCE-SMITH is a professor of economic history of Asia and Africa at the School of Oriental and African Studies of the University of London, chief editor of the *Journal of Global History*, a contributor to the *New Cambridge History of Islam* (2010), and author of *Islam and the Abolition of Slavery* (2006). He writes on diasporas, labor, sexuality, and consumption.

ROJA FAZAELI teaches in the School of Religions and Theology, Trinity College, Dublin. A recipient of the Government of Ireland Scholarship in Humanities and Social Sciences, she has also been a visiting scholar at the Institute for Research on Women and Gender, Columbia University, New York City, and the Feminist Legal Theory Project, Emory University School of Law, Atlanta.

ANISSA HÉLIE was raised in Algiers. She teaches history at John Jay College of Criminal Justice, City University of New York, and previously taught at Amherst College and Mount Holyoke College. From 2000 to 2005, she was the executive director of the London coordination office for the organization Women Living under Muslim Laws. She works on issues of Islam, gender and sexuality, religious fundamentalism, and war and conflict. She is involved in international feminist networks as a board member and as an advocate.

ANTHONY LUYIRIKA KAFUMBE is a principal legal officer at the East African Community Secretariat in Tanzania. He holds law degrees from Makerere University, in Uganda, and the University of Pretoria, in South Africa, and a PhD from the University of Glasgow, in Scotland. His research interests include human rights for women.

SAIDA KOUZZI is a legal officer of the Maghreb Regional Office of Global Rights, an international human rights capacity-building NGO, where for over twelve years she has collaborated with local NGOs to promote women's legal rights. Previously, she worked at a human rights law firm in Rabat and was a long-time active member of local NGOs. She has a law degree from the Université Mohammed V, in Rabat.

ANTHONY MARCUS is an associate professor of anthropology at John Jay College of Criminal Justice, City University of New York. He participated in the post-tsunami international reconstruction effort in the Maldives in 2006 and 2007 and has researched, written on, and been involved in international development projects in Guatemala, Kenya, Kazakhstan, Dubai, the Maldives, Indonesia, Nepal, and Sri Lanka.

CLAUDIA MERLI is a lecturer in anthropology at Durham University. She specializes in medical anthropology, and her main field of research pertains to reproductive health, bodily practices related to postpartum male and female genital cutting, and biopolitics. She is the author of *Bodily Practices and Medical Identities in Southern Thailand*.

YÜKSEL SEZGIN is an assistant professor of political science at John Jay College of Criminal Justice, City University of New York. He has taught comparative religious law and women's rights at the University of Washington and Harvard Divinity School; held research positions at Princeton University, American University in Cairo, and the University of Delhi; and served as a consultant to the United Nations Entity for Gender Equality and the Empowerment of Women.

KATJA ZVAN ELLIOTT expects to receive her PhD from the University of Oxford in 2012. She is studying the impact of women's rights and development discourses on married women and single adult (educated) girls in a Berber-speaking Moroccan community. Her first academic publication is "Reforming the Moroccan Personal Status Code: A Revolution for Whom?," *Mediterranean Politics* 14, no. 2 (2009): 213–27.

INDEX

eftar, 288, 308

Egypt: abortion laws, *16*; Arab Spring, 303; divorce, 243, 248–250, 254–256, 265nn13–14, 266n17; divorce statistics, 256, 266n19; ethno-religious community rules, 243; female circumcision, 129, 137; hermeneutic communities, 254; *khul‘* divorces, 254–256; Law No. 1 (2000), 249, 255; Law No. 44 (1979), 254, 266n17; Law No. 100 (1985), 254; marriage contract, 217n26; maternal mortality, 7; Muslim population, xviii; personal status codes, 217n26, 263n2; polygyny, 254, 266n17; women-led law reform, 254–255; women's rights, 254–256

Ehrlich, Eugen, xxv

El Hajeb, Morocco, 50–51, 56

Encyclopaedia of Islam, 126, 183

Encyclopedia of Women and Islamic Cultures, 126

Engels, Friedrich, 98

ensoulment, 13–14, 28nn40–41

equity. *See istihsan*

Eritrea: abortion laws, *16*; maternal mortality, 7

eslamgariy-e dini (political Islamism), 279, 308

Espace Draa de la femme et du développement (Zagora), 69n15

Espace Oasis Tafilalet pour le développement (Rissani), 69n15

Estrada-Claudio, S., 27n16

Ethiopia, Muslim population, xviii

Europe, Muslim population, xviii

Evening Weekly (Maldives), 106

extramarital relationships, 104–105, 109, 120n12, 166n1, 216n21. *See also* adultery

Fahim, Kareem, 304

family: changing ideas about, 192; feminist dependence on, 290–291

Family Code (Algeria, 1984), 212, 215n8, 217n27

Family Code (Morocco, 2004): attitudes toward, 147; definition, 308; divorce, 40, 206; effectiveness, 37–38; gender equality, 148–149; impact, 149; and marital relationships, 147–168; marital tutors, 217n28; marriage contracts, 193, 215n8; marriage rights, 198; misconceptions, 162, 198, 217n24; mutuality of rights, 307; patriarchy in, 148–149; preamble, 214n3; prenuptial agreements, 149; problems with, 43; public opinion, 149, 162; *talaq tafwid*, 217n27; as top-down reform, 43, 68n13

Family Codes. *See* Personal Status Codes

Family Courts Law (Israel, 1995), 257

family law: basis in Islamic precepts, 191; codification impact, 215n11; Israel, 246–247; and marriage contracts, 205; misunderstandings, 205; Uganda, 221. *See also* Islamic family law; personal status systems

family law reform, 243–272; de facto/de jure, 96; divorce reform, 97, 107; in governance, 115; Maghreb, 205; Maldives, 95–97, 106–107, 111–117; top-down approaches, 97–98, 116–117. *See also under* Islamic family law; personal status systems

family planning: Bangladesh fatwas, 21; as imperialist, 10–11; in marriage contracts, 205; in Quran, 14; recommendations for access, 10. *See also* abortion; contraception; menstrual regulation/extraction

Faqih, Khul'oud, 266n27

Farzaneh (Iranian feminist journal), 277, 296n28

Fassi, Hatoon al-, 304

fatiha, 199, 217n25, 218n31

Fatima, as role model, 278, 284

fatwa/fatawa, 13, 28n42, 30n66, 308

Fazaeli, Roja, 91n78

Feillard, Andrée, 126

female circumcision: age at, 134-136, 180; conservative movements, 136-140; definition, 308; Egypt, 129, 137; as entry into Islamic faith, 130, 136, 138; eradication strategy, 142; in hadiths, 185n6; incidence, 131-132; Indonesia, 124-128, 130-139, 141-142; intensification of practice, 140-141; Java, 124, 125, 128, 131-137, 139, 141; justifications for, 129-131, 137, 138, 141, 180; Malaysia, 132, 139, 180; male circumcision links, 130, 134, 135-136; mass rituals, 141; opponents, 136-140; origins and spread, 124-125, 127-128; procedures, 132-133; in Quran, 129, 178, 179; reformist movements, 136-140; as ritual purification, 136; severity, 132-134; as sexuality regulator, 130-131, 137; Southeast Asia, 124-146, 170-171; symbolic procedures, 133; Thailand, 130, 133, 136, 137, 140, 169-188; as transition to adulthood, 130, 134-135; vocabulary, 128; Yemen, 135

female genital cutting (sunat): age at, 173; case studies, 174-177; of converts, 173, 176, 177; decision makers, 173-174, 176, 178-179, 183, 184-185; definition, 308, 313; as entry into Islamic faith, 173, 176, 177; eradication strategies, 184-185; gender and decision-making on, 169, 173, 178-179, 180-182; history, 170-171; justifications for, 181; men's opinions, 177-182; modernist views, 172, 177, 179-180, 184; opinions on necessity of, 174, 175, 176, 177, 178, 181-182, 184; as postpartum practice, 173-174; practitioners, 172, 175; in Quran, 179; religious education and, 169, 172, 179-184; seniority and, 169, 173, 174-176; severity, 170, 175; Southeast Asia, 170-171; Thailand, 130, 133, 136, 137, 140, 169-188; traditionalist views, 172, 177, 179-180; women's roles, 173-177

feminism: abortion and, 8-9; Islamic legal tradition interpretations, xvi-xvii, xix-xxi; schism with Islam, xvi; Sharia-fiqh distinctions, xix; and struggle with state and religion, 77-82. See also Iranian feminisms

feminist dependency paradigm, 287-292; family dependence, 290-291; foreign dependence, 289-290; negative state dependency, 287-291; positive dependency, 291-292

fetus, 13-14. See also ensoulment

FGC. See female genital cutting (sunat)

fiqh, xix, 285, 308-309

Fitna (video), xv

folk Islam, 95-96, 98, 107

former Soviet republics, maternal mortality, 7

Formichi, Chiara, 126

fragmented confessional personal status systems, 263n2

Freedman, Lynn, 22

Fromm, Erich, 292

Fulu, E., 119n1

fundamentalism: and abortion rights, 19-24; anti-imperialism campaigns, 142; arguments used, 20-21; cross-religious alliances, 24-25; definition, 30n63; gender ideology, 283, 289; Southeast Asia, 140; strategies, 291-292. See also Hindu Right; Muslim fundamentalists; Muslim religious right

Gambia: abortion laws, 17; maternal mortality, 7; population control, 8

Gaza Strip, abortion laws, 16

Gender and Community (Narain), 72-73

gender equality: and gender roles, 98-99, 162-163; Iran, 280-281, 286; Maldives, 114; Morocco, 148-149; religious right's objection to, 11

gender ideology, 289

gender roles: and gender equality, 98-99, 162-163; influences on, 166; Morocco, 156-164, 167n9 genital cutting. *See* female circumcision; female genital cutting; male circumcision

Gerami, Shahin, 291

get (halachic bill of divorce), 246–247, 264n7, 265n10, 309

girls. *See* children; teenagers

Global Rights (NGO), 216n18, 309

Global Rights Maghreb: marriage contract project, 195–197, 216n19; Morocco violence against women law campaign, 42, 44, 46–49, 51, 63–66, 69n16, 70n29

Gorji, Monir, 277, 278, 295n19

grassroots reforms: effectiveness, 254; engaging women, 44–49; marriage contract reform, 195–197, 213; Morocco violence against women law, 42–49, 69n16; NGO involvement, 42–43, 44; training, 44, 69n16

Guam, divorce rate, 104

Gujarat, India, pogrom against Muslims, 81–82

Gumaa, Ali, Grand *Mufti* of Egypt, 29n42

Gus Dur, 138–139

Hadhramaut, Yemen, female circumcision, 135

hadiths: abortion, 14; circumcision, 129; definition, xv, 129, 309; divorce, 255; family planning, 23; female circumcision, 123, 129, 137, 140, 169–170, 178, 179, 183–184, 185n6; in Islamic legal tradition, xix; reinterpretations, 169; women's rights, xix

Hadler, Jeff, 133

Hagar (Hajar), 130

Haghighatjoo, Fatemeh, 279–280, 282–283, 298n52

hajagha, 287–289, 299n73, 309

Hajar (Hagar), 130

hajj celebrations, 156, 312

Halakhah, 246, 256, 264n4, 309

halal (lawful), 28n42, 139, 309

Halperin-Kaddari, Ruth, 247

Hama Jamiyya (Maldivian coalition), 114, 116, 117, 118

Hamid, Sayeda, 260

Hammani, Ahmad, 18–19

Hanafi, 79, 83, 309

Hanbali, 83, 309

haqq, 83–84

haram (prohibited), 14, 288, 309

Hashemi, Fereshte, 298n63

hawza (school of Shi'a religious learning), 276, 279, 296n25, 309

health care: adverse trends, 11; privatization, 11, 27n27

hermeneutic (interpretive) communities, 252–254

Herzfeld, Michael, 104

hijab, 274, 278, 286, 294nn9–10, 309

Hindu law: genital mutilation, 127; succession, 251–252, 259

Hindu Right, 72, 74, 81–82, 258

Hindu Succession Act (India, 1956), 251, 259

HIV-positive women, abortion access, 23

Hoffman, Katherine, 158

hokumat, 281, 309

Hossain, Sara, 21

Hosseinkhah, Maryam, 275, 277–278

households, multigenerational, 152–155, 167n16

huis clos, 63, 70n33

Hujjat ul-Islam, 296n25, 309

human rights: approaches to change, xxii–xxiii; authority, 82, 83; Islamic legal tradition, xvi–xvii, xix–xxi, 82–85; multivocalization of, xix–xx; and reproductive rights, 10; secular paradigm, 82, 83, 91n71

Huntington, Samuel, xvi

Ibn Battuta, 101, 105, 119n6

Ibn Hanbal, 129

Ibn Khaldun, 119n3

Ibrahim (Abraham), 130, 179

ICPD (International Conference on Population and Development), 10–11, 24–25, 27n28

iddah (alimony), 107

iddat: definition, 309; India, 74, 75, 88n27, 251, 258–259, 260; maintenance, 74, 75, 88n27, 233, 251, 258–259, 260

ijtihad: definition, 13, 28n37, 276, 310; egalitarian, 280; female jurists, 276; as feminist methodology, 285, 286, 295n20; legitimacy, 91n78

Ilahiane, Hsain, 154

illegal abortion, 6, 12, 26n2

illegitimate children, 199, 216n21

Imam, Ayesha, 14–15

immigrants, abortion access, 23

imperialism: abortion, 8–9, 27n26; contraception, 10–11, 27n26; female circumcision bans, 142

Imrana (India, 2005), 79–80

incarcerated women, abortion access, 23

incest, and abortion laws, 13–14, 29n42

India: adultery, 81; anti-Muslim movement, 72, 81–82; British colonial legacy, 72–73; CEDAW, 76, 88n34, 88nn37–38; community norms, 79–81, 243; Constitution, 73, 74–75, 79, 86nn12–13, 87n21; CRC, 76; Criminal Procedure Code, 74; divorce and maintenance, 73–75, 77–78, 88n27, 243, 249, 250–251, 258–259, 260; dual subordination of Muslim women, 71–92; female circumcision, 133; Hindu Succession Act, 251, 259; impact litigation, 258–259; inheritance and succession, 80, 86n10, 251–252, 259; Islamic feminism, 259–260; Islamic law, 72–75, 78; Islamic legal schools, 72; Islamic Personal Law, 75, 78; legal frameworks, 72–77; legislative reform, 259; marriage contracts, 260; marriage rights, 80, 88n38; minority rights, 73, 86nn12–13; Muslim population,

xviii, 71; Muslim sexuality discourse, 81–82; Muslim Women's Act, 74, 77, 251, 258–259; Penal Code, 81; personal law system, 79, 80–81, 258, 259–260, 263n2; property rights, 251–252; rape, 79–80, 90n57; religious freedom, 73, 86n13; religious law reform efforts, 253; self-ruling communities, 253–254; sexual rights discourse, 77–82; Sharia, 72, 88n27, 253–254, 260; Special Marriage Act, 243; State Women's Commission, 80; *talaq*, 250–251; Uniform Civil Code, 73, 86n14, 258; violence against women, 81–82; women's courts, 254, 259–260, 265n15; women's rights, 76, 88n38, 258–260

Indonesia: abortion, 6, 14, 16; female circumcision, 124–128, 130–139, 141–142; maternal mortality, 7; Muslim population, xviii, 125, 141; population control, 8; top-down approach to women's rights, xxiv

Indonesian Council of Ulemas (MUI), 14

infanticide of girls, 14

inheritance and succession: India, 80, 86n10, 251–252, 259; intestate, 86n10, 219, 227–232, 234–235, 237, 239n21, 251, 310; and marriage, 99, 224; Quran, 234–235; testate, 232, 236, 313; Uganda, 219, 223, 224, 227–232, 234–235, 236, 237, 239nn21–22

International Coalition for *Agunah* Rights (ICAR), 256

International Conference on Population and Development (ICPD), 10–11, 24–25, 27n28

International Convention on the Elimination of All Forms of Racial Discrimination, 290

International Convention on the Rights of the Child (CRC), 76, 88n35, 290

International Covenant on Civil and Political Rights, 77, 290

International Covenant on Economic, Social and Cultural Rights, 290 intestacy rules: definition, 310; India, 86n10, 251; Uganda, 219, 227-232, 234-235, 237, 239n21

Iran: abortion, 8, *16*, 22-23; Assembly of Experts for the Constitution, 277; civil code, 293n2; Constitution, 286, 289; contraception, 23; education of women, 274, 293n3, 294n8; fundamentalism, 22; gender equality, 280-281, 286; human rights treaties, 290; interrogations, 287-289, 299n73, 300n86; Islamic Revolution, 277-278, 284; marriage age, 295n22; maternal mortality, 7; Muslim population, xviii; NGOs, 290, 300n87; One Million Signatures Campaign, 280, 281, 289, 291, 297n40; Parliament, 22-23, 282-283, 310; population policies, 18, 22-23; women in government, 282-284, 296n32; women's rights, 278, 290-291; women's rights movement, 276, 287-289, 300n81. *See also* Iranian feminisms

Iranian feminisms, 273-302; categories, 274, 282-287; CEDAW, 286; Constitution, 286; dependence on foreign funding, 289; dependency paradigm, 287-292; funding, 289, 300n80; gender equality, 286; hijab, 286; Islamic feminism, 275-285, 292; Islamic nonstate feminism, 284-285, 292; Islamic state feminism, 282-284, 292; misunderstandings about, 275, 294n13; Muslim feminism, 285-286, 292; negative state dependency, 287-291; positive dependency, 291-292; revolutionary ideals, 278, 279, 282, 284; secular feminism, 286-287, 292; sexuality, 286

Iran-Iraq War (1980-1988), 273, 293n11

Iraq: abortion laws, 14, *16*; condemnation of ICPD, 10-11; maternal mortality, 7; Muslim population, xviii

Islam: female circumcision, 124-125, 127-128; maintenance during marriage, 248; polygyny, 233-234; schism with feminism,

xvi; sexual rights, 82-85; Western depictions of, xv, xxiii-xxiv; women's position, xv-xvi. *See also* Sharia

Islamic Consultative Assembly, 22-23, 310

Islamic family law: conflict with statutory laws, 237; maintenance after divorce, 233; patriarchy in, 117-118; reform, 118; women's property rights, 233-236. *See also* family law; personal status systems

Islamic feminism: definitions, 275-281; diversity within, 281; India, 259-260; Iran, 275-285, 292; methodologies, 295n20; reformist thought, 280-281; *vs.* Muslim feminism, 279, 281, 285, 286

Islamic law: in action, xxv-xxvi; extramarital sex, 120n12; gender-sensitive reinterpretation, 284; India, 72-75, 78; marital property rights, 201, 215n8; marriage contracts, 192; as misnomer, 13; rape, 79-80; reform, 285; secular law dialectic, 95-96, 97, 116-117; *vs.* Islamic legal tradition, xvii, xix; widows, 235

Islamic legal tradition: feminism and human rights discourse, xvi-xvii, xix-xxi; feminist interpretations, xix; human rights in, 82-85; *vs.* Islamic law, xvii, xix. *See also ijtihad*

Islamic nonstate feminism, 284-285, 292

Islamic orthodoxy: female circumcision, 137; Indonesia, 126

Islamic Personal Law, 310

Islamic Revolution (Iran, 1979), 277-278, 284

Islamic state feminism, 282-284, 292

"Islamic" vs "Muslim," 14-15

Islamization, and abortion, 8, 20-24

isma, 206, 217n27, 310

Ismaili branch of Shi'a, 72, 308, 310, 313

Israel: alimony and child support, 257-258; civil family courts, 265n11; divorce, 243, 246-247, 264n6, 264n8, 265n10; ethno-religious community rules, 243; Family Courts Law, 257; Jewish marriage and

legislative advocacy, 57–63

Lehnerer, Melody, 291

Lesser Sunda Islands, circumcision, 136

Libya: abortion laws, *16*; Arab Spring, 303, 304; maternal mortality, 7

literacy, 69n17, 216n22

"living law," xxv

low-income women, abortion access, 23

mabaraat, 86n10, 311

MacFarquhar, Neil, 304

Madura (island), Indonesia: female circumcision, 131, 139; Islamic orthodoxy, 126

maghnae, 273, 293n4

Maghreb marriage contracts, 191–218; current reality, 194–195; customary law, 193; family law reform, 205; future inquiry and action, 210–213; importance, 199–200; Islamic law, 192; legislation, 192–193; negotiated conditions, 208–210; personal experiences, 206–210; personnel, 211–212; polygamy, 194, 215n16; procedures, 211; project lessons learned, 197–212; project strategy, 195–197; rationale and justification, 191–195; reality, 194–195; rights-protective clauses, 200–206; women's knowledge of, 197–199; women's opinions and perceptions, 199–206. *See also* Algeria; Morocco; Tunisia

mahakim shar'iyya, 263n1, 311

Mahboubeh. *See* Abbasgholizadeh, Mahboubeh

mahila adalat, 254, 265n15, 311

mahr (dowry or bridal gift), 250

mahr al-muajjal (dowry), 255, 311

maintenance: for children, 223; Egypt, 249, 255; India, 73–75, 77–78, 88n27, 250–251, 258–259; Islamic family law, 233; Israel, 248; Maldives, 107, 111; during marriage, 148–149, 248; Uganda, 233

Majlis Ulama Indonesia (Council of Indonesian Ulama), 139

Makhlouf Obermeyer, Carla, 18, 23

Malay Peninsula: female circumcision, 130, 139, 142; Islamic orthodoxy, 126; male circumcision, 130

Malaysia: abortion laws, 15, 17, *17*; female circumcision, 132, 139, 180; maternal mortality, 7; Muslim population, xviii; National Fatwa Committee, 17; Sisters in Islam, 20

Maldives: background, 101–102; CEDAW, 96, 107, 114; cultural intimacy, 108–109; democratization, 102; divorce, 95–123; divorce fees, 107, 112; divorce rate, 104, 106, 107, 119n2, 120n10; divorce reform, 97; domestic violence, 114; economy, 115–116; extramarital sex, 104–105, 109, 120n12; family law reform, 95–97, 106–107, 111–117; folk Islam, 95–96, 107; gender equality, 114; gulf-oriented Islam, 102, 105–106, 110, 113; history, 101, 105; Islamicists, 113; "liberal/bad/sloppy" Muslims, 104–105, 109, 119n6; marriage, 97, 100, 104, 105, 108–113, 119n5; Ministry of Family and Gender, 107; overview, 96; polygamy, 97, 114; population, 96; post-divorce maintenance, 111; property rights, 108, 115–116; remarriage, 112–113; scholarly literature, 106, 119n1; sexuality of women, 104, 106, 109, 119n7; *taliq*, 95–123; teenage sex, 120n12; top-down family law reform, 116–117; tsunami and aftermath, 102, 103; weddings, 110–111

Malé, Maldives: economy, 115; population, 102; tsunami recovery, 103

male circumcision: Berbers, 156; of converts, 136, 180; female circumcision links, 130, 134, 135–136; Java (island), Indonesia, 127–128; mass rituals, 141; medicalization, 172; as obligatory, 174, 180, 181; in Quran, 179, 185n7; reasons for, 181

Mali: abortion laws, *16*, 25; maternal mortality, 7

Maliki /Malekite, xvii, 72, 83, 179, 214n2, 311

Maloney, Clarence, 106

mamzerim, 247, 265n9, 311

manteaux, 293n5

marital tutors, 206, 209, 217n28

Markaz Mosharekate Zanan (Center for Women's Participation), 283-284

marriage: age at, 148, 161, 295n22; agrarian societies, 99-100; arranged, 110-111, 206; Berbers, 147-168; changes in, 160-163; as civil contract, 192; companionate, 100, 106, 107-108; divided loyalties, 153-155; evolution of traditions, 163-165; family tensions, 153-155; India, 80, 88n38; and inheritance, 99, 224; Iran, 295n22; Israel, 245-247, 264n6; Jewish, 246-247; maintenance, 148-149, 248; Maldives, 97, 100, 104, 105, 108-113, 119n5; Morocco, 147-168, 194; officiants, 207, 210, 211-212, 217n29; in personal status systems, 245-246; prenuptial agreements, 97; property rights, 105, 108, 201, 204, 215n8, 219, 222-227; as protection for women, 117, 118; punishment for violating traditions, 154-155; purpose of, 105; rape in, 90n57; relationship with society, 98-100; spousal roles, 166; Uganda, 222-227, 238nn8-10. *See also* divorce; domestic violence; marriage contracts; remarriage; weddings

Marriage Act (Uganda, 1904), 223, 238n8

Marriage and Divorce Bill (Uganda, 2010), 225-226

Marriage and Divorce of Mohammedans Act (Uganda, 1906), 223, 238n9

marriage contracts: advocacy to local authorities, 213; Algeria, 192-193, 207-209, 211-212, 215n8, 217n30, 218n31; children's rights, 199; contents, 194, 204-206; current status, 194-195, 208; customary law, 193; domestic violence clauses, 204, 205-206; Egypt, 217n26; enforcement difficulties, 199-200, 204; family planning clauses, 205; future inquiry and action, 210-214; grassroots awareness raising, 213; importance of, 199-200; India, 260; Islamic law, 192; Maghreb, 191-218; marital relations improvement, 201; misunderstandings about, 197-199, 211-212; model marriage contract, 196, 213, 216n20; Morocco, 164, 193, 194, 207-208, 212, 215n8, 217n30; national legislation, 192-193; negotiated by male relatives, 206-207; personnel responsible for, 211-212; procedures, 211; property rights, 193, 194, 198-199, 215n8; purposes, 191-195, 197, 199; research project, 195-197; rights-protective clauses, 193, 195, 196, 197-198, 200-206, 208-210, 211, 218n31; right to work outside the home, 205; sexual relations legitimization, 199; spousal rights notification, 207-208, 217n30; Tunisia, 193, 198-199, 207-208, 212, 215n8, 217n26, 217n30; verbal agreements, 198, 208-209, 218n33; women's experiences with, 206-210; women's knowledge of, 197-199; women's opinions of, 199-206; as women's rights tool, 191-192, 195-197. *See also* prenuptial agreements

Marriages of Africans Act (Uganda, 1904), 223, 238n11

marsoum qadai (legal circular), 257

maternal mortality: definition, 26n10; geography, 6-7, 26n15, 27n16; in MDFs, 11, 27n30; in Muslim-majority countries, 7; statistics, 6; and unsafe abortion, 5-7, 12

matrimonial property, 225-226, 311

Mauritania: abortion laws, 16; maternal mortality, 7

Mavoi Satum (women's organization), 266n22

McLennan, John, 98

MDFs (Millennium Developments Goals), 11-12, 27nn29-31

ME. *See* menstrual regulation/extraction

MENA Region. *See* Middle East and North Africa regions

menstrual regulation/extraction, 18, 311

mentally disabled women, abortion access, 23

Merli, Claudia, 126

Mernissi, F., 78

mesorevet get, 264n7

Middle East and North Africa regions (MENA): abortion laws, 15, 17; definition, 311; maternal mortality, 7. *See also specific countries*

migrants, abortion access, 23

Millennium Developments Goals (2000-2015), 11-12, 27nn29-31

Miller, Alice, 76

Minangkabau people, 126, 138

Minivan News (Maldives), 105-106

Mir-Hosseini, Ziba, 275-276, 280, 281

Mission Islam, 8

Mitakshara coparcenary system, 251-252, 259

Moghadam, Valentine M., 289-290

Mohajerani, Ayatollah, 283

Mohammed VI, King (Morocco), 68n13, 147, 214n3

Mohd. Ahmed Khan vs. Shah Bano Begum & Ors (India, 1985), 73-74, 78, 312

Moore, Ruth, 131

Moosa, Ebrahim, 83-84, 91n71

Mormons, cross-religious alliances, 25, 30n79

Morocco: abortion laws, *16*; divorce, 40, 193, 206; gender equality, 148-149; gender roles, 156-163; illegitimate children, 216n21; literacy, 69n17, 216n22; Malekite school of Sunni Islam, 214n2; marital relations changes, 160-163; marital tutors, 206, 217n28; marriage, 147-168, 194; marriage contracts, 164, 193, 194, 207-208, 212, 215n8, 217n30; marriage sta-

tistics, 194; marriage traditions, 163-165; maternal mortality, 7; Ministry of Justice, 42; Ministry of Social Development, Family, and Solidarity, 42, 60, 61-63; multigenerational households, 152-155; Muslim population, xviii; polygamy, 148, 198; property rights, 194; rape laws, 41; State Secretariat in Charge of the Family, Children and Persons with Disabilities, 42; violence against women, 38-42; violence against women units, 52, 70n26; women's daily lives, 155-156; women's social world, 152-156. *See also* Family Code (Morocco, 2004); Maghreb; violence against women law, Morocco efforts

Moudawana. *See* Family Code (Morocco, 2004)

Mozafari, Kaveh, 280

MR. *See* menstrual regulation/extraction

mu'akhar saddaq (dowry), 249, 255, 311

Mubarak, Hosni, 303

muftis, 28-29, 30n66, 139, 308, 311

Muhammadiyah, 137-138

MUI (Indonesian Council of Ulemas), 14

mujtahidas, 276, 295n22, 311

mukhbirun (informants), 248

multigenerational households, 152-155, 167n16

Muslim feminism, 285-286, 292; *vs.* Islamic feminism, 279, 281, 285, 286; *vs.* secular feminism, 286

Muslim fundamentalists, 24-25. *See also* Muslim religious right

Muslim jurisprudence, 12-15. *See also* Sharia

Muslim-majority countries: abortion laws, 15-19, *16-17*; maternal mortality, 7

Muslim personal law, 74, 226

Muslim Personal Law Application Act (India, 1937), 73, 86n10, 253

Muslim Personal Law Bill (Uganda, 2010), 225

Muslim religious right, 8–9, 10–11. *See also* Muslim fundamentalists

Muslims: diversity, 3–4; geographical distribution, *xviii*; population, xvi–xvii, xviii, 71, 171, 235; sexuality in India, 81–82

"Muslim" vs "Islamic," 14–15

Muslim Women's (Protection of Rights on Divorce) Act (India, 1986), 251, 258–259

Muslim Women's League, 27n28

nafaqa. See maintenance

Nahdatul Ulama (NU), 138–139

Nahjul Balagheh, 278, 296n30, 311

Nairobi. *See* Women's Conference (Nairobi, 1985)

Najmabadi, Afsaneh, 279

Narain, Vrinda, 72–73, 80–81

Nasir, Jamal, 148

National Mobilization Caravan (Morocco), 47–49, 51

Nawawi, Muhi al-Din Yahya al-, 129, 132, 134, 178, 181

Negeri Sembilan, Malaya, female circumcision, 130–131

neocolonialism and population control, 8

New Family (self-ruling community), Israel, 253

New Guinea, female circumcision, 127

Newland, Lynda, 126

Niger: abortion laws, *16*; maternal mortality, 7; property rights for widows, 263n3

Nigeria: abortion laws, *16*, 20–21; fundamentalism, 20–21; maternal mortality, 7; Muslim population, xviii; population control, 8; property rights, 263n3

nikah (marriage), 255, 260, 311

nikahnama (Islamic marriage contract), 260

niqab, 179

NU (Nahdatul Ulama), 138–139

Oceania, Muslim population, xviii

Old Group (Kaum Tua), 172, 177, 183, 184

Oman: abortion laws, 15, *16*; maternal mortality, 7

One Million Signatures Campaign (Iran), 280, 281, 289, 291, 297n40

One Million Signatures Campaign (Morocco), 149

orthodox Islam: female circumcision, 137; Indonesia, 126

Ortiz, Tomás, 127, 132

Ottoman Law of Family Rights (1917), 248

Oued al-Ouliya, Morocco, 150–152, 165. *See also* Taddert, Morocco

overpopulation. *See* population control

Pakistan: abortion, 6, 15, *16*; maternal mortality, 7; Muslim population, xviii; top-down approach to women's rights, xxiv

Palestinian Authority: female judges in Sharia courts, 258, 266n27

Panchayat system, 74–75, 79–80

parental gender roles, 157

parental rights, 273, 291, 293n2

Parker, Lyn, 126

patriarchy, 98–100, 108, 113–118, 148–149

Patthalung, Thailand, 177

Payam-e Hajar (Iranian magazine), 285

Peacock, James, 133

Peletz, Michael, 183

penal codes. *See* civil and penal codes

"Pénalisation, Protection, Pas de Tolérance" (Criminalization, protection, no tolerance) (poster), 46–47

People of the Maldive Islands (Maloney), 106

People's Union for Democratic Rights, 81–82

Persatuan Islam (Persis), 140

personal law. *See* personal status systems

Personal Status Code (Tunisia, 1956), 193, 214n1, 312

Personal Status Codes (Morocco), 147–148. *See also* Family Code (Morocco, 2004)

Personal Status Laws (Egypt), 217n26

Personal Status Ordinance of the Coptic
Orthodox Community (Egypt, 1938), 249
personal status systems: definition, 244;
fragmented confessional, 263n2; and
human rights, 244-245; ideal types, 244,
263n2; India, 79, 80-81, 258, 259-260,
263n2; marriage in, 245-246; Personal
Status Codes, 3; reform, 259-260;
religion-based, 244-245, 252, 263n3; unified confessional, 263n2; unified semiconfessional, 263n2; women-led reform,
252-253, 257, 258; and women's rights,
245-252, 261, 263n3. *See also* family law;
Islamic family law
pesantren (boarding schools), 132, 312
Philippines: female circumcision, 127, 130,
132, 135, 136; male circumcision, 130; maternal mortality, 27n16
physically disabled women, abortion access, 23
plural legal systems, 220, 221-222, 228, 232, 263n3
politico-legal approach to rights change,
xxii-xxiii, xxiv, 97-98
Politics as a Vocation (Weber), xxv
politics of change, xxi-xxv, 1-92; abortion
policy, 3-36; Muslim women in Indian
legal culture, 71-92; violence against
women law in Morocco, 37-70
polyandry, 230
polygamy: Maghreb, 194, 215n16; Maldives,
97, 114; Morocco, 148, 198; prohibitions, 215n16, 218n31; and property rights,
226, 227; and spousal support, 233-234;
Uganda, 226, 227, 229, 233-234
polygyny: definition, 230; Egypt, 254,
266n17; inheritance rights, 230, 235;
Islam, 233-234; in Quran, 266n17;
Uganda, 229, 230, 235
population control: coercive, 8; criticisms
of, 8-9; current status, 27n17; definition,
8; political pragmatism, 18-19, 22-23;
practices, 8

pragmatist feminism, 298n47, 307
pregnancy. *See* abortion; birth celebrations; maternal mortality; teenagers,
pregnancy
prenuptial agreements, 97, 114, 149, 158, 162.
See also marriage contracts
prenuptial classes, 97, 107
pricking, 312. *See also* female genital cutting *(sunat)*
professional women, career limitations,
273, 293n3
property rights: cohabitation, 228, 237;
customary and religious law, 219; on divorce, 118, 193, 219, 222-227; enforcement,
239n22; India, 251-252; Islamic family
law, 233-236; land ownership, 226-227;
Maldives, 108, 115-116; during marriage,
105, 108, 201, 204, 219, 222-227; marriage
contracts, 193, 194, 198-199, 215n8; matrimonial property, 225-226; Morocco,
194; Nigeria, 263n3; and polygamy, 226,
227; reform proposals, 219, 236-237; statutory law, 219; Tunisia, 198-199; Uganda,
219-242; of widows, 219, 227-232, 263n3.
See also inheritance and succession
Public Trustee Act (Uganda), 228
Putranti, Basilica, 126, 133, 136

Qaddafi, Muammar El-, 303
qadi/qudah, 30n66, 248, 266n27, 312
Qatar: abortion laws, 14, 16; maternal mortality, 7
qazi, 260
qsar/qsour, 150-151, 163, 165, 312
Quran: abortion, 13-14; divorce, 266n17;
family planning, 14; female circumcision, 129, 178, 179; inheritance of property, 234-235; Islamic feminism and, 276;
Islamic legal tradition, xvii; male circumcision, 179, 185n17; polygyny, 266n17;
reinterpretations, 285; Surah An-Nisaa,
234, 313

rabbinical authorities, 264n6, 264n8

rabbinical courts, 246, 247, 256–257, 265n10

Rabbinical Courts (Enforcement of Divorce Decrees) Law (Israel, 1995), 247

Rahbar, Negar, 281

Rahnavard, Zahra, 298n63

Rajid, Abdul, 137

Ramali, Ahmad, 138

rape: and abortion laws, 13, 14, 18–19, 28n42; as harm to community, 82; India, 79–80, 90n57; Islamic law, 79–80; in marriage, 90n57; Morocco laws, 41

Redwan, Zeinab, 255

refugees, abortion access, 23

Rehendi Khadeeja (Maldivian sultana), 101

Reid, Anthony, 131

religion-based personal status laws, 244–245, 252, 263n3

religious law: gender norm reinforcement, 71, 77–78, 79; as product of human agency, 262; reinterpretation, 252–253, 262; women-led reform, 253; and women's rights, 252–260, 263n3

remarriage, 112–113

reproductive health, adverse trends, 11

reproductive rights, 9–12, 76–77. *See also* sexuality and sexual rights

Republic of Maldives. *See* Maldives

Resistance Committee Judicial Powers Statute (Uganda, 1988), 228

rights change, approaches to, xxii–xxiii, xxiv

Road of One Thousand Kasbahs, Morocco, 150, 312

Roman Catholic Church, cross-religious alliances, 24–25

rule of law, 53, 312

rural women: abortion access, 22, 23; Algeria, 198, 218n31; desire for change, xxiv; effectiveness of top-down change for, xxiv; Kyrgyzstan, 22, 307; Morocco, 44–45, 48, 147–168; Uganda, 221; violence against, 39, 49

Rural Women's Union (ALGA), 22, 307

Ruse, Austin, 25

Russia, divorce rate, 104

Saeed, Abdullah, 98

Saidzadeh, Hujjat ul-Islam Seyed Mohsen, 276–277, 295n19, 296n25

Salim, Haji Agus, 138

salish, 21, 30n67

Sarah, 129–130

Sarekat Islam, 138

Satun Province, Thailand: background, 171–172; female genital cutting, 170, 174–177; household composition, 178–179, 183, 185n4; Muslim legal innovations, 183, 185n10; Muslim population, 172; population, 172

Saudi Arabia: abortion laws, 17; alliance with Mormons, 31n79; condemnation of ICPD, 10–11; maternal mortality, 7, 7; Muslim population, xviii; women's rights, 304

scholarships, 294n8

Schriecke, B. J. O., 127

secular feminisms, 286–287, 292

secular law: gender norm reinforcement, 71, 77–78, 79; human rights in, 82, 83, 91n71; Islamic law dialectic, 95–96, 97, 116–117. *See also* civil and penal codes

Sefati, Zohreh, 295n22

Sekhon, Joti, 74–75

Seleh, Ali Abdullah, 303

self-ruling communities, 253

Senegal: abortion laws, 16; maternal mortality, 7

separated spouses, rights of, 231

sexuality and sexual rights: circumcision as regulator, 130–131, 137; definition, 76; extramarital relations, 216n21; extramarital relationships, 104–105, 109, 120n12, 166n1, 216n21; feminist analysis, 77–81; forbidden practices, 299n74; India, 77–82; international norms, 75–77; Iranian feminisms, 286; and Islam, 82–85; Maldives, 104, 106, 109, 119n7; and Muslim women, 76; patriarchal management, 80, 81; in religious and secular discourse, 77–85; sexual rights, 76–77. *See also* adultery; reproductive rights

sexual violence. *See* rape; violence against women

Shafii: definition, 312; female circumcision, 124, 125, 129, 138–139, 169–171, 178, 183–184; *istihsan*, 83

Shafii, Al-, 91n78

shah, definition, 312

Shah Bano. See Mohd. Ahmed Khan vs. Shah Bano Begum & Ors (India, 1985)

Shaheed, Farida, 13

Shahidian, Hammed, 294n13

Shaikh, Sa'diyya, 13, 28n37, 28n39, 28n41

shalish, 21, 30n67

Sharia: Coptic use, 250; definition, xix, 312; divorce and maintenance, 74, 75, 248, 254–255; *fiqh* distinctions, xix; human rights, 84–85; India, 72, 88n27, 253–254, 260; Israel, 248, 265n11; Maldives, 95–123; reform, 95–123; *vs.* Western law, 83; women's rights, 89n46, 248

Sharia courts: alimony and child support, 257–258; female *qadis*, 258; Israel, 243, 248, 257–258; reform, 257–258

Shari'ati, Ali, 278

Shenhav, Sharon, 256–257, 266n23

Sherkat, Shalah, 294n13

Shi'a, xvii, 83, 129, 313

Shinawatra, Thaksin, 171–172

Shmais, A., 266n17

Shojaee, Zahra, 283–284

Sidqi, Hala, 250

Siegel, James, 135

Sierra Leone: abortion laws, 17; maternal mortality, 7

Singapore: female circumcision, 133, 139; Islamic Religious Council, 139

single mothers, 216n21

Sisters in Islam, 20

Snouck Hurgronje, Christiaan, 128, 134

Sobhan, Salma, 21, 30n66

social change, politics of, xxi–xxv

sociocultural approach to rights change, xxii–xxiii, xxiv

Somalia: abortion laws, 16; maternal mortality, 7

Souss region, Morocco, marriage contracts, 193, 215n11

South Africa, abortion laws, 25

South Asia, maternal mortality, 26n15

Southeast Asia: female circumcision, 124–146, 170–171; fundamentalism, 140

Southern Thailand: background, 171–172; genital cutting, 169–188

Soviet republics, former, maternal mortality, 7

statutory guardian, definition, 313

statutory laws, 237. *See also* civil and penal codes; secular law

sub-Saharan Africa, maternal mortality, 7, 26n15

succession. *See* inheritance and succession

Succession Act (Uganda), 223, 228–232, 236, 237, 239n21

Sudan: abortion laws, 14, 16; condemnation of ICPD, 10–11; maternal mortality, 7; Muslim population, xviii

Sufism, 178

sukoun, 193, 215n11, 313

Sulawesi (island), Indonesia: female circumcision, 127, 130, 131, 132, 133, 134, 136; male circumcision, 130

Sulu, Philippines, female circumcision, 131

Sumatra (island), Indonesia: female circumcision, 131, 133, 134, 138; Islamic orthodoxy, 126

Sunan Abu Dawud (hadith), 179, 184, 185n6